POPULAR WOODWORKING

complete book of tips, tricks & techniques

BY THE EDITORS OF POPULAR WOODWORKING

POPULAR
WOODWORKING
BOOKS
CINCINNATI, OHIO
www.popularwoodworking.com

READ THIS IMPORTANT SAFETY NOTICE

To prevent accidents, keep safety in mind while you work. Use the safety guards installed on power equipment; they are for your protection. When working on power equipment, keep fingers away from saw blades, wear safety goggles to prevent injuries from flying wood chips and sawdust, wear headphones to protect your hearing, and consider installing a dust vacuum to reduce the amount of airborne sawdust in your woodshop. Don't wear loose clothing, such as neckties or shirts with loose sleeves, or jewelry, such as rings, necklaces or bracelets, when working with power equipment. Tie back long hair to prevent it from getting caught in your equipment. People who are sensitive to certain chemicals should check the chemical content of any product before using it. The authors and editors who compiled this book have tried to make the contents as accurate and correct as possible. Plans, illustrations, photographs and text have been carefully checked. All instructions, plans and projects should be carefully read, studied and understood before beginning construction. In some photos, power tool guards have been removed to more clearly show the operation being demonstrated. Always use all safety guards and attachments that come with your power tools. Due to the variability of local conditions, construction materials, skill levels, etc., neither the author nor Popular Woodworking Books assumes any responsibility for any accidents, injuries, damages or other losses incurred resulting from the material presented in this book. All prices and materials listed for supplies and equipment were current at the time of original publication and are subject to change. Glass shelving should have all edges polished and must be tempered. Untempered glass shelves may shatter and can cause serious bodily injury. Tempered shelves are very strong and will just crumble if they break, minimizing personal injury.

METRIC CONVERSION CHART

TO CONVERT	TO	MULTIPLY BY
Inches	Centimeters	2.54
Centimeters	Inches	0.4
Feet	Centimeters	30.5
Centimeters	Feet	0.03
Yards	Meters	0.9
Meters	Yards	1.1
Sq. Inches	Sq. Centimeters	6.45
Sq. Centimeters	Sq. Inches	0.16
Sq. Feet	Sq. Meters	0.09
Sq. Meters	Sq. Feet	10.8
Sq. Yards	Sq. Meters	0.8
Sq. Meters	Sq. Yards	1.2
Pounds	Kilograms	0.45
Kilograms	Pounds	2.2
Ounces	Grams	28.4
Grams	Ounces	0.035

Published by Popular Woodworking Books, an imprint of F&W Publications, Inc., 4700 East Galbraith Road, Cincinnati, Ohio, 45236. 800-289-0963. First edition.

Visit our Web site at www.popularwoodworking.com for information on more resources for woodworkers.

Other fine Popular Woodworking Books are available from your local bookstore or direct from the publisher.

08 07 06 05 04 5 4 3 2 1

Library of Congress Cataloging-in-Publication Data

A catalog record for this book is available from the Library of Congress at <http://catalog.loc.gov>.

ACQUISITIONS EDITOR: Jim Stack
EDITED BY: Jennifer Ziegler & Amy Hattersley
DESIGNED BY: Brian Roeth
PAGE LAYOUT BY: Donna Cozatchy
PRODUCTION COORDINATED BY: Robin Richie

special thanks

Jennifer Ziegler, associate editor of Popular Woodworking Books, researched and compiled all the materials in this book. She perused issue after issue of *Popular Woodworking* magazine and copy after copy of Popular Woodworking book selections to find the best how-to tips, tricks and techniques.

Additional thanks go to Brian Roeth for his design of this book. Brian was given photos, materials lists, hardware lists, captions, body text, tips, sidebars, etc., and created a visually appealing book that clearly tells the reader "how- to" without clutter or confusion.

The book production department here at F+W Publications is second to none. They continue to keep our woodworking books on time and within budget. All that while pouring over each proof page to double- and triple-check for proper colors, correct layout, proper alignment of photos, text, key lines, etc. Not to mention they find the best printers available. It's a huge and mostly thankless job that is absolutely essential to the book publication process.

A great product isn't worth anything without dedicated salespeople selling our books. They know the product well and are excited about sharing the information in our books with as many readers as possible.

Many thanks to all of you for your continued outstanding efforts!

JIM STACK
Acquisitions Editor
Popular Woodworking Books

ACKNOWLEDGEMENTS

Sioux Bally, Heartstone Arts

Matt Bantly

Tom Begnal

Nick Engler

Bob Flexner

Kara Gebhart

Glen Huey

Bill Hylton

Don McConnell

Al Parrish

Scott Phillips

Danny Proulx

Gene Sasse

Christopher Schwarz

Troy Sexton

Steve Shanesy

Jim Stack

Jim Stuard

David Thiel

Linda Watts

contents

SHOP

MATERIALS

SHARPENING

TOOLS

JOINERY

SHELVING & CABINETRY

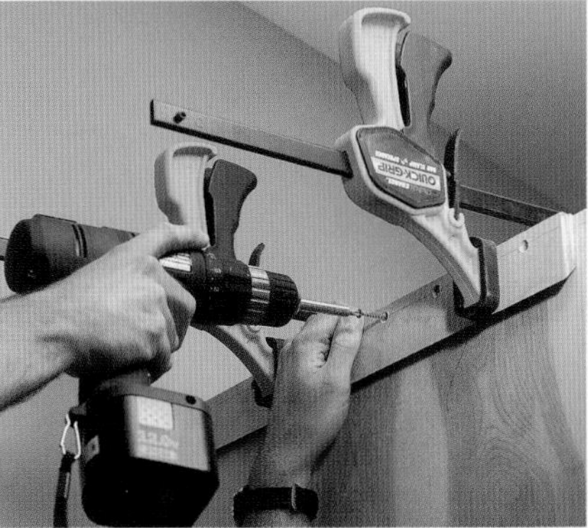

FINISHING

REFERENCE MATERIALS

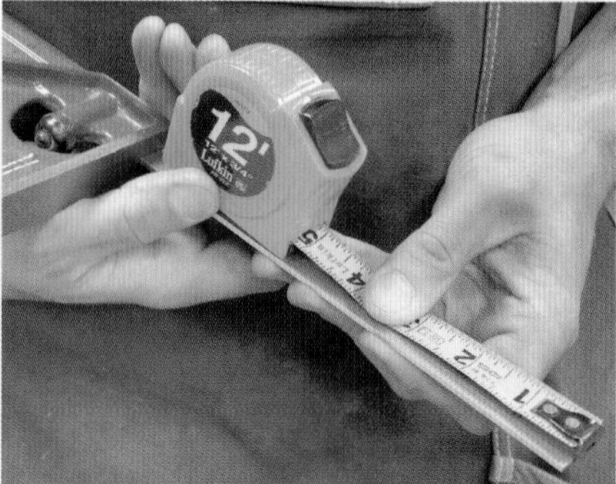

introduction

Keep this book in your shop for all your reference needs!

We, the editors of Popular Woodworking, have compiled this book for those woodworkers who question their tools and materials. Is your shop less than perfect? Then check out the shops of some of America's finest woodworkers for their tips and tricks. Unsure of what tools you need and which to buy? Information for every major tool is featured in this book. Not sure what type of wood will work best for your project? Check out our section on selecting lumber. Do you have questions about finishing and how to take care of your finished masterpiece? We have provided a large section from Bob Flexner with everything you need to know on how to get and keep a beautiful finish for years to come. What are you waiting for? Dig in and use this book for all your woodworking needs!

what makes an ultimate workshop?

BY DAVID THIEL

Tom Willenborg's assembly room is a study in organization and function. Everything has a place and he makes sure no space is wasted.

Most woodworkers have seen Norm Abrams' shop on *The New Yankee Workshop* and drooled over both the machinery and the acres of work space. For many, it's the ultimate shop.

Unfortunately the average woodworker is more likely faced with using the garage or basement. That doesn't mean it can't be an ultimate workshop; it just means you need a different approach to layout and organization while recognizing that compromises are necessary.

Speaking of compromises, DIY, the Do It Yourself Network, recently set out to demonstrate to viewers how to set up a woodworking shop, an auto mechanic shop and a gardening work area! If you want to see the clever ways DIY solved this space problem, visit www.diynet.com to check the air times for the five-part miniseries, *The Ultimate Workshop II*.

Ultimately, everyone's needs and wallets will determine what their shops are. And for every woodworker, the ultimate workshop is likely to be very different from his or her neighbor's.

A Tale of Two Shops

We had the chance to look at two woodworkers who approached their ultimate shops in different ways. We learned from them, and we hope you will also.

Tom Willenborg is a children's advocacy attorney in northern Kentucky in his early 50s who has been woodworking for 30 years. While his wife abandoned their basement to his hobby in 1990, it wasn't until two years ago that he decided the space could be used better. So he excavated the floor to gain ceiling height and added a two-story loft for his ultimate shop.

The second shop belongs to George Jaeger, who worked as a human resources manager for 38 years at an international machinery manufacturer. While woodworking was always a hobby, it wasn't all-consuming until his retirement in 1992. He and his wife moved into a fairly new house that included a 32' × 40' barn that screamed to be turned into a woodshop.

High-Tech, High-Concept

Willenborg's shop is hidden in the basement of his 1927 farmhouse. Formerly part of a large parcel of land, it now sits on about an acre with urban sprawl and a widening road encroaching.

His basement workshop underwent changes during the 10 years he'd been woodworking there. A non-load-bearing wall had been removed to gain some space, and a crawl space had become a room for a dust collector and bathroom.

But after 10 years of stooping under heating ducts, he decided it was time to do it right. He removed the concrete floor and dug down 12". It was a messy job that he doesn't recommend, but it was the cornerstone of his plan for his 1,250-square-foot shop.

To gain even more headroom, he sunk his central dust collection ducting in the new concrete floor, choosing 8" PVC (polyvinyl chloride) pipe for the main run, and 6" and 4" branches running to the individual machines. Oneida Air Systems helped him plan the system, and he added the new Ecogate automatic blast gate system to the 16 drops in the system.

The main assembly room (opening photo) lets in natural light through rooftop skylights. Double doors serve as the entry to the shop. The cabinetry offers an amazing amount of storage, while still leaving space for assembly and finishing. It also has a cleverly tucked-away router table built into the island top.

The work flow in Willenborg's shop was a compromise. While each room has a purpose, the flow is backwards from tradition, with his lumber storage furthest from his jointer and table saw.

Willenborg decided that with his busy job as an attorney, the time in the shop was too short to be spent setting up tools. So all his machinery is dedicated to one purpose. There's no drill press with a mortising attachment here. In fact, he even bolted a second table saw to his main saw, making it a combo machine with a dado stack always at the ready.

You'll also find another time-saving device on the wall of the lumber prep room. A series of pipe clamps allows for quick and space-saving panel glue-ups.

Speaking of saving time, tucked away near his dust collector room and lumber racks is a bathroom. While it took more work than the average bathroom (with no handy sewage hookup, the waste has to be pumped out), Willenborg didn't want to have to run upstairs to answer nature's call.

Most of the equipment in his shop was upgraded during his recent renovation, as well. In keeping with his ultimate plan, all the machinery is top-quality and even color coordinated.

Is this a lot of work just for a basement shop? Well, working within the given constraints, Willenborg built a shop that he's happy to spend as much time in as he can. While it might not be yours, it is his ultimate shop.

Gimme That Countryside

While Willenborg chose to make the most of his existing house, Jaeger and his wife chose their retirement home with an existing barn in mind for his shop.

As you approach Jaeger's place along the back roads of the northern Kentucky countryside, you can appreciate the beauty and solitude. You might also think of the distance to the nearest lumberyard. For some woodworkers, that distance might be too far.

The Jaegers' home had been built with all the contemporary comforts only a few years before, and the former owner

The clamp wall allows Willenborg to glue up lots of solid panels efficiently (they can be mounted in the rack in two horizontal tiers) without dragging clamps all over the shop. When glued up, the panels are tucked against the wall and out of the way.

Woodworkers are nothing if not creative. One fine example in Willenborg's shop is the double table saw (below), combining a standard 10" cabinet saw with a 10" contractor's saw mounted in the right-hand wing. Willenborg always leaves an 8" dado stack set up in the contractor's saw to save time. The well-organized and fully stocked lumber racks (left) show a good sense of organization and recycling. The racks were purchased from a going-out-of-business home-improvement store. A good assortment of clamps are tucked out of the way behind the lumber, but still within easy reach.

Why is George Jaeger smiling? Well, it could be the excellent deal he got on the complete Stanley 45 plane lying on his bench. Or it could be the majestic view surrounding his enormous stand-alone shop (inset, left). Either way, when you look at the spacious, well-organized and well-appointed shop interior (one-quarter of which is shown), it's easy to see Jaeger has created his ultimate workshop.

had added an ample barn (32' × 40') with sliding cargo doors at either end and about 12' of headroom.

Inside Jaeger's shop is a great collection of machines and tools he's gathered over the decades. Some of the machinery he even made himself, such as his tilting-top router table and shaper. Most of the equipment has an acquisition story behind it that shows as much joy at the getting as in the using.

The 1,280 square feet of storage in his shop is almost an embarrassment of space. In fact, there's so much room in his shop that Jaeger stores his fishing boat below his lumber racks.

The shop has most amenities: heat (no air-conditioning . . . yet), excellent lighting from windows and a score of both fluorescent fixtures and incandescent task lights (it seems fluorescents do funny things to spinning forms on the lathe).

One thing is missing, however. During our visit, Jaeger's wife suggested that we "make use of the facilities" before heading out to the shop.

Willenborg took advantage of being able to create what he needed in his shop space. The Oneida cyclone dust collection system (below right) is built into a separate room, with the ducting running under the poured concrete floor. Where the ducting meets the machines, he incorporated Ecogates (top right) that automatically open and activate the cyclone collector when the machine is turned on.

Jaeger wanted efficient dust collection, but also wanted it tucked away. His dust collection room was built out from the existing wall, forming a bump-out with worktop space on either side. To avoid losing any of the natural light pouring in from the windows, he added an interior window to the bump-out. A lift-off door panel (shown removed at bottom left) allows easy access for emptying the bags. A small Plexiglas access door (top left) lets him not only see which blast gate is open, but allows easy access while still keeping the room sealed.

While Jaeger also recognizes the importance of adequate dust collection in his shop, his solution is a bit lower-tech than Willenborg's. A large filter-bag dust collector is tucked away in a closet, with a special access door to change which blast gates are open. Jaeger did add an extra window to the closet to avoid losing any natural light.

A nice collection of hand tools rounds out the shop's equipment. It's Jaeger's ultimate workshop. You might have different ideas for your own shop, but that's the beauty of woodworking. It's a little different for everyone, and what we bring to it makes it our own, ultimately.

CHAPTER 2

the ultimate home workshop

BY DAVID THIEL

When DIY, the Do It Yourself Network, asked Popular Woodworking to help produce its *The Ultimate Workshop* series, we sent DIY a barrage of tips and advice the staff had accumulated over decades of professional and home-shop woodworking.

We looked at all our advice — enough to fill a book — and boiled it down into an essential guide for anyone planning their own ultimate home workshop.

But what is an ultimate home shop? It depends on you. However, whether you're going to build reproduction furniture using only hand tools, or make plywood shelves for the den, many of the ideas presented here will help you set up your ultimate home workshop the right way, the first time.

Location, Location, Location

Most woodworkers can put their shop one of two places: the garage or (in about half the country) the basement. If you're lucky or wealthy, you might have a separate outbuilding to consider.

If you're in a part of the country with basements, they can make handy shops. Basements are usually prewired for electrical outlets and lighting, and already have plumbing and heat. But a basement shop poses problems, too. You need to get lumber, large equipment and finished projects up and down steps. The size of your doors, the number and slope of your steps and any corners you might have to turn can make a basement shop impossible.

Another basement problem is ceiling height. Older homes may have only 6' or 7' ceilings — less than optimal when working with taller projects.

Finally, basement shops test the patience of your family with the dust and noise. Here's a tip for quieting your basement shop: If the ceiling has drywall, add a second layer. If the ceiling is open rafters, so much the better. Add insulation, then add a layer of drywall.

If you don't have a basement, or it's already got a pool

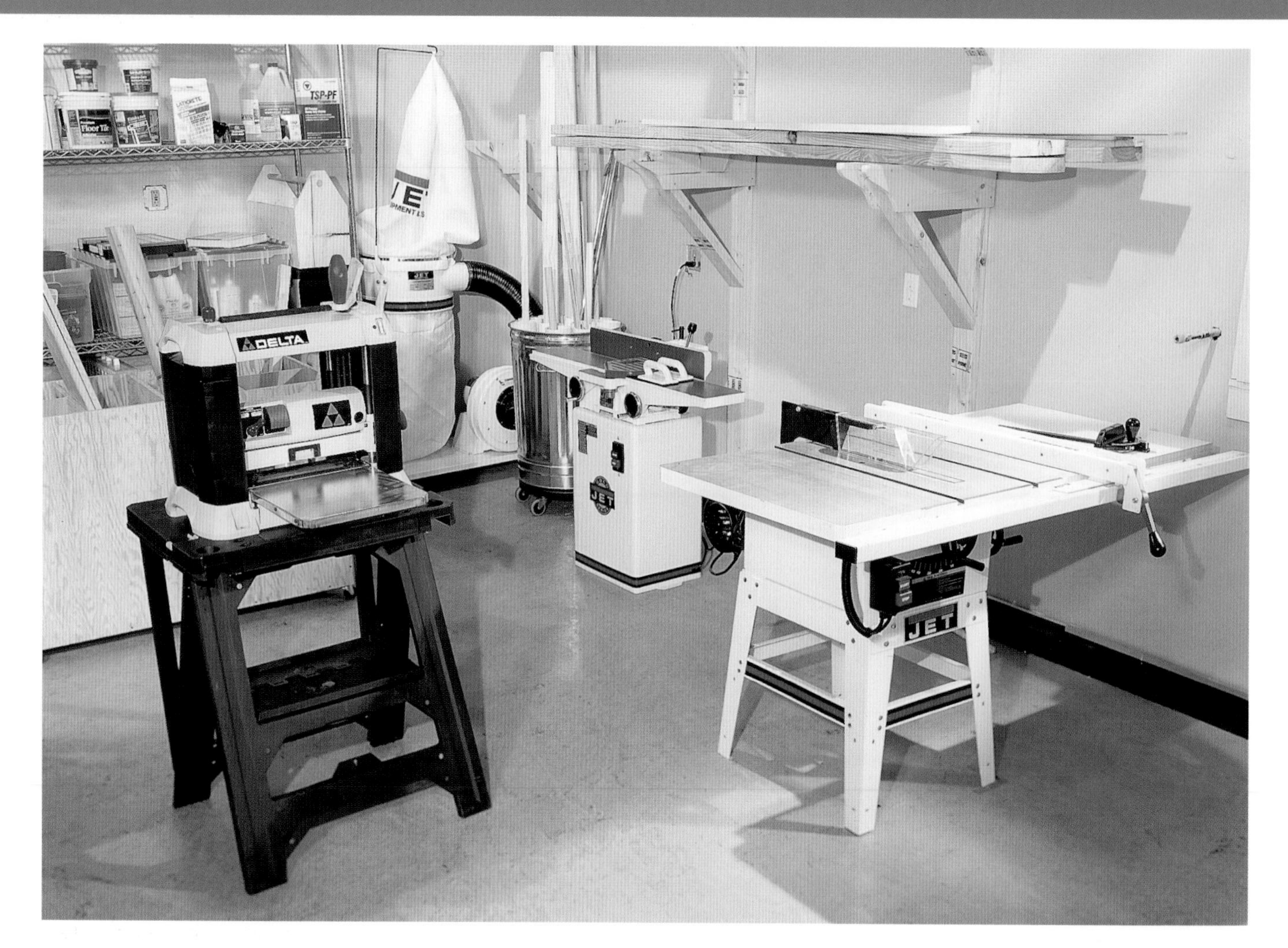

table in it, a two-car garage makes a great workshop, offering easy access through large doors, a solid poured concrete floor and a location that's unlikely to get you in trouble when you make dust.

With a garage shop, your first decision is whether the cars will stay out permanently or just when you're woodworking. If your workshop will include some major machinery, the cars will be experiencing some weather.

Other concerns with a garage shop include: upgrading your electrical system (more outlets and perhaps 220-volt service), plumbing and lighting the shop (and heating in colder climates).

A third option may or may not be available to you. If you have an outbuilding on your property (or the space and funds to build one), they make great shops without the noise and dust concerns. If you're building, this also allows you to get everything just the way you want it.

Once you've decided where your workshop will be, it's time to decide how it will be used.

Not Just For Woodworking

We all know that a lot more happens in a home workshop than just woodworking. Hundreds of home fix-up projects take place there, from painting a closet door to rewiring a lamp.

So even though you're planning on lots of woodworking, don't overlook the needs of other projects. Plan on extra storage for paint cans, mechanic's tools and a drawer or two for electrical tools and supplies. But before we worry about storage, let's pick some tools and machines.

Picking Your Tools

If woodworking will be an occasional activity, or space is at a high premium, consider buying benchtop machines. You can do a lot of work with a benchtop drill press, planer and band saw. While they're not as versatile as their floor-model big brothers, we recommend them for the small shop.

On the other hand, we don't recommend benchtop table saws for any but the tiniest of shops. While a benchtop saw might be smaller, it's also less powerful and less accurate. Find a way to squeeze a contractor's saw or cabinet saw in your shop on a mobile base.

The same goes for the jointer. Like the table saw, benchtop jointers just don't satisfy the needs of most woodshops. We recommend carving out a section of floor space along the wall for a stationary 6" or 8" jointer.

This corner essentially makes up the machining area in the shop. Lumber is stored within easy reach above the jointer, with the planer positioned ready to be used by simply turning around from the jointer. With the wood milled, it's a simple step to the table saw to cut the pieces to final size. The stand for the planer is designed to knock down quickly and fold flat against the wall. The planer itself stores under a cabinet, or even under the right-hand wing of the table saw. The portable dust collector is stored in the corner, but it can be attached quickly to any of the three machines in this corner for clean and safe working conditions.

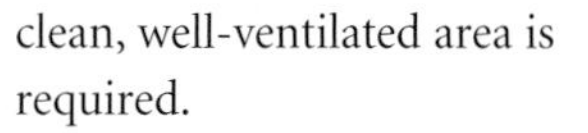

With these five machines (and an assortment of portable and hand tools), you'll be ready to build cabinets and shelves. However, if turning is your passion, a lathe may be at the top of the list, and the jointer and planer may disappear altogether. It's your choice.

You'll want to have other tools, including a miter saw, scroll saw and bench grinder, as you go along if you don't already own them, and they don't take up much space.

Placing Your Machines

Once you know what machines will be in your workshop, you need to determine their location. Allow for infeed and outfeed space and place them near machines they're used with most frequently.

Each machine requires space for itself and space to use the tool. With a table saw, you need to be able to maneuver a 4' × 8' sheet of plywood to the back, front and left side of the saw. This means a pretty big footprint for the machine when in use (you can overlap the "in-use" footprints of multiple machines). We've added a diagram below that shows the necessary working footprint for each major machine. We suggest you draw your shop on graph paper, cut out the tools and try different arrangements to see what works.

The trick to positioning your machines in your shop is to create an orderly flow of work from raw lumber to the finished product. The work flow always starts where the wood is stored, or where it enters the workshop. Next, the lumber is prepared for use by jointing, planing and sawing to the proper dimensions. Conveniently, the machines required for these steps are also the ones that need the most power and create the most dust, allowing you to locate your power and dust collection in a "machining" area, with these machines close to one another.

From the machining phase, the next step is joinery and assembly, usually requiring hand tools, a band saw, drill press and handheld power tools, such as a router, biscuit joiner and brad nailer. A stable workbench or assembly table is ideal for this step.

The assembly area should be located out of the way of the machining area, but not so far away that you end up carrying lots of milled lumber across the shop. Your hand and small power tools should be easily accessible (stored in handy drawers or on the wall), and quick access to clamps will make things easier, as well.

Once assembly is complete, the third phase is finishing. No matter what finish you use, a clean, well-ventilated area is required.

When applying a varnish or shellac finish, the vapors given off as the finish dries are flammable and should be kept away from any ignition points, such as water heaters or space heaters. In concentrated exposure, the vapors can also be harmful to you, so ventilation is important. Also, when storing solvent-based finishes (such as varnishes) a fireproof storage cabinet is a must.

If you're going to use a spray-on finishing system, ventilation is even more critical to move the overspray away from your lungs.

From here, the rest of your shop will fall into place in the space left. Keep in mind that to save space, many tools can be stored under cabinets until needed.

Putting Things Away

While we've talked about where your lumber storage should be in the work triangle, we haven't talked about how to store the lumber.

Three types of wood are stored in a workshop: sheet goods (such as plywood), rough or full-size lumber, and shorts and scraps. Shorts and scraps are the pieces you can't bring yourself to throw away. Not only are there usually more of these pieces, but they're

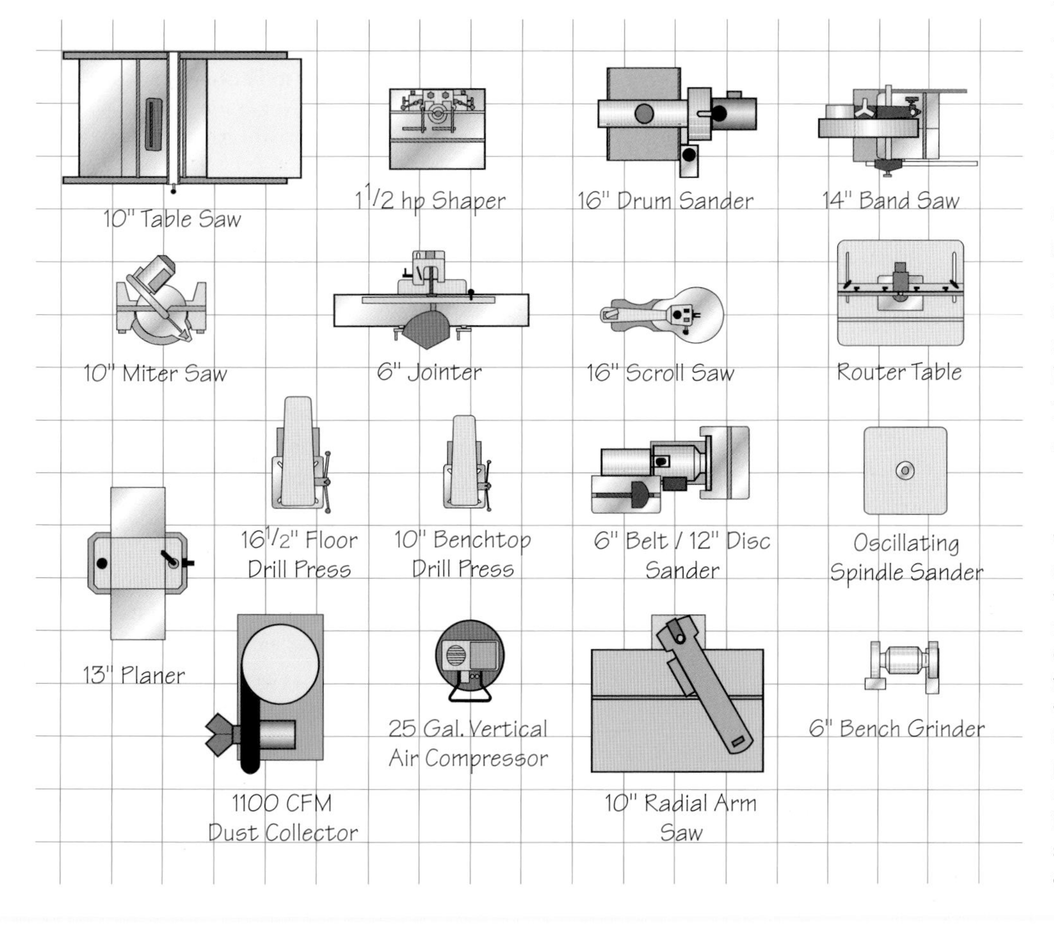

We know that not everyone has the same size work space, so we thought we'd give you some templates to photocopy and cut out to plan your own shop. The grid is a 1/4" pattern in full size (one square equals 1'), which will work with most graph paper you buy in tablets at the store. (Trust me, paper tools are much lighter to move around.) Also, when organizing your tools, remember to include space for the wood on the infeed and outfeed sides.

harder to store than plywood or rough lumber because of their odd shapes and sizes. Let's start with the easy stuff first.

Plywood takes up the least amount of space when stored standing on edge. Most of us don't store more than a few sheets of plywood, so this can often be stored in a 10"- to 12"-deep rack that can slip behind other storage or machinery. This keeps it out of the way but accessible.

Rough lumber is best stored flat and well supported to keep the wood from warping. Keeping it up off the floor also keeps it away from any water that might get into your shop. A wall rack with a number of adjustable-height supports provides the easiest access while keeping the wood flat and dry.

Shorts are the hardest to store, but a rolling box with a number of smaller compartments holding the shorts upright allows easy access to the pieces, and it keeps them from falling against and on top of each other. For plans for a good bin (and 24 other shop projects), get a copy of the book *25 Essential Projects for Your Workshop* published by Popular Woodworking Books.

Carrying on with the storage concept, one category that deserves special attention is finishing materials. While waterborne finishes are gaining in popularity, flammable finishes in cans, bottles and jars should be stored in a fireproof storage box and kept clean and organized at all times. A tall cabinet with lots of adjustable shelf space makes room for the many sizes of finishing supplies.

Other workshop storage needs fall into the cabinet and shelving category. Just because a tool sits on the floor against the wall doesn't mean you can't hang a cabinet or shelving above it. In fact, in many cases the tool's accessories and supplies belong on a shelf right above it. And don't hesitate to go all the way to the ceiling with storage. Even though the top shelves are harder to get to, we all have things in our shops that don't get used very often.

Many of us have purchased a tool that had a base tossed in to sweeten the deal. It seems like a good idea, but if you stop and think about it, it's truly wasted space. Throw away that stamped-steel base and build a storage cabinet to go underneath the tool.

When choosing base storage cabinets, you'll have to decide whether you need drawer cabinets, door cabinets or both. If you're storing large, odd-shaped items (belt sanders, arc welders), a drawer can be a real problem. They're designed to hold only so much. A door cabinet is a better place to store bulky items.

On the other hand, if you're storing smaller items (door hinges, glue, seldomly used jigs), a door cabinet can be a great place to lose these items. Items seem to migrate to the back of the cabinet; and until you're down on your knees peering into the hole, you won't find them. While drawers can get pretty junky if you're not careful, you'll at least be able to stand up and stare down into the drawer to look for your lost metric tape measure.

Beyond doors or drawers, you have two general choices in cabinets — buy 'em or make 'em. If you make your own cabinetry, you will almost certainly get exactly what you need for the best space utilization. You'll also likely save some money, but it'll take a fair amount of time.

Buying shop-grade cabinets from a home center can work out well. Any number of utility cabinets are available in all shapes, sizes and finishes.

One other option is plastic or metal storage units, designed specifically for a workshop. These units offer features that are set up to maximize tool use and convenience.

Beyond cabinets, open shelves are good for storage, but they're a bit of a trade-off.

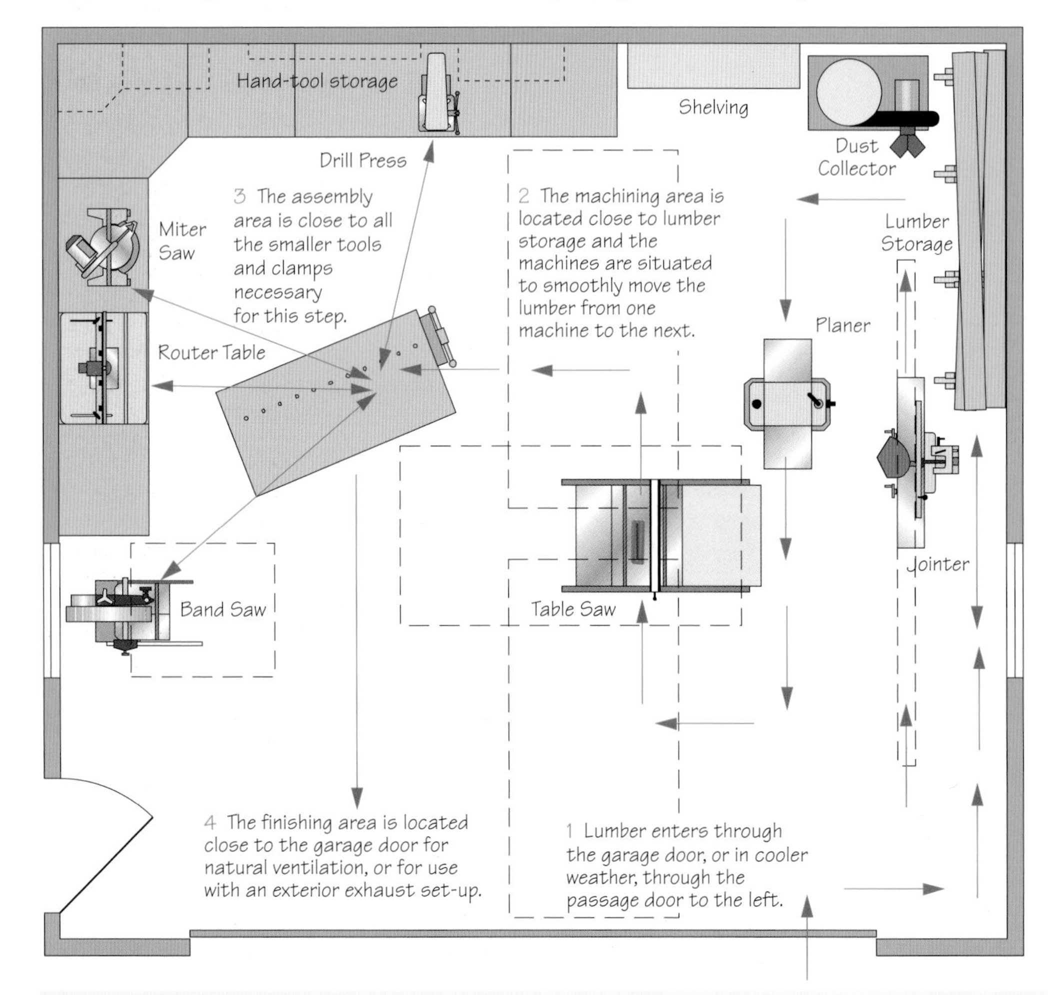

Our example of work flow in a two-car garage. This is the same shop as shown in the other photos, so you know it works on more than paper. Just follow the red arrows to the easiest path for woodworking. The dotted lines show approximate infeed and outfeed room for lumber.

The cabinets you choose for your shop can be premade kitchen cabinets, cabinets you make yourself, or cabinets designed for your woodworking needs, as shown in the photo. These cabinets offer simple drop-in platforms for a variety of benchtop tools, with slide-in/slide-out storage for easy access. Storage options include drawers and doors, depending on your needs. Each of the units is capable of easy dust collection hookup for any benchtop tool, and one of the drop-in panels will allow the cabinet to function as a downdraft table. But don't forget the lowly pegboard for storing hand tools. It still provides the easiest, least expensive and most adjustable hanging storage around.

While you can easily see what you're looking for, so can everyone else — whether it's attractive or not.

Wire-frame shelving is not a good choice for storing small pieces. And knowing the weight limit of the shelves will keep you from picking up all your wood screws from the shop floor when the shelf collapses. Also, while you may view deeper shelves as being capable of storing more (which they are), recognize that smaller items on the shelf can get pushed to the back and get lost.

Where'd I Put That Hammer?

Certain hand tools (hammers, screwdrivers, chisels and handsaws) are always being reached for — frequently when only one hand is free. For that reason these and other hand tools are usually stored hanging within easy reach on the wall.

All sorts of ways exist to hang hand tools on a wall. Some woodworkers build special cabinets for their hand tools. The more common solution is pegboard. It's inexpensive, versatile and easy to mount. With a variety of hooks to choose from, you can make pegboard storage adapt to almost anything. And pegboard doesn't have to be dark brown. More frequently it's being offered in colored plastic, or you can simply paint your own.

But pegboard isn't the only simple option for hanging tools. You've likely seen slat wall in department stores holding up socks and ties. This material is essentially a ¾" board with T-shaped grooves cut in it and a colored plastic laminate on top. It provides much of the versatility and convenience of pegboard, but looks nicer doing it. It'll cost a little more, but it's your choice.

Then there are the workshop experts who mount things right to the wall. By using drywall molly bolts (or covering your walls with painted particleboard) and a variety of hanging storage accessories available in any home-improvement store, you can make a wall of tools that will be uniquely your own. In fact, many folks add outlines of the tools on the wall (or on pegboard) so they know exactly where it belongs — and more importantly, if it's missing.

Power, Lights, Ventilation

Now that you know where everything belongs, it's time to power it up. While it's one thing to be able to check the

A good workbench is one item you should build into your plans from the start. We've put the bench in this shop so it's central to all the activity. It's just a short step away from the saw and planer, and only a few feet away from all the hand tools and other benchtop tools. And with it isolated in the center of the room, all four sides of the workbench can be used. You can order complete plans for this bench (which costs just $175 to build) from our Web site at www.popularwoodworking.com. The plans are $9.95.

tool manuals for the power requirements, it's quite another thing to go about hooking up that power yourself. If you're uncertain about adding new breakers or running wiring, we recommend you get a licensed professional to help you out. But you can help them out by determining the voltage requirements for your tools, whether 110 or 220 volts, and also how many amps each tool requires.

You'll need to provide adequate amperage for each grouping of tools. A contractor's saw will usually require a 110-volt, 20-amp connection, but you can use that same circuit for your planer or jointer because these machines are seldom used simultaneously. Band saws and drill presses can also share a circuit. Another way to improve motor performance and safety is to use a heavier-gauge wire (12 gauge versus 14 gauge) for your stationary tools.

Other things to include in your power requirements are lighting, bench outlets and any ambient air cleaners. Even if you're blessed with lots of windows in your shop, we all work on cloudy days and in the evenings. So proper lighting can be critical. Make sure you have plenty of general lighting throughout your shop, and add task lighting over dedicated work areas, such as your workbench, and over tools that require careful attention to detail, such as the band saw or scroll saw.

Don't skimp on power outlets. Heck, put one everywhere you can imagine plugging in a tool, radio or fan. Make sure a good power strip with numerous outlets is mounted near your bench because cordless-tool battery chargers will use them up fast.

Wood dust is bad for the lungs. By properly using dust collection to keep the larger dust particles out of the air to start, and air cleaners to pull the smaller particles out of the air, the workshop can be a safe and lung-friendly place.

Dust collection is usually set up one of two ways — either with a central collection system using metal or plastic ductwork and a single large dust collector, or with multiple dedicated collectors (though often these can be shared by more than one machine).

A central dust-collection system is a fairly involved topic that entire books have been written about (see *Controlling Dust in the Workshop* by Rick Peters [Sterling Publications]). You need to determine the amount of air movement required to collect from the many different machines, make

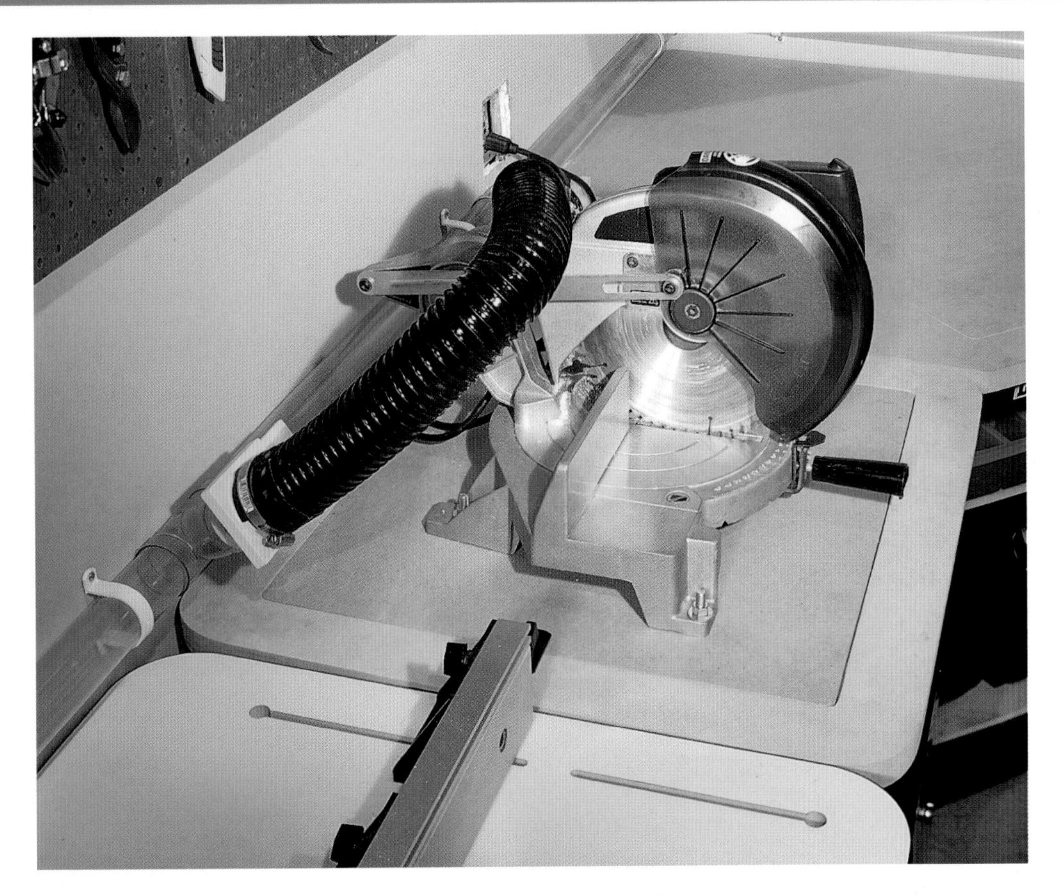

Here's a little closer look at the interchangeable drop-in panels and dust-collection hook-ups for the bench-top tools.

sure your collector is capable of that performance, and locate and use blast gates in the ductwork to maximize the performance of the machine. If a central dust-collection system is your preference, you should spend some in-depth research time on the topic and maybe even consult a professional for advice.

Smaller portable dust collectors are often more affordable and can provide adequate collection for a couple of machines. By using multiple hoses and closeable gates to control which machine is being collected, one machine can do double or triple duty. Each machine is rated by the cfm (cubic feet per minute) of air that it is capable of handling. We've included a quick reference chart that rates each machine by the suggested cfm required to extract dust. By using the chart, you can easily determine the size and number of dust collectors you need.

Ambient air cleaners pull the dust from the air that the dust collectors miss. They are designed to exchange a specific amount of air determined by the size of your shop. Choose the air cleaner (or cleaners) to best serve your space, then let them go to work. Air cleaners require less attention than a dust collector, but you do need to clean or change the filters on a regular basis so they operate properly.

Another air-quality decision is finishing. Because of the volatile and harmful vapors given off by solvent-based finishing products, they will be labeled for use in a well-ventilated area. Whether that means a dedicated finishing area with appropriate air-extraction equipment, or just making sure the garage door is open and a good fan is in use, finishing should take place in an area that ensures safety from explosion and from inhalation of fumes.

MACHINE DUST-COLLECTION STATISTICS

MACHINE	REQ'D CFM
12" Planer	350
13"+ Planer	400
Shaper	400
Band saw	400
Radial-arm saw	350
Table saw	350
Disc sander	300
Jointer	350
Drill press	300
Scroll saw	300

STATIC PRESS.	LOSS/FT.
4" Duct	0.055 in./ft.
5" Duct	0.042 in./ft.
6" Duct	0.035 in./ft.
7" Duct	0.026 in./ft.
8" Duct	0.022 in./ft.

ernie conover's shop

BY SCOTT PHILLIPS

It is my opinion that the recent impressive growth in woodworking in this country can be traced to the American Revolution. My theory is that it's the independent American spirit that inspires woodworkers to dream of new things and to create new projects. One of our country's biggest dreamers is Ernie Conover of Conover Workshops (www.conoverworkshops.com). Conover is a woodworker, turner, tool manufacturer and educator who has made all those things work together in one place: a workshop that most folks would fantasize about.

Born and raised in Ohio, Conover holds a degree in business administration. During the early 1970s he plied his skills as an intelligence officer in Germany, then during the next 15 years he co-founded and developed Conover Woodcraft Specialties. The company manufactured a unique line of reproduction hand tools and produced the Conover 16" lathe. In the course of this endeavor he identified the need for quality educational woodworking classes, and that eventually led to Conover Workshops.

Located in the bucolic village of Parkman, Ohio, Conover Workshops is in the center of Amish country, surrounded by rural America at its best. Conover and his wife, Susan, own a farmhouse and a 3,500-square-foot gable-roofed vintage barn. Throughout the years they have industriously added rooms to the farmhouse and many tools to the barn.

First and foremost, Conover Workshops is a school. In his classes, Conover teaches students first how projects are designed. Next, he focuses on hand and power tool techniques used in making projects.

This is a European style of teaching woodworking, and it puts a great deal of emphasis on mastering all hand and power tool skills. Each project in the class is designed so students' fundamental skills progress as they tackle each successive project in the course.

Conover's barn workshop is divided into four large work zones. On the ground floor is a small store that sells refurbished old hand planes, chisels, layout tools, books and more.

Next to the store is the lathe area, which is a turner's paradise. Conover is one of the country's leading turners, and has been instrumental in helping to grow the American Association of Woodturners, so it should come as no surprise that 10 lathes (Nova and Conover), with a variety of Sorby and Crown chisels and sharpening aids, are located here.

Two-thirds of the second-floor space is dedicated to many handmade and Ulmia workbenches. Conover limits most classes to eight students for personal attention. The hardwood floors are much easier on the back and feet and make it a comfortable area to work in. The ladder in the background accesses the third-floor attic that stores an eclectic collection of jigs, fixtures and tools.

On the second floor there's one huge room with large banks of windows that is home to more traditional handmade and Ulmia workbenches than I have seen in one well-organized space. The barn's massive hand-cut and hand-fit beams help to inspire an interest in learning things the right way. The workbenches are arranged so that 8 to 10 students each have their own work areas. Various guest instructors, all leaders in their respective fields, share their talents at Conover Workshops, offering courses in a soup-to-nuts, hands-on series of classes leaning toward hand-tool techniques, with a healthy reverence for the safe use of power tools.

The fourth work zone is a smaller room on the barn's upper level that has mostly

The Unisaw in the prep area has a crosscut sled and, when needed, a traditional Unifence. The saw is on a mobile base so students can move it to work with longer or wider workpieces. A drum sander offers an affordable way to surface even highly figured woods such as curly maple. Notice that the central dust-collection piping is carefully tucked in out-of-the-way places for efficient use.

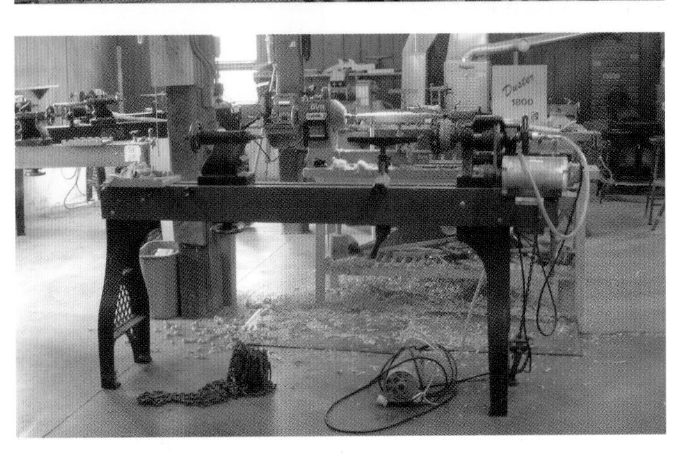
The ground floor work area features one of the classic Conover lathes. I also noted some Nova lathes. The 8" bench grinders help students master the art of quick and easy sharpening. The antifatigue mats make working on concrete much more comfortable. Ample windows and many banks of lights provide great illumination that leads to less eyestrain and better work.

Delta tools, including a Unisaw, band saw and drill press. There's also the standard complement of small power tools. Conover has perfected crosscutting jigs that produce flawless work on the table saw. He has experimented with a number of high-quality table saw blades and has settled on CMT blades.

Tool chests (handmade, of course) housing razor-sharp chisels are located in strategic locations throughout the shop area. Conover has studied many different woodworking traditions and embraces them all for their various strengths. But for sharpening bench chisels he prefers using traditional Japanese waterstones.

One of Conover's gifts is the ability to sharpen any tool to perfection. He uses every imaginable sharpening tool, yet he prefers using an 8" grinder with the Wolverine grinding jig system to sharpen lathe chisels. He hones all his spindle turning tools, but he prefers to leave a burr (a fine wire curl) on the edge of all face-plate lathe chisels, including some scrapers that can be used for both styles of turning.

The woodshop barn is as comfortable as an old hat. The smell of years of woodworking wafts into every niche. Throughout the years, the barn has accumulated jigs and fixtures for cutting every imaginable dovetail. In the third-story storage loft are woodworking contraptions that only a fellow tinkerer could understand. Mortising jigs, finger-joint fixtures, cast iron workbench legs — stuff every woodworker would love to have.

Perhaps his secret to making this barn so productive is the fact that a second storage barn (much smaller) is linked by a crane to his main barn. When he needs something special he just hoists it into the main barn. It looks like he has enough stationary equipment in the spare barn to sink a ship.

Most shops like Conover's tend to have wood and lumber jammed into every corner. Not here. Conover stocks carefully. I saw only about 1,000 board feet of wood, neatly stored. That's it. When asked, he said that he provides wood for featured projects, but also wants students to feel free to bring their own lumber. Figured hard maple, cherry and walnut are his most frequently used woods.

One interesting addition will be the timber-frame post-and-beam L-shaped wing that the Conovers are adding to the main barn. This space is going to be built with traditional mortise-and-tenon hand-cut joints. Conover will use this addition to house a fine collection of metalworking tools, which he inherited from his father, who is one of the most inventive men that I have had the good fortune to meet. It's fair to say Conover is a chip off the old block.

During his three decades of woodworking, Conover has made just about every style of furniture. He has a keen eye for design, but prefers to focus on the joy of the woodworking process and sharing that process with his students. I get the impression that there is nothing in the world Conover would rather do than to be working with people who have a passion for woodworking. Maybe that is why he is constantly grinning like a child in a candy store. Maybe that's what makes him a good teacher.

sam maloof's shop

BY DAVID THIEL

Most woodworkers are aware of who Sam Maloof is. The son of Lebanese immigrants, Maloof turned his skill for graphic design and a passion for woodworking into a career that has made him one of the most sought-after and successful craftsmen in the world. His signature pieces — sculpted chairs and rockers — are made using intricate joints and have lines that draw you from one detail to the next, while the shape invites you to sit in perfect comfort.

What many woodworkers don't realize is that Maloof now has a new shop. His old shop in Alta Loma, California, was relocated because his shop of 50 years was in the way of progress — or more correctly, in the way of the 210 Freeway. Because of Maloof's stature, the property was considered worthy of preservation, and the house and shop were moved intact to a new location three miles north of the original site. The shop space continues in use, while the original house now serves as a gallery and museum, displaying a dizzying array of pieces from throughout Maloof's career, as well as a glimpse into his 50-year marriage with his late wife, Alfreda.

On the day before his 87th birthday, Maloof took time out of his hectic schedule to lead a tour of his new workshop, home and lumber-storage facilities. During the tour, what was striking was that despite his fame and success, Maloof even today still simply thinks of himself as "just a woodworker."

Sam Maloof strikes a pose with a love seat in midconstruction. The piece includes his trademark sculpted appearance with hard and soft lines blended together into seamless elegance.

Sam and the Boys

Though acknowledging his advancing age, Maloof continues to have an active part of every piece of furniture. "Any of the boys [his three employees] can do what I do," he says. "But I just don't want to walk out and do nothing. I'd die! So I still work."

The "boys" are Larry White, Mike Johnson and David Wade. White was 19 and looking for a summer job in 1962 when he became Maloof's first employee. He spent seven years with Maloof, then went out on his own. In 1992, events conspired to allow White to come back to work with Maloof.

Johnson was an industrial arts major in college when he and his wife saw Maloof at a local mall. His wife encouraged him to go talk to Maloof, which he did. It just so happened that Maloof had a job opening and told him to stop by. That was in 1981, and Johnson has been with Maloof ever since.

Wade, a journeyman craftsman with Maloof's operation since 1989, liked working with wood in high school. One day a girl in a class noticed the parts to a project of his stashed under his desk.

"If you like wood," she said to Wade, "you should meet my grandfather, Sam Maloof." Well, the budding woodworker knew a good thing when he saw it and is now a solid member of the Maloof shop.

Always after Amazing Wood

Maloof always has been picky about who works in his shop — just like he is picky about his wood. After a visit to his shop you can see how it is a never-ending obsession.

Maloof's pieces are made predominately from walnut, though maple and zircote are also strong sellers. While zircote is beautiful, Maloof doesn't really like working with it because of the toxic dust.

Right before lunch that day, a local landscaper stopped by to chat with Maloof. He was taking down some Torrey pines (5'-6' across and maybe 100' straight). He'd found trees for Maloof in the past and wanted to know if he wanted these. Sure, Maloof says, and they worked out the arrangements. But Maloof also brought up a particular walnut tree he'd seen and wanted to know when he could get that one. The tree wasn't scheduled to come down anytime soon, but Maloof knew where the good wood was, and he was keeping his eye on it.

Of the buildings on his property, two are dedicated to lumber storage, and Maloof is currently overseeing the construction of a third. He designed the new structure with a peak to mirror the San Gabriel mountain peaks looming directly behind the building.

The wood storage sheds hold thousands of board feet of quilted maple, figured walnut, rosewood, ebony and zircote. It's more than most woodworkers could use in a lifetime, but not Maloof. "Those pieces — you can see how wide they are [5' wide and easily 2" thick] — those are beautiful. They're fiddleback walnut, and I'm making a dining table for the kitchen in the other house, and the other will be a conference table."

In "Sam's shop" (more accurately the machining room), templates for a dizzying array of chair designs line the wall. Standing at the ready is a 20" planer, 12" jointer and, tucked in the left of the photo is a Laguna 20" band saw, one of four band saws currently in the shop.

On the opposite side of the room above is a 12" table saw and heavy-duty shaper. More templates adorn the walls (they're fixtures in most of the rooms), and a chalkboard and props stand at the ready for weekend lectures where Maloof walks attendees through the construction process of one of his chairs.

Building a Maloof Piece

David Wade describes the process of making a piece of Maloof furniture. "Sam does all the sculpting on the band saw, does the joinery and the wood selection and puts everything together. But it's a continual back-and-forth process. He'll put a seat together, then I'll get it and carve out the shape, then it goes back to him. He puts the back legs on, then it goes to Mike or Larry and they start shaping it. When that's shaped, it goes back to Sam and he'll do the arms. Everyone gets their hands on it."

The process starts in one of the wood storage rooms with Maloof picking 5"-to-7" width, 8/4 material for the seats in the rough. Backs will be 12/4 or 14/4. Maloof heads straight to the band saw to cut the lumber to size, then lays out the pieces using one of the hundreds of patterns hanging in the shop.

Maloof rough-sculpts the pieces on the band saw. He also will use the templates as shaping patterns, nailing the template to the piece, then heading to the shaper and using the template to guide the shaper as with a flush-trimming router bit.

"It would take me a lot longer if I didn't cut them out like I do on the band saw [free-handing the large chunks of wood rapidly through the machine]," Maloof says. "I can make a couple items in 15 minutes, but if I were doing it all by hand, it would probably take me four or five hours." But he doesn't recommend his free-hand shaping method, because of the safety factor. "I didn't know any better when I started . . . It's sorta dumb. You can say that, too. It's sorta dumb."

He's had his choice of band saws throughout the years, working his way up from a 14" cast iron Rockwell band saw with an extension block, to his current 32" Agazzani.

In the assembly room you pass a rack full of clamps. Pipe, bar and C-clamps are organized and handy. While none are brand-new, all are in good shape even after years of use.

"I use machines wherever possible," Maloof says. "But I'd say 90 percent of it is handwork. You can't do it with a machine. There's no way. There isn't a machine made that would do the things that we do by hand. It's very time-consuming . . . but we don't let anything out of the shop that we don't like. We'd rather cut it up and throw it away."

With the pieces rough, the rest is shaping. Wade explains this part of the process:

"There's a lot of detail work, a lot of shaping to get the hard lines established. And then sanding from there. We use pneumatics, files and Nicholson No. 49 10" rasps. The Dynabrade's really helpful for sanding, and we use electric quarter-sheet sanders. [There's a] lot of hand sanding. We've made foam blocks in different shapes that we use to get into the curves."

Wade recommends Klingspor sanding products, saying they seem to cut better than any other papers they've used, last longer and don't load up as much. With all the sanding that goes on, they rely on air cleaners and attic fans to keep things clean. On Fridays the shop gets a thorough cleaning. Wade says he's even resorted to a yard blower.

Finishing Remarks

The last step is putting on the finish. Maloof developed a two-part finish 50 years ago and continues to use it on all his pieces. The first step is the poly/oil (one-third semigloss urethane, one-third raw tung oil and one-third boiled linseed oil). The second step is wax/oil. (Same as the first mix, but leaving out the urethane and adding a couple of handfuls of shredded beeswax per gallon to the mixture. This is heated in a double boiler until the wax melts.)

You can buy Maloof's finishes pre-mixed from Rockler Woodworking and Hardware. That's what's on his shelves, and that's what they use.

"Four coats of the poly/oil and one coat with the wax/oil, and it gives it a nice sheen," Maloof says. "It's a friendly finish. It's real easy to apply. Just rub it on and rub it off. No need for a spray booth. It's friendly down the road, too. If you do have a dent or a cup ring or something, it's easy to repair."

The Maloof team works a standard 40-hour week, but the guys also help out with Maloof's Saturday workshop lectures.

"I know a lot of people, very good friends of mine, that just think I'm crazy doing what I do, as far as giving workshops," Maloof says. "They say, 'You don't owe anybody anything, you've been doing it for so long.' But I still enjoy giving workshops. I like to share what

In the fitting room, Johnson (far left) and White use a variety of hand sanding and sculpting tools to final-fit the pieces. A 14" band saw stands handy, and a large and small lathe are available for any turning needs. The photo above shows the lathe tools and some spindles ready to be fitted into the back splat.

In the assembly room, more templates dot the walls, while partially assembled pieces wait for the next step. A 10" cabinet saw sits amidst rough-sanding machines, including an edge sander, large disc sander, spindle sander and contour sander.

I do. I don't have any secrets."

Maloof's past is all around him, with many pieces coming back to his shop for repairs or on their way to museums. Though Maloof has a lifetime of experiences already, his zest for life has not decreased. He remarried recently, and to who else but a former customer.

Maloof had built a dining table for a couple early in his career and throughout the years they'd stayed in touch. Beverly and her husband had divorced over time, and then Maloof's first love, Alfreda, "had to leave" as he explains her 1998 death.

Sometime later, Beverly "invited me to her house for lunch and I couldn't see the grain through the finish [in the table he'd made]. It looked awful. So I told her I'd come by and pick it up and redo it for her. I did, and I think that's the reason she married me."

Maloof continues to take orders on new furniture pieces and has about a four-year waiting list at this time. With his newly formed Sam and Alfreda Maloof Foundation for Arts and Crafts (see the sidebar at right for more details), his plate is full, but his work will continue to delight and dazzle generations to come.

As Johnson and White fit the back splat on a love seat, you might think they're getting close to being done. There are still many hours of sanding and shaping before this piece will bear the Maloof maker's mark.

MALOOF FOUNDATION

The Sam and Alfreda Maloof Foundation for Arts and Crafts, established in 1994, is committed to creating a preeminent center that preserves the Maloofs' legacy and fosters the arts and crafts movement. The work of the foundation recognizes the ever increasing role of the crafts in our world of machine-made products — the reconnecting of human values with natural forms and materials.

A principal responsibility of the foundation is protection and conservation of the art, furnishings, structures and grounds entrusted to it. The foundation is also making the Maloof Center available to the public, artists and researchers, and developing a variety of programs, including visiting craftsmen, workshops and arts and crafts exhibits.

Sam Maloof continues to create furniture at the new site and add to his fine art collection that encompasses work from all media, including many renowned artists such as Maria Martinez, Millard Sheets, Paul Soldner, Kay Sekimachi and Bob Stocksdale.

Friends' contributions help conserve and maintain the foundation's art collection, structures and grounds, as well as support foundation programs that seek to create an awareness of the way in which crafts enrich our culture.

To learn more about becoming a member of the Maloof Foundation, or to get tour information, contact them at:

P.O. Box 397, Alta Loma, CA 91701
909-980-0412
www.malooffoundation.org
E-mail: malooffoundation@earthlink.net

To learn more about Sam Maloof's remarkable life and his woodworking, we suggest:

Sam Maloof, Woodworker by Sam Maloof, published by Kodansha International

The Furniture of Sam Maloof by Jeremy Adamson, published by the Smithsonian American Art Museum.

LEFT TO RIGHT: Larry White, Mike Johnson, Sam Maloof, David Wade, Slimen Maloof (Sam's son) and business manager Roz Bock.

warren may's shop

BY SCOTT PHILLIPS

For years I've wanted to make my own Appalachian-inspired, mountain lap dulcimer. These wooden wonders have been part of American culture since before the American Revolution. Dulcimers are easy enough to make, yet tricky to perfect. Woodworker Warren May of Berea, Kentucky, just might have figured out the best way to make these four-stringed instruments. I recently visited this dulcimer maker and learned a few things about designing a workshop to make his projects — and yours — easier.

May's workshop is located on about 40 acres of gently rolling hills, about five miles from Berea. It's forested with mixed hardwoods. Many of the huge black walnut and cherry trees will be harvested in coming years to be turned into mountain dulcimers and fine furniture. Yep — even though May's shop (he has three employees) has completed more than 12,000 dulcimers, he still has time to produce dozens of pieces of fine furniture to sell every year.

After looking around his shop, I decided that May and Thomas Edison might be distant relatives. May uses machines that you would find in a well-equipped home shop. But every machine is decked out with shop-made jigs and fixtures. In some cases he's built or modified power tools (including an incredible "gang fret saw"; more on that later). And sometimes he's taken an unlikely object, such as in-line skate wheels, and built a safety device, such as a resawing featherboard for his band saw. May works with both hand and power tools. And perhaps his continued success is a result of the hand-worked details he adds to every piece before it leaves his workshop.

In May's shop there are huge windows on every available wall. The abundance of natural light makes the shop much easier to work in. The electric heat pump is nice, too. It keeps the 2,500-square-foot shop conditioned and comfortable year-round.

May's motorized "gang fret saw" allows the fret board to be held against the fence on the sliding table, as the table carriage is pushed over the blades. It's a tool that's hard to imagine, let alone make. But May's invention has helped him make instruments with exacting precision — and save time.

For dust collection, May has a big impeller that exhausts chips directly out the back of his shop into a recycling pile. Dust collection is more than a convenience in this shop. May's finishing room is adjacent to the main shop and must be kept virtually dust-free.

The finishing area is outfitted with a sizable exhaust fan. When he applies his usual sanding sealer followed by multiple light coats of lacquer, the fan really reduces overspray, smell and fumes.

I asked May what the toughest part of making a dulcimer is and he pointed to the fret board. All frets (metal strips perpendicular to the

The in-line skate wheel featherboard makes frequent resawing activities on May's band saw safe, precise and pretty easy.

May's clamping jig is a set of 5/16" bolts that are held in a special pattern frame. Each of the multiple dulcimer profiles requires a matching "spring clamping jig." All bolts are spaced properly to place just the right amount of pressure at exactly the right spot. While one jig costs about $30 to make, it replaces about 40 spring clamps and makes a better product.

strings) must be perfectly spaced and fitted to produce perfect tonality. So he designed a saw that will cut all the slots for the frets in the neck of a dulcimer at once. This "gang fret saw" looks like a miniature direct-drive table saw (with more than a dozen blades) and a sliding table. All the 2"-diameter circular saw blades have thin kerfs that fit the metal fret strips perfectly.

Almost any musical instrument maker will tell you that gluing up the body takes lots of time and clamps. So May invented a spring-loaded jig to glue up the bodies that uses only one clamp. I'm not lying. The photo on the left explains it better than words can.

Many dulcimer parts require very thin, resawn wood. Here, May uses a generic-brand 1-hp band saw with a 5/8" Lenox resaw blade. May frequently uses a Teflon-like spray, Bostik DriCote, to coat the blade. This reduces blade friction and minimizes pitch and resin buildup. Ultimately, this extends blade life.

And, of course, there's the in-line skate wheels. He uses the urethane-coated bearings to make a spring-tensioned featherboard that pushes material firmly against his band saw's fence. The wheel material won't mar the wood or let it slip.

In a dulcimer, the sound holes, along with the shape and thickness of the sound board (the wide top board), impart the tonal qualities to the finished instrument. Often, May will take advantage of nature's own bookmatched limb holes, knots or natural openings to form the sound holes. Or he'll use the scroll saw to cut hummingbirds, floral or heart-shaped openings. His love of handwork is evident in the beveled edges carved on each sound hole design and the carved details on the tuning head.

Often, delicate-edged details require extra support. A unique blend of thick viscosity cyanoacrylate (superglue) mixed with rosewood dust makes a solid backing in seconds. A catalyst isn't required, because a chemical in the dust accelerates the curing. Remember to wear a mask when working with rosewood; this species can cause allergic reactions.

I've been in hundreds of woodshops in the last 20 years. No two are alike. May's shop is a long, rectangular building that he built on a budget and has added to as needed. His shop has grown and evolved over the years. My day with May gave me new ideas that will help make my work better and easier.

WORKSHOP AND RETAIL STORE

To see outstanding dulcimers surrounded with elegant furniture, I went to the Warren A. May Woodworker store in Berea. Warren and his wife, Frankye, work closely to offer a wide selection of wooden objects for every budget. It is fair to say they have something for everyone. I bought a $400 dulcimer (my wife really needed it for her birthday) that not only looks perfect but the notes that escape it just sing. Their store is on the same block as Berea's famous Boone Tavern and is where he and Frankye both made and sold dulcimers and furniture in their early years. Today, they have the store set up for sales and the country woodshop perfected for woodworking.

The store always has a selection of Kentucky-style furniture. Warren May describes it as honest, well-made, solid hardwood furniture with folk-inspired handwork in the finishing touches. Hand tool work is part of the tradition of fine Kentucky-made furniture. Over the last 200 years, Kentucky has developed a unique style of honest furniture design — simple, solid walnut, cherry and maple designs accented with hand beading, diamond keyhole accents, line inlay of contrasting woods and shaped aprons. Some folks might misjudge this style as Shaker simplicity with decorative highlights. I believe the Kentucky style started before Shaker times and in turn, may have influenced the "western" Shakers' furniture.

His popular Kentucky sideboard uses inlaid maple diamond keyhole escutcheons. Beaded drawer fronts hide the perfect handmade dovetails inside. Frankye May made a sign nearby that says, "Please do not remove the drawers, trust me they are made correctly." Many drawers have been dropped over the years when folks got a little too excited about the perfect details. All the pieces are finished to a beautiful sheen.

The Mays have been in their store for 27 years and at the country woodshop for 15 years. Earlier, Warren May taught industrial arts to high school students. Today, he continues to teach, but now it's how to play the dulcimer. His energy and skills are contagious. He believes anyone can play a well-made instrument, and I have to agree. Dulcimers are easy to learn to play, and he can teach anyone the basics in just one sitting. They're almost as easy to play as humming into a kazoo — and that is part of their magic.

kelly mehler's shop

BY SCOTT PHILLIPS

The lifeline of Berea, Kentucky, is Chestnut Street. It takes every visitor to the heart of Berea College. This school has been teaching progressive concepts for over a century, programs to keep inspired individuals prospering. This atmosphere touches everyone in Berea, or maybe the people of Berea just are independently unique. Either way, Kelly Mehler's shop on Chestnut Street fits this place like a glove.

Mehler's first passion is custom woodworking. But on the side he finds time to author books, articles and videos, teach classes at the Marc Adams School of Woodworking, give seminars at the woodworking shows, and host many workshops across America every year.

The first thing that is striking about his place is that Mehler converted a vintage automotive dealership into his woodshop. Aged brick walls frame huge banks of windows that light up his shop. Years ago, cars probably occupied every inch of both the showroom and the "garage." Today air-drying wood fills that space, and its aroma makes all woodworkers feel right at home.

When I walked through the 24"-wide door into the garage-turned-woodshop I got a little envious. Natural light from the southern exposure streamed in on his vintage machines. Well-insulated 15'-high ceilings lift the eyes to explore every nook and cranny.

Kelly Mehler: Best known for his landmark *The Table Saw Book*, first published in 1993, Mehler also is a frequent lecturer on the woodworking show circuit and an instructor at the Marc Adams School of Woodworking. Mehler works only with solid wood and is known for his grain-matching talents.

His shop space totals about 3,000 square feet. This includes a small entrance showroom that features graceful furniture accented by beautifully figured wood that Mehler builds from select logs. When asked to describe his design style, he smiles because most folks see a unique furniture form.

It all is solid, beautifully selected and matched-grain native woods that blend the best of Shaker, traditional and contemporary forms. Mehler says he buys rare logs, then has them sawn so he can use matching boards for every piece he makes. He says he air-dries most of his own lumber because of the rich colors this technique produces. After more than 30 years in the business he has amassed a small fortune in special wood. But don't even think about offering to buy some of it. My guess is that in the back of his mind he has plans for every board.

When I visited, Mehler's latest project was to update his well-known *The Table Saw Book* (Taunton Press), so his shop was temporarily loaded with about every table saw on earth. It was interesting to see "all" table saws at once. It reminded me that most saws are copies of a few basic designs.

So which saw does he like for the home woodworker? Mehler says he's kind of partial to the DeWalt DW746. Mostly, though, Mehler warns woodworkers away from buying a saw based only on price.

"We spend $2,000 on a computer that lasts about five or six years," he says. "Yet often we try to pinch pennies when we buy tools that last a lifetime."

I couldn't agree more. Spend the extra dollars for quality, and you'll always be happy. Just don't tell everyone at home about your purchase.

Mehler (center) demonstrates his Felder combination machine. It's amazing how the splitter moves up and down with the blade. Why can't we have this on all U.S.- and Taiwanese-made saws?

During my visit to Mehler's shop in Berea, Kentucky, nearly every square foot of floor space was occupied by a table saw. Every place there wasn't a table saw, there were huge racks of wood.

Mehler's band of heavy-metal machines includes this massive planer. My only question is: Where is its mobile base?

And get rid of the box before you take it home. Wives are cagey about empty, expensive-looking packaging. Don't tell anyone I told you this.

When Mehler is done with all these saws, you can bet he'll stick with his 5-hp Austrian-made Felder combination machine (they cost between $5,000 and $15,000 and can be set up to do just about every machining job in a wood shop). It occupies the center of the shop and maybe Mehler's heart.

Another interesting part of Mehler's shop is his vintage heavy-duty machinery that he has purchased wisely (and inexpensively) over many years and after a little horse trading. I covet his 36" 1910 Oliver band saw, which he uses primarily for resawing. His 24" Crescent planer looks as big as the Rock of Gibraltar. It also was interesting to see that his dust-collection system ducts directly outside to minimize shop cleanup time and maximize woodworking time. His industrial-grade spray booth is tucked in a far corner behind his clamp rack.

Perhaps his favorite "tool" is his German-style European workbench that looks loaded with great stories. This well-worn bench is where Mehler uses hand tools to cut dovetails, fit joints, and make the wood just about sing.

Everywhere you look you'll see that this man has carefully grown his shop with just the right tools for his needs. So passionate is Mehler about tools that he's lately been getting involved in the debate about safety and guards in the U.S. market. Mehler consults for many different companies regarding shop safety and design. He is a member of an Underwriters Laboratories Inc. advisory council and focuses on improving power tool safety.

When Mehler is asked what is the most important piece of safety equipment on a table saw, the splitter comes to the top of his list. Why? Because, he maintains, the splitter reduces the risk of a kickback dramatically. He also says that European manufacturers can teach American tool companies many great ideas on improving tool guards.

For example, he showed me how the Felder table saw's splitter actually was designed to move up and down with the saw blade. The splitter can be used for nonthrough groove and shoulder cuts because of this feature — again, minimizing the risk of kickback. Also, European guards on jointers make it hard to even get your hands near the cutterhead while jointing a board. The guard is positioned to make a woodworker raise his or her hand over the danger zone. Very smart design! And by the way, Mehler practices what he preaches. Even his old 12" Oliver jointer was set up with a great guard.

Mehler's portfolio of furniture is extensive, and it's obvious he specializes in matching and coordinating the grain in a piece of furniture. When I visited, Mehler was working on a tiger maple chest, a rift-sawn red oak hope or blanket chest (with hand-cut dovetails) and a large case-on-case piece.

He probably works 60 hours a week and clearly loves what he does. I bet if he had to just do one thing, it would be to teach woodworking to as many folks as possible. If you have an opportunity to work with him, don't pass it up. You will find your time well spent with this American master.

scott phillips' shop

BY SCOTT PHILLIPS

When I first designed and outfitted my workshop for *The American Woodshop* in 1970, I thought I'd have everything set up perfectly within a year. It's now 32 years later, and I think I might be close to getting my "dream shop" the way I want it.

Most shops are clever adaptations of existing space. They're usually packed with wood and tools, and there's never enough room for everything — especially wood. Five years ago, I started looking for a new woodshop, in part to make producing my public television series easier to shoot. Many people would say that it's easier to buy or fix up an existing space. I can't argue with that logic, because they would be right. But I decided that to get everything the way I wanted it, I'd have to start from scratch.

Zoning issues ruled out most locations. I finally found two acres that were zoned for business but were in a rural setting. It's in the city limits (we shoot my show in Piqua, Ohio) so I still get all the city services.

The first step was to sketch out what I thought I needed (my dream shop looked great on a napkin), then to double the size. Expect to spend about $30 to $40 per square foot if your shop is built on a concrete slab with a traditional footer. Next, I enlisted the help of the Upper Valley Joint Vocational School in developing a design for the building. The students and teachers added a lot to the shop project, providing invaluable plan designs and drawings.

The construction is stick-built with a concrete pad footprint of 32' × 92'. The roof is metal with a 9/12 pitch and 10'-high ceilings inside. If you're doing math in your head, that gives me a 2,944-square-foot shop, but it isn't all available for building projects.

I partitioned the 12' × 32' built-on porch for those necessary moments to stop and ponder my plans, and the front part of the building includes an office, project gallery, restroom and utility room. That brings the main woodshop room down to 64' × 32' — only 2,048 square feet. But it's still a luxury with plenty of room for everything I do.

My machines are set up for both 110- and 220-volt power. To keep everything running, I selected a 110/208 three-phase Square D 200-amp breaker panel. This gives me voltage flexibility and also saves me money when I run three-phase tools and utilities.

The shop thermostat, which is zoned so the electric three-phase heat pump can be used efficiently, keeps things comfortable. The heat pump works both as a furnace and an air conditioner, with central ductwork in the attic and all registers in the ceiling. The main shop return air duct is equipped with an electrostatic prefilter that acts just like the world's biggest ambient air cleaner. And because I have learned that 80 percent of all heat and air-conditioned energy is lost through the ceiling, I opted to blow R38 virgin fiber-

This shot gives you a feel for the full length of the shop, with everything fairly organized. There's lots of room now; the trick is to keep from filling the place up with more tools. You can see the large garage door in the back that makes moving lumber, equipment and projects in and out much easier, as well as letting that warm summer air in. I know you're wondering about the rug. Well, it's actually a temporary sound dampener for when we shoot the TV program. It seems sound bounces off the door pretty badly.

To keep the shop as dust-free as possible, I upgraded all the dust collectors with 1-micron efficiency bags that help keep airborne dust out of the air. I also use 4" and 5" hose, connectors and blast gates to maximize airflow efficiency and collection capacity. Keeping the collector close to the machines also improves performance. Oh, see the rescued barn door in the background? That's going to be a new tool storage cabinet for the shop.

glass into the attic.

Lighting is one of the most important aspects in any shop, and you just can't beat working with natural light. I installed lots of 48" × 62" double-hung windows. These let in daylight, make things easy on the eyes and save on the lighting bill. For when the sun isn't shining, I installed dual 8' fluorescent low-noise/high-output daylight fluorescent tubes. The tubes produce an 87 cri (color-rated index), are a good buy and come very close to the daylight spectrum. This translates into less eye fatigue and better work.

Where dust collection is concerned, most people make setting up a system too complicated. I opted to use three 1,100 cfm (cubic feet per minute) dust collectors and kept all hose and pipe runs short and sweet. A remote on/off switch for a dust collector is a real time-saver. An ambient air cleaner by the workbench where I sand the most picks up dust that the other systems don't catch.

My shop basically is divided into complementary tool zones. This is called the workstation concept, where tools are arranged to work most effectively together. For instance, a compound miter saw, table saw, jointer and planer are perfect companions. When these four tools are positioned together, 90 percent of furniture project preparation can be completed in this one zone. Plus, this makes it easy to hook up all the tools to a dust collector and saves time when moving from tool to tool during construction.

It also makes sense to put all the hand tools in cabinets by the best light so you can use your workbench most efficiently. Any time a woodworker has to walk across the shop to fetch a tool, you can bet the setup can be improved. Maybe this is why it's taken me 32 years to get my new shop just about right.

I still believe in the versatility of casters and mobile bases, because this allows me to easily reposition tools for large workpieces and store them when they're not needed.

One huge luxury in the new shop is the 18' × 9' insulated garage door at the back of the shop. On good-weather days, the door goes up and the joy of working in great light and air is exhilarating. Often, I roll the

The single most important tool in my shop is the 352-pound European-style Ulmia workbench. This heavy-duty bench can't be pushed around and is like an aircraft carrier with lots of room to do whatever I want. It also has a tilting drawer, which (confession is good for the soul) is one great catchall with a lock. The drawers never stay neatly arranged if much work is getting done in the shop. I prefer to keep the bench pulled away from the wall so I can work on all sides of it as necessary.

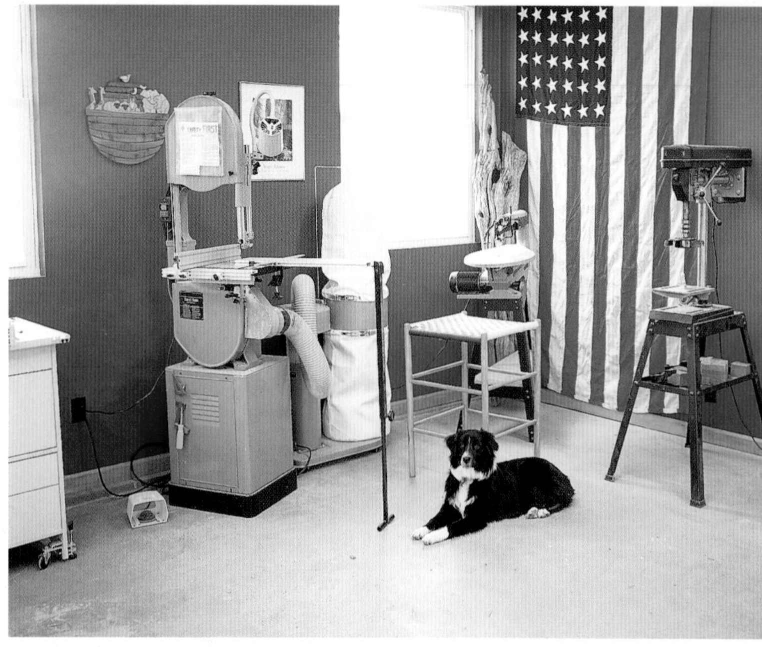

I almost forgot one of the most important parts of my new shop: Callie. Every woodshop needs a shop dog. She keeps me company, chases dropped tools and generally keeps things lively. This is just one of Callie's favorite places to hang. The well-lit corner provides a great place for fine work on the scroll saw. One addition to my machinery that I highly recommend is the foot pedal by the band saw to turn the dust collector on and off. It saves a few steps and makes it easier to remember to keep the dust out of the air.

planer or sanders outside and let the chips fall where they may. Plus, when it comes time to use my high-volume, low-pressure spray finishing system, you can't beat the ventilation. When the weather's not good enough to open the door and spray, environmentally friendly finishes such as water-based polyurethane, shellac, wiping gels and true oil finishes are easy and safe to use.

A few extras (I didn't tell my wife, Suzy, about these things) are the in-floor concrete electrical plates that cost about $300 each installed, extra incandescent track lighting to add highlights, three monster fire extinguishers (required) and a security system that protects a lifetime of accumulated tools and also will call the fire department in case it detects smoke.

I did run into some snags. First, I'm 25 percent over my budget. I expected that, and so should you if you build a new shop. I had to install a retention pond to control the roof and parking lot runoff ($8,000); the shop lane and 20-car parking lot had to be paved to comply to code ($10,000); architect's fee ($2,000, even if you do most of your own preliminary design work and have the help of JVS students); engineer's site plan and required building permits ($1,250); and extra gravel for the access lane and raising the elevation grade for the slab floor ($4,000). And then there's the miscellaneous extras: emergency exit signs, locking gate, plumbing extras and landscaping (another $3,000).

There were some good things about the process, too. Over the years I've accumulated thousands of board feet of Midwestern hardwoods, and I've always dreamed about having a barn for lumber drying and storage. My new property came with a beauty of a barn! The post-and-beam work in the barn dates back to 1840, according to a local historian. All posts are hand hewn. Though the barn is in relatively good shape, it does need some fixing up. I figure about one year's work. But guess what? I have to make the barn comply with local covenants. That means another $20,000 in roofing and siding!

george reid's shop

BY SCOTT PHILLIPS

During the last 30 years I have journeyed to every corner of our country to visit people who have mastered unique aspects of woodworking. But I didn't have to go far from home to meet one of the most impressive artisans, master woodworker George Reid of Kettering, Ohio.

Reid and I have been good friends for 18 years, and I never will forget the first time I walked into the Reid home. Heirloom antiques adorned every room. Because I collect antique furniture, I quickly calculated that Reid had a king's ransom in antiques in his modest home. But then came the real shock: Reid told me they weren't antiques. He had made them all.

At 88, George Reid is still working every day. Here he's sitting at his workbench with two recently completed miniatures. Each miniature includes completely accurate handcut dovetails on the drawers with raised solid-panel bottoms. The Delta drill press you see behind him is 1940s vintage. It's all original except the motor, which he salvaged from his first 1940s-era bench saw and upgraded with a length of link belt.

Reid's eye for proportion and dimension not only gives him the ability to build reproduction Chippendale, Queen Anne, Sheraton, Hepplewhite and other classic furniture styles (both full-size and exquisite miniatures), it has given him the grace to carve them beautifully. His carving is what sets him apart from just about any other cabinetmaker I know. Lots of folks can build the furniture; few can really master the carving.

Other than his signature and date on every custom piece, you cannot distinguish his work from museum originals. Even more impressive, Reid doesn't just make copies. He has studied the classical furniture styles to a degree where he can think and design like an 18th-century cabinetmaker. He can handle sensitive furniture restoration, as well as design new pieces in the classic styles, sometimes even adding additional detail that would be appropriate for that period.

Three views of a miniature Chippendale chair. Reid's chairmaking skills are simply astonishing. Photos of the originals are indistinguishable from his copies.

From the Farm to the Woodshop

Raised on a family farm near Fletcher, Ohio (the farm is still in his family), Reid grew up with a strong work ethic. If you wanted something, you made it; and the milking stool that was his first woodworking project is still in his den being used as a footstool.

Working with his hands on the farm led to a love of wooden models, including his perfectly built scale model of a stagecoach. That model was eventually shown to folks at Wright Field (now Wright-Patterson Air Force Base) in Dayton, Ohio. Impressed, the Army Air Corps hired Reid to make scale airplane models for use as training props and for movies during World War II. The original stagecoach is still on display in his home.

After the war, Reid made the acquaintance of a local businessman who was selling the newest hi-fi components in his store in downtown Dayton. His customers were anxious for the radio pieces, but they wanted them housed in cabinets that would complement their existing furniture. Reid started building these cabinets, many matching quality furniture pieces, and that work led to a study, and love, of furniture styles.

He has always worked by referral only, no walk-in trade. His practical head for business led him to always keep detailed records on how many hours each job took so he was able to charge an accurate price that was both fair and rewarding.

After Reid made furniture for a prosperous golf pro, the stream of new customers was continuous. Word of mouth from happy customers (who always turned into lifelong friends) still keeps him busy in his shop on weekdays and some Saturdays.

Modest Shop, Modest Tools

When you stop by to see Reid in his 28' × 32' basement shop, you'll likely find him wearing his white shop apron. In the breast pocket is the folding carpenter's rule that was issued to him at Wright Field during the war. He uses it every day, but he comments that it has gotten a little too close to the saw once or twice, pointing out the nicks.

The pictures shown here represent a small portion of the work Reid has created, working in the same shop for 60 years. It should humble all woodworkers who complain about not having enough space or tools.

The machines in his shop are mostly late 1940s vintage, which he purchased new shortly after leaving Wright Field.

With barely a scratch on it, this early Delta jigsaw sits in the back corner of Reid's shop, by the lathe. There is not a spot of rust on the cast iron top. The secret? Reid says he merely wipes it down after use to remove fingerprints.

Reid has made some amazing turnings on this well-made Craftsman lathe. Reid doesn't profess to be a turner, but his amazing work belies that statement.

No tilting arbor here. Reid built most of the furniture in his career using this tilt-top table saw and a high-speed steel blade. After about 60 years of use, the saw still has a lot of life left in it.

They are in immaculate condition, and many still have the original manuals hanging handy. The shop itself is just as meticulously maintained. Chalk that up to necessary organization for working in a small space, and to avoid tracking dust all over the house.

As you peer around his shop, your eye takes in clamps neatly stored in the basement joists. His original workbench (with a white oak top) is still as sturdy as the day he made it 60 years ago, and it sees continuous use. This is where he does almost all his carving, including period ball-and-claw legs and bombé chest miniatures.

His first major purchase was a 1941 Delta tilt-top table saw. It was his only table saw until he received a Delta Unisaw in 1997. The tilt saw is still used right alongside the Unisaw. Most of his Delta tools were purchased in the 1940s and are still used to make furniture. A Delta benchtop drill press near his bench has been upgraded with a balanced pulley and PowerTwist belt. His Delta shaper has performed flawlessly for years, to the point that he doesn't own a router.

A sanding station is positioned near a heavy-duty shop vacuum to save time sanding. He keeps his shop orderly by doing a thorough cleaning once a day. Ultimately there is no substitute for elbow grease.

A 12" Boice-Crane planer, a

This miniature chest-on-chest is perfect in every detail, from the shell carving to the broken pediment. While his miniatures use less wood, Reid estimates that they take almost as much time as building a full-size piece.

1940s Craftsman band saw and lathe, a 6" Delta benchtop jointer by a smaller workbench and a Delta jigsaw (scroll saw to us today) round out the list of stationary machines.

His small power tools are limited to a couple of vintage corded drills, a belt sander, finishing sander, a rotary flattop oilstone grinder and a few other common corded tools.

Hand Tools Make the Difference

Reid's hand tools are his prize possessions and are the tools that let his skills shine. They are decades old, but in better shape than when new because of his years of care.

His hand tools include a selection of more than 300 great carving chisels, most from one set he purchased from the son of a leading woodcarver of Pullman train cars. It's an amazing set that's been used to carve ornately detailed period reproductions for many years. Many of Reid's reproductions are built directly from measured drawings of original museum pieces drafted by renowned furniture designer and craftsman Lester Margon in the 1930s, and later published in the 1940s.

When asked what work he respects, Reid cites the Garvan Collection of period furniture at Yale University as the "purest" American collection to be found. Reid credits Francis Garvan for purchasing a piece of furniture only after it was first thoroughly inspected by a master cabinetmaker.

The most important lesson George shares with other woodworkers is to study design every chance you get, in museums, books, plans and magazines. Pay particular attention to dimension, scale and proportions. Take time to understand the designs you are interested in, and just build it.

Reid is a Renaissance man who will never stop exploring and learning. Congratulations on creating some of the most awe-inspiring woodworking ever seen, and a woodshop that is still growing and thriving after more than 60 years — an accomplishment that few individuals can boast.

After seeing some of the amazing detailed Lester Margon drawings that George Reid uses for his work, we wanted to see and know more. If you'd like to see his work, his *Construction of American Furniture Treasures* is available as a reprint in paperback from Dover Publications.

The hand-cut dovetails on this miniature Hepplewhite sideboard are tighter than most examples you'll find on full-size furniture. Most of the miniature hardware Reid orders from Ball and Ball Antique Hardware Reproductions (he's been a regular customer since the 1940s), but sometimes he has to make his own.

Reid made the hardware for this William & Mary miniature, which sits in his dining room on top of a full-size Queen Anne lowboy. The turnings are exquisite.

drawer slide basics

BY STEVE SHANESY

Every woodworker remembers a moment of paralyzing fear when they had to do some task for the first time. Mine occurred when asked to make my first drawer while working in a custom cabinet shop. I'd watched the "old guys" make drawers, but now it was my turn. I allowed the proper 1" side-to-side clearance ($^1/_2$" for each side), and the drawers themselves turned out fine. Then it came time to install the drawers. The shop foreman handed me a box of epoxy-coated under-mount slides and walked away. No instructions. Nothing. It was time to learn the hard way.

To help you avoid that paralyzing fear, we decided to share some of our hard-won experience with you on installing drawer slides. Following are instructions on the two most common slides available from home-improvement stores, catalogs and retail stores: under-mount slides and full-extension side-mount slides.

About the Slides

Under-mount slides are more common and less expensive — about half the price of side-mount slides. They're easy to position and mount on the drawer box and have enough adjustability to make installation pretty foolproof.

SOME BASIC DRAWER SLIDES

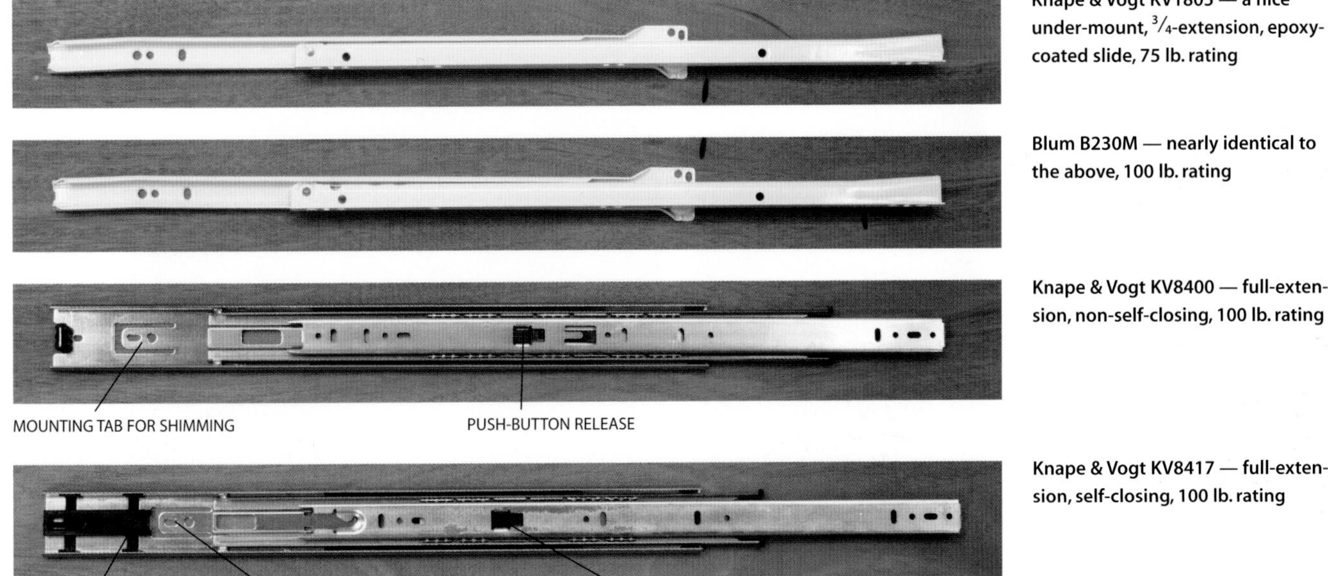

Knape & Vogt KV1805 — a nice under-mount, $^3/_4$-extension, epoxy-coated slide, 75 lb. rating

Blum B230M — nearly identical to the above, 100 lb. rating

Knape & Vogt KV8400 — full-extension, non-self-closing, 100 lb. rating

Knape & Vogt KV8417 — full-extension, self-closing, 100 lb. rating

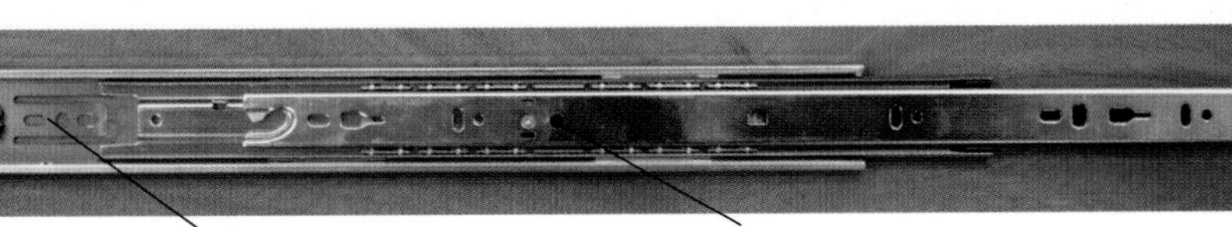

Accuride 3832SC — full-extension, self-closing, 100 lb. rating

These slides allow you to open the drawer three-quarters of the way out of the cabinet, which means you'll still end up digging around at the back of the drawer. But under-mount slides are attractive, smooth-running, quiet and affordable.

Many side-mount slides let you pull the drawer box clear of the cabinet (these are called full-extension slides), making the entire drawer accessible. The side-mount slides also allow a little better use of the cabinet space because they require less clearance room to install or remove the drawer. They're also available in higher weight-holding capacities, which make them popular for use with larger drawers.

Both can be used in either face-frame cabinetry (cabinets that have a solid-wood picture frame placed over the opening, forming a lip around the front edge of the cabinet) or frameless European cabinets (cabinets with no front lip, allowing maximum use of the interior space).

Installation Tips

While many of the slide manufacturers are more helpful than my former shop foreman by including installation instructions with their slides, the information is superficial and won't provide everything you need to know for easy installation.

The following photos and text provide information for installing both under-mount and side-mount slides in both frameless and face-frame cabinets. These basics will simplify the leap to more advanced hardware (such as pocket doors, for example).

The photos walk you through installing the top drawer in a cabinet. If your cabinet has only a top drawer (with a door below), you're in great shape. If you need a bank of drawers, here are some additional tips you need to know.

How Many and How Big?

Start by determining the amount of interior height available in the cabinet, then determine how many drawers you need. When deciding the number and use of your drawers, remember that drawer interiors usually should be no shallower than 2" and no deeper than 10".

Next, take this interior drawer dimension and add $^1/_2$", which is typically the part of the drawer that is not usable space: the bottom itself and the space below the bottom. Now add the necessary clearance space above and below the drawer. The amount of space is determined by the type of slide (as discussed with the photos). Generally $^1/_2$" of space below the drawer is adequate, and $^1/_2$" to $1^1/_2$" above is typical.

Using the above formula, your 2" lap drawer will require 4" of space when using an under-mount slide. With the drawer heights now in hand, mark them out on your cabinet's interior side, then work backwards to locate the correct slide-mounting locations. Double-checking your math is easy once the slides are on the drawers themselves.

When installing multiple drawers of the same height, a template can save time. Use a piece of $^1/_4$"-thick plywood that is cut to the height of the necessary drawer space. Then mark and drill the location holes for the cabinet slides in the template. By placing the template on the floor of the cabinet, then moving up the side, you can quickly drill the pilot holes for all your slides.

You're now ready to tackle drawer slides without fear!

INSTALLING UNDER-MOUNT SLIDES

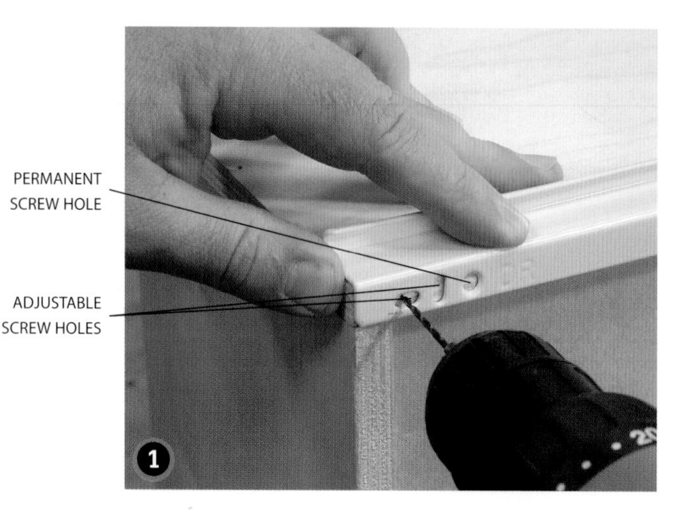

With the under-mount slides, it's easy to determine their mounting location on the drawer. Most of the parts are stamped with DL (drawer left) or DR (drawer right) to make it simple. Slip the drawer slide over the bottom edge of the drawer side and hold the front end (without the roller) flush against the front edge of the drawer box. If you're not using a false-front drawer design, the slide will butt directly against the back of the drawer front. Drill a 5/64" pilot hole in the center of the front-to-back adjustment hole to avoid splitting the drawer side.

The slides should come with screws, but some economy slides don't. If not, a No. 6 x $^1/_2$" screw is your best bet. Depending on the manufacturer, the included screws may be roundhead or flathead. If you have to buy your own screws, opt for the flatheads. That way you won't run into any situations where the rounded head impedes the slide. Two screws (one at either end) in the adjustable slots will do for now. Once the drawers are adjusted, you'll put the permanent screws in their holes.

TOP OF CABINET

CENTER OF MOUNTING HOLE

3

When under-mount slides are slid into, or out of, the drawer case, the drawer must be lifted to allow the rollers to clear each other. Because of this, leave space above the drawer. One inch is sufficient to provide clearance. To determine where to mount the cabinet slides, slip the two slide halves together, then position your drawer to determine top clearance. Measure to the center of the mounting holes on the slide, and that is your cabinet-mounting dimension. The three standard types of drawer fronts are: overlay (where the drawer front is completely outside the cabinet box), lipped (where a rabbet cut in the back of the drawer front allows the front to fit partially into the cabinet box), or inset (where the drawer front is fully contained in the cabinet box). Depending on your drawer front, you'll need to flush or recess (usually $^3/_4$") the front end of the slide on the cabinet sides accordingly.

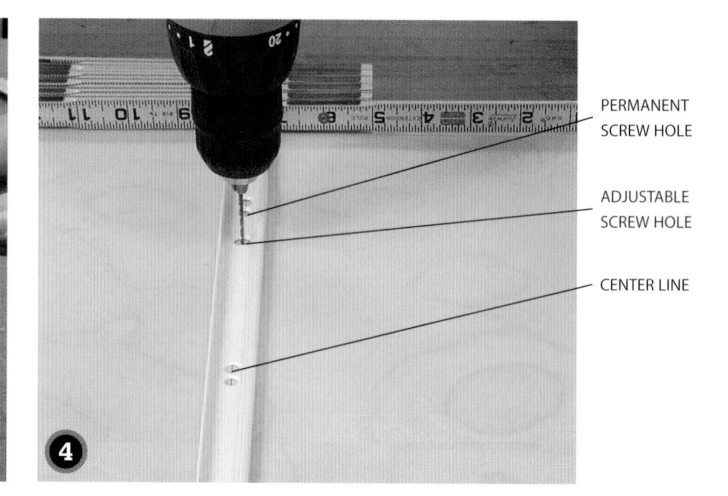

Transfer to the cabinet side the dimension determined from measuring the slide location on the drawer. You can make a mark at the front and rear of the cabinet sides, then connect the marks. Or if you have a good square that you trust, you can simply draw the line that way. It's not a bad idea to check the measurement even if you use the square. While the slides are adjustable, if the square moves $^1/_8$" while making your line, adjustment will be much more difficult. Make a pilot hole at the front and back of the slide using the vertical adjustment slots, then mount the slides. To install the drawer, rest the wheels of the drawer slides on the top of the wheels on the cabinet slides while lifting the front of the drawer. The drawer will drop into the track, then you can level the drawer and slide it into place. Check your fit and you're done.

INSTALLING SIDE-MOUNT, FULL-EXTENSION SLIDES

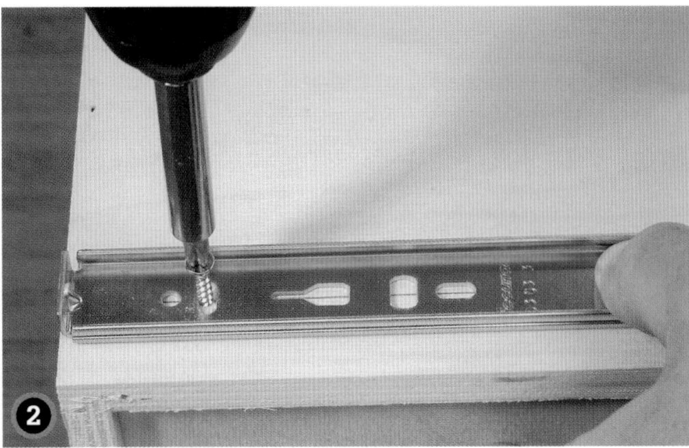

Side-mount slides can be attached to the drawers at any location on the side. We'll mount these at the bottom of the drawer. First, determine the center line of the assembled slide. Side-mount slides have no left or right slide, so we simply use a combination square to take the measurement to the center of the mounting holes. It's then a simple matter to transfer the center location to the drawer sides. Next, disassemble the slide. Check the instructions to see how your slide works. Usually you lift a lever or push a button on both slides simultaneously.

While these slides have no left or right, they do have a front and back. Once the slide is disassembled, orientation can get confusing, so take a close look at the slide before you separate the two parts. Hold the front edge of the drawer slide slightly back from the front edge of the drawer. No more than 1/8" is necessary, and 1/16" is preferable. Again, drill a pilot hole in the center of a top-to-bottom adjustable slot, then attach the drawer member.

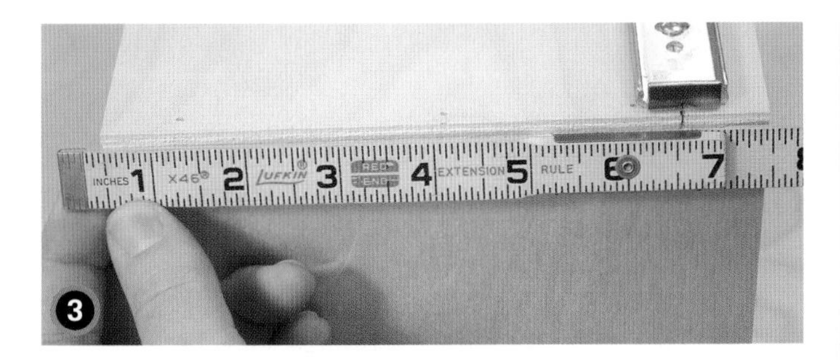

To determine the location of the cabinet member of the slide, measure to the center line of the drawer side member. Side-mount slide pieces push directly into one another without the lifting necessary on under-mount slides. Because of this it's not necessary to leave a space above the drawer side, but it's still not a bad idea in case the drawer becomes too full at some time. We allow a 1/2" space above the drawer box on side-mount slides, just to be safe.

ADJUSTABLE SCREW HOLE

Transfer the dimension to the cabinet side and mark a line from the front to the back of the cabinet side. After marking the necessary spacing for the drawer front (in the photo we're allowing a 3/4" setback for an inset drawer), hold the cabinet member in place and attach the slide using the adjustable slots. On side-mount cabinet slides, use the front-to-back adjustable slots; that's why we used the top-to-bottom slots on the drawer members. To install the drawer, extend the slides on the cabinet fully, align the slide halves and slide the drawer into place.

HOW TO INSTALL EITHER TYPE OF SLIDE IN A FACE-FRAME CABINET

The above photos show a frameless cabinet, but these slides work with face-frame cabinets, too. The only difference is compensating for the lip of the frame. To make the slides work on face-frame cabinets, simply add build-up strips behind the slides. You may be able to use scrap plywood or composite board to bring the slides flush with the frame edge. However, if the frame-lip dimension isn't a perfect 3/4", you'll need to run some solid material through the planer to the perfect thickness — which is flush with the inside edge of the face frame.

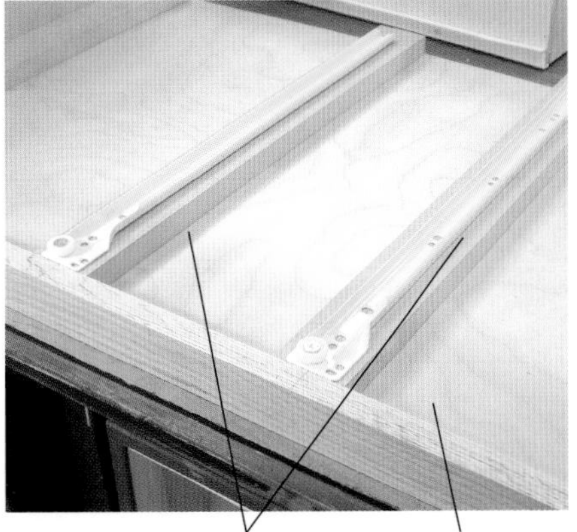

BUILDUP STRIPS FACE FRAME

ADJUSTING THE DRAWERS

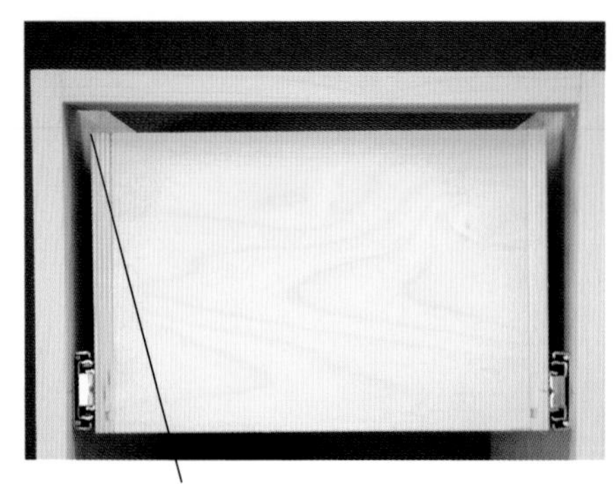

With the drawer slid into place you can see how things are starting to fit. The view of the drawer (left) shows it lower on the left side. The photo at right (getting a look from the side of the cabinet) indicates that the drawer is lower in the back than at the front. Remove the drawer, loosen the screws in the adjustable slots and move the slides to accommodate the changes. The problems shown are all height adjustments and will be adjusted on the drawer slide members. When the drawer is level, attach the false front and check front-to-back alignment. Any necessary adjustments here will be made on the cabinet-side slides. When everything is in good shape, carefully pilot-drill the center of the permanent screw holes on both the drawers and the cabinets slides, and put in the screws. If the screws aren't perfectly centered in the permanent holes, they can pull the slides out of adjustment.

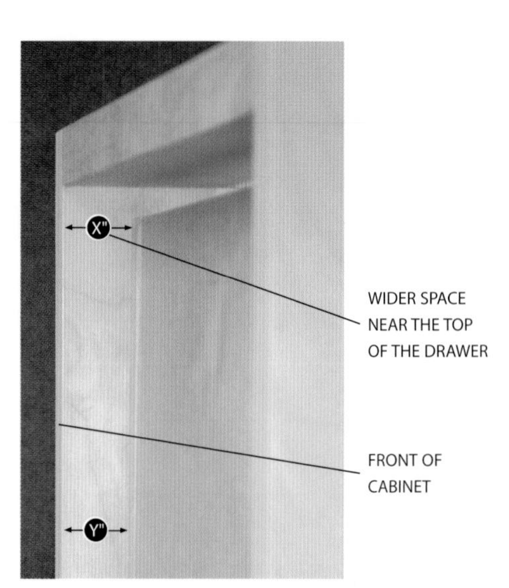

TABS KEPT FLAT FOR A PROPER-FITTING DRAWER

TABS EXTENDED TO COMPENSATE FOR UNDERSIZE DRAWER

Fitting drawers that are too small is easier than fitting drawers that are too big. If you err on the small side, it's easy to fix on the side-mount slides. Each slide has mounting tabs that can be bent away from the slide body to fit closer to the drawer. When the proper spacing is gained, the permanent screws are installed, locking the tabs in place.

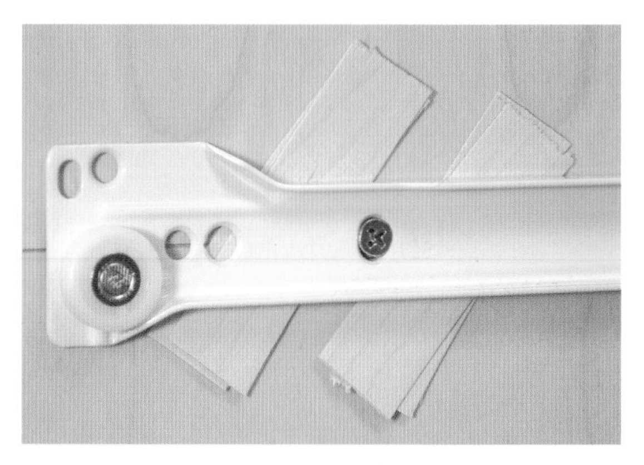

The under-mount slides don't have tabs to help fit undersize drawers. That's when shims come to the rescue. Almost any material can serve as a shim. In the photo above, we're using pieces of self-adhesive edge tape. These pieces can be stacked to reach the appropriate spacing and will stick to one another, as well as to the slide. Make sure you shim on either side of the screw hole. The shims shown are simply slid in place to test the fit. When correct, they will be slid behind the slide so they aren't visible.

A SIMPLE WAY TO ADD A DRAWER FRONT

As you may have noticed, we like using false-front drawers. While not appropriate for period furniture, they're easy to adjust. Inset drawers are one of the most difficult type of drawers to build because there is little room for error. By using a false-front design, the drawer box can be installed and fitted into the cabinet without worrying about the front. Then the drawer fronts can be made to perfectly fit the opening. While the fronts can be simply screwed in place through the drawer-box front, we've found an even better way. Using drawer-front adjusters mounted in the false front, you gain $^3/_{16}$" adjustment vertically or horizontally. Essentially the mounting screw wiggles in the plastic housing. This allows a precise amount of fitting for the drawer front and also makes attaching the fronts easier.

PERMANENT SCREW HOLES ONCE PERFECT FIT IS ESTABLISHED

MACHINE SCREW FOR ADJUSTER

RECESS FOR DRAWER PULL SCREW HEADS

HOLES FOR DRAWER PULLS

DRAWER FRONT ADJUSTER'S PLASTIC HOUSING

gluing up panels

BY CHRISTOPHER SCHWARZ

For several years I was fortunate to live down the road from a logger. When he would come across a tree he thought might interest me, he'd give me a call. I'd excitedly put on my boots and gloves and prepare for some intense hiking through rough terrain. The brush would snap and crack under our feet, and the thorns would snag our clothing as we trekked through woods and across muddy fields.

The results were well worth the long hike; I now have stacks of richly colored walnut and cherry boards stashed in the barn. Some boards are as wide as 2', and the narrow boards are wide enough for many show surfaces such as door panels, desk lids and small tabletops.

However, in spite of my stash of lumber on steroids, there are still times that I need to glue several boards together to make a wide panel. Large tabletops, sides for casework and bottoms for drawers all come to mind. When I combine several boards to make a tabletop or other large panel, I want the finished panel to appear as one solid board as much as possible. After all, one of the many reasons I enjoy woodworking is because of the natural beauty of the material. I don't want to spoil the qualities of the wood by gluing together poorly selected boards with distracting mismatched grain and color.

Matchmaker, Make Me a Match

When selecting boards for a panel, you'll find that the best color and grain match comes from boards sawn from the same tree. In fact, I prefer planks that were sawn consecutively.

You can purchase matching lumber from one of the small specialty hardwood dealers that advertise in the pages of *Popular Woodworking* magazine.

The prices are higher from these merchants, but I think it's worth the extra cost for the premium matching lumber. If you're searching for matching boards at a large, commercial lumberyard, be aware that the boards usually are mixed together with those from other trees. It requires a lot of organization and effort to keep the boards sorted by individual trees. Nevertheless, you still can find matching boards.

What to Look For

As you sift through the stacks at lumberyards (be sure to ask permission and keep the stack neat), look for defects, saw kerfs and width. Knots, worm holes and other natural defects will line up in consecutive boards. You also can look for short kerfs left over from the logger's chain saw. As you spot boards with interesting figure, set them aside and search for their relatives.

Although it's not as easy to spot as knots or saw kerfs are, the grain pattern itself can be a good way to identify matching boards. If you're looking at rough lumber, you'll find it helpful to skim the surface with a block plane. (However, to avoid being kicked out of the lumberyard, be sure to check with the lumber dealer before you try this technique.) Cutting two shorter lengths from one long board also can lead to a good match. But, again, ask for permission first.

Be careful to match the figure along the glue joint. Some types of figure match well, while others don't. There are many types of grain or figure. Cathedral grain and radial grain are most common. They're primarily a result of how the log was sawn: Sawing "around the log" yields cathedral grain, while plain sawing (not rotating the log) yields boards with cathedral grain in the middle and radial grain

When gluing panels, you'll get the best color and grain match by finding boards that were sawn consecutively from a tree. Look for knots, bark, saw kerfs and other clues that the boards were next to one another in their previous life. Look carefully at the photo and you'll see a sap streak that is consistent.

along the edges.

I prefer plain-sawn boards because it's easier to match the straight grain that appears along the boards' edges. Besides, boards sawn in this way typically are wider, and the resulting figure appears more natural to my eye than the figure from lumber sawn using other methods.

After carefully selecting the best boards for the panel, the next step is to arrange them in order for glue-up. My old high school woodworking textbook stated that the boards should be arranged so that the annual rings on the ends of each board alternate up and down. The idea was that as the boards cupped either direction they would keep the overall panel flat.

This outdated idea typically results in a washboard surface with disjointed grain and color at all the seams, which is why I don't do it. Instead, I arrange the boards for the best color and grain match, and I ignore the annual rings. Warpage isn't a problem because I use dry (preshrunk, prewarped) lumber and allow it to acclimate to my shop before milling it. Afterwards the construction of the piece will keep it flat.

For example, a door panel is held flat by the door frame, and a desk lid is restrained and held flat by its two breadboard ends.

Mill It to Size

To create a flat glued-up panel, it's essential to begin with flat planks. And be aware that rough lumber is seldom flat. Neither is dressed or planed

PHOTO AT LEFT **A dry run is essential when clamping up panels. Put the wood in the clamps and check for bows using a straightedge. It could be your wood isn't flat or your clamps are contorting your panels.**

Sometimes the best way to find out if a board matches its neighbor is to look at the grain patterns. Take a block plane with you to the lumberyard to skim off a little of the rough-sawn stuff to get a look at the grain.

PHOTO BELOW **Joint all your edges before gluing up a panel. Some people like to use a sprung joint that has a slight bow in the middle. I find it unnecessary.**

lumber, because it was not flattened on a jointer before it was planed. You can flatten the boards on a large jointer (I have a large 16" jointer for this purpose) or use a long hand plane such as a No. 6, No. 7 or No. 8. But first, cut each board approximately 1" longer than needed. This will help remove some of the warp.

After flattening one face of each board for the panel, plane the boards to final thickness. Then joint all the edges of the stock and use care to ensure that the edges are 90° to the face.

To ensure strong, long-lasting joints in the panel, it's important that the edges are straight. Some woodworkers prefer that the joint is slightly concave; this is sometimes referred to as a "spring" or "sprung" joint.

The idea is to place greater pressure at the ends to keep the joint tight in this area if the ends dry out and shrink. Although a spring joint works effectively, I find that it isn't necessary. I simply joint the edges straight. However, convex edges should be corrected before glue-up. Otherwise they will introduce tension on the ends of the joint and it will most likely fail.

If you don't own a jointer, a jointer plane, such as this No. 7, can joint a perfect edge. It takes a bit of practice, but isn't as difficult as you might think.

No Biscuits, Please

While some woodworkers use a number of devices such as splines, dowels and biscuits to strengthen an edge joint and aid with alignment, I simply spread the glue and apply the clamp pressure. Edge joints don't need additional strength; the joint is already stronger than the surrounding wood. And aligning is a breeze; just gently push and pull on the boards as you tighten the clamps.

Gluing Up

The glue-up procedure should be performed on a flat surface; otherwise you can glue a twist into the panel. Sawhorses work well, but unless the panel is extremely large I usually just work on my bench, which is large and flat.

Before you begin, make sure that your clamps are straight; a bent pipe clamp also can cause the panel to twist. As I position the clamps, I alternate them over and under the work to equalize the pressure. I space the clamps approximately 12" apart, closer if the wood is very hard or there are more than two boards in the panel.

I always perform a dry run to check the flatness of the panel and the fit of the joints before applying glue to the edges. Any potential problems are spotted easily in the dry run and corrected before the glue is applied. Before I disassemble the dry run I mark the pieces to ensure that I arrange the boards correctly during the actual glue-up, preventing unnecessary stress.

When spreading glue you'll want just enough to wet the surface. I like to see a few drops of squeeze-out; it lets me know that the joint isn't glue starved. But too much glue leads to a big sticky mess and boards that slide out of position as clamp pressure is applied.

I begin by clamping in the middle of the panel and work to the ends. I push or pull the boards at the ends until they're aligned at the clamp. Then I apply pressure to that area.

Fingertips are quite sensitive and they can feel a few thousandths of an inch of misalignment. Once everything is aligned and all the clamps are in place I allow the glue an hour or so to dry. Then I remove the clamps and scrape away the soft beads of glue along the joint line.

Keep It Flat

Once the glue has set, continue to work the panel to keep it flat. If left lying around, the panel can warp as the humidity changes.

Finally, always apply finish to both faces of a panel. Otherwise, the unfinished face will react sooner to changes in the weather and cause the once perfectly flat panel to warp.

choose the right lumber

BY CHRISTOPHER SCHWARZ

Like many legendary lumber tales, our story begins with a farmer and an old barn out in the middle of nowhere.

You see, there was this farmer out in the middle of nowhere, and about 25 years ago a storm blew down the biggest walnut tree on his land. The farmer had a friend at a sawmill cut up the tree, and the old guy put the wood in his barn to use someday.

Someday never came. The farmer died, one of his relatives called us, and we went out to this secluded hamlet with visions of 24"-wide clear planks in our heads.

But like many lumber tales, ours ended when we scaled up to the barn's hayloft. Up there we found a mound of moldy, rotting, bug-infested, unstickered wood that wasn't even good enough to burn.

Finding lumber off the beaten path has both risks and rewards. For every time we've bought black cherry for $1 a board foot (kiln-dried but ungraded), we've probably had three or four times when we came up empty-handed. Or worse, we bought wood that looked good to us as we loaded the truck, but it turned out to be junk.

Because we can't always rely on foraging for wood, we're also regular customers at commercial lumberyards. Sure, the price can be a bit higher, but the lumber is graded, so you know what you're going to get. And the supply is more predictable than hunting for the old barn in the woods.

No matter who you are, unless you own a sawmill, finding the best material for your projects is going to be a challenge. Even professional cabinetmakers are constantly foraging for new sources for wood.

But it is possible to find quality lumber — no matter where in the country you live. To verify this, we tracked down several woodworkers from relatively hardwood-deprived states such as Florida, Arizona and Texas (all of whom belonged to a woodworking club, by the way). According to these wood scroungers, it is possible to find quality lumber. You just have to know where to look.

And when you do find some wood, you need to figure out if it's worth buying. This means you have to get familiar with the lumberyard lexicon. You need to know these terms so you can ask for (and get) exactly what you need. To help you on that point, at the end of this chapter we've included a glossary of the common terms and expressions you'll hear at the lumberyard.

Once you've boned up on the lumberyard-ese, it's time to start your search. Here are the strategies we use to keep the racks in the *Popular Woodworking* shop (and at home) full of good wood.

FANCY (AND FREE) FIREWOOD

Three years ago in Moscow, Ohio, Steve Koller and his father, Eugene, were loading a pickup truck with odds and ends from a pallet company — wood they would use to heat their homes. Steve began noticing the dark color of some of the pallet wood, so he took a piece of it to his shop and cut it in half. At that moment Steve realized he and his father had just brought home an entire truckload of walnut. While some were small pieces, others ranged in size from 18" to 24" long, 6" wide and 3" thick.

The next week, Steve and his father went to the pallet company for some more firewood, only to discover they had brought home a pickup truck full of cherry. But their luck soon ended. According to Steve, since then, the pallets have been the norm: oak and poplar.

How much lumber did you need? Commercial lumberyards and mills are an excellent source of consistent, graded lumber with few surprises.

Commercial Lumberyards

Believe it or not, you might not be aware of all the lumberyards that carry hardwoods in your area. Some are small family operations that rely more on word of mouth than marketing. Your first steps should be to check the yellow pages (look under "lumber, retail") and visit the WoodFinder Web site (www.woodfinder.com), which can help you find suppliers within a 200-mile radius.

Some lumberyards deliver even small loads, and others are worth the drive, so don't discount the stores that are out of town. If you're still not having luck finding basic hardwoods

Popular
Woodworking

such as red oak and poplar, call a local cabinet shop and ask where you can find hardwoods locally.

And don't forget to look for lumber mills if you live near hardwood forests. Some of these mills sell direct to the public, and the prices can be pretty good.

Wood by Mail

It might seem nuts to buy lumber through the mail, especially when you consider that you're buying it sight-unseen and have to pay for shipping. But many of the big mail-order lumber suppliers actually are quite competitive in price, and the wood is of a high quality.

Editor Steve Shanesy recently visited Steve Wall Lumber Co. (www.walllumber.com) in North Carolina and was impressed by what he saw in the racks. Wall offers special 20-board-foot bundles of lumber in 3' to 5' lengths that ship via UPS.

Woodcraft (www.woodcraft.com) sells domestic and exotic woods by the board or in bundles. Paxton (www.paxtonwood.com) sells wood by the bundle, and so do many other large lumberyards. WoodFinder lists many other mail-order companies, too.

LUMBER IS MEASURED IN QUARTERS

For new woodworkers, one of the most confusing aspects of buying lumber is figuring out the terminology for thicknesses. Rough lumber (which has not been surfaced) is sold in "quarters." Each quarter represents $\frac{1}{4}$" of thickness in its rough state. So four-quarter lumber (written as 4/4) is 1" thick in its rough state; 5/4 is $1\frac{1}{4}$" and so on. When the lumber is surfaced by the mill it loses thickness. That's why 4/4 lumber is $\frac{3}{4}$" thick when it's surfaced. Here's a chart that you can use as a quick reference:

ASK FOR	ROUGH, THICKNESS	SURFACED THICKNESS
4/4	1"	$\frac{3}{4}$"
5/4	$1\frac{1}{4}$"	1"
6/4	$1\frac{1}{2}$"	$1\frac{1}{4}$"
8/4	2"	$1\frac{3}{4}$"
10/4	$2\frac{1}{2}$"	$2\frac{1}{4}$"
12/4	3"	$2\frac{3}{4}$"

PHOTO AT LEFT Editor and Publisher Steve Shanesy pulls out one of his monster walnut boards. The lumber, all 1,100 board feet, came free from a neighborhood tree. A number of boards were up to 30" wide. Steve hired a Wood-Mizer sawmill operator to cut the logs.

Join the Club

Of course, there are ways to make the search easier. Perhaps the best way is to join your local woodworking club or guild.

Almost every club seems to have a resident wood scrounger who is more than happy to point you to places that are off the beaten path. Some clubs even organize purchases of lumber for their members; buying in volume drives down the price. And if you're looking for a small quantity of a particular species, it's likely that one club member will have a few extra board feet of that species to sell. They'll probably offer it to you at a great price, too.

Don't know if there's a club in your area? Go to www.betterwoodworking.com/woodworking_clubs/woodworking_clubs.htm to find one near you. We highly recommend joining a club.

Mobile Mills

Outside every window, of course, are thousands of board feet of lumber. And whenever Mother Nature is roused, the downed trees in your neighborhood are a potential gold mine of wide, clear stock. It's just a matter of first moving the bole — the straight part of the trunk below the branches that yields clear and stable wood. Moving the bole is perhaps the most difficult task.

Then you have to find someone to mill the logs into suitable thicknesses for drying. Luckily, this is pretty easy. Wood-Mizer Products, Inc., which manufactures portable band-saw mills, maintains a list of sawyers who perform custom cutting. Contact Wood-Mizer at www.woodmizer.com. In addition to Wood-Mizer owners, there are probably other sawyers in your area who will do the job. Check with your local woodworking club (another good reason to join).

Finally, you have to learn how to properly sticker your green wood for seasoning. It's not rocket science, but there are some rules to follow.

A LOG IN EVERY PORT

In 1992, Donald Boudreau and his wife, Carol, sold everything they owned, bought a teak 49' sailboat, named it *Domicile* and began fulfilling their dream of sailing around the world.

While in Rio Dolce, Guatemala, Boudreau wanted to make a cutting board that also would cover the top of his stove. A local gave him some wood to use for the project. Later, Boudreau realized it was goncalo alves (tigerwood). It was Bourdreau's first experience with exotic wood. He soon began collecting exotic wood wherever they docked.

Six years and many islands later, the couple was in New Zealand with an expensive wood collection and grandchildren waiting for their return back home. So they sold the boat and shipped the wood to South Florida where they planned to make their new home near Fort Lauderdale.

Once in Florida, Boudreau put his exotic wood collection aside and spent three years building every piece of furniture for their new home. With the home furnished, Boudreau began building award-winning boxes using the exotic wood he purchased on his trip and has been collecting since.

At any given time his shop is filled with 50 to 60 different species of wood totaling several hundred board feet. While he has found several Florida dealers who import Latin American wood, Boudreau says he also buys 4/4 hardwood flooring, shops on the Internet and, when necessary, hops on a plane to make a purchase.

Donald Boudreau and his wife sailed this sailboat around the world, collecting tropical hardwoods in Central America, South America and the South Pacific.

Farmers with Barns

Farmers are out there with barns full of lumber. And garages are stacked high with premium wood left behind by deceased woodworkers. But how do you get your hands on it?

Basically, it's a matter of putting the word out among your friends, relatives and co-workers that you're a woodworker and on the prowl for wood. Tell enough people, and

You need a few things to move logs: cant hooks, a strong back and lots of friends (all shown at right). It's grueling work, but it's worth it.

you'll eventually hear from the friend of a friend who wants to dispose of some boards. Sometimes you get lucky. We once bought a garage full of impressive lumber that one woodworker (who could not take it with him to the afterlife) had amassed over several decades.

Classified Ads, Auctions and Offcuts

You can find wood in somewhat surprising ways. Believe it or not, wood shows up pretty regularly in the classified ads of the daily newspaper and local free shopping papers.

And while you're poring over the classifieds, keep an eye out for auctions at farms and cabinet shops. When these places go under, there can be good deals on wood (and machines). Bear in mind that haunting auctions is both time-

HARDWOOD LUMBER GRADES: THE BASICS

When you buy wood at a lumberyard, it has been graded — essentially separated into different bins based on how many defects are in each board. The fewer the defects, the more expensive the board. Grading hardwood lumber is a tricky skill with rules set by the National Hardwood Lumber Association. (Grading softwood is different; these rules do not apply.)

Here are some of the basic guidelines graders follow as they classify each board.

FIRSTS: Premium boards that are at least 6" wide, 8' long and $91\frac{2}{3}$ percent clear of defects.

SECONDS: Premium boards that are at least 6" wide, 8' long and $81\frac{2}{3}$ percent clear of defects.

FAS: The two grades above are typically combined into one grade called FAS, or "firsts and seconds," which must be at least $81\frac{2}{3}$ percent clear of defects.

FAS 1-FACE: One face must meet the minimum requirements of FAS; the second face cannot be below No. 1 common.

SELECTS: While not an official grade, this refers to boards that are at least 4" wide, 6' long and with one face that meets the FAS 1-FACE requirements. Essentially, these are good clear boards that are too narrow or too short to fit in the above grades. This and the FAS grades are good choices for nice furniture.

No. 1 COMMON: Boards that are at least 3" wide, 4' long and $66\frac{2}{3}$ percent clear of defects.

No. 2 COMMON: Boards that are at least 3" wide, 4' long and 50 percent clear of defects.

NOTE: There are exceptions to these rules. For example: walnut, butternut and all quarter-sawn woods can be 5" wide instead of 6" wide and still qualify for FAS.

STAIRCASE SLIP-UP

Duncan Alldis (now retired) and a friend had a workshop in Croydon, Surrey, England. One day, a friend of his son stopped by and asked if Alldis would be interested in the parts from an old three-flight mahogany staircase. The young man had been hired to remove and dispose of the staircase, and he thought Alldis might like to buy the parts he salvaged from the job.

Alldis often used mahogany in his shop. So he calculated its value and told the (now smiling) young man how much he could offer.

The next day the young man arrived at Alldis's workshop with a pile of stairs. Alldis took one look at the wood and knew it wasn't mahogany. Closer examination verified this fact, and the young man, noticing Alldis's frown, asked if he still wanted the wood.

Alldis said he would take the wood but also said that the price would have to be recalculated. The young man told Alldis that any money would be appreciated. You can imagine the young man's surprise when Alldis handed him the original payment and told him he would need a few days to work out an additional payment.

Once cleaned, each of the handmade staircase's treads amounted to a beautiful 2" × 8" × 32" piece of 100-year-old Burmese teak. The mahogany staircase quickly became the most glorious stack of Burmese teak Alldis had ever seen.

Straight from the woods, this pile of cherry is being stickered as we go. When complete, we painted the ends with a special paint (which is wax suspended in a water-based emulsion) to retard end checking.

consuming and addictive.

Some people buy lumber through eBay, an online auction Web site (www.ebay.com). Shipping can be a real killer ($1 a pound), so tread cautiously and do the math before you buy from online auctions.

Finally, for the true bottom-feeder, there's always the waste stream. Find out if there's a pallet factory, furniture manufacturer, veneer mill or construction site in your area. Their waste might be perfect for your woodworking.

We've cut up pallets made from mahogany, ash and other desirable species. In fact, most of the projects in Jim Stack's *Building the Perfect Tool Chest* (Popular Woodworking Books) were built in our shop using wood discarded from pallets. A cabinet shop that built a lot of face frames once sold us their falloff, which was the perfect size for chair spindles. All you have to do is ask.

And speaking of asking, make sure when you climb up to that hayloft to check out that wood in the barn that you ask if there are any hornets' nests waiting up there. There's more than one way to get stung when hunting for lumber.

STICKER SHOCK

Twenty-five years ago Gene Nurse, from Dartmouth, Nova Scotia, Canada, went to the lumberyard on his lunch break to buy some wood for a mahogany desk he wanted to build. When he arrived, the man who usually worked the desk wasn't there and a young teenager was in his place.

The sticker price on the pile of undressed mahogany indicated that the lumber was a typical $3 (Canadian) a board foot. Nurse said the young man, not knowing the difference between dressed and undressed lumber, said that the sticker "must be a mistake for that crappy stuff. They must have meant 30 cents a board foot."

After trying to dissuade the guy several times, Nurse loaded up his truck with 500 board feet of mahogany. Price: $150.

Feeling guilty, Nurse went back and explained what had happened to the man who usually worked the desk. The man thought the story was funny, said it was their mistake and let Nurse keep the wood. But next time, the man said, Nurse should deal with him personally.

BYOB: Bring your own bole. All over the country, independent sawyers such as Ed Motz can mill the logs you find into rough slabs. Moving it and drying it usually is up to you.

THE LANGUAGE OF LUMBER

AIR-DRIED LUMBER: Wood that has been dried from its freshly cut state by stacking it (usually outside) with stickers between. Air-drying reduces the moisture content to about 12–15 percent. Wood for interior use needs to be dried further.

BOARD FOOT: A piece of wood that is 1" thick by 12" wide by 12" long in the rough — or its cubic equivalent.

CHATTER MARK: A defect caused when the board was surfaced at the mill and the knives mar the surface.

CUPPED: A board with edges higher than its middle. The cup is always to the sap side of the board.

DEFECT: An imperfection in the board that will change how it is graded (and its price).

DIMENSIONAL LUMBER: Lumber that is surfaced on all four sides (S4S) to specific thicknesses and widths: 1×4s, 2×8s, etc. Note that with this lumber the finished thickness and width are less than the stated size. For example, a 1×4 typically will measure 3/4" × 3 1/4".

END CHECK: Separation of the wood fibers at the end of a board, almost always a result of drying.

FLITCH: A log that is sawn into veneer with the sheets stacked in the same order as they come off the log. Good for bookmatching.

GREEN LUMBER: Wood that has been freshly cut from the tree, typically with a moisture content of 60 percent or higher.

HEARTWOOD: The part of the tree between the pith (the very center) and the sapwood (the whitish outer layer of wood).

HONEYCOMB: A separation of the wood fibers inside the board during drying. It might not be evident from the face of the board.

KILN-DRYING: An artificial way to reduce the moisture content of wood using heat and forced air.

KNOT: A circular woody mass in a board that occurs where a branch or twig attached to the tree.

LINEAL FEET: A wood measurement based only on a board's length and not its width or thickness; usually used to refer to mouldings.

MINERAL STREAK: A typically green or brown discoloration, which can be caused by an injury to the tree.

MOISTURE CONTENT: The percentage of a board's weight that is water.

PITCH: A resinous, gummy substance typically found between the growth rings of softwoods.

PITH: The small and soft core of a tree that the wood grows around. It's undesirable for woodworking.

PLAIN (FLAT) SAWN: A method of milling a log that results in the growth rings intersecting the face of the board at an angle less than 45°.

QUARTER-SAWN: A method of cutting a log at the mill that results in the growth rings intersecting the face of the board at more than 45°. Quarter-sawing wastes more wood and requires more effort. But quarter-sawn wood is more stable.

RANDOM WIDTHS & LENGTHS: While softwoods and cabinet woods such as red oak and poplar can be found as dimensional lumber, many hardwoods cannot. These hardwoods are cut in different widths and lengths to get the best grade.

RIFT-SAWN: A method of cutting a log that results in the growth rings intersecting the face of the board at an angle between 30° and 60°. More stable than plain-sawn wood; less stable than quarter-sawn.

ROUGH: A board as it comes from the sawmill; not surfaced or planed.

SLR1E: The acronym for "straight-line ripped one edge," meaning the board has one true edge.

S2S: Planed on two faces; the edges are rough.

S3S: Planed on two faces and one edge; one edge is rough.

S4S: Planed to a smooth finish on all four long edges of a board.

SAPWOOD: The lighter colored wood between the heartwood and bark; typically weaker than the heartwood.

SHAKE: A split that occurs before the tree is cut, usually from the wind buffeting the tree.

SHORTS: High-quality lumber that is less than 6' long.

SOUND KNOT: A knot that is solid across the face of the board and shows no sign of decay.

STRAIGHT-LINE RIP: A perfectly straight edge that is suitable for gluing.

SURFACE CHECK: A shallow separation of the wood fibers.

TWIST: A defect that occurs where the board has warped into a spiral.

WANE: The presence of bark on the edge or corner of a piece of wood.

WARP: A general term for a distortion in a board where it twists or curves out of shape.

WORM HOLES: A void in the wood caused by burrowing insects (killed during kiln-drying).

THANKS TO PAXTON, THE WOOD SOURCE FOR ASSISTANCE WITH THIS GLOSSARY.

modern materials and hardware

BY DANNY PROULX

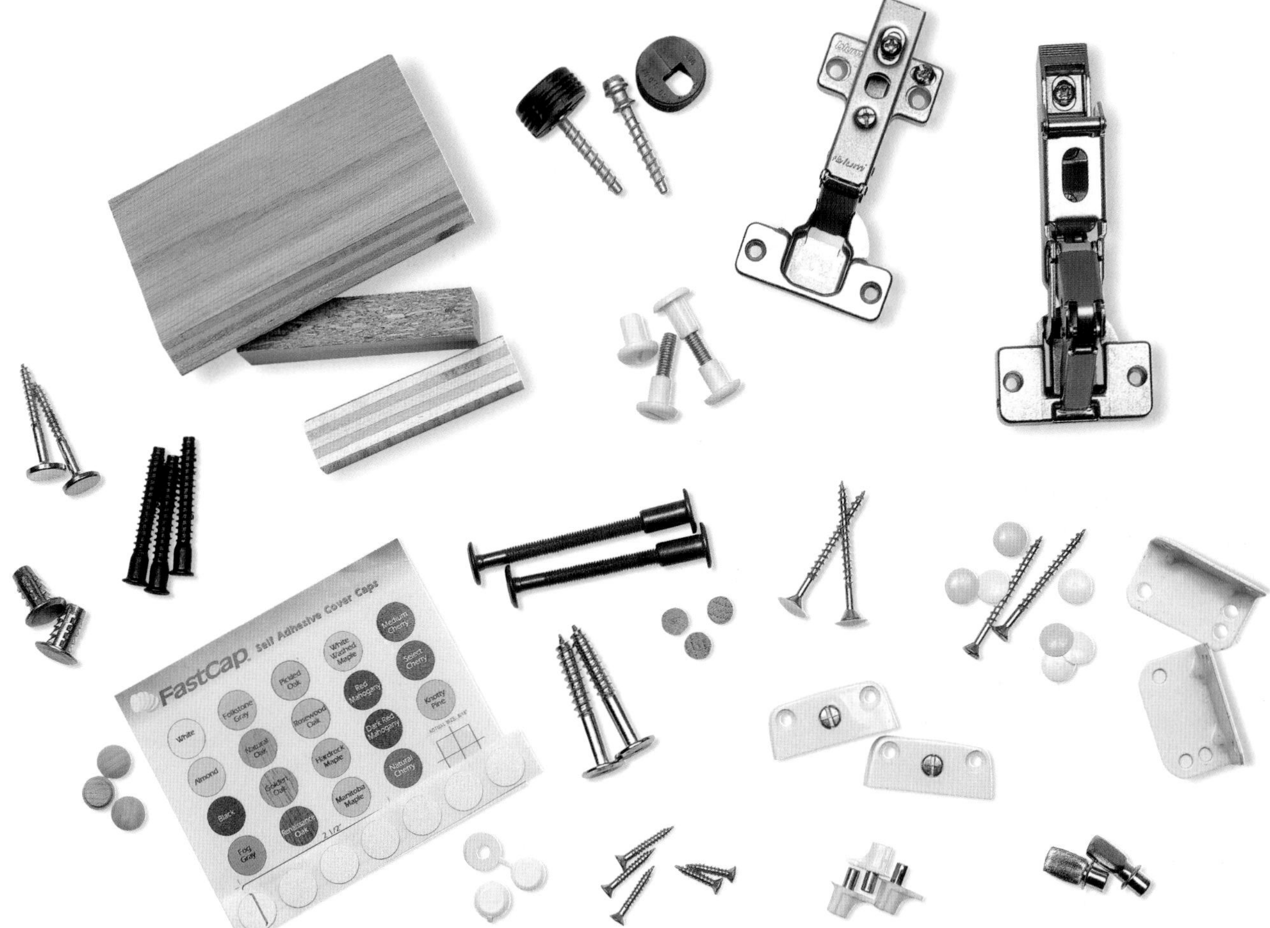

The last few years have been exciting for those of us in the building materials and hardware business. Modern plywood, improved particleboard (PB), melamine-coated particleboard (MPB) and medium-density fiberboard (MDF) have made a tremendous impact on how we build cabinets.

We've come to realize that our forest products must be managed carefully. Wood that was once burned or discarded as garbage has now become a valuable resource. Improved management of that wood has been a blessing to all of us who care about our forests.

That so-called garbage wood is now used to manufacture all forms of particle core and fiberboards. It has become popular as a cabinetmaking material in the commercial casework industry and is now being accepted by the hobbyist woodworker.

Some of us used these composite boards when they were first introduced and may have been disappointed. Today, there are grades and standards, and the products are far superior to the early offerings.

Although low-cost sheet material is available, it isn't good value for your money and should be avoided. Ask the supplier for cabinet-grade products and pay a little more to get high-quality material. Most often, it's only a few dollars a sheet more, but it's well worth the money. You can make a lot of furniture from one sheet of MPB, so a few extra dollars isn't a major issue.

These modern sheet goods and hardware have opened a whole new world. You don't have to be an expert cabinetmaker to build great-looking projects. And you don't need a fully equipped shop. You can build most of these projects with only a few inexpensive tools.

Joinery Techniques

The butt joint, using modern hardware, is the most common joinery method. Most adhesives are not suited to properly join many of the coated materials, with the exception of wood veneer material. Melamine, which is a paper soaked in resins and fused to PB, cannot be glued with standard wood adhesives. We therefore depend on high- quality fasteners to build our cabinets.

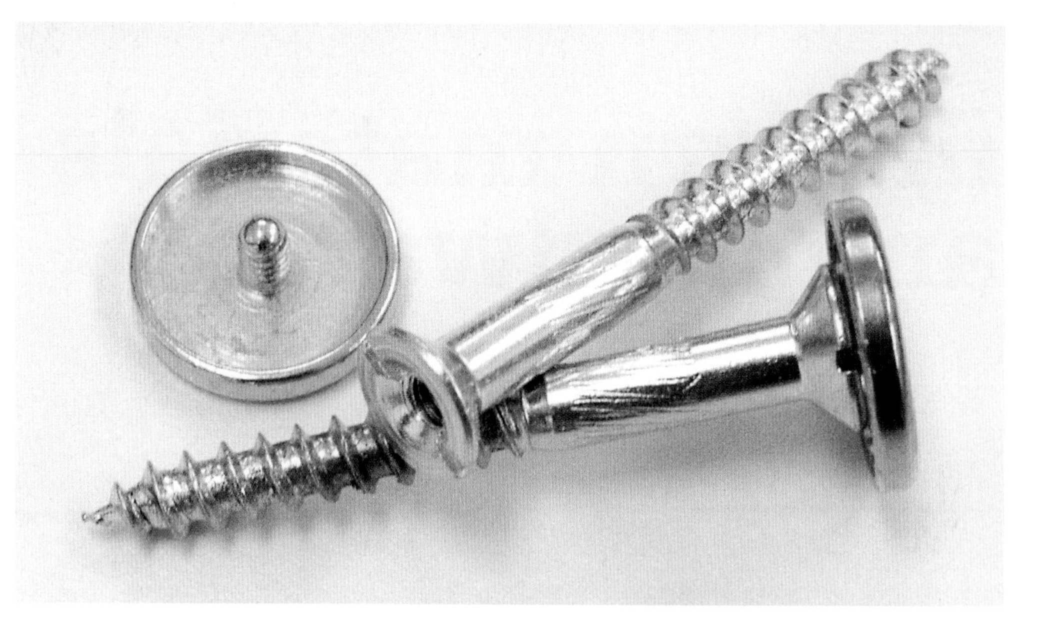

Some decorative screws for PB have screw-on caps that are available in many finishes. These caps can be matched to complement the coated PBs surface. And when properly located on the project they look great.

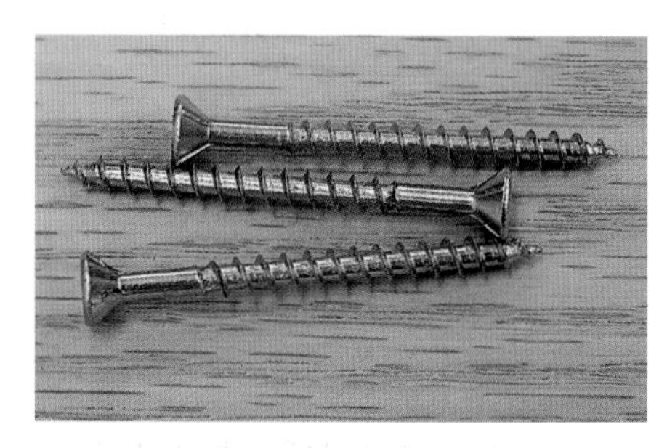

PB or chipboard screws are available from most hardware suppliers. They have a thin shaft with a coarse thread and are specially designed to hold PB securely.

When working with wood-veneer-covered PBs, we have dozens of wood screw-hole coverings available. The plug and button are the two common types, but many other styles are available.

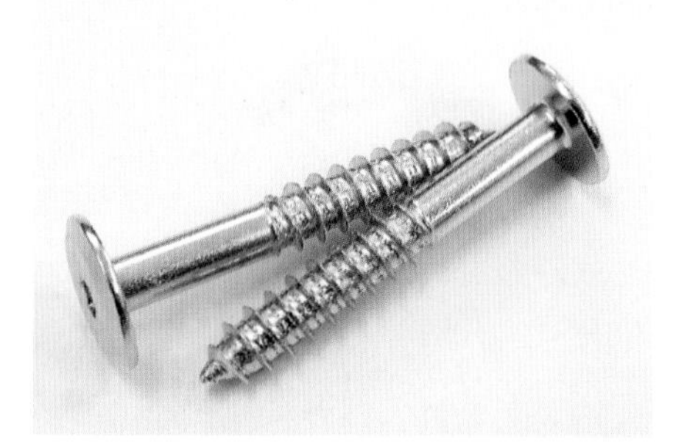

Variations of PB screws include ones with decorative heads. These are meant to be seen and add a finished look to the cabinet.

Plastic screw-hole coverings are also available. Some are plastic caps held on by the screw, and others are push-on styles that fit in the screw head.

A PB screw is available that, until recently, had been used only by professional cabinetmakers. It's a great fastener, with superior holding capabilities, but you should be aware of a couple of issues when using this screw.

First, the screw is tapered and requires a special, and somewhat expensive, drill bit. Second, this fastener has a large-diameter body and coarse thread. You must drill an accurate pilot hole and drive the screw straight into that hole for a positive hold. Poor drilling techniques or improper driving will push the screw through the finished surface or weaken the joint.

However, once you become accustomed to using the screw you'll appreciate its fastening power. When you need a strong joint that is able to withstand stress, this is the fastener to use.

Furniture that can be taken apart is a necessary requirement for some people. That need has led to the development of a whole range of joinery bolts. Furniture can be quickly taken apart and rebuilt without damage.

Cabinet and furniture makers have developed many applications for this type of fastener. It's often seen on children's beds and storage shelving systems. The Europeans have expanded the use of these bolts and developed an extensive line of knockdown furniture.

Hidden Joinery Hardware

Many types of quick-connect-and-release right-angle butt joinery hardware items are available. Often, a screwdriver is all that is needed to assemble the furniture. And it can be taken apart quickly if the need arises. It may not be purist woodworking, but these fasteners do have a place in modern cabinetry.

Another version of bolt joinery uses a finished end cap. The bolt is often hidden and only the cap is visible. The head is about $\frac{1}{2}$" in diameter and is drawn tight to the material surface.

These cap nuts provide a sound mechanical connection. They are also used on high-stress joints such as bed frames.

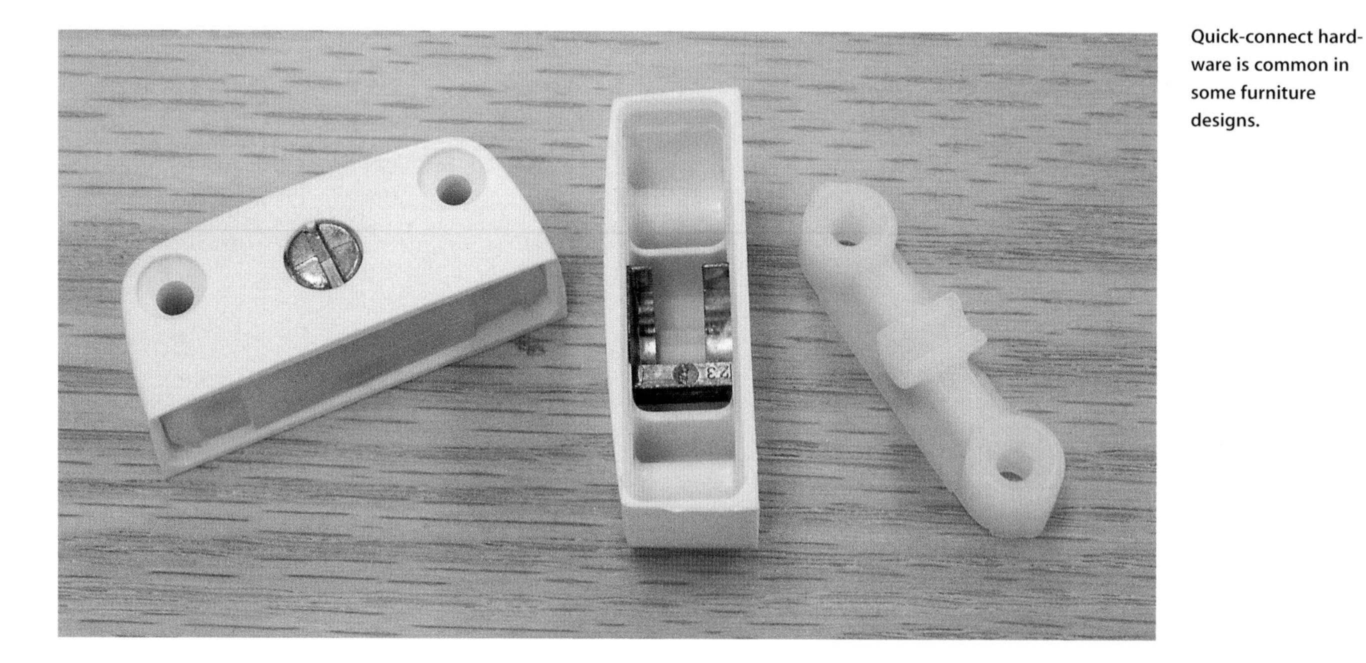

Quick-connect hardware is common in some furniture designs.

Most quick-connect hardware operates on a cam lock system, as shown here.

HIDDEN AND TRADITIONAL HINGES

To some degree, the modern European or hidden hinge has replaced the traditional-style hinge. But in certain applications, our old standby model is the hinge of choice.

In the last few years door-mounting hardware from Europe has become a popular alternative. The so-called Euro hidden hinge is now widely used as the standard kitchen cabinet door hardware.

The hidden hinge usually requires a 35mm hole drilled in the door. That task seems a bit challenging to some people, but it's a straightforward process.

Most woodworkers experience a learning curve when first working with the hidden hinge. For instance, these hinges are classified with terms such as *full overlay*, *half overlay* and *inset*. The distance the door covers the cabinet side member (gable end) is called overlay.

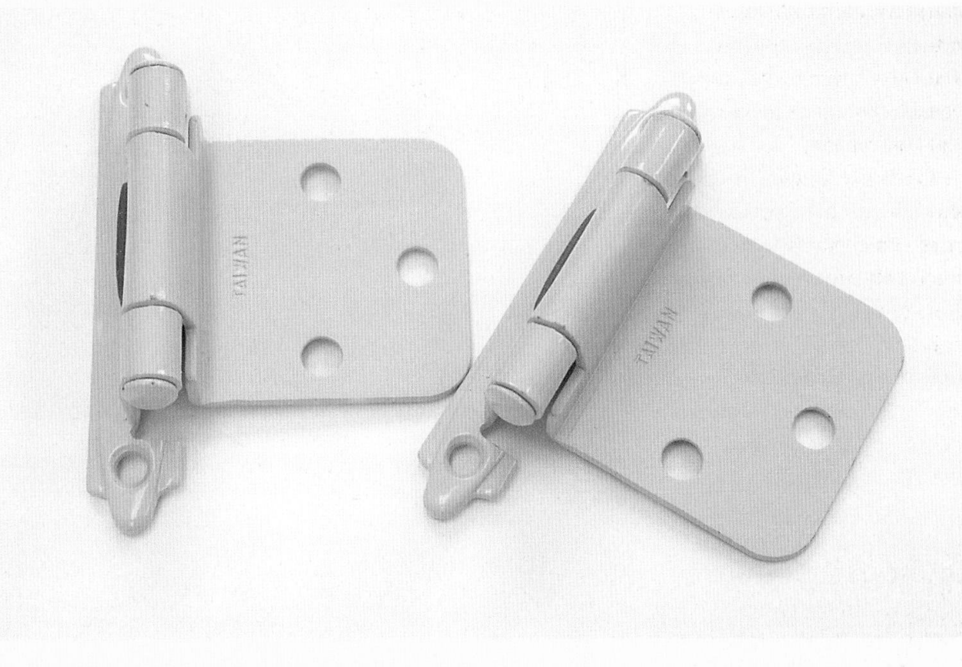

The old standby traditional-style hinge can still be used for overlay doors. It is easily mounted to the door and then onto the cabinet face. It provides a 180° swing.

Parts of a Hinge

The hidden hinge comes in two parts: the hinge, or boss, which is mounted on the door, and the mounting plate, which is attached to the cabinet side or gable end of the cabinet.

The boss is attached to the mounting plate with a screw or a clip pin. The clip-on method is popular because you can remove the door from the mounting plate without disturbing any adjustments.

Degrees of Operation

Hidden hinges are also classed in terms of degrees of opening. For standard door applications, the 100°-to-110°-opening hinge is common. But you can purchase hinges that will allow the door to open from 90° to 170°. The term simply refers to the number of degrees of swing that the door can open from its closed position.

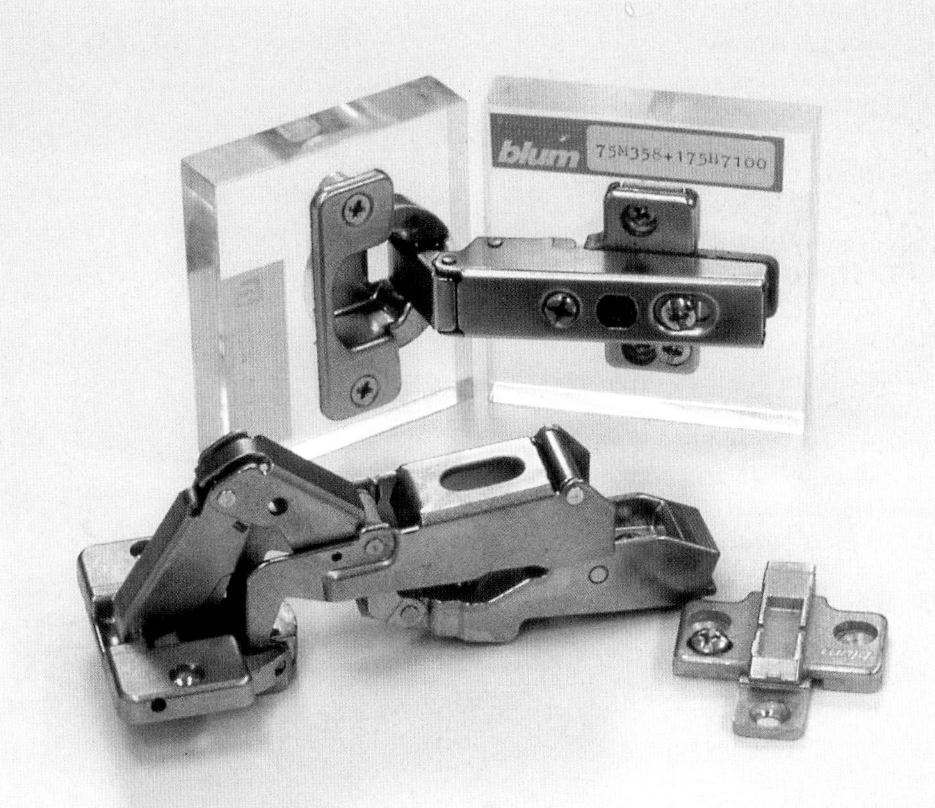

The Euro hinge and mounting plate system is used on many modern cabinets. It provides great flexiblity in door mounting options.

Adjustable Shelving

The fixed shelf is gone! Nowadays, everyone wants adjustable shelves in their cabinets. This feature makes sense because it increases the flexibility of any cabinet.

Adjustable shelving is easy to install. All that is required are accurately drilled columns of holes and good-quality shelf pins.

Adjustable shelving is made possible by the dozens of shelf pin styles now available.

Assembly Brackets

Attaching countertops during a kitchen project is often accomplished using metal brackets. It's the best method for securing something, like a kitchen countertop, which will have to be replaced in the future.

These brackets come in many shapes and sizes. They provide a quick-connect capability and add strength to any project. They are sometimes used with other joinery hardware to provide extra hold when joint stress is an issue.

Metal brackets of all shapes and sizes are used in the cabinet-making industry.

Drawer Glides

Modern hardware now gives us the opportunity to vary drawer styles and construction methods. Side- and bottom-mounted glides with three-quarter and full extension capabilities, along with positive stops and closing features have opened a world of design opportunities.

Low-cost metal drawer glide sets that consist of two bottom-mounted drawer runners and two cabinet tracks are simple to install. Installing the new drawer hardware demands special attention to the drawer body width, as most of the hardware requires precise clearances to operate properly. Otherwise, building high-quality drawers is well within the abilities of any woodworker or hobbyist.

Bottom-mounted drawer glides simplify the drawer construction process.

Sheet Goods

Coated and plain particle core and plywood boards are stable materials that are suitable for many cabinet applications. These products are the most common building materials in today's furniture industry.

The melamine-coated decorative panels come in a wide range of colors. And best of all, they're already finished. The wood veneer boards can be stained, glued, joined and used like solid wood.

All the colored panels and wood veneers have complementary edge tape that is attached with glue. In some cases, solid-wood edging is installed to protect and accent the beauty of these boards.

High-Pressure Laminates

High-pressure laminates are the best materials for kitchen countertops. But they are also appropriate for many other cabinet applications.

Modern sheet goods have opened many cabinet design possibilities.

Wood and melamine edge tapes are available for all the boards.

Dozens of decorative panel colors and textures are available.

High-pressure laminates are available in many colors.

CUTTING MELAMINE PB CHIP-FREE WITHOUT A TABLE SAW

A table saw with a special melamine-cutting blade (called a triple-grind with carbide teeth) is the ideal tool when working with modern sheet goods. But you can get chip-free cuts without a table saw.

A good circular saw, with a fine-tooth blade, will cut these boards cleanly if you follow a two-step process. A table saw chips melamine board on the underside during cutting, and the opposite is true for a radial-arm saw. The blade rotation has a great deal to do with material damage.

To get a good cut with a circular saw, set the blade to cut 1⁄16" into your board. Clamp on a saw guide and make the first cut. Now, lower the blade until it's 1⁄16" deeper than the material thickness and make the final cut. It won't be perfect, but it will give you a reasonable cut.

If you want to achieve the perfect cut with veneers and melamine board, use a circular saw and a router.

Clamp a guide to the board and cut the material with your circular saw 1⁄8" longer than required. Next, install a carbide-tipped, straight-cutting bit in your router. Set the guide so your router will cut off the 1⁄8" added length. Proceed slowly and hold the router firmly. You are cutting through glue and wood chips. The operation is noisy and dusty, so wear safety glasses, a dust mask and keep your hands firmly on the router.

The final cut will be clean and chip-free. It takes a little extra time, but the results are worthwhile — perfect cuts every time.

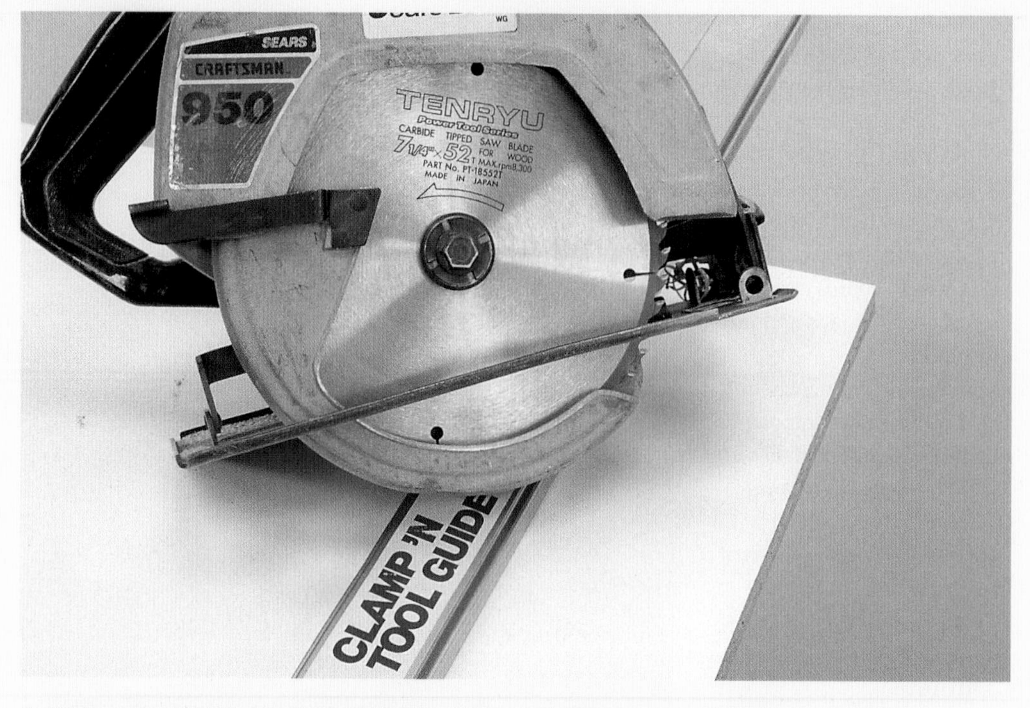

Particleboard and wood veneer sheets can be successfully cut chip-free without a table saw.

For a perfect chip-free cut, use a circular saw and a router.

INSTALLING DOORS WITH HIDDEN HINGES THE EASY WAY

Door mounting jigs are available at all woodworking stores. If you plan to use the hidden hinge for many of your projects, these jigs are worthwhile.

If you're using the hidden hinge only occasionally, here's a quick and easy installation method without using a jig.

This method works with all hinge-mounting applications. It's based on using a 95° to 110° standard opening hinge. If you plan on installing a nonstandard hinge, such as the 170° model, install the door with a standard hinge boss mounted in the door, then replace the hinge boss with a 170° boss after the door has been hung.

First, drill the 35mm holes in the door and mount the hinge boss.

Secure the hinge boss in the hole, making certain it's at 90° to the door edge.

Attach the mounting plate to the hinge boss.

Place the door on the cabinet in its 90° open position. A 3/16" thick spacer, between the door edge and the gable end edge, sets the correct door gap. Insert screws through the mounting plate to secure them to the cabinet side.

Doors with hidden hinges can be installed without jigs.

Align the mounting plate with a square before securing with screws.

The proper door gap is set using a 3/16" thick spacer. Secure the hinge plates with 5/8" PB screws.

manufactured woods

BY TOM BEGNAL

Softwood plywood is used primarily for general construction applications such as wall and roof sheathing, siding and subflooring. In the woodworking shop, softwood plywood is used for jigs, fixtures, shelves, shop cabinets and much more. When building furniture, however, softwood plywood is rarely used as a substrate for plastic laminate or high-quality veneer because the uneven plywood surfaces tend to be visible even after a veneer or laminate is applied.

Plywood is made by gluing thin sheets of wood, called veneers or plies, at right angles to each other. This cross-grained construction results in a wood product that is exceptionally strong. Also, it creates outstanding dimensional stability, which means the plywood changes little in length and width, even as the relative humidity changes.

Softwood plywood is almost always made using an odd number of veneers, usually three, five or seven. Using an odd number of veneers allows the grain of the two outside veneers (one in front and one in back) to run in the same direction.

During manufacture, small defects in the veneers (such as knots and splits) are removed with special cutters. A wood or synthetic plug (sometimes called a patch) is used to repair the cutout.

APA — The Engineered Wood Association (formerly the American Plywood Association) is the major trade association for the softwood plywood industry. Its member mills produce approximately 80 percent of the softwood plywood made in the United States. Most softwood plywood is made into 4' × 8' panels, although 4' × 9' and 4' × 10' panels are also available.

standard thicknesses

FRACTION (IN)	METRIC EQUIVALENT (MM)
1/4	6.4
5/16	7.9
11/32	8.7
3/8	9.5
7/16	11.1
15/32	11.9
1/2	12.7
19/32	15.1
5/8	15.9
23/32	18.3
3/4	19.1
7/8	22.2
1	25.4
1 3/32	27.8
1 1/8	28.6

species group number

Softwood plywood is made from over 70 species of wood. The species are divided into five groups numbered in descending order of strength and stiffness, with Group 1 being the highest and Group 5 the lowest.

GROUP 1	GROUP 2	GROUP 3	GROUP 4	GROUP 5
Apitong	Cedar, Port Orford	Alder, Red	Aspen, Bigtooth	Basswood
Beech, American	Cypress	Birch, Paper	Aspen, Quaking	Poplar, Balsam
Birch, Sweet	Douglas Fir 2*	Cedar, Alaska	Cativo	
Birch, Yellow	Fir, Balsam	Fir, Subalpine	Cedar, Incense	
Douglas Fir 1*	Fir, California Red	Hemlock, Eastern	Cedar, Western Red	
Kapur	Fir, Grand	Maple, Bigleaf	Cottonwood, Eastern	
Keruing	Fir, Noble	Pine, Jack	Cottonwood, Black (Western Poplar)	
Larch, Western	Fir, Pacific Silver	Pine, Lodgepole	Pine, Eastern White	
Maple, Sugar	Fir, White	Pine, Ponderosa	Pine, Sugar	
Pine, Caribbean	Hemlock, Western	Pine, Spruce		
Pine, Loblolly	Lauan, Almon	Redwood		
Pine, Longleaf	Lauan, Bagtikan	Spruce, Engelmann		
Pine, Ocote	Lauan, Mayapis	Spruce, White		
Pine, Shortleaf	Lauan, Red			
Pine, Slash	Lauan, Tangile			
Tan Oak	Lauan, White			
	Maple, Black			
	Mengkulang			
	Meranti, Red			
	Mersawa			
	Pine, Pond			
	Pine, Red			
	Pine, Virginia			
	Pine, Western White			
	Spruce, Black			
	Spruce, Red			
	Spruce, Sitka			
	Sweet Gum			
	Tamarack			
	Yellow Poplar			

*Douglas Fir grown in Washington, Oregon, California, Idaho, Montana, Wyoming, Alberta and British Columbia are classified as Douglas Fir 1. Those grown in Nevada, Utah, Colorado, Arizona and New Mexico are classified as Douglas Fir 2.

exposure durability

Exposure durability classification is a measure of the strength of the softwood plywood glue bond as it relates to weather and the resulting moisture.

EXPOSURE DURABILITY CLASSIFICATION	DESCRIPTION
Exterior	Has a fully waterproof bond. Designed for permanent exposure to weather or moisture.
Exposure 1	Has a fully waterproof bond. Designed for applications where high moisture conditions might be encountered in service, or where long construction delays are expected prior to providing protection.
Exposure 2	Intended for protected applications that could get occasional exposure to high humidity and water leakage.
Interior	Made with interior glue; intended for interior applications only.

softwood plywood outer veneer grades

Softwood plywood outer veneers (face and back) are graded on the basis of natural growth characteristics of the wood and also the allowable size and number of repairs that may be made during manufacture. In addition to the grades below, some manufacturers also produce an N grade, which has the highest-quality veneer and is available by special order only.

OUTER VENEER GRADE	DESCRIPTION
A	Has a smooth, paintable surface. Not more than 18 neatly made repairs permitted. Repairs can be wood or synthetic.
B	Has a solid surface. Shims, sled or router-type repairs and tight knots to 1" across grain permitted. Wood or synthetic repairs permitted. Some minor splits permitted.
C Plugged	Plugged Improved C veneer. Splits limited to 1/8" width; knotholes or other open defects limited to 1/4" × 1/2". Wood or synthetic repairs permitted. Admits some broken grain.
C	Tight knots to 1 1/2". Knotholes to 1" across grain and some to 1/2" if total width of knots and knotholes is within specified limits. Synthetic or wood repairs permitted. Discoloration and sanding defects that do not impair strength are permitted. Limited splits allowed. Stitching permitted.
D	Knots and knotholes to 2 1/2" width across grain and 1/2" larger within specified limits. Limited splits are permitted. Stitching permitted. Exposure durability classification limited to Exposure 2 or interior.

Grade Designations

Softwood plywood grades are usually identified in one of two ways: either (1) in terms of the veneer grade used on the face and back of the plywood or (2) by a name suggesting the plywood's intended use (including APA Performance Rated Panels).

Grade Designation by Face and Back Veneer Grades

A softwood plywood that's identified by the veneer grade on the face and back might be stamped A-B. Such a designation indicates that the face has an A-grade veneer, while the back has a B-grade veneer. Some other examples of grade combinations include A-A, B-C, B-D and C-D.

Grade Designation by Intended Use

Plywood that is identified by a name suggesting the intended use might be stamped Underlayment or Marine. This type of grade designation also includes the APA Performance Rated Panels, which are identified by such names as APA Rated Sheathing, APA Rated Sturd-I-Floor or APA Rated Siding.

Span Ratings

APA Performance Rated Panels (APA Rated Sheathing, AP Rated Sturd-I-Floor and APA Rated Sidings) are further identified with a span rating. On APA Rated Sheathing, the span numbers are shown as two numbers separated by a slash, for example, 32/16 or 48/24. The left-hand number indicates the maximum recommended spacing of supports when the plywood is used for roof sheathing. The right-hand number indicates the maximum recommended spacing of supports when the plywood is used for subflooring. The span rating is shown as a single number on AAPA Rated Sturd-I-Floor and APA Rated Siding. All span ratings are based on installing the plywood panels with the long dimension across three or more supports.

Grade Mark

Manufacturers label plywood with a grade mark. The grade mark provides useful information about the plywood product. Depending on the grade designation, the grade mark can be applied to the back or edge of the plywood.

Grade Mark for Plywood Identified by Face and Back Veneer Grades

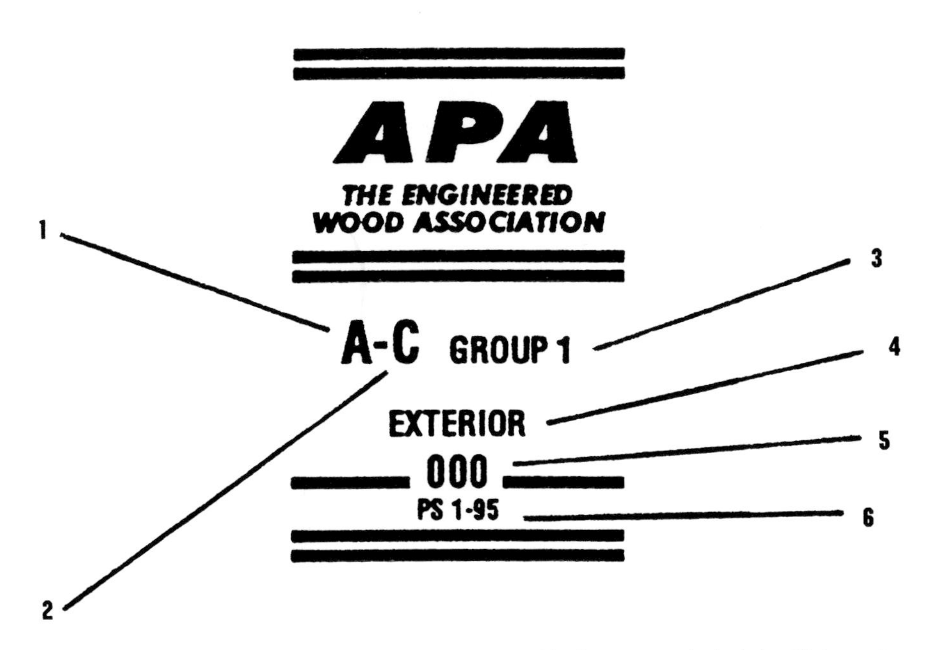

The grade mark for plywood that is identified by the face and back veneer grades includes (1) the grade of the face veneer, (2) the grade of the back veneer, (3) the species group number, (4) the exposure durability classification, (5) the lumber mill that produced the panel (shown as a number) and (6) the applicable product standard.

Grade Mark for Plywood Identified by Intended Use*

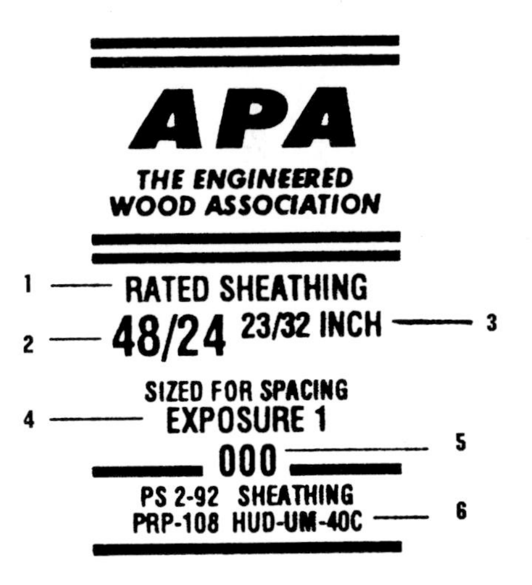

This grade mark can vary a bit, but in general includes (1) the panel grade designation, (2) the span rating, (3) the thickness, (4) the exposure durability classification, (5) the lumber mill that produced the panel (shown as a number) and (6) the applicable product standard.

*Grade mark shown is for an APA Performance Rated Panel.

Hardwood Plywood

Hardwood plywood is used primarily for appearance applications. It provides an attractive wood surface that, as a general rule, costs less than solid-stock hardwood lumber of the same species. Also, because of its construction, hardwood plywood is dimensionally stable, which means that little expansion and contraction occurs as the relative humidity changes.

The plywood panel side that has the higher-grade outer veneer is called the face or the face side. The side with the lower-grade veneer is called the back. When the two outer veneers are the same grade, the panel doesn't have a back but rather has two face sides.

The material sandwiched between the two outer veneers is called the core. Hardwood plywood cores can be made from either softwood or hardwood veneer (not necessarily the same grade as the outer veneers), softwood or hardwood lumber, particleboard, medium-density fiberboard (MDF) or hardboard.

When hardwood plywood has five or more plies, the first layer of veneer under the outer veneer is called the crossband. The crossband is assembled at right angles (90°) to the grain of the outer veneer. In addition, the term *crossbanding* is used to describe all the inner layers of veneer that have a grain direction running at right angles to the outer veneers.

The type and quality of hardwood plywood can be affected by a variety of factors, including (1) the wood species of the face veneer, (2) the grade of the face veneer, (3) the wood species of the back veneer, (4) the grade of the back veneer, (5) the construction of the core and (6) the type of glue bond.

When purchasing hardwood plywood, a number of thickness, width and length combinations are available. However, the most commonly found hardwood plywood panel sizes are 4' × 6', 4' × 8' and 4' × 10'. Commonly found thicknesses are shown in the following chart. Other thicknesses might be available; check with your dealer.

hardwood plywood thicknesses

FRACTION (IN)	METRIC EQUIVALENT (MM)
1/8	3.2
1/4	6.4
3/8	9.5
1/2	12.7
5/8	15.9
3/4	19.1
7/8	22.2
1	25.4
1 1/8	28.6

categories of wood species commonly used for face sides of hardwood plywood

Wood species most commonly used for the face side (or sides) of hardwood plywood are shown here. The species are grouped by category based primarily on the modulus of elasticity and specific gravity of the wood. The modulus of elasticity and specific gravity provide a measure of wood strength and stiffness. The categories are shown in descending order of strength and stiffness, with the highest values in category A and the lowest in category D.

You'll note that a few softwood species are shown in the chart. Softwoods that are considered decorative are used as face veneers on some hardwood plywoods.

CATEGORY A	CATEGORY B		CATEGORY C		CATEGORY D
Apitong	Ash, Black	Magnolia, Southern	Alder, Red	Meranti Shorea spp.	Aspen, Bigtooth
Ash, White	Avodire	Mahogany, African	Basswood	Pine, Ponderosa	Aspen, Quaking
Beech, American	Birch, Paper	Mahogany, Honduras	Butternut	Pine, Sugar	Cedar, Eastern Red
Birch, Sweet	Cherry	Maple, Black	Cativo	Pine, Eastern White	Cedar, Western Red
Birch, Yellow	Cucumber Tree	Maple, Red	Chestnut	Pine, Western White	Willow, Black
Bubinga	Cypress	Spruce, Red	Cottonwood, Black	Primavera	
Hickory	Elm, Rock	Spruce, Sitka	Cottonwood, Eastern	Redwood	
Kapur Dryobalanops spp.	Fir, Douglas	Sycamore	Elm, American	Sassafras	
Keruing Dipterocarpus spp.	Fir, White	Teak	Elm, Slippery	Spruce, Black	
Maple, Sugar	Gum	Walnut, Black	Hackberry	Spruce, Engelmann	
Oak, Red	Hemlock, Western	Yellow Poplar	Hemlock, Eastern	Spruce, White	
Oak, White			Lauan, Shorea spp.	Tupelo	
Pecan			Lauan, Parashorea spp.		
Rosewood			Lauan, Pentacme spp.		
Sapele			Maple, Silver		
Tan Oak					

hardwood plywood — standard grades for face veneers

The grades, based primarily on appearance features, are shown in descending order of quality, with best appearance veneers in grade AA and the lowest in grade E.

GRADE	GENERAL DESCRIPTION
AA	Highest-quality veneer with an excellent appearance. For use in high-end applications such as quality furniture, case goods, doors and cabinets, and architectural paneling.
A	Allows a few more imperfections than grade AA but remains a high-quality panel.
B	Exhibits more imperfections than grade A, but still an attractive panel for many applications.
C, D and E	Veneer has sound surfaces, but allows unlimited color variation. Permits repairs that increase in size and number from grade C to grade E. Generally used where a more natural appearance is desired or where the surface is hidden.
SP (Specialty Grade)	Grade is limited to veneers that have characteristics unlike any found in grade AA through E. Species such as wormy chestnut and bird's-eye maple fall into grade SP. Acceptable characteristics are as agreed upon by buyer and seller.

hardwood plywood — back grades

The grades are shown in descending order of quality, with grade 1 the highest and grade 4 the lowest.

IMPERFECTION	GRADE 1	GRADE 2	GRADE 3	GRADE 4
Sapwood	Yes	Yes	Yes	Yes
Discoloration & stain	Yes	Yes	Yes	Yes
Mineral streaks	Yes	Yes	Yes	Yes
Sound tight burls	Yes	Yes	Yes	Yes
Sound tight knots	Max. dia. 3/8"	Max. dia. 3/4"	Max. dia. 1 1/2"	Yes
Max. number of tight knots	16	16	Unlimited to 1/2", max. 16 from 1/2" to 1 1/2"	Unlimited
Knotholes	No	1/2" repaired	1*	4
Max. combined number of knotholes and repaired knots	None**	All repaired; unlimited to 3/8", no more than 8 from 3/8" to 1/2"*	Unlimited to 3/8", no more than 10 from 3/8" to 1"	
Wormholes	Filled***	Filled***	Yes	Yes
Splits or open joints	Six 1/8" x 12" repaired	Six 3/16" x 12" repaired	Yes, 3/8" x 1/4" length of panel*	1" for 1/4 panel length, 1/2" for 1/2 panel length, 1/4" for full length of panel
Doze (dote) and decay	Firm areas of doze	Firm areas of doze	Firm areas of doze	Areas of doze and decay OK provided serviceability not impaired
Rough cut/ruptured grain	Two 8" dia. areas	5 percent of panel	Yes	Yes
Bark pockets	1/8"-wide repaired	1/4"-wide repaired	Yes*	Yes
Laps	No	Repaired	Yes*	Yes

*Available repaired if necessary.
**Pin knots and repaired pin knots allowed.
***Unfilled wormholes shall be a maximum of 1/16" dia.

inner veneer grades for veneer-core hardwood plywood

Grade designations are based on the allowable openings in the veneers.

DESCRIPTION	GRADE J	GRADE K	GRADE K	GRADE L	GRADE M
Thickness of crossbands adjacent to faces	Any thickness	Thicker than $^1/_{10}$"	$^1/_{10}$" and thinner	Any thickness	Any thickness
Knotholes and other similarly shaped openings (max. dia.)	None	$^3/_8$"	$^3/_4$"	1"	$2^1/_2$"
Splits, gaps and other elongated end or edge openings. Each opening is visible on only one end or edge of panel (max. width)	$^1/_8$"	$^1/_4$"	$^1/_4$"	$^1/_2$"	1"

hardwood plywood types

Three hardwood plywood types are available. With each one the glue bond offers different moisture resistance qualities.

TYPE	DESCRIPTION
Technical (Exterior)	Fully waterproof. Meets panel construction criteria for special applications such as marine and aircraft.
Type I (Exterior)	Fully waterproof. Allows lower-grade inner veneers than technical. Not to be used when continuously exposed to moisture in critical applications such as marine and aircraft.
Type II (Interior)	Moisture resistant, but not waterproof. For interior use only.

common hardwood plywood core constructions

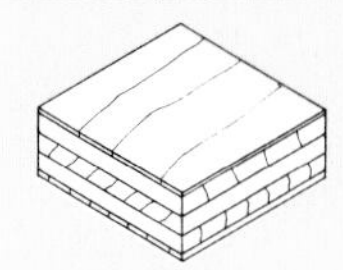

VENEER-CORE: Made of veneers (usually three, five or seven), which can be either hardwood or softwood; species mixing not allowed.

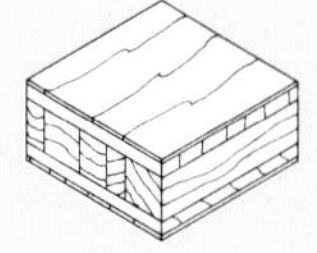

LUMBER-CORE: Made from three, five or seven plies of edge-glued solid lumber; can be either hardwood or softwood; species mixing not allowed. Grades available are Clean, Sound and Regular. A regular grade clear-edge version is available with edge strips at least $1^1/_2$" wide to facilitate edge moulding and shaping.

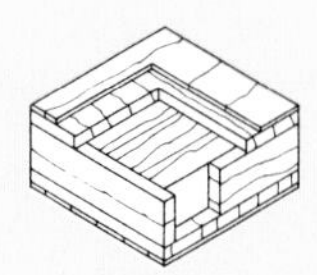

BANDED LUMBER-CORE: Bands must be made from clear stock; other specifications are as agreed upon by buyer and seller. Bands can be applied to one or two ends (B1E, B2E); one or tow sides (B1S, B2S); two ends, one side (B2E1S); two sides, one end (B2S1E); or two sides, two ends (B4).

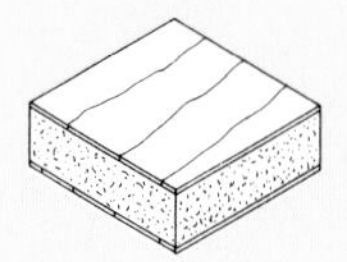

PARTICLEBOARD-CORE: Made with either three or five plies of particleboard.

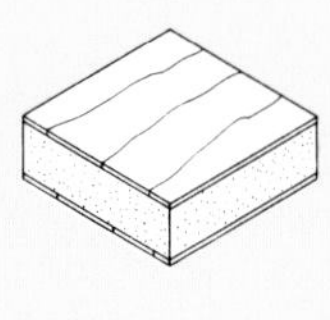

MDF-CORE: Made with three plies of medium-density fiberboard.

HARDBOARD-CORE: Made with three plies of hardboard.

characteristics of hardwood plywood panels

CORE TYPE	FLATNESS	VISUAL EDGE QUALITY	SURFACE UNIFORMITY	DIM. STABILITY	SCREW HOLDING	BENDING STRENGTH	AVAILABILITY
Veneer Core (all hardwood)	Fair	Good	Good	Excellent	Excellent	Excellent	Readily
Veneer Core (all softwood)	Fair	Good	Fair	Excellent	Excellent	Excellent	Readily
Lumber Core (hard- or softwood)	Good	Good	Good	Good	Excellent	Excellent	Limited
Particleboard Core (medium density)	Excellent	Good	Excellent	Fair	Fair	Good	Readily
MDF Core	Excellent	Excellent	Excellent	Fair	Good	Good	Readily
Hardboard Core (standard)	Excellent	Excellent	Excellent	Fair	Good	Good	Readily
Hardboard Core (tempered)	Excellent	Good	Good	Good	Good	Good	Limited

Matching

Hardwood plywood face veneers can be matched in different ways to create panels that have considerable visual appeal. Face veneers are matched in one of three general ways:

1. Matching between adjacent veneers. Examples of matching between veneers include bookmatching, slipmatching, pleasing match and random.

2. Matching of panel faces. Veneer is matched from one panel to another, usually to create symmetry in a room. Examples: running match, balance match and center match.

3. Matching for special effects. Examples: checkerboard match, diamond match and sunburst match.

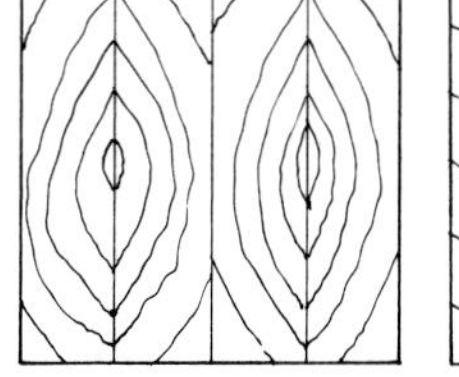
BOOKMATCHING

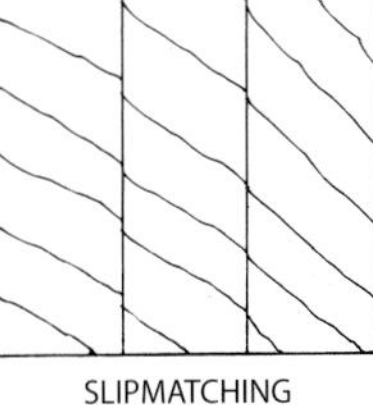
SLIPMATCHING

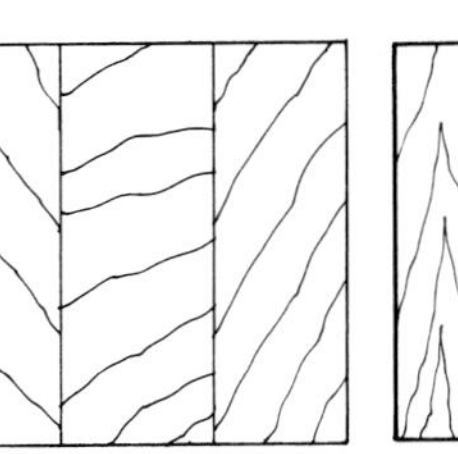
PLEASING MATCHING

RANDOM

Typical Hardwood Plywood Edge Stamp

Hardwood plywood is labeled with a mill stamp that provides useful information about the panel. To avoid marring the face and back veneers, manufacturers generally stamp the panel edges with a mark called an edge stamp.

A typical edge stamp includes (1) the thickness of the plywood, (2) the grade of the face veneer, (3) the grade of the back veneer, (4) the wood species of the face, (5) the number of plies and type of core, (6) the identifying mill number and (7) the applicable standard.

1 2 3 4 5 6 7

Particleboard

Particleboard is made by mixing small particles of wood with synthetic resin and bonding them under heat and pressure. By modifying the manufacturing process, the manufacturer can make particleboard into several different grades for various applications.

Particleboard grades are identified by a letter (or letters) followed by a hyphen and a number or letter. The letter designates the particleboard density as follows:

H = high density, generally above 50 pounds per cubic foot (pcf)

M = medium density, generally between 40 and 50 pcf

LD = low density, generally less than 40 pcf

The number following the hyphen indicates the grade identification within a particular density. For example, M-1 indicates medium-density particleboard, grade 1. The higher the grade identification number, the higher the strength qualities of the particleboard. For example, grade M-2 has better strength characteristics than grade M-1.

Any special characteristics are listed after the grade identification number. For example, M-2 Exterior Glue indicates medium-density particleboard, grade 2 made with exterior glue.

The chart below lists some of the important physical properties for each grade.

particleboard grades (selected requirements)

GRADE	MODULUS OF RUPTURE (PSI)	MODULUS OF ELASTICITY (PSI)	HARDNESS (POUNDS)	SCREW HOLDING FACE (POUNDS)	EDGE (POUNDS)
H-1	2393	348,100	500	405	298
H-2	2973	348,100	1000	427	348
H-3	3408	398,900	1500	450	348
M-1	1595	250,200	500	NS**	NS**
M-S*	1813	275,600	500	202	180
M-2	2103	326,300	500	225	202
M-3	2393	398,900	500	247	225
LD-1	435	79,800	NS**	90	NS**
LD-2	725	148,700	NS**	124	NS**

NOTES:
Grades PBU, D-2 and D-3, used as flooring products, are not shown.
*Grade M-S refers to medium-density "special" grade. This grade was added after grades M-1, M-2 and M-3 were established. Grade M-S falls between grades M-1 and M-2 in terms of physical properties.
**NS = not specified.

Medium-Density Fiberboard (MDF)

Medium-density fiberboard is made by mixing processed wood fibers with synthetic resin (or other suitable bonding material) and bonding them under heat and pressure. By modifying the manufacturing process, the manufacturer can make MDF into several different grades for various applications. Thicknesses from 3⁄16" to 1½" are available, but the ¾" thickness is the one most commonly found.

MDF is organized into product classifications rather than grades. The classifications are based on the density of the product. A two-letter designation identifies each classification. The classifications are as follows:

HD = high density, generally above 50 pounds per cubic foot (pcf)

MD = medium density, generally between 40 and 50 pcf

LD = low density, generally less than 40 pcf

MDF products with special characteristics are identified with either a letter, a number or a term that identifies the characteristic. For example, MD-Exterior Glue indicates that the MDF has a medium-density classification that meets exterior glue requirements.

The chart lists some of the important physical properties for each grade.

medium density fiberboard classifications (some selected requirements)

PRODUCT CLASSIFICATION	MODULUS OF RUPTURE (PSI)	MODULUS OF ELASTICITY (PSI)	SCREW HOLDING FACE (POUNDS)	EDGE(POUNDS)
INTERIOR MDF				
HD	5000	500,000	350	300
MD (0.825" thick or less)	3500	350,000	325	250
MD (more than 0.825" thick)	3500	350,000	300	225
LD	2000	200,000	175	150
EXTERIOR MDF				
MD-Exterior Glue 0.825" thick or less)	5000	500,000	325	250
MD-Exterior Glue (more than 0.825" thick)				

Hardboard

Hardboard is made from wood chips that are converted into fibers and then bonded under heat and pressure. Other materials can be added to improve such characteristics as moisture and abrasion resistance, strength, stiffness and hardness. Hardboard is available either smooth-one-side (S1S) or smooth-both-sides (S2S).

hardboard panel thicknesses

NOMINAL THICKNESS		THICKNESS RANGE (minimum-maximum)	
INCHES	MILLIMETERS	INCHES	MILLIMETERS
1/12 (0.083)	2.1	0.070–0.090	1.8–2.3
1/10 (0.100)	2.5	0.091–0.110	2.3–2.8
1/8 (0.125)	3.2	0.115–0.155	2.9–3.9
3/16 (0.188)	4.8	0.165–0.205	4.2–5.2
1/4 (0.250)	6.4	0.210–0.265	5.3–6.7
5/16 (0.313)	8.0	0.290–0.335	7.4–8.5
3/8 (0.375)	9.5	0.350–0.400	8.9–10.2
7/16 (0.438)	11.1	0.410–0.460	10.4–11.7
1/2 (0.500)	12.7	0.475–0.525	12.1–13.3
5/8 (0.625)	15.9	0.600–0.650	15.2–16.5
11/16 (0.688)	17.5	0.660–0.710	16.8–18.0
3/4 (0.750)	19.1	0.725–0.775	18.4–19.7
13/16 (0.813)	20.6	0.785–0.835	19.9–21.2
7/8 (0.875)	22.2	0.850–0.900	21.6–22.9
1 (1.000)	25.4	0.975–1.025	24.8–26.0
1 1/8 (1.125)	28.6	1.115–1.155	28.3–29.3

hardboard classifications

CLASS	GENERAL DESCRIPTION
Tempered	Highest strength, stiffness, hardness and resistance to water and abrasion. Available in all thicknesses from 1/12" to 3/8".
Standard	High strength and water resistance. Hardness and resistance to water and abrasion less than that of tempered class. Available in all thicknesses from 1/12" to 3/8".
Service-tempered	Has better strength, stiffness, hardness and resistance to water and abrasion than service class. Available in 1/8", 3/16", 1/4" and 3/8" thicknesses.
Service	Good strength, but not as strong as standard class. Available in 1/8", 3/16", 1/4", 3/8", 7/16", 1/2", 5/8", 11/16", 3/4", 13/16", 7/8", 1" and 1 1/8" thicknesses.
Industrialite	Moderate strength. Available in 1/4", 3/8", 7/16", 1/2", 5/8", 11/16", 3/4", 13/16", 7/8", 1" and 1 1/8" thicknesses.

why you should freeze your tools

BY CHRISTOPHER SCHWARZ

About 150 years ago, Swiss watchmakers noticed that extreme cold changed the properties of their metal clock parts for the better. So after manufacturing their gears or what have you, some watchmakers would then store the parts in caves during the cold Swiss winters and let them freeze.

Unwittingly, they had given birth to what is now commonly known as cryogenics.

During the last century, toolmakers and metal heat treaters have explored what extremely cold temperatures do to tooling, metals and other materials. And they have come to some remarkable conclusions. For certain types of metals, cooling them to -320° Fahrenheit can make them at least twice as resistant to wear as untreated metal.

The wear resistance is permanent. You have to treat your tooling only once, and it will remain that durable forever, experts say. And the price of cryogenically treating your tooling is becoming quite reasonable. We found that treating about four pounds of metal will cost you about $30 to $50. (If you treat a lot of items, the cost can be as little as $1 a pound — and prices continue to drop). Cryo labs themselves are also becoming more common because commercial heat treaters are investing in the technology so they can offer the service to their customers. If you live in an industrial area, you'll probably be able to find a cryo lab locally. But even if you live in the sticks, you can ship your tooling to cryo labs for treatment.

So what's the catch? If cryo is so amazing, why doesn't anyone sell cryogenically treated planer knives or router bits? Many of the manufacturers we talked to, including Freud Tools, had experimented with the process in its early days and found it had little or no effect.

That's not surprising, says Bill Bryson, author of the book *Cryogenics* (Hanser Gardner Publications) and the president of the company Advisor in Metals in Milton, New Hampshire.

"Back in the 1970s it was a free-for-all, and it hurt the industry," Bryson says. "People were dumping tools in liquid nitrogen and they were cracking, or they weren't tempering the tools after the [cryogenic] process."

As a result, cryogenics got a bad rap in the steel and tooling industry, Bryson says. Not only for the early mistakes that were made but because some people thought that cryogenics would hurt sales. If tooling lasted twice as long, they might sell only half as many tools.

But during the last 30 years, heat treaters and cryogenic advocates began figuring out more about how, why and when cryogenics works. And today, most people in the industry acknowledge that it works well for certain types of

Many carbide tools are good candidates for cryogenic treatment. Before you treat your carbide-tipped saw blade or router bits, check with the manufacturer to see if the carbide is new or recycled — some companies use carbide recovered from old tools. For some reason, recycled carbide doesn't improve after cryogenic treatment.

CRYO: IT'S NOT JUST FOR TOOLS ANYMORE

Sure, cryogenics can make your tools last longer, but it also has a lot of other benefits, some practical and some wild. Here's a short list of claims we've gathered from books, magazine articles and the Internet:

- **PANTY HOSE:** Nylon stockings that have been cryogenically treated are less likely to develop runs.
- **GOLFING:** Cryogenically treated golf clubs hit balls 3 percent to 5 percent farther. Cryogenically treated balls can be hit farther.
- **RACING:** Small-block Chevy engines have been treated and found to have significantly less cylinder wear during a racing season. Many other racing professionals have also used cryo.
- **FIREARMS:** Treated rifles are more accurate.
- **MUSICAL INSTRUMENTS:** Cryogenically treated instruments have a better tonal quality and the valves slide more easily.
- **GUITAR STRINGS:** It doesn't even have to be the entire instrument. Some people treat guitar strings and say it improves their tone.
- **SPORTS:** Baseball bats that have been frozen hit balls 2 percent to 4 percent farther.

metals, Bryson says, particularly the more complex alloys (more on that later).

In the home woodworking market, we've seen only a few cryogenically treated tools on the market. A few years ago, Vermont American announced it would sell Ice Bits, cryogenically hardened screwdriver bits. Hock Tools recently began offering a line of cryogenically treated A2 plane blades. The cryo blades cost between $5.50 and $12.50 more than the same-size high-carbon steel blades. And toolmakers Bridge City Tool Works and Steve Knight, owner of Knight Toolworks, also offer cryogenically treated blades.

But cryogenic treatment can help woodworkers with a lot more than plane blades or screwdriver bits, Bryson says. Just ask James Larry Poole of P&K Custom Cabinets in Lula, Georgia.

A couple of years ago Poole sent out his carbide-tipped sawblades, router bits and shaper cutters to a lab for treatment.

"It really makes them last longer," he says. "I had one saw blade in particular that just would not wear out."

Poole used to be involved in car racing, and he had heard about the benefits of cryogenically treating some car parts, including crankshafts and pistons. So when a friend of his from the racing business started a cryo lab, Poole decided to see if it would help his tools.

"You really can tell the difference," he says. "I get twice the life at least . . . so it's worth the money."

But before you start gathering all the cutting tools in your shop to take to a lab, you need to know some things.

In a Nutshell: What Cryo Does

A little science is needed to understand what cryogenics does, but it's easy to digest. When tooling is made, the manufacturer heats it to make it hold an edge. During heat treatment, the structure of the

WHERE TO GO FOR CRYO

If you can't find a cryogenics lab or a heat treater locally, a few labs across the country provide the service. Please see the suppliers list at the back of the book and contact them for pricing and shipping information.

steel changes. As it is heated, the steel has a structure called austenite, which is softer and has a coarse, irregular grain. When the blade is quenched (reduced quickly in temperature), the austenite changes into martensite, which has a finer grain and is more resistant to wear.

The problem is that the transformation from austenite to martensite is never 100 percent. If a tool is carefully heat treated, it might end up with 90 percent martensite and 10 percent austenite. Commercial heat treating typically results in 75 percent martensite, Bryson says. In low-quality tooling, it can be as low as 50 percent martensite.

By carefully cooling the tooling to -320°F and then thoroughly retempering the metal, nearly all the austenite is transformed into martensite. Bryson says it's proven to be a 99.9-percent transformation or more.

All tooling will benefit from cryogenics, Bryson says. But if the steel is an alloy containing cobalt or tungsten, the cryogenic process will create very fine microcarbides, which add even more durability to the edge.

The alloy A2 steel, which is now found on some hand plane blades, contains carbon and chrome, so it reacts well to cryogenic treatment. High-speed steel (HSS) contains molybdenum (which makes the tool resistant to heat), chromium and sometimes tungsten, which makes it ideal for cryo treatment. You'll find HSS in your planer knives, your jointer knives and in other cutting tools. As a rule with metals, the higher the alloy content, the better the cryogenics will work.

But what about carbide tools? Will saw blades and router bits benefit from cryogenic freezing? According to Bryson, that depends.

If the carbide is newly manufactured and not recycled from old carbide tooling, cryogenic treatment works, Bryson says. Carbide that has been reclaimed or recycled is not improved.

"And we don't know why," he says.

In new carbide, cryogenic treatment strengthens the binder between the individual carbides, he says. Cryogenically treated bits should last twice as long between sharpenings, Bryson says, though some people report even longer times between sharpenings.

Tools that are difficult or expensive to resharpen, such as this Forstner bit, are prime candidates for cryogenic treatment.

Beware of the Thin Film

Perhaps one of the strangest aspects of cryogenic treatment is something that experts have yet to fully explain. It seems that after a tool has been frozen and then retempered, some report you won't get the added wear resistance until the tool is resharpened.

Bryson says a layer of metal that's between 0.00007" and 0.0001" thick on the outside remains untreated. After you remove this layer by sharpening, the tool works great. Bryson calls this the "thin film phenomenon," and he says it's one of the reasons some people thought cryogenics was a crock in the early days. People would treat their sharp new tools, put them to use and see almost no difference in the tool's life. But if you sharpen the tools after treatment, Bryson says, that's when you see the full benefits of cryogenic treatment.

How to Shop for Cryo

Several ways exist to cryogenically treat tools, and experts say some are better than others.

- Warmer cryo: Some labs use dry ice to cool the tools. Dry ice will take the temperature down to -109°F. This process works, but you won't get a full transformation of austenite to martensite.
- Quick dip: Some labs dip the tools into liquid nitrogen (-320°F), leave it there for a short period of time, remove the tools and let them return to room temperature. This process can cause the tools to shatter from thermal shock. It also can transform only the outer layer and leave the core untreated. Many of the experts we talked to do not recommend this procedure.
- Long bath: Other cryo labs use gaseous nitrogen to reduce the temperature slowly; they keep it there for 20 hours or more (using either gas or liquid nitrogen), and then slowly return the tools to room temperature. Bryson says he's tried a variety of methods, and the equipment he prefers (and sells to other cryo labs) takes the temperature down using gas and then soaks the tools in liquid nitrogen. Either process works, however.

Hock Tools' plane blade is made from A2 tool steel that has been cryogenically treated. Cryogenics can more than double the time between sharpenings on plane blades.

IN SEARCH OF PROOF CRYO REALLY WORKS

To many people, cryogenics sounds too good to be true. So we went looking for some stories to back up the claims we'd read so much about.

Ron Hock, the founder of Hock Tools, offers A2 plane blades that have been cryogenically treated — in addition to his line of high-carbon steel blades that he's offered for years.

He says he began offering the A2 tools after other plane blade manufacturers, such as Veritas Tools, began selling A2 blades. Hock says he isn't entirely convinced that A2 can be made as sharp as his high-carbon blades, but it does appear to wear longer and be slightly more corrosion-resistant.

"It was adding the cryo that tipped it for me," Hock says. "Without the cryo improvement, I wouldn't use the A2."

Hock says he's getting good reports back from customers who are seeing longer edge life.

Thomas Lie-Nielsen, the founder of Lie-Nielsen Toolworks in Warren, Maine, was also looking for answers. He was considering switching to a different type of blade for his line of high-quality planes. For years he's used a high-carbon steel that he carefully heat-treated. Lie-Nielsen was considering switching to A2 that was cryogenically treated.

So he took three A2 blades (some of which had been cryogenically treated) and three high-carbon blades and made 300 identical cuts with each. Lie-Nielsen says it was obvious that the A2 blades retained their edge longer than the high-carbon blades.

One of the keys to getting the best results is to choose a lab that has some knowledge of heat treatment and metallurgy and is willing to soak the tools for a long time, says Randall Barron, professor emeritus at Louisiana Tech University's Department of Mechanical Engineering. Barron's pioneering research in the 1970s, 1980s and 1990s helped convince many industries to use the process in manufacturing.

Barron's studies showed that bringing the temperature down to -320°F created a more durable tool. Plus, his research showed that soaking the tools for hours was what led to the creation of the microcarbides, which lend additional wear resistance.

No matter which process is used, after the tools return to room temperature, the tools need to be retempered because the new martensite is fragile and can shatter, experts say. This retempering process is almost always included in the price for the cryo treatment.

Bryson recommends that the tools be tempered at 300°F to 350°F for two hours for every inch of thickness of the tool. He also says you should make sure that the items are not stacked on top of one another during tempering.

How Well Does It Work?

How well cryogenics works, of course, is the big question. Some of the claims seem outright outrageous. A dowel maker claimed his A2 knives lasted 800 percent longer. A titanium aircraft bit that once lasted for 15 holes was replaced by a common bit that had been cryogenically treated that would last for 200 holes.

Most cryogenics labs will tell you it's reasonable to expect your tooling to last two or three times longer between sharpenings. Considering how inexpensive cryogenic treatment can be, you'll make your money back after one sharpening.

Even if cryogenic processing really works, don't be surprised if you don't see cryogenic planer blades for sale in woodworking catalogs.

Professor Barron says that one of the studies he did in the early days was for a manufacturer of razor blades. The company wanted to see if the cryogenic process could improve the dies they used in making the blades.

"I asked if they wanted to treat the razor blades to make them last longer," he says with a chuckle. "They said no, because then they might not make as much money."

sharpening plane irons and chisels

BY CHRISTOPHER SCHWARZ

When I took my first class in woodworking some years ago, the first thing the instructor showed us was his shop-made waterstone pond.

With a reverence and care reserved for religious artifacts and small injured animals, the teacher brought the pond out from its special place in his cabinet. For more than an hour he talked with a furrowed brow about secondary bevels, wire edges and polishing the back of our edge tools.

All of us in the class did our best to stifle our yawns. I kept looking at the rows of chisels and backsaws and wondered when we were going to get to the important part.

Within a week we all realized that we should have paid more attention to the sharpening lecture. Soon there were only two sharp chisels in the shop for a class of 10 students, and we quarreled over them. Trimming tenons with the equivalent of a butter knife was no fun.

So I made it a point to learn to sharpen well. And I've been fortunate to be able to use a variety of methods, including: oilstones, diamond stones, waterstones, ceramic stones, sandpaper, electric grinders and the Tormek system.

Each system has its good and bad points. Some are simple, others don't make a mess, some are less expensive and most systems can put an astoundingly good edge on tool steel.

For me, the two most important qualities a sharpening system needs are that it must be fast and it must produce the keenest edge. I'll pay a little more and suffer a little mess to get a good edge in a hurry.

That's because I'm more interested in woodworking than I am in the act of sharpening. I have no desire to look at my edges under a microscope or fret about tiny imperfections in the metal. I'm not the kind of guy who wants to meditate on my power animal as I proceed up to 500,000 grit. I want to be done with it and get back to the good part.

Familiarity Breeds a Keen Edge

The steps I'm about to describe will work with every sharpening and honing system I know of on the market. That's because no matter what system you use, sharpening is about one thing: Grinding and polishing the two intersecting planes of a cutting edge to as fine a point as possible.

The tools you use to get there are up to you. But here are a few words of advice: Pick a sharpening system and stick with it for a good long time before you consider giving it up. Many woodworkers that I've talked to jump around from system to system, trying to find the best thing (and spending a lot of money).

If you stick with one system, your edges will improve gradually as you get better and better at using your particular set of stones or sandpaper. Skipping around from one system to the next will only stunt your sharpening skills.

Second, please buy a honing guide. It's a big old lie that these things slow you down. In fact, these simple and inexpensive guides are quick to set up and ensure your edge will be perfect every time you sharpen.

However, don't buy a whole rolling army of honing guides. I use a $10 Eclipse-style guide (the gray side-clamp contraption shown in most of the photos) for sharpening my chisels and most plane irons. I also own the Veritas honing guide. It excels at sharpening skew chisels and specialty plane irons that won't fit in the Eclipse guide, such as irons for shoulder planes.

Each honing guide holds the blade a little differently, and few of them are ever perfectly square. That's OK, because what you're after with a honing guide is repeatability. Use the same guide over and over, and your edges will come out the same every time.

If you don't polish the backside of your newly acquired chisels and plane irons, your cutting edges will always be jagged and easily dulled. You need to polish just the area up by the cutting edge. This is a process you'll only have to do once.

Polish Your Backside

There are three sharpening operations that must be performed on all chisels and plane irons that are new to you. First you must polish the flat backside (sometimes called the "cutting face") of the tool. Next you grind the cutting bevel. Finally you hone and polish a small part of that cutting bevel, which most people call the "secondary bevel."

Keep in mind that these three steps are only for tools

PHOTO AT RIGHT Learning to sharpen your edge tools will open a lot of doors in woodworking. Sharpening is half the battle when learning handplanes, turning and carving.

GRINDING THE EDGE

To begin grinding your edge, put the tool in your honing guide and adjust it until the cutting bevel is flat on your stone. Eyeball it at first. After a couple of passes on the stone you'll know if you're off or not.

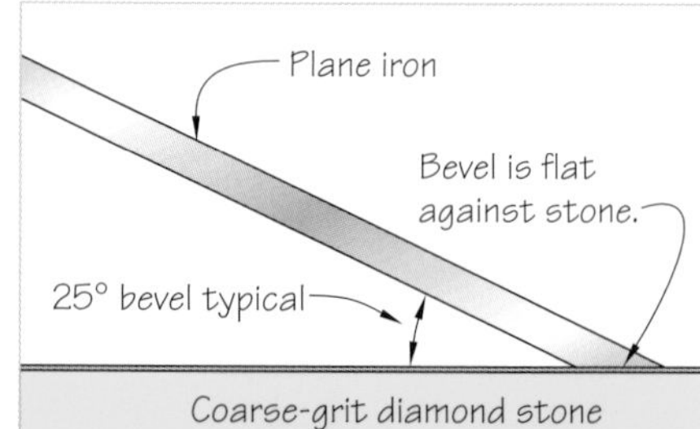

Flat-grinding your cutting bevel should not take long on a coarse diamond stone. If you're having trouble gauging your progress, color the cutting bevel with a permanent marker and you'll get a quick snapshot of where you stand.

When honing narrow chisels, this is the best way I've found to keep things steady and square. Put one finger on the cutting edge; put the other behind the jig to move it.

When you're done grinding, this is what your edge should look like.

that you have newly acquired. Once you do these three things, maintaining an edge is much easier. You'll probably only have to polish the backside once. You'll have to regrind an edge mostly when you hit a nail or drop the tool. Most sharpening is just honing and polishing the secondary bevel.

Begin with the backside of the tool. This is the side of the tool that doesn't have a bevel ground into it. It's one-half of your cutting edge so you need to get it right.

Start sharpening by rubbing the backside back and forth across a medium-grit sharpening stone or sandpaper. You don't need to polish the entire back, just the area up by the cutting edge. I begin this process with a 1,000-grit Norton waterstone, then do the same operation with the 4,000-grit and then the 8,000-grit stone. The backside should look like a mirror when you're finished.

The Not-so-daily Grind

The next step is to grind the cutting bevel of the tool. You can do this on an electric grinder that has a tool rest, which will produce a slightly curved cutting bevel called a hollow-ground edge. Or you can do it on a coarse sharpening stone, which will produce a flat-ground edge.

A lot has been written about the advantages and disadvantages of each system. In comparing my hollow-ground edges vs. flat-ground edges I personally have found little difference between them in terms of edge durability.

I grind using a diamond stone for three reasons. First, it will never destroy a tool due to overheating (which can happen with electric grinders). Second, I use the diamond stone to flatten the waterstones. And third, the diamond stone is great for touching up my router bits.

I use DMT's extra-coarse stone for grinding my edges.

Put the tool in your honing guide and set it so the cutting bevel is dead flat against the stone. Most tools come ground at a 25° bevel, which is good for most woodworking tasks. Mortising chisels should be set for 30°; tools designed only for light paring can be set for 20°.

Don't get too worked up about angles as you begin sharpening. Somewhere in the 25° neighborhood will be fine for most tools.

I use mineral spirits to lubricate my diamond stone. Most people use water, but a sharpening guru at DMT turned me on to mineral spirits. It evaporates slower than water and won't allow rust to build up easily on the stone.

Rub the cutting bevel against the diamond stone and check your progress. You want to grind the entire cutting bevel of the chisel or plane iron all the way across. If you set the tool properly in the jig, this should be about 5 to 10 minutes of work.

As you progress on this coarse stone, you should make a substantial burr on the backside of the tool. This is called a "wire edge," and you'll want to remove it by rubbing the backside on your finest-grit stone a couple of times. Never rub the backside on your coarse stone. That just undoes all your polishing work there.

How you hold the jig is important, too. For plane irons and wide chisels, put a finger on each corner of the tool up near the cutting bevel and use your thumbs to push the jig. For narrower chisels, put one finger on the tool by the cutting bevel and push the jig from behind with one finger.

With the cutting bevel ground, it's time to refine the leading edge to a keen sharpness.

Honing: The Fun Part

Honing is quick and painless if your stones are flat and you've done the first two steps correctly. The first thing to do is to reset the tool in your honing guide. Loosen the screw that clamps the tool and slide the tool backwards about 1/8". Retighten the screw.

This will set the tool so only a small part of the cutting bevel will get honed. This speeds your sharpening greatly.

Start honing with a 1,000-grit waterstone, soft Arkansas oilstone or 320-grit sandpaper. I use the 1,000-grit Norton waterstone. Lubricate your stones as recommended by the manufacturer. Rub the tool back and forth on the stone. Turn it over and check your progress. You should see a secondary bevel appear up at the cutting edge. Rub your thumb along the backside; you should feel a small burr all the way across the cutting edge. If there's no burr, then you're not sharpening up at the edge; so continue honing until you feel that burr.

Once you have that burr, remove it by rubbing the backside across your 8,000-grit stone. Go back to your 1,000-grit stone and refine the secondary bevel some more until all the scratches on your secondary bevel look consistent. Use less and less pressure as you progress on this stone and remove the wire edge on the backside as you go.

Put the 1,000-grit stone away and get out a 4,000-grit waterstone, a hard black Arkansas oilstone or 600-grit sandpaper. Go through the same process you did with the 1,000-grit stone. Remove the wire edge on the backside with your 8,000-grit stone. At this stage, the bevel should look a bit polished in places.

WHY I SWITCHED TO WATERSTONES

There are a lot of sharpening systems out there. And while I haven't tried every one of them, I've tried most. After much experimentation, I settled about five years ago on a system that used DMT diamond stones and oilstones. My system worked pretty well, but the oilstone part was slow, and my final cutting edge was always "almost" perfect.

Last summer I got my hands on a set of Norton's new American-made waterstones and it was like a door had been opened for me. These things cut wicked fast. And the edge they produce is darn near perfect.

They feel different from many Japanese waterstones I've used. The best way to describe the difference is that the Norton stones give you different "feedback" as you sharpen. The 4,000-grit Norton actually feels like it is cutting (it is). The 4,000-grit Japanese stones I've used have a more rubbery feel to them in use in my opinion. And they didn't seem to cut as fast at that level. The 8,000-grit Norton waterstone also provides great feedback to the user.

The downside to all waterstones is that they need to be flattened regularly. For this job, I use a DMT DuoSharp stone with the coarse grit on one side and the extra-coarse on the other. I also use this same diamond stone for grinding the cutting edge of all my chisels and plane irons.

The most economical way to get started with this system is to buy a Norton combination waterstone that has 1,000 grit on one side and 4,000 grit on the other. Then buy an 8,000-grit Norton waterstone for polishing. Norton also makes a 220-grit waterstone, but if you buy the DMT diamond stone you won't need it.

Norton waterstones and the DMT DuoSharp stone are a great combination. The DMT handles the grinding jobs and flattens the Norton waterstones.

Finally, you want to polish the secondary bevel with your finest-grit stone or 1,500-grit sandpaper. I use an 8,000-grit Norton waterstone. There are Japanese waterstones at this grit level, too, however there are no comparable oilstones. A translucent oilstone is somewhat close.

Polishing is a little different. You're not going to feel a wire edge on the backside of the tool. Work both the secondary bevel and the backside of the tool on the 8,000-grit stone and watch the scratches disappear. When they're gone, you're done.

Test the edge using your fingernail — see the photo 5 on page 77 for details. Some people finish by stropping their edges at this point with a piece of hard leather that has been charged with honing compound. I don't find it necessary. In fact, if you're not careful, you will round over your cutting edge while stropping.

Remove the tool from your honing guide, wipe it down with a little oil to prevent rusting and go to work on some end grain.

The tool should slice through the wood with little effort. And if that doesn't convince you of the value of sharpening, I don't know what will.

HONING THE EDGE

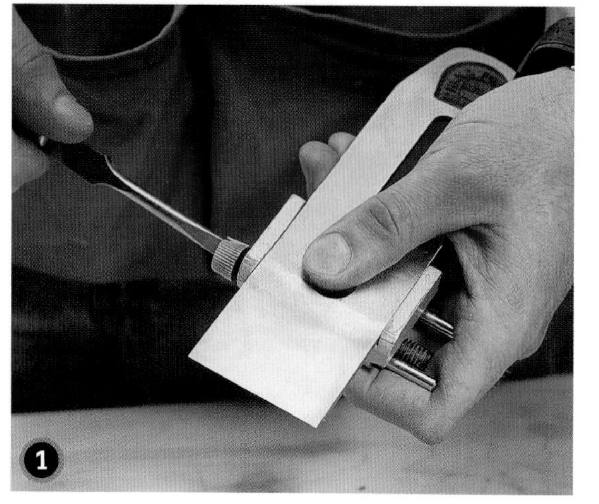

Before you begin honing the secondary bevel, loosen the clamp on your honing guide and nudge the blade backwards in the guide about $^1/_8$".

Begin with a 1,000-grit stone and rub the tool back and forth across the work. Try to wear the stone evenly by moving the tool in a regular pattern.

After a dozen licks, turn the tool over and remove the burr from the backside by rubbing it a couple of times over the 8,000-grit stone.

After honing the tool on the 1,000-grit stone, this is what the secondary bevel should look like.

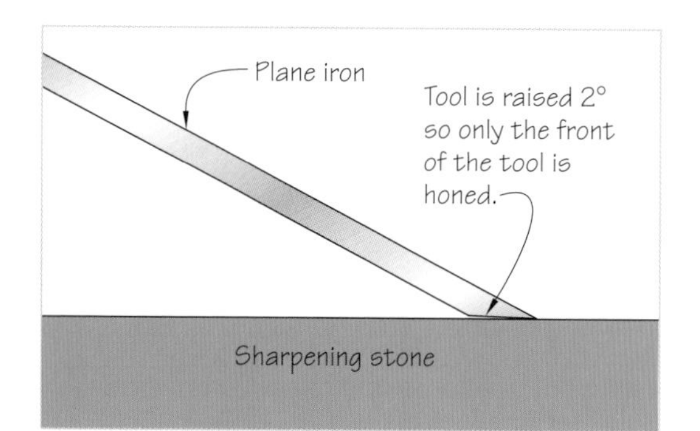

SHAPTON STONES: THE LATEST THING IN SHARPENING

If you think white-lab-coat wizardry is reserved for the manufacturers of power tools, think again. Some of the highest-tech science-fiction stuff happens in the knuckle-dragging hand tool industry: think unbreakable "nodular" cast iron, cryogenically treated tool steel and super-strong "rare earth" magnets that are incorporated into both tools and jigs.

And now the latest innovation is in sharpening. Shapton waterstones from Japan are all the rage among the sharpening gurus, who say the stones cut faster and wear longer than other stones. They also can be expensive. Shapton stones come in several grades, and a basic setup of three stones can cost you anywhere from $130 to $220 — plus you'll need some way to flatten them.

MORE HONING AND POLISHING

Continue honing the edge by switching to a 4,000-grit stone. Remove the burr on the backside with the 8,000-grit stone.

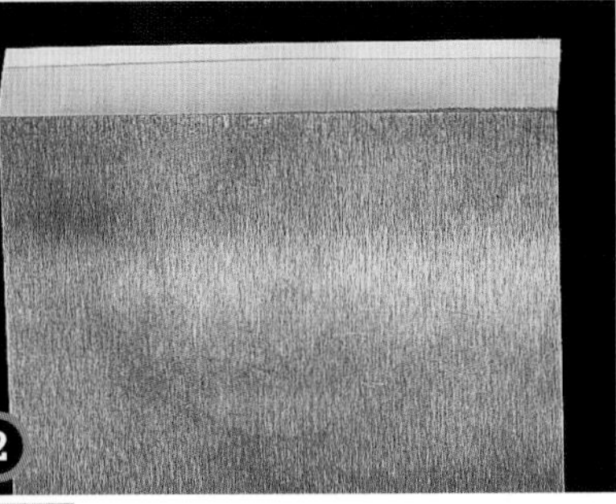

After working the 4,000-grit stone, here's what the secondary bevel should look like. It got a little bigger and it is more polished.

Repeat the same process on the 8,000-grit stone. You are almost finished. Tip: If your corners aren't getting polished, move the tool back $^1/_{32}$" in the jig.

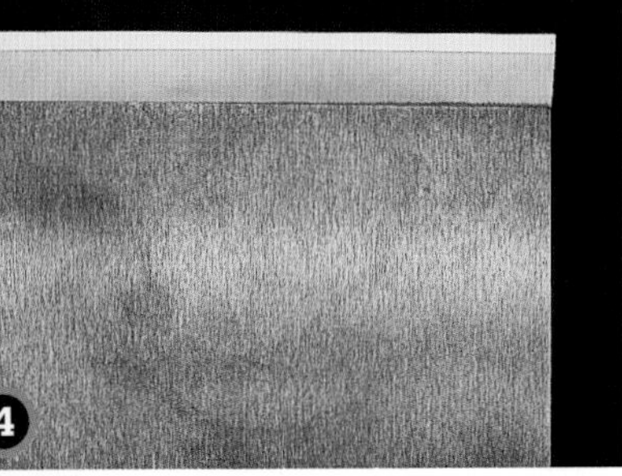

Polish the secondary bevel on the 8,000-grit stone until it is a mirror.

Here's how to test your edge without flaying your finger open. Pull your thumbnail across the edge at about a 90° angle. If the edge catches and digs in immediately, you're sharp. If it skids across your thumbnail, you have more work to do.

TWO JIGS FOR ALMOST EVERY JOB

There are a lot of honing guides on the market these days. After trying out most of them, I'm convinced these two will handle almost all your edge tools.

The gray side-clamp jig you see at every woodworking show and store is the workhorse in my sharpening kit. You can find this tool for about $7 to $13.

None of these gray jigs I've inspected grind a perfectly square edge, but they're real close. Be sure to tighten the jig's clamp with a screwdriver when you fix the tool in the honing guide.

The Veritas guide found at Lee Valley Tools can handle many oddball tools. It easily clamps skew chisels, shoulder-plane blades, irons that are tapered in width and some not-so-stubby Japanese chisels. I don't use this jig as much for my run-of-the-mill plane blades and chisels with straight sides. It's much easier to clamp these in the gray side-clamp jig and go.

The Veritas jig will help you hone tools that would normally have to be sharpened freehand. It's a good investment.

very scary sharp

BY NICK ENGLER

Some years ago, Steve LaMantia of Seattle, Washington, posted a long, rambling letter to the Internet news group rec.woodworking (better known as "Wreck Wood") entitled "The D&S Scary Sharp™ System." Once you waded through Steve's superlatives, exclamations and stream of consciousness, his message boiled down to just this: You can put a very fine cutting edge on hand tools with sandpaper. That's right — sandpaper. (To read Steve's original message, check out www.shavings.net/scary.htm)

Other travelers through Wreck Wood spotted Steve's post, tried his methods and posted their own raves. The news spread, sandpaper stock soared, and the term scary sharp became part of the popular woodworking lexicon. All of which amused those who remember woodworking before so much virtual sawdust was flying about.

About 40 years ago, I participated in a rite of manhood known as the Boy Scouts of America. There, in the old *Handbook for Boys*, wedged between square knots and Morse code, is this advice: Sharpen your pocketknife with sandpaper.

Well, it was good advice then and better advice now. Continuing developments in abrasives make sandpaper an excellent sharpening material. In many ways, it's easier to use, less expensive to get started with and more versatile than traditional sharpening stones.

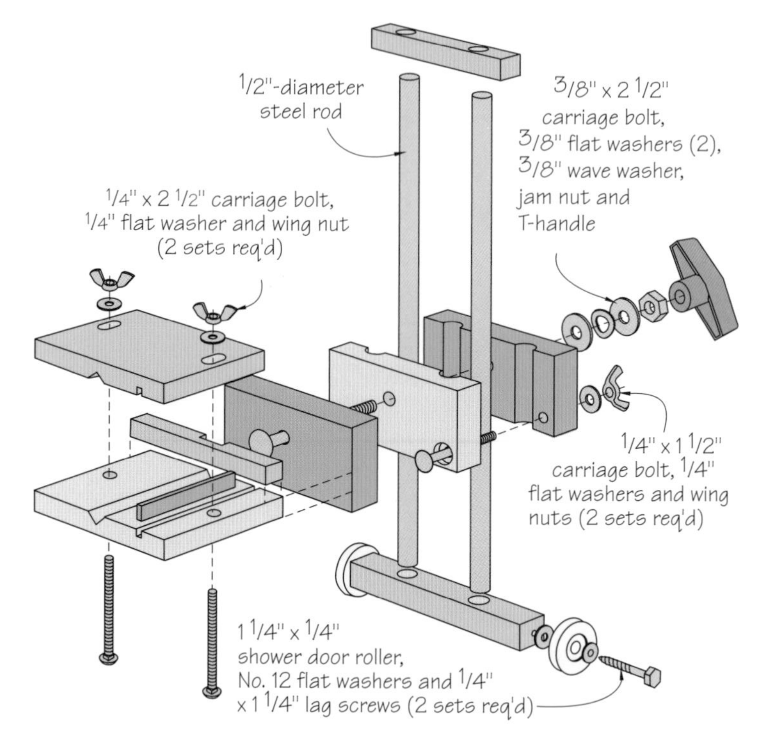

Sandpaper — It's Not Just for Sanding Anymore

The most common abrasives in sandpaper are aluminum oxide and silicon carbide, both of which were originally intended to abrade steel. Their application to woodworking was an afterthought. Point of fact — these are the very same abrasives in India stones, grinding wheels, ceramic stones, even Japanese waterstones. Sandpaper is just another form of the abrasive you may already use for sharpening.

The difference is that sandpaper comes in a much wider range of grits than stones and grinding wheels. Grits between 50 and 2,000 are readily available, and if you look around, you can find sandpaper as coarse as 36 and as fine as 12,000. It's this range that gives sandpaper the edge (pun intended) over other sharpening materials. Traditional stones start between 100 and 200 grit. The finest Arkansas stone is roughly equivalent to 900, the finest ceramic and diamond stones are about 1,200, and the finest waterstone, 8,000 in the Japanese grit system, is close to 2,000 in our American system.

Why is range important? Because proper sharpening

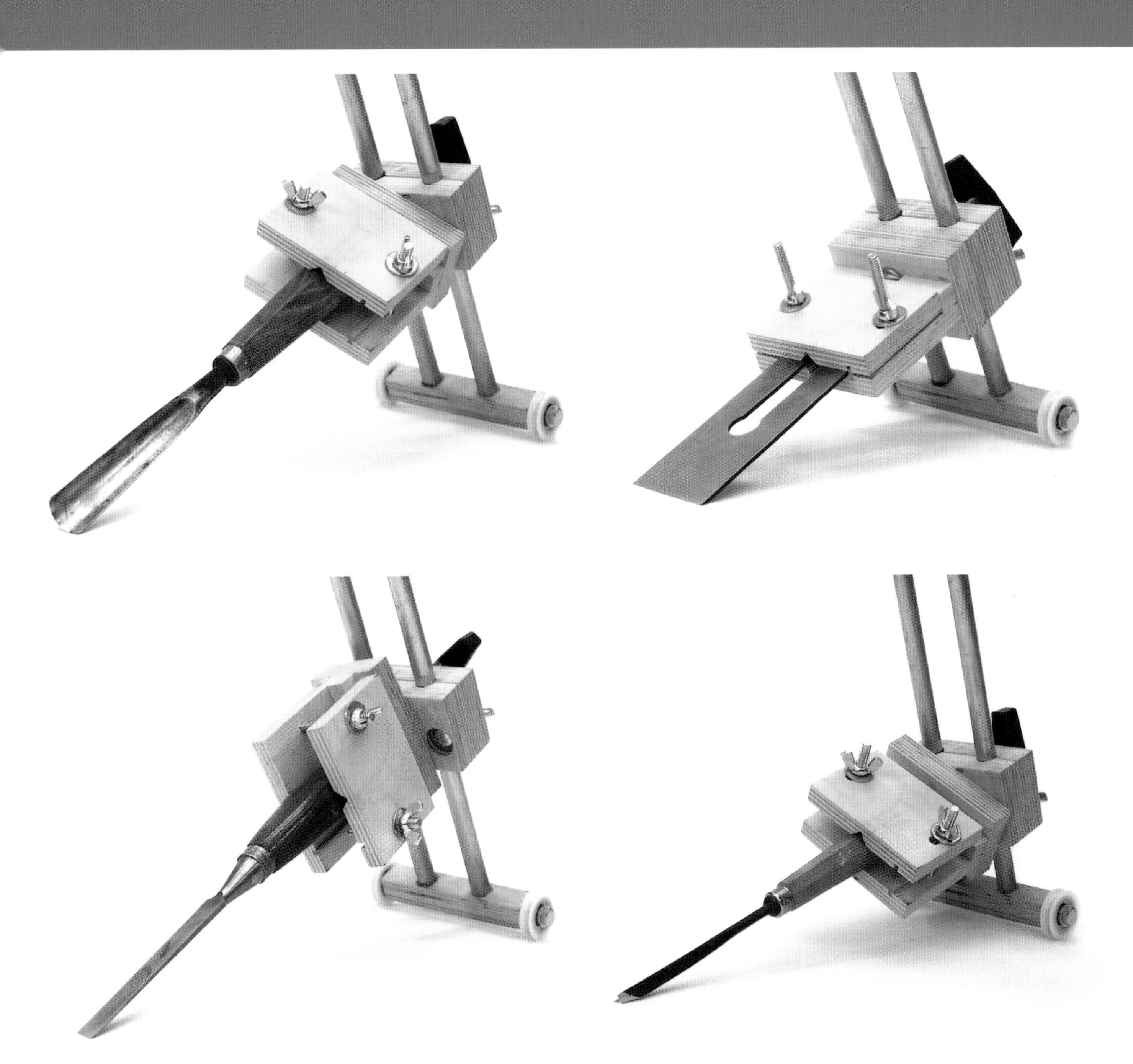

In addition to chisels, the guide will accommodate gouges, plane irons, skews and parting tools.

technique requires that you hone with progressively finer grits, much like sanding a wooden surface. You can't put a superkeen, scary sharp edge on a tool with just one stone. Start with coarse abrasives to quickly condition the edge and repair any nicks. This leaves deep scratches in the steel and makes the edge jagged. The chisel is sharper than it was, but not sharp enough. You must continue sharpening with progressively finer abrasives. As you work your way up through the grits, the scratches grow smaller and the edge becomes keener.

Sandpaper not only extends the range from coarse to fine, it gives you more steps in between. If you've ever tried to jump from 80-grit sandpaper to 150 when sanding wood, you know how long it can take to work out the scratches left by the coarser grit. It takes less time and you get better results if you work your way up in increments. So it is with sharpening.

The Secret Formula

Stones have it all over sandpaper in one respect: They are rigid. To use sandpaper for sharpening, you must mount it to a flat, rigid surface. Steve and those who came after him recommended $\frac{1}{4}$"-thick plate glass, but this isn't rigid enough. It will flex slightly if your workbench isn't dead flat or if a bit of sawdust is under one corner.

Instead, I use a marble slab to back up the sandpaper. (Talk about rigid!) You can purchase a precision-milled granite block known as a reference plate from a machinist's supplier, or you can take your straightedge to a cooking supply store and find a reasonably flat marble pastry stone (for rolling out pie dough) for a quarter of the cost. I have a 20"-square pastry stone that mounts eight different sandpaper grits — four on each side.

You can use ordinary sand-

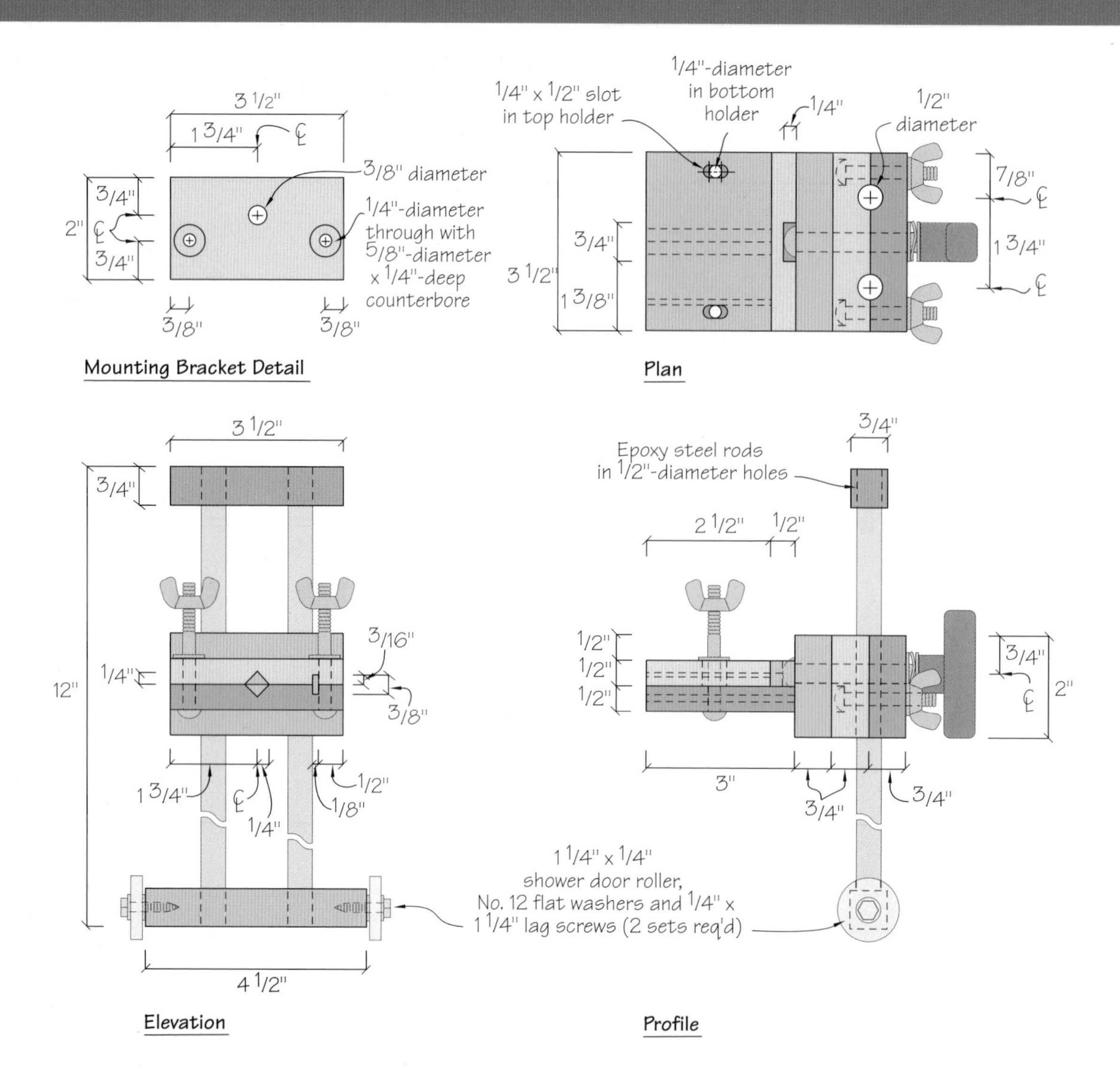

The basic Scary Sharp™ system consists of a selection of sandpapers and a rigid backing plate. I add a stiff brush and a honing guide.

paper and stick it to the marble with a spray adhesive; this yields good results. However, I prefer self-adhesive 8"-diameter sanding discs. Because these are made for machine sanding, they have an "open coat" — 40 percent less abrasive on the surface. They cut a little slower, but they last much longer. The open coat prevents the metal filings (the swarf) from becoming impacted between the grits and "loading" the paper. I also look for stearate-impregnated paper; this, too, reduces loading.

For most sharpening tasks, I work my way through four grits — 120, 300, 600 and 1,500. I keep these all on one side of the pastry stone. On the other side, I have 50, 100, 220 and 2,400. The two coarse grits are to recondition badly damaged edges. The 220 provides an intermediate step between 120 and 300 when I'm flattening the backs of large chisels and plane irons. And the superfine 2,400 is the last step when I'm flattening something.

As you sharpen, brush away the swarf frequently. I use the stiff bristles on the back of a file card. This keeps the abrasive clean and helps prevent loading.

After honing, strop your tools on a piece of leather charged with a superfine abrasive polishing compound. If leather is hard to come by, a couple of pieces of typewriter paper adhered to a rigid surface work just as well.

The last step in my sharpening process is stropping. This is the secret ingredient in every successful sharpening formula, no matter what abrasive material you use. Stropping removes tiny burrs and refines the cutting edge, making it as keen as it can possibly get.

To adjust the holder to rotate, snug the jam nut against the washers, but don't collapse the wave washer. Hold the jam nut from turning with an open-end wrench and tighten the T-handle against it.

For this step, I've mounted a piece of leather to a hard maple board and "charged" it with chromium oxide, a polishing compound. (You might also use jeweler's rouge or tripoli.) Why not mount the leather to the pastry stone? Leather is considerably thicker than the sandpaper. Because of the type of honing guide I use to maintain the sharpening angle, it's important that the stropping surface be at the same level as the other abrasives. I've planed the wood to adjust for the thickness of the leather.

The Secret Weapon — The Very Scary Honing Guide

Yes, I use a honing guide. I know that some experienced sharpeners look down on these jigs as "training wheels," but I don't. If the first secret to successful sharpening is to hone with progressively finer grits, the second secret is to maintain a precise cutting angle as you do so. And you can be much more precise with a guide. After all, if our hands were all that good at maintaining an angle, we wouldn't need planes to hold plane irons.

One of the reasons some folks don't like honing guides is that the current commercial crop is difficult to adjust and not especially versatile. The homemade jig that I've developed holds a chisel by its handle rather than the blade. Because the jig makes a large triangle with the abrasive surface and the tool, it's easier to adjust and maintain the sharpening angle.

The tool holder conforms to every chisel handle that I've been able to find, and it's wide enough to accommodate an iron from a jointer plane. Additionally, the holder pivots, and it can be locked in place or adjusted to roll around an axis. This makes it possible to sharpen not only chisels and plane irons, but also gouges, skews and parting tools.

The tool holder mounts to two grooved brackets that slide along steel rods. To adjust the angle at which the guide holds the tool, slide the brackets up or down on the rods and tighten the wing nuts that lock them in place. To secure the holder, rotate it to the desired angle and tighten the T-handle. To adjust the holder so it will roll as you sharpen a gouge, insert a jam nut between the T-handle and the washers. Tighten the jam nut until it just begins to compress the wave washer. Hold the jam nut from turning and tighten the T-handle against it.

As shown, this honing guide will accommodate hand tools up to 18" long. For longer tools, extend the steel rods.

band saws

BY THE EDITORS OF *POPULAR WOODWORKING* MAGAZINE

Band saws are versatile and easy-to-use machines that every shop should include. With very little instruction, you can perform rips, crosscuts, scroll work and even resaw lumber. And they don't take up a lot of space in your work area.

Mounting a Blade

When you buy a band saw, it will likely come supplied with a 3/8" steel blade that will handle many ordinary tasks, but it might not be the blade you'll choose to purchase again when it becomes dull. Check the box below for our preferences on a couple of top-notch aftermarket blades.

When choosing a blade, remember that more teeth per inch (tpi) is best for fine (but less aggressive) cuts. Fewer tpi produces faster, rougher cuts.

With either your standard blade or an upgraded choice, the important thing is to get the blade in the right location on the wheels and tensioned properly. Most blades are designed to ride on the center of the "tire" on the wheels. With the power off and the blade lightly tensioned around the wheels, you can spin the wheels and see where on the wheels the blade tracks. By adjusting the pitch of the upper wheel (follow your band saw's instructions for this), you can move the blade until it tracks in the center.

To tension the blade appropriately, most band saws have a scale near the tension knob that will show you where to tension the blade according to the width of the blade.

Guide Setup

A band saw has two types of guides: the thrust bearing, which supports the blade from behind, and the side guides, which keep the blade from shifting left or right during a cut. There are two sets of these guides, one above the table and one below.

With the blade tracking correctly in the center of the wheels, the thrust bearing should be adjusted to the distance of one folded dollar bill away from the blade. Set this way the bearing will contact only the blade during a cut.

The side guides, if of the block design, should also be set to the width of a folded bill on either side of the blade. This way the guides will support the blade without pinching. If you have roller guides on the sides, these can be adjusted to actually touch the blade. Either type of side guides should be set at the back of the gullet behind the

BEFORE YOU BUY

- **BENCHTOP VS. STATIONARY.** Prices for benchtops range from $100 to $210, but average about $175. Stationary models average in the $500 to $800 range. Benchtop saws tend to run on universal or smaller horsepower motors and also offer smaller capacity in throat depth, resaw and blade width. If cash and space allow, buy a stationary model.
- **MOTOR.** An induction motor is preferable. The most common 14" stationary model will offer a 3/4- or 1-hp motor. This is sufficient for most band saw work. If you will be doing more resawing, try for a larger (1 1/2-hp) motor.
- **GUIDES.** Guides are critical to performance. All band saws use a ball-bearing rear thrust (guiding the back of the blade), but the side supports can be guide blocks or bearing guides. The blocks can be metal, synthetic or ceramic. In most cases, guide blocks are adequate to the task, though replacing standard metal guides with synthetic or ceramic will allow tighter tolerances.
- **BLADES.** Don't skimp on your blades, and use the right blade for the task. For resawing on a 14" saw, a quality 3/8" or 1/2" blade is recommended. We like a 3/8", 3/4 variable-pitch carbide blade from Lenox. Though pricey, it does an amazing job. If you have a larger (18") saw, a wider blade (3/4" to 1") can be tensioned appropriately for resaw work. For tight turns, a thinner 1/8" or 1/4" blade is preferable. For general band saw use, we're fond of a 3/8" Timberwolf blade from Suffolk Machinery.

teeth on the blade to avoid damage.

Making the Cut

Making any type of cut on a band saw is fairly simple. You want to cut to the waste side of your cut line, not down the center, unless your line isn't that critical.

Adjust the upper guides to just above the work to keep less blade exposed and allow the guides to properly support the blade.

One thing that will happen on a band saw, unlike other saws, is drift. A band saw blade (nearly all of them) will want to pull to one side of the cut or the other. This means you have to adjust how you feed the wood into the blade to compensate for this drift. Even if you're cutting a straight line, you may have to angle the wood into the blade to cut straight. Once you've made a few cuts on the band saw, you'll start to compensate automatically.

If you use your fence with your band saw, you also will need to angle it to compensate for drift when ripping or resawing.

Once you get comfortable with the band saw, it will become one of the most valuable machines in your shop.

RECOMMENDATIONS

Occasional User

- **DELTA BS200.** A compact, easy-to-use benchtop machine, with nice features.
- **GRIZZLY G1052.** Similar benefits to the above Delta. This model replaces plastic with metal, making a stouter tool.
- **GRIZZLY G0555.** This machine makes it affordable to move off the benchtop to a 14" band saw with lots of features and the option of a 6" riser block for resawing.

Serious Home Woodworker

- **DELTA 28-206.** This band saw has a 1-hp motor, a quick tension release, an improved 4" dust port and more. A solid buy.
- **JET JWBS-14CS.** This band saw has all the features a woodworker should have.

Advanced Woodworker or Professional

- **DELTA 28-241.** A new version of a reliable predecessor, this one adds a $1\frac{1}{2}$-hp motor, improved tensioning spring to support wider blades and more.
- **JET JWBS-16 AND JWBS-18.** Two well-appointed one-piece band saws that offer strength, stability and increased capacity.
- **LAGUNA LT18.** Unquestionably a professional-quality saw that's worth the price.

THESE TOOLS HAVE BEEN TESTED OR USED BY THE EDITORS OF *POPULAR WOODWORKING* MAGAZINE AND HAVE EARNED THEIR RECOMMENDATION. ALL SUPPLIES AND EQUIPMENT WERE CURRENT AT THE TIME OF ORIGINAL PUBLICATION AND ARE SUBJECT TO CHANGE.

When using block-style guides, the proper distance from the blade is easily gauged by simply folding a $1 bill and pushing the guides against the blade with the bill as a spacer. And, yes, a $20 bill also will work.

STATS

MODEL	SIZE IN.	RESAW CAP. IN.	TABLE TILT LEFT, RIGHT	BLADE GUIDES	MAX. BLADE (IN.)	HP	VOLTS	WEIGHT (LBS.)	COMMENTS
BENCHTOP									
Craftsman 21409	9	3 3/4	3, 45	M	3/8	1/3	120	40	table extension
Craftsman 21459	9	3 1/2	0, 45	M	3/8	1/3	120	35	work light
■ Delta BS200	9	3 3/4	3, 45	CB	3/8	1/3	120	33	work light
■ Grizzly G1052	9	4 1/8	15, 45	BB	3/8	1/2	110	100	with rip fence
Ryobi BS901	9	3 1/2	0, 45	BB	3/8	1/3	120	30	
Tradesman 8166	9	3 1/2	0, 45	BB	3/8	1/3	115	40	T-slot, miter gauge
Wilton 99162	9	3 1/8	0, 45	CB	3/8	1/3	120	43	work light
Tradesman 8168	10	4	0, 45	BB	3/8	1/3	115	45	T-slot, miter gauge
Craftsman 21450	11	3	0, 45	M	3/8	1/3	120	32	three wheels
Grizzly G8976	12	3 7/8	0, 45	BB	3/8	3/4	110	38	three wheels
FLOOR									
Delta 28-195	10	7	3, 48	CB	1/2	1/2	120	75	
Craftsman 22432N	12	5	10,45	M	1/2	5/8	120	154	open stand
Jet JWBS-120S	12	6	10, 45	M	1/2	1/2	115	138	open stand
Craftsman 22424	14	6	15, 45	NA	3/4	1 1/2	NA	154	
Delta 28-276	14	6 1/2	3, 45	M	3/4	3/4	115	220	quick tension release
■ Delta 28-206	14	6 1/2	3, 45	M	3/4	1	115	245	quick tension release
Delta 28-231	14	6 1/4	3, 45	M	3/4	1 1/2	115	205	open stand, 14" × 14" table
■ Delta 28-241	14	6 1/4	3, 45	M	3/4	1 1/2	115/230	230	closed stand, 14" × 14" table
General 90-100M1	14	7	0, 45	M	3/4	1	115/230	210	2 speeds with fence
General 90-125M1	14	6	0, 45	M	3/4	1	115/230	230	2 speeds with fence
Grizzly 1019	14	6 1/4	10, 45	M	3/4	3/4	110/220	203	with rip fence
Grizzly G1019Z	14	6 3/8	15, 45	M	3/4	1	110/220	165	open stand
■ Grizzly G0555	14	6 1/2	15, 45	BB	3/4	1	110/220	210	w/tension lever & fence
Jet JWBS-140S	14	6	10, 45	P	3/4	3/4	115/230	183	microadj. top guides
■ Jet JWBS-14CS	14	6	10, 45	P	3/4	1	115/230	197	microadj. top guides
Jet JWBS-14MW	14	6	10, 45	P	3/4	1	115/230	206	3 speeds
Jet JWBS-C140S	14	6	10, 45	BB	3/4	3/4	115/230	186	Carter guides
Jet JWBS-C14CS	14	6	10, 45	BB	3/4	1	115/230	200	Carter guides
Jet JWBS-C14MW	14	6	10, 45	BB	3/4	1	115/230	209	Carter guides, 3 speeds
Laguna LT14	14	8 5/8	15,45	CB	1	1 1/2	220	230	
Lobo BS-0143	14	6	10, 45	NM	1/2	3/4	115	167	
North State WA-14M	14	6 1/4	10, 45	M, BB	3/4	1	115/230	250	
Powermatic 44	14	9	15, 45	BB	3/4	1	115/230	212	
Ridgid BS1400	14	6	10, 45	M	3/4	3/4	115/230	195	Lifetime warranty
Shop Fox W1672	14	7 3/16	0, 45	NM	1	1	110/220	215	with fence
Star WBS14	14	6	10, 45	NA	3/4	3/4	115/230	188	
Star WBS143	14	6 3/4	10, 45	NA	5/8	3/4	115/230	195	3 speeds
Tradesman 8157	14	6 1/4	10, 45	BB	1/2	1	115/230	162	
Transpower SB500	14	6	10, 45	NM	3/4	1	110	180	
Bridgewood BW-15BS	15	6	-10, 45	M	1	3/4	115	151	
Craftsman 24393	15	8 1/2	0, 45	M	3/4	3/4	115	234	3 speeds
General 490-1	15	6 3/4	-10, 45	M	3/4	1	115	320	
Grizzly G1148	15	7 1/2	10, 45	M	3/4	1	110/220	164	2 speeds
Agazzani B-16	16	10	5, 45	ES	1	2	230	288	
Grizzly G1073	16	7 3/4	10, 45	M	1	2	110/220	456	with rip fence
Grizzly G1073Z	16	7 3/4	10, 45	M	1	2	110/220	408	
Hitachi CB75F	16	11 13/16	0, 45	P, BB	3	2.8	115	309	
■ Jet JWBS-16	16	10 1/4	10, 45	ES	1 1/4	1.5	NA	310	
Laguna LT 16	16	12	0, 45	ES	1	1 1/2	220	320	
Laguna LT 16 HD	16	12	5, 45	ES	1 3/8	3	220	385	
Laguna LT 16 SEC	16	12	5, 45	BB/ES	1	2 1/2	220	320	
Lobo BS-0163	16	10	10, 45	ES	1	1 1/2	115	270	
Mini Max MM16	16	13	NA	ES	1 1/4	3 1/2	230	450	
Shop Fox W1673	16	8 5/8	10, 45	NM	1 1/4	1 1/2	110/220	265	
Transpower SB600	16	10	10, 45	CB	1	1 1/2	110	270	
Bridgewood PBS-440	17	12	0, 45	ES	13/16	3	230	480	fence; foot brake; USA motor
Craftsman 24396N	18	11	0, 45	M	1	1	115	330	2 speeds
Agazzani B-18	18	12	5, 45	ES	1 3/8	2 1/2	230	370	
General 90-260M1	18	9 3/8	10, 45	CB	1 1/4	1 1/2	115/230	495	2 speed with fence
Grizzly G1012	18	10	5, 45	M	1 1/4	2	220	350	3 speeds

MODEL	SIZE IN.	RESAW CAP. IN.	TABLE TILT LEFT, RIGHT	BLADE GUIDES	MAX. BLADE (IN.)	HP	VOLTS	WEIGHT (LBS.)	COMMENTS
FLOOR (CONTINUED)									
Grizzly G4186Z	18	$9\frac{3}{8}$	10, 45	M	$1\frac{1}{4}$	2	110/220	345	with rip fence
■ Jet JWBS-18B	18	$10\frac{1}{4}$	10, 45	ES	$1\frac{1}{2}$	$1\frac{1}{2}$	115/230	346	with rip fence
■ Laguna LT18	18	12	5, 45	ES	$1\frac{3}{8}$	3	220	451	
Laguna LT18SE	18	16	5, 45	ES	$1\frac{3}{8}$	5	220	473	
Lobo BS-0181	18	$9\frac{3}{4}$	10, 45	ES	$1\frac{1}{2}$	$1\frac{1}{2}$	230	350	
Lobo BS-0183	18	$9\frac{1}{2}$	10, 45	ES	$1\frac{1}{2}$	2	230	360	
Mini Max S45	18	$10\frac{1}{4}$	0, 45	ES	$\frac{3}{4}$	$2\frac{1}{2}$	230	320	
North State WBS1803	18	$10\frac{1}{2}$	10, 45	M	$1\frac{1}{2}$	2	115/230	425	
North State WBS18L	18	10	0,45	M	1	2	115/230	330	
Transpower SB800	18	9	10, 45	CB	1	2	220	390	
Delta 28-640	20	11	4, 45	BB	1	2	230	585	
Agazzani B-20	20	13	5, 45	ES	$1\frac{1}{2}$	3	230	458	
General 390	20	$12\frac{1}{2}$	12, 45	M	1	2	230	865	
General 90-360	20	$11\frac{3}{8}$	0, 45	M/BB	$1\frac{3}{8}$	2	220	836	
Grizzly G1258	20	$13\frac{7}{8}$	10, 45	BB	$1\frac{1}{4}$	3	220	640	foot brake
Jet JWBS-20	20	12	10, 45	ES	$1\frac{1}{2}$	2	NA	500	w/rip fence, foot brake
Laguna LT20	20	14	10, 45	ES	$1\frac{3}{8}$	5	220	545	
Lobo BS-0202	20	$11\frac{3}{4}$	10, 45	ES	$1\frac{3}{4}$	3	230	620	
Mini Max MM20	20	$15\frac{3}{4}$	NA	ES	$1\frac{1}{2}$	5	230	523	
North State WBS-20	20	11	10, 45	BB	$1\frac{1}{2}$	3	230	700	foot brake
Powermatic 2013	20	$12\frac{3}{8}$	15, 45	BB	$1\frac{1}{2}$	2	230	950	fence, work light, brake
Seco SK-20BS	20	11	10, 45	BB	1	3	220	620	
Star WBS20L	20	12	10, 45	BB	$1\frac{1}{2}$	3	230	575	
Transpower SB1000	20	$11\frac{1}{2}$	10, 45	NA	$1\frac{3}{4}$	3	220	650	
Woodtek 959571	20	$12\frac{1}{2}$	0, 45	BB	1	2	230	551	
Bridgewood PBS-540	21	14	0, 45	ES	$1\frac{3}{8}$	5	220	595	fence; foot brake; USA motor
Agazzani B-24	24	$15\frac{3}{4}$	5, 45	ES	$1\frac{1}{2}$	4	230	600	
General 90-600	24	$13\frac{3}{4}$	0, 45	M/BB	3	3 or 5	230	990	
General 90-460	24	$13\frac{3}{8}$	10, 45	M/BB	$1\frac{3}{8}$	3	220	705	
Grizzly G3619	24	$13\frac{3}{4}$	10, 45	BB	2	5	220	748	
Grizzly G3620	24	$15\frac{3}{4}$	10, 45	BB	2	$7\frac{1}{2}$	220	748	
Laguna LT24	24	$15\frac{1}{4}$	10, 45	ES	$1\frac{1}{2}$	5	220	725	
Lobo BS-0242	24	$11\frac{3}{4}$	10, 45	ES	$1\frac{5}{8}$	3	230	728	
Mini Max MM24	24	15	NA	ES	$1\frac{1}{2}$	5	230	748	
North State WBS24	24	11	10, 45	BB	$1\frac{1}{2}$	5	230	800	
Powermatic 2415	24	14	15, 45	BB	$1\frac{1}{2}$	3	230	1,050	fence, work light, brake
Grizzly G9963	$26\frac{1}{2}$	18	0, 45	NM	3	$7\frac{1}{2}$	220	1,100	
Grizzly G9966	$26\frac{1}{2}$	18	0, 45	NM	3	$7\frac{1}{2}$	220	1,100	
Powermatic BW-900	36	20	3, 45	BB	$1\frac{3}{4}$	$7\frac{1}{2}$	230/460	2,200	

key

M= metal
BB=ball bearing
CB=Cool Blocks
NM=non-metal
P=plastic
ES=European-style ball bearing
NA=not applicable
■ *PW* Recommends

ALL SUPPLIES AND EQUIPMENT WERE CURRENT AT THE TIME OF ORIGINAL PUBLICATION AND ARE SUBJECT TO CHANGE.

CHAPTER 18

biscuit joiners

BY THE EDITORS OF *POPULAR WOODWORKING* MAGAZINE

Biscuit joiners are easy tools to learn to use. If it takes you more than 5 minutes to cut your first joint, you probably took a coffee break between opening the box and firing up the tool. That said, knowing some finer points about using the tool will make it even faster and more accurate.

Joint Layout

The less measuring you do, the less likely you are to cut slots that don't match up. For that reason, we recommend that you put the two parts you're joining together and mark lines for the biscuit slots across the joint. You'll never miss this way. When joining panels, a good rule of thumb is to place your first biscuit 2" from each edge and then put one every 5" to 7" between. Use the largest-size biscuit your material and your joint will allow.

Fence Setup

If the fence isn't parallel to the cutter, your joint will be cockeyed. Make sure your fence is locked down securely and parallel to the slot that the cutter emerges from. Double-check the angle your fence is locked at. If the fence doesn't fit your joint like a glove, the angle of your slot will be a bit off.

Cutting the Slot

Biscuit joiners are such quick tools, it's easy to get sloppy. First, clamp your work to your bench. If you're using the fence, use one hand to hold the fence tightly against the work and the other to plunge the barrel of the tool. Injuries are rare with this tool; but when they do occur, it's usually because the tool wasn't held down adequately and the blade raced up your arm.

Gluing and Clamping

You can put glue in the slots or paint glue on the biscuits; it's your choice. Either way, be sure to go easy on the clamping pressure. It's easy to contort a frame made with biscuits. If you're using polyurethane glue in your biscuit joints, you should quickly dip the biscuits in a cup of water before inserting them into the slots. Polyurethane glue needs moisture to cure, and the biscuits need moisture to swell up and lock the joint tight.

When to Use Biscuits

One of the biggest questions facing woodworkers is when

BEFORE YOU BUY

- **FENCE.** Most biscuiting tasks don't need a complicated fence: The two most basic angle settings (0° and 45°) will handle most biscuiting tasks, and 135° comes in handy, too. What's critical is that you want to make sure the fence will easily lock parallel to the cutter. Adjust the fence up and down to check the ease of its movement. Make sure that when it locks down, it stays down. And don't forget to examine how the fence grips the work. Some woodworkers prefer rubber; some prefer pins. Neither method works great, so don't sweat it.
- **MOTOR.** Don't sweat the motor either. We've used all these machines, and the motors have enough power to handle all standard biscuiting tasks.
- **BLADES.** If you have a choice, buy a tool that has antikickback technology on the blades. Check how easy it is to change the blade. It's not a frequent operation, but it shouldn't require major tool surgery.
- **SLOT SIZES.** Every standard biscuit joiner can cut slots for #0, #10 and #20 biscuits. But some machines offer smaller cutters for making face-frame joints. If you make face frames, you should consider one of these machines.
- **SWITCH.** Some people like locking triggers, and others like a thumb toggle. Determine your favorite and buy accordingly.

RECOMMENDATIONS

Occasional User

- **FREUD JS100.** This tool will handle 90 percent of your biscuiting tasks — especially if you build cabinets. For the money, you can't buy a better entry-level tool.

Serious Home Woodworker

- **FREUD JS102.** For a few dollars more than the JS100 you get a more adjustable fence, a blade that's easier to change and a price that still beats most tools.
- **MAKITA 3901.** Though an older design, this tool is accurate and totally reliable, as you would expect with a Makita tool. It's also lighter in weight than some newer tools, which makes a difference if you use it all day.

Advanced Woodworker or Professional

- **PORTER-CABLE 557.** Hands down, the 557 is the most versatile biscuit joiner on the market today. The fence is capable of almost any sort of gymnastics. The tool also comes with a smaller cutter for face-frame biscuits. We also recommend the Porter-Cable brand of biscuit. In our tests, they were extremely consistent in thickness and few were unusable.
- **LAMELLO CLASSIC C2.** Lamello invented biscuit joinery, and the company's European-made tools are precision instruments in every way. The price of the tool is high, but many professionals are glad to pay it. Lamello also makes a wide range of specialty biscuits, from knockdown hardware biscuits to hinges that can be installed with a biscuit joiner. Check it out at www.csaw.com.

THESE TOOLS HAVE BEEN TESTED OR USED BY THE EDITORS OF *POPULAR WOODWORKING* MAGAZINE AND HAVE EARNED THEIR RECOMMENDATION. ALL SUPPLIES AND EQUIPMENT WERE CURRENT AT THE TIME OF ORIGINAL PUBLICATION AND ARE SUBJECT TO CHANGE.

STATS

	CRAFTSMAN 17501	CRAFTSMAN 27730	DEWALT DW682K	■ FREUD JS100	■ FREUD JS102	■ LAMELLO CLASSIC C2	LAMELLO TOP 20S	■ MAKITA 3901	■ PORTER-CABLE 557	RYOBI JM80K
FENCE										
# of detents	6	2	2	3	3	5	5	3	7	4
Material	Plastic	Aluminum	Aluminum	Aluminum	Aluminum	Aluminum	Aluminum	Aluminum	Aluminum	Steel
Angle capacity	0°–135°	0°–90°	0°–90°	0°–135°	0°–135°	0°–90°*	0°-90°*	0°–90°	0°–135°	0°–135°
Size in inches	$3\frac{3}{4} \times 5\frac{1}{4}$	$2\frac{1}{2} \times 4\frac{3}{4}$	$2\frac{1}{2} \times 4\frac{5}{8}$	$2 \times 4\frac{3}{4}$	$2 \times 4\frac{3}{4}$	$2\frac{1}{2} \times 5$	$2\frac{1}{2} \times 5$	$2\frac{3}{8} \times 5$	$3\frac{3}{4} \times 5\frac{1}{4}$	$3\frac{3}{4} \times 5\frac{1}{4}$
MOTOR										
Amps/no load	3.5	2.8	2.7	2.8	2.7	2.64	4.0	2.47	3.08	3.55
Amps/load	6.7	6.75	5.89	3.89	4.49	4.07	5.89	4.93	5.29	6.08
Amps variance	3.2	3.95	3.19	1.09	1.79	1.43	1.89	2.46	2.21	2.53
dB/no load	102	104	103	103	104	105	101	102	98	101
BLADE										
# of teeth	8	6	6	6	6	6	6	6	6/4	8
Antikickback	Yes	No	No	Yes	Yes	Yes	Yes	Yes	Yes	Yes
Blade kerf	0.159	0.155	0.150	0.155	0.154	0.154	0.133	0.153	0.159	0.191
Hole kerf	0.165	0.166	0.154	0.164	0.157	0.159	0.159	0.156	0.159	0.191
Variance	0.006	0.011	0.004	0.009	0.003	0.005	**	0.003	0.000	0.003
OTHER STATS										
Cord length	10'	8'	8'	7'8"	7'8"	8'	8'	8'	8'	10'
Weight in lbs.	6.3	6.7	6.9	6.8	6.8	6.6	6.6	6.2	7.5	6.8
Body style	In-line	Right angle	Right angle	Right angle	Right angle	Right angle	Right angle	Right angle	Right angle	In-line
Size biscuits	0,10,20	0,10,20, max	0,10,20, max	0,10,20, A,B,max	0,10,20, A,B,max	0,10,20, S,D, max	0,10,20, S,D, max	0,10,20, S,D, max	0,10,20, S,D, max,FF	0,10,20
Nonskid material	R/face	Pins	Pins	R/pads	R/pads	R/pads	R/pads	R/face	Grit face	R/face
Dust collection	Box	Bag/VP	Bag/VP	Bag/VP	Bag/VP	Bag/VP	Bag/VP	Bag/VP	Bag/VP	Bag/VP
PW RATINGS										
Blade change	2	3	3	3	4	4	4	5	4	2
Ergonomics	2	3	4	3	3.5	4	4	4	4	2
Overall performance	2	4	4	3	4	5	5	4	5	2

key

* Angles past 90° (including 135°) can easily be achieved by attaching the 90° fence and adjusting the angle of the adjustable fence.

** Blade geometry for the Top 20S is different than all the other blades. The scoring teeth are offset. As a result, the variance is not a measure of runout.

R=rubber, FF=face frame

Ratings on a scale of 1 to 5 with 5 being outstanding and 1 being unacceptable.

■ = *PW* Recommends

ALL SUPPLIES AND EQUIPMENT WERE CURRENT AT THE TIME OF ORIGINAL PUBLICATION AND ARE SUBJECT TO CHANGE.

biscuits are appropriate. Here are the facts:

- Long-grain joints: Some woodworkers use biscuits to align boards being glued up for a tabletop. Biscuits will help align the boards, but they will not offer additional strength. The long-grain-to-long-grain joint is stronger than the wood itself.
- Face frames: Biscuits are great for face frames — as long as your stock is wider than $2\frac{3}{8}$". Otherwise, you'll need to use smaller specialty biscuits, dowels or a mortise and tenon.
- Continuous-stress joints: Don't use biscuit joints on chairs.
- Tables: If you're joining a leg to an apron, use two biscuits in each joint to add strength.
- In $\frac{1}{2}$" plywood: In thin material, biscuits can "telegraph" their shape through the surface of the plywood. To prevent this, we recommend you use #0 or #10 biscuits and go easy on the glue.

To biscuit a partition in the middle of a panel, lay the partition flat on its mate at the location where they will be joined. Cut the slots in the partition.

Using the lines you marked on the partition, cut the slots in the cabinet side using the partition as a fence.

drill presses

BY SCOTT PHILLIPS

The drill press is a somewhat underappreciated machine in most shops. While it doesn't see constant use, when you need one it's invaluable. To drill a quantity of consistent, accurate and similar holes (like about 200 shelf pin holes in a bookcase), the drill press is your best buddy. And it serves as a nice spindle sander if you add a simple attachment.

Drill presses are probably one of the least expensive machines in a shop, pound for pound and feature for feature. Whether you opt for a smaller benchtop model, a well-appointed benchtop model or one of the beefy floor models, it's going to be a good deal.

Setting the Speeds

There aren't a lot of things to know about using a drill press. Probably the most important thing is to use it at the proper speed. To get the best performance (and life span) out of a bit, the drill press should be used at a particular speed. In general, smaller twists or brad-point bits (under 3⁄8" in diameter) should be run faster, anywhere from 2,000 to 3,000 rpm. Midsize bits (1⁄2" to 3⁄4") should be run in the 1,500 rpm range, and anything larger should spin at 1,000 rpm or slower.

Spade and Forstner bits fall into a slightly different catego-

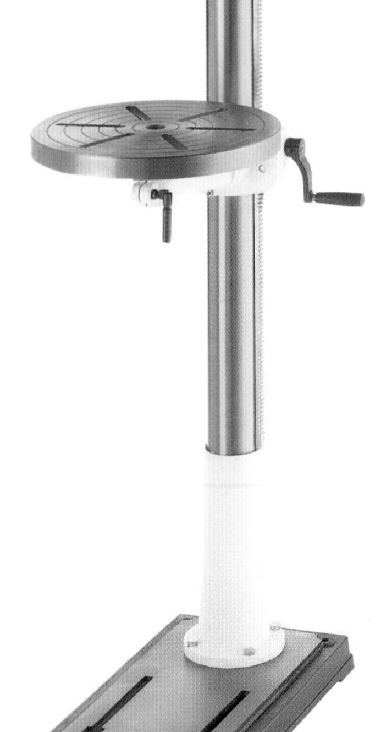

RECOMMENDATIONS

Occasional User

- **GRIZZLY G7943.** For the basic benchtop drill press, this model answers all the needs for a very low price.
- **GRIZZLY G7945 OR G7946.** Either the benchtop or floor model of this radial drill press offers greater capacity than a standard drill press.
- **DELTA DP250 & DP350.** The only benchtop drill presses offering variable speed without changing belts.

Serious Home Woodworker

- **GRIZZLY G7944.** This is a great price for a 14" floor-model drill press, and it's a good machine, too.
- **DELTA 17-965.** A step up in size to this 16½" unit makes it a pro-shop option at a good price.

Advanced Woodworker or Professional

- **GRIZZLY G7948.** We say "pro" here because of the capacity. At 20", this baby can handle all your needs.

THESE TOOLS HAVE BEEN TESTED OR USED BY THE EDITORS OF *POPULAR WOODWORKING* MAGAZINE AND HAVE EARNED THEIR RECOMMENDATION. ALL SUPPLIES AND EQUIPMENT WERE CURRENT AT THE TIME OF ORIGINAL PUBLICATION AND ARE SUBJECT TO CHANGE.

BEFORE YOU BUY

- **BENCHTOP VS. STATIONARY.** Interestingly enough, this is one category where you can get almost the same exact machine features in either a benchtop or a floor design, though the capacity is often greater on floor-model machines. The added benefit of stationary machines is the increased height from table to quill, but that isn't something that every woodworker needs. You might benefit more by using the area under the benchtop drill press for storage.
- **MOTOR.** Essentially an accurate drill, a drill press doesn't need a very large motor to be competent. One-half horsepower is adequate, though if it's affordable, larger motors will offer more torque for the bigger bits.
- **VARIABLE SPEED.** Using bits at their proper rated speeds will improve performance as well as tooling life span. Most drill presses require moving the belts manually to change the speed. The easier the belts are to reconfigure, the more likely you'll take the time to change the speed.
- **STOPS.** Two types of depth stops are normally used on drill presses: either a threaded shaft with jam nuts or an internal limiter that stops the handle motion. Both work and are more of a personal preference. Some models will offer both systems for even more options and flexibility.
- **OSCILLATING MOTION.** Each year, new oscillating models are added to the drill press lines. These add a valuable feature to any drill press, making it a more versatile machine.

STATS

MODEL	SIZE IN.	RESAW CAP. IN.	TABLE TILT LEFT, RIGHT	BLADE GUIDES	MAX. BLADE (IN.)	HP	WEIGHT (LBS.)	COMMENTS
BENCHTOP								
Delta DP115	4	1/2	2	660–3,235	N	1/4	39	5 speeds
Grizzly G7942	4	1/2	2	620–3,100	Y	1/3	50	5 speeds
Jet JDP-8	4	1/2	2	620–3,100	N	1/6	42	square table, front switch
Tradesman 8055S	4	1/2	2	620–3,100	N	1/4	42	5 speeds, also available w/3" vise
Woodtek 829785	4	1/2	2	620–3,100	N	1/4	40	5 speeds
Shop Fox W1667	4 1/4	1/2	1 5/8	620–3,100	N	1/2	49	oscillating, 5 speeds
Craftsman 24809	4 1/2	1/2	2	620–3,100	N	1/3	48	5 speeds, w/fence, vise
Craftsman 21909	4 1/2	1/2	2	620–3,100	N	1/3	48	5 speeds, w/fence
Delta DP200	5	1/2	2 1/4	620–3,100	Y	1/4	70	5 speeds
■ Delta DP250	5	1/2	3 1/4	500–3,100	Y	NA	NA	Continuous variable speed
Jet JDP-10	5	1/2	2 1/2	540–3,600	N	1/3	70	5 speeds
Ryobi DP101	5	1/2	2 1/4	570–3,050	Y	1/4	68	5 speeds
Tradesman 8062S	5	1/2	2 1/4	620–3,100	N	1/4	59	5 speeds, 3" vise
Delta DP300	6	1/2	2 3/8	620–3,100	Y	1/3	78	5 speeds
■ Delta DP350	6	1/2	3 1/4	500–3,100	Y	NA	NA	continuous variable speed
Fisch DP2000	6	1/2	2 1/2	500–3,100	Y	1/3	80	6 speeds
CShop Fox W1668	6 5/8	5/8	3 1/4	250–3,050	Y	3/4	115	oscillating, 12 speeds
■ Grizzly G7943	7	5/8	3 1/4	140–3,050	Y	3/4	160	12 speeds
CJet JDP-14J	7	1/2	3 1/4	195–3,630	Y	1/2	132	work light
CJet JDP-14M	7	5/8	3 3/8	460–2,500	Y	1/2	132	MT-2 taper, work light, ind. PB switch
CGeneral 34-02-M-1	7 1/2	1/2	4 1/2	460–4,910	N	3/4	174	6 speeds
CGeneral 75-100-M-1	8 1/2	5/8	3 1/4	340–2,800	Y	3/4	180	12 speeds
FLOOR								
Tradesman 8080S	6 1/2	5/8	3 3/8	250–3,100	Y	1/2	156	12 speeds
■ Grizzly G7944	7	5/8	3 1/4	140–3,050	Y	3/4	172	work light, vise
Jet JDP-14JF	7	1/2	3 3/8	195–3,630	Y	1/2	156	taper, work light, ind.
Jet JDP-14MF	7	5/8	3 1/4	460–2,500	Y	3/4	167	MT-2 taper, work light
Lobo DP-016F	7	5/8	3 1/2	240–3,800	Y	1/2	135	16 speeds
Yorkcraft YC-19FDP	7	5/8	3 5/16	140–3,050	Y	3/4	176	12 speeds,work light
Powermatic 1150HD	7 1/4	1/2	6	150–4,200	Y/N	1	432	Variable speed
Craftsman 22915	7 1/2	5/8	3 1/8	250–3,100	Y	2/3	166	12 speeds
Craftsman 22935	7 1/2	5/8	4 13/16	300–3,300	Y	1	440	Variable speed
General 34-01-M1	7 1/2	1/2	4 1/2	460–4,910	N	3/4	196	6 speeds
Powermatic 1150-A	7 1/2	1/2	6	400–5,300	N	3/4	323	5 speeds
Ridgid DP1550	7 1/2	5/8	3 3/4	250–3,100	Y	1/2	162	ambidextrous handle
Lobo DP-186F	8	5/8	3 5/16	190–2,640	Y	3/4	170	16 speeds w/foot pedal
Delta DP400	8 1/4	5/8	3 3/8	250–3,000	Y	3/4	194	12 speeds
Delta 17-925	8 1/4	1/2	6	150–3,200	Y	3/4	230	variable speeds
■ Delta 17-965	8 1/4	5/8	4 7/8	215–2,720	Y	3/4	195	16 speeds
Jet JDP-17FSE	8 1/4	5/8	3 3/8	200–3,000	Y	3/4	168	MT-2 taper, also avail. w/work light
Woodtek 816-805	8 1/4	5/8	3 1/4	250–3,000	Y	3/4	165	12 speeds
Grizzly G7947	8 1/2	5/8	4 3/4	210–3,300	Y	1	275	12 speeds, work light
Bridgewood BW1758F	8 1/2	5/8	3 5/16	250–3,900	Y	3/4	150	work light
Craftsman 22917	8 1/2	5/8	3 1/4	200–3,630	Y	3/4	195	16 speeds
General 75-200-M-1	8 1/2	5/8	3 1/4	340–2,800	Y	3/4	200	12 speeds
Powermatic 1170	8 1/2	5/8	3 1/4	190–3,500	Y	1	188	16 speeds
Shop Fox W1680	8 1/2	5/8	3 1/4	150–3,050	Y	1	200	12 speeds
Tradesman 8106S	8 1/2	5/8	3 3/8	200–3,630	Y	1	183	16 speeds
Grizzly G9749	9 5/8	5/8	6 7/16	300–2,000	Y	1 1/2	685	
Craftsman 22920	10	3/4	4 22/32	150–4,200	Y	3/4	282	12 speeds, work light
Jet JDP-20MF	10 1/4	3/4	4 3/8	150–4,200	Y	1 1/2	288	MT-3, square table, work light
■ Grizzly G7948	10	5/8	4 3/4	210–3,300	Y	1 1/2	312	12 speeds/ light
Powermatic 2000	10	5/8	4 1/2	130–2,770	Y	1 1/2	340	12 speeds
Powermatic 2000HD	10	1/2	6	200–1,820	Y	2	606	variable speed
Bridgewood BW2501F	10 1/4	5/8	4 5/8	150–4,200	Y	3/4	266	work light
Grizzly 9746	10 1/4	5/8	5 1/8	60–2,900	Y	1	682	12 speeds
Jet JDP-20MF	10 1/4	3/4	4 5/8	150–4,200	Y	1 1/2	288	12 speeds
Woodtek 816-812	10 1/2	5/8	4 13/16	180–4,200	Y	1	346	12 speeds
Grizzly G9747	10 3/4	5/8	5	60–2,900	Y	1 1/2	682	12 speeds
General 75-500-M-1	11	3/4	4 1/2	130–2,770	Y	1	340	
Lobo 222F	11	5/8	4 3/4	190–4,300	Y	1	360	12 speeds

STATS

MODEL	SIZE IN.	RESAW CAP. IN.	TABLE TILT LEFT, RIGHT	BLADE GUIDES	MAX. BLADE (IN.)	HP	WEIGHT (LBS.)	COMMENTS
RADIAL								
Delta 11-090	16	1/2	3 3/8	580–3,450	Y	1/3	120	5 speeds
Shop Fox W1669	16	5/8	3 1/4	550–3,470	Y	1/2	100	5 speeds, bench top
Shop Fox W1669	16	5/8	3 1/4	550–3,470	Y	1/2	150	5 speeds
■ Grizzly G7945	17	5/8	3 1/4	550–3,470	Y	1/2	100	bench top
■ Grizzly G7946	17	5/8	3 1/4	550–3,470	Y	1/2	150	5 speeds
Grizzly G9986	22 1/2	5/8	3 1/4	200–3,000	Y	1/2	400	
Yorkcraft YC-16RDP	17 1/4	5/8	3 1/4	550–3,470	Y	1/2	81	5 speeds

ry, with smaller bits (1/4" to 5/8") operating best around 2,000 to 2,400 rpm, and larger bits (up to 1 1/2") running around 1,500. Larger Forstner bits (1 1/2" to 2") should be operated in the 500 rpm range.

Other Helpful Thoughts

Most drill press operations are similar to using a corded or cordless drill. If you are drilling all the way through a piece, use a backing board to keep the hole from tearing out on the backside. Go slow and let the bit do the cutting. Make sure the bit is perfectly perpendicular to your work before drilling.

One thing that is peculiar to a drill press is the tendency with the higher torque to catch a piece and spin it out of your hand. Whenever possible, attach a fence to the table to keep the piece from spinning, or clamp the wood to the table. The torque can be impressive, so don't underestimate it.

key

Y = yes

N = no

■ = *PW* Recommends

ALL SUPPLIES AND EQUIPMENT WERE CURRENT AT THE TIME OF ORIGINAL PUBLICATION AND ARE SUBJECT TO CHANGE.

dust collectors

BY THE EDITORS OF *POPULAR WOODWORKING* MAGAZINE

Dust collectors are rapidly gaining popularity with many home woodworkers for three reasons: We're more aware of the health dangers posed by fine dust; we're trying to reduce the risk of a fire; and the dust collection machines themselves are becoming more affordable every year. This category is the fastest growing in our guide.

In fact, there's so much to know about this topic that you should read the revised edition of Sandor Nagyszalanczy's *Woodshop Dust Control* (Taunton Press).

The Basics

These simple machines have a fan pulling dust from a machine through a flexible or metal duct into a collection container. What sets the machines apart from one another is the wide variety of sizes, how they filter the chips and how they hold the waste.

The basic dust collector is a hose connected to the motor/fan housing, with two cloth bags attached. The dust is pulled

BEFORE YOU BUY

- **DUST COLLECTOR.** Available in a variety of capacities, these machines are hooked to one or more machines to collect wood chips and dust. They can employ a bag or canister filter to collect much of the fine airborne dust.
- **AIR CLEANER.** These boxlike units are designed to pull fine dust particles from the air. They're used in addition to a dust collector or collection system in a shop. An air cleaner is a true benefit, but it's possibly a luxury.
- **CYCLONE COLLECTOR.** Similar in purpose to a standard collector, cyclones add a collection stage to separate out larger chips and provide more efficient dust collection. Benefits include easier waste disposal and less need for ambient air cleaners.
- **CFM AND PRESSURE — NOT HP.** CFM (cubic feet of air moved per minute) and the static pressure (the strength of air suction) of a collector are statistics to watch for when evaluating dust collection systems, not horsepower. In general, a 12" planer should be hooked to a collector with 500 cfm capability. With two machines being used simultaneously, 1,200 cfm is suggested.
- **BLAST GATES AND DUCTING.** To maximize efficiency, collectors can be connected to multiple machines using ductwork or hoses. Blast gates direct the airflow from one machine at a time to improve efficiency.
- **FILTER EFFICIENCY.** Collector efficiency is rated by the micron efficiency of the filters. A dot measuring approximately $\frac{1}{16}$" wide equals 615 microns. Dust smaller than 2 microns can remain in the lungs and cause health problems. In our opinion, a filter rated at 30 microns isn't efficient enough. Spend the extra money for 5-micron bags. And if health is your driving influence in choosing dust collection, we strongly recommend you upgrade to 1-micron bags.

RECOMMENDATIONS

Occasional User

- **GRIZZLY G8027.** A great price for a basic dust collector for the small shop.

Serious Home Woodworker

- **PENN STATE DC1B-XL.** A quality machine with upgrades that make it a bargain.
- **GRIZZLY G1029.** For a few dollars more you can add a lot more power to your dust collection with this unit.
- **DELTA AP200.** For better efficiency, this rugged air cleaner makes a nice partner for your dust collector.

Advanced Woodworker or Professional

- **POWERMATIC 75.** Quiet, efficient and powerful, this is a good choice in a busy shop.
- **PENN STATE DC4-5.** This model offers more power and upgrades at a great price.
- **JDS AIR-TECH 750.** These premium air cleaners are designed for pro use.
- **CYCLONES.** We've just started testing cyclones in our shop, but we feel they offer an affordable alternative for the busy woodshop.

THESE TOOLS HAVE BEEN TESTED OR USED BY THE EDITORS OF *POPULAR WOODWORKING* MAGAZINE AND HAVE EARNED THEIR RECOMMENDATION. ALL SUPPLIES AND EQUIPMENT WERE CURRENT AT THE TIME OF ORIGINAL PUBLICATION AND ARE SUBJECT TO CHANGE.

BRAND & MODEL	HP	MAX. CFM	MAX. STATIC PRESSURE (IN. OF WATER)	SAWDUST CAPACITY (CU. FT.)	NO. OF PORTS, PORT DIA. (IN.)	VOLTS	WEIGHT (LB.)	DECIBEL LEVEL	BAG EFFICIENCY (MICRONS)	COMMENTS
SINGLE STAGE										
Shopsmith DC3300	1/2	330	NA	4	3, 2 1/2	115	64	NA	NA	
Woodmaster 820	1/2	680	4.4	NA	1, 4	115/230	50	NA	NA	
Delta AP300	3/4	550	NA	NA	1, 4	115/230	NA	NA	30	
Jet DC-610	3/4	610	6.9	1.8	1, 4	115	64	55-60	30	
Woodtek 911-047	3/4	250	NA	20 gal.	1, 4	115	18	70-80	10	
Belsaw MC-CT-50S	1	700	5.5	2	1, 4	115	46	62-82	30	
Belsaw MC-CT-80A	1	700	5	2.2	1, 4	115/230	70	52-74	30	
Belsaw MC-CT-90C	1	700	5.5	2.2	1, 4	115/230	73	62-80	30	
Craftsman 29979	1	650	8.5	1.5	1, 4	120	68	55-65	30	
Delta AP400	1	650	8.5	2.6	1, 4	115/230	57	63-73	30	
General 10-005 M1	1	750	5.5	20 gal.	1,4	120	76	52-62	2	
Grizzly G1163	1	450	2.8	2	1, 4	110/220	52	NA	30	
■ Grizzly G8027	1	500	2.8	2	1, 4	110/220	79	NA	30	
Jet DC-650	1	650	7.8	2.7	1, 4	115	84	60-70	30	
Jet DC-650SB	1	650	7.8	3.1	1, 4	115	58	55-65	30	
Jet DC-650TS 2 Stage	1	650	7.8	44 gal.	1, 4	115	38	60-70	5	
Lobo DC-1190	1	730	8.5	2.5	1, 4	115/230	78	60-70	30	
North State CT-50S	1	700	5.5	3.5	2, 4	115/230	80	55-66	15	
Penn State DC 5	1	914	9.4	1.5	1, 4	110	18	75	30	avail. w/5 mic bag
■ Penn State DC1B-XL	1	850	6	3.5	2, 4	110	66	62	5	avail. w/1 mic bag
Seco UFO-40	1	500	5.5	2.5	1, 4	115/230	40	55-65	20	
Seco UFO-70	1	655	5.5	2.5	1, 4	115/230	71	60-70	20	
Seco UFO-70F	1	655	5.5	2.5	1, 4	115/230	88	60-70	20	
Seco UFO-80	1	655	5.5	2.5	1, 4	115/230	88	60-70	20	
Seco UFO-90	1	655	5.5	2.5	1, 4	110	68	60-70	20	
Star S3810	1	700	4.5	2.2	1, 4	115/230	70	70-80	35	
Star S3811	1	700	4.5	1.5	1, 4	115/230	70	70-80	35	
Sunhill UFO-90	1	610	5.5	2.5	1, 4	110/220	70	55	20	
Transpower DC747	1	700	6.5	2	1, 4	115	65	NA	NA	
Woodtek 802-124	1	400	5.5	2.5	2, 4	115/230	85	74	5	
Woodtek 864-367	1	380	5.5	3.5	2, 4	115/230	47	64	5	
Yorkcraft YC-015A	1	500	2.76	17.8 gal.	1, 4	110/220	63	NA	15	
Delta 50-850	1 1/2	1,200	11.4	6	2, 4	115/230	100	69-79	30	
General 10-105 M1	1 1/2	1,250	6.5	42 gal.	1,5	115/230	110	80-90	2	
Grizzly G1028z	1 1/2	1,300	10.3	5.4	2, 4	110/220	115	60-80	30	
JDS DUST FORCE	1 1/2	1,280	12	42 gal.	1, 5/2, 4	110/220	106	67	30	
Jet DC-1100	1 1/2	1,100	11.5	7.4	1, 6; 2, 4	115/230	103	70-80	30	avail. w/canister filter
Jet DC-1200FS	1 1/2	1,200	10.5	3.5	2,4	115/230	125	70-80	30	
Penn State DC2-5	1 1/2	1,100	8.5	5.8	2, 4; 1,6	110/220	130	67	5	avail. w/1 mic bag
Penn State DC3-5XL	1 1/2	850	8.5	5.4	1, 4	110	46	62	5	avail. w/1 mic bag
Belsaw MC-1DC	2	1,059	8.3	5.2	1,5; 2, 4	230	123	67-87	30	
Bridgewood BW-002A	2	1,059	9.1	5.8	1, 5; 2, 4	110/220	117	NA	1	
Delta 50-851	2	1,500	13.7	6.5	3, 4	230	175	62-82	30	
General 10-110	2	1,600	8.3	42 gal.	1,5; 2, 4	240	132	66-77	2	
■ Grizzly G1029	2	1,550	12.3	5.4	2, 4	220	130	65-85	30	
Jet DC-1200-1	2	1,200	10.5	3.5	2, 4	230	143	65-80	30	1 or 3 phase, avail. w/CF
Lobo DC-101	2	1,290	9.5	5.2	2, 4	115/230	155	65-80	30	

key

NA = not available;

CF = canister filter;

mic = micron

■ *PW* Recommends

BRAND & MODEL	HP	MAX. CFM	MAX. STATIC PRESSURE (IN. OF WATER)	SAWDUST CAPACITY (CU. FT.)	NO. OF PORTS, PORT DIA. (IN.)	VOLTS	WEIGHT (LB.)	DECIBEL LEVEL	BAG EFFICIENCY (MICRONS)	COMMENTS
SINGLE STAGE (CONTINUED)										
North State UFO-101	2	1,182	9.5	5.4	3, 4 & 5	115/230	140	NA	15	
Seco UFO-101	2	1,182	7.5	5.2	2, 4; 1,5	115/230/460	139	65-80	20	
Shop Fox W1666	2	1,550	12.3	5.4	2,4	110/220	130	NA	30	
Star S3820	2	1,182	8.3	5.2	1, 5; 2, 4	230	135	67-87	35	
Sunhill UFO-101	2	1,182	7.5	5.2	2, 4	110/220	143	69	20	
Transpower DC2000	2	1,200	6.5	4	2, 4	115/230	143	NA	NA	
Woodtek 805-930	2	790	8.3	4.4	2, 5	230	123	76	5	
Penn State DC250SE	2	1,350	9.5	5.8	2, 4;1,6	110/220	145	65	5	avail. w/1 mic bag
Belsaw MC-2DC	3	1,836	8.7	10	1,6; 3,4	230	150	75-95	30	
Belsaw MC-CT-201H	3	1,836	8.7	10	1,6; 3,4	230	156	75-95	30	
Bridgewood BW-003A	3	1,836	5.8	13.5	1, 7; 4, 4	220	184	NA	1	
Delta 50-852	3	2,100	18.1	12.5	4, 4	200/220	200	77-91	30	
General 10-210	3	2,300	8.7	83 gal.	1,6; 3, 4	240	165	75-85	2	
Grizzly G1030	3	2,300	16.7	10.8	3, 4	220	170	75-90	30	
Jet DC-1900-1	3	1,900	10.2	10.7	1, 6; 2, 4	230	198	75-90	NA	1 or 3 phase
Lobo DC-102	3	2,600	11.5	10.5	1,6; 3,4	115/230	178	75-90	30	
Lobo DC-103	3	1,700	10.5	8.2	1,5; 2, 4	115/230	145	70-85	30	
North State UFO-102B	3	1,883	9.5	5.4	4, 5 & 6	230	181	75	15	
■ Penn State DC4-5	3	2,300	10.2	11.6	3, 4;1,7¾	220	200	75	5	
■ Powermatic 75	3	1,900	12.4	10	1, 8 or 6; 3, 4	230	215	80-90	5	1 mic bags avail.
Seco UFO-102A	3	1,883	NA	5.3	1,6; 3,4	NA	179	NA	NA	
Seco UFO-102B	3	1,883	9.1	10.4	1,6; 3, 4	115/230/460	179	70-80	20	
Star S3830	3	1,850	5.8	10.4	1, 6; 3, 4	230	165	75-95	35	
Sunhill UFO-102B	3	1,883	9.1	10.5	3, 4	230	181	78	20	
Sunhill UFO-103	3	2,683	10.4	17.7	4, 4	230	363	NA	20	
Transpower DC3000	3	1,850	5.6	5.3	3, 4	115/230	178	NA	NA	
Transpower DC4000	3	1,968	5.8	6.7	4, 4	115/230	250	NA	NA	
Woodmaster 1033	3	2,688	9.2	NA	1, 7	220	140	NA	NA	
Woodtek 864-381	3	1,180	8.6	8.8	1, 6	230	194	78	5	
Grizzly 9958	4	3,560	16.8	26	4,4	220	320	NA	1	
Bridgewood BW-005A	5	3,500	9.7	196 gal.	1, 9; 4,4	220	227	NA	1	
General 10-510	5	5,100	16	144 gal.	4, 4	240	370	75-85	2	
Grizzly G5954	5	4,820	17	26	4, 4	220	375	NA	1	
Lobo DC805	5	3,800	13	18.7	4, 4	220/440	310	70-85	30	
North State	5	4,850	17	NA	1,8; 4,4	220/440	380	75	NA	
Seco UFO-103B	5	2,683	NA	21	1,7; 4,4	NA	254	NA	NA	
Sunhill UFO-535DS	5	3,200	11	18	1,8	220/440	400	NA	20	
Powermatic 5000	7½	5,000	16.5	21.36	1, 10; 5,4	230	534	75-90	30	
Powermatic 5600	10	5,600	17.8	21.36	1,10; 5,4	230	563	75-90	30	
Seco UFO-104D	10	4,167	NA	58	1,9; 6,4	NA	728	NA	NA	

key

NA=not available

*Max CFM taken with cyclone and filters in place.

+3 phase available.

■ = *PW* Recommends

ALL SUPPLIES AND EQUIPMENT WERE CURRENT AT THE TIME OF ORIGINAL PUBLICATION AND ARE SUBJECT TO CHANGE.

through the fan, or impeller, then into the bag section. The smaller particles of dust are forced into the upper bag and trapped against the material; the heavier chips drop into the lower bag to await dumping later. This style is a good collector for most home-shop needs.

For more efficient dust collection, purchase better filter bags; better yet, add an air cleaner. These units scrub the ambient air to remove fine dust particles.

Some new dust collectors on the market have replaced the filter bag with a paper filter canister. These units are rated at about 2-micron efficiency.

For the ultimate, we're pleased that cyclone collectors (once only a commercial machine) are now becoming quite affordable.

Similar to a dust collector, a cyclone adds another separating stage, using centrifugal force to spin the debris. This action more efficiently divides the medium to lighter particles, trapping them in a filter canister or in dust bags. The heavier particles drop into a lower container.

STATS

BRAND & MODEL	CFM EFFICIENCY	# FILTERS (LB.)	DUST REMOVAL	WEIGHT,	DECIBELS
AIR CLEANERS					
Bridgewood CTP-500-2	500	1	97% @ 5 mic	21	NA
Bridgewood CTI-1400	1,400	2	99% @ 5 mic	72	NA
Craftsman 16995	200	2	93% @ 5 mic	14	NA
Craftsman 29972	300	2	95% @ 5 mic	45	NA
■ Delta AP200	850	2	98% @ 5 mic	50	NA
Delta 50-875	1,000	2	NA	55	NA
Delta 50-870	1,900	2	98% @ 5 mic	85	50
General 10-600 M1	1,400	3	98% @ 5 mic	86	64
Grizzly G9954	220	1	99.7% @ 5 mic	15.5	NA
Grizzly G9955	400	2	99.7% @ 5 mic	18.75	NA
Grizzly G5955	510	2	98% @ 3 mic	40	NA
Grizzly G9956	1,400	3	99.7% @ 5 mic	79	NA
JDS Air-Tech 10-16	1,000 or 1,600	3	99% @ 5 mic	92	65
■ JDS Air-Tech 750	200 to 750	3	99% @ 5 mic	62	61
JDS Air-Tech 8-12	800 or 1,250	3	99% @ 5 mic	86	63
JDS Air-Tech 2400	2,410	3	99% @ 5 mic	203	67
Jet AFS-1000	500; 70; 1,044	2	99% @ 5 mic	54	NA
Jet AFS-1500	750; 900; 1,300	3	99% @ 5 mic	75	NA
Jet AFS-2000	800; 1,200; 1,700	3	99% @ 5 mic	110	NA
Penn State AC465 cfm KIT	465	2	85% @ 1 mic	40	60
Penn State AC930 cfm KIT	930	2	85% @ 1 mic	45	65
Penn State AC620	620	2	85% @ 1 mic	42	60
Penn State AC 930	930	2	85% @ 1 mic	51	67
Penn State AC2500-s	2,500	2	85% @ 1 mic	130	67
Woodtek 923-838	340	2	98% @ 0.5 mic	35	55
Woodtek 923-859	510	2	98% @ 0.5 mic	30	55

STATS

BRAND & MODEL	HP	MAX. CFM	MAX. STATIC PRESSURE (IN. OF WATER)	SAWDUST CAPACITY (CU. FT.)	NO. OF PORTS, PORT DIA. (IN.)	VOLTS	WEIGHT (LB.)	DECIBEL LEVEL (MICRONS)	BAG EFFICIENCY	COMMENTS
CYCLONE										
Blue Tornado 102	2	1,350	10.5	1, 6	115/230	NA	NA	NA	NA	
Blue Tornado 103	3	2,170	11.2	1, 7	230	NA	NA	NA	NA	
Bridgewood BW-CDC2	2	1,500	13	15 gal.	1, 6 or 2, 4	220	160	NA	15 mic	
Bridgewood BW-CDC3	3	2,400	16	15 gal.	1, 8 or 3, 4	220	175	NA	15 mic	
Oneida 1.5 Component	1.5	800*	9	5, 8, & larger	1, 6	115/208–240+	115–145	72–78	99% @ 2 mic	
Oneida 2 Component	2	1,100*	9	5, 8 & larger	1, 7	115/208–240+	125–195	72–78	99% @ 2 mic	
Oneida 2 Commercial	2	1,220*	10.2	5, 8 & larger	1, 7	115/208–240+	140–300	75–81	99% @ 2 mic	
Oneida 3 Commercial	3	1,800*	11	5, 8 & larger	1, 8	208–240+	175–400	75–83	99% @ 2 mic	
Penn State Tempest 2	$1\frac{1}{2}$	750	5	35 gal.	1, 5	110/220	118	63	100% @ 5 mic	avail. w/.5 mic cart.
Penn State Tempest	2	1,000	6	35 gal.	1, 5	110/220	125	65	100% @ 5 mic	avail. w/.5 mic cart.
Penn State Tempest 4	3	1,350	6.8	35 gal.	1, 5	220	154	73	100% @ 5 mic	avail. w/.5 mic cart.
Woodsucker	2	925	8.75	NA	1, 6	220	NA	NA	NA	

key

NA=not available

*Max CFM taken with cyclone and filters in place.

+3 phase available.

■ = *PW* Recommends

ALL SUPPLIES AND EQUIPMENT WERE CURRENT AT THE TIME OF ORIGINAL PUBLICATION AND ARE SUBJECT TO CHANGE.

hand tools

BY DON MCCONNELL

With chisel and mallet at the ready, I paused, knowing that soon there would be no turning back. In that moment, I also became aware that the painter working on the landing nearby was watching with puzzled curiosity. His curiosity turned to shock as I struck the chisel with the first mallet blow.

The previous afternoon, while sanding the continuous, three-story custom handrail, I had discovered a small but deep area of blowout. In many situations, it might not have warranted such a radical repair, but this would be quite visible and was part of an elliptical stairway that was one of the focal points of this high-end house. Additionally, I knew the site manager to be extremely detail oriented, and unlikely to tolerate a "paint and putty" approach in such a critical place.

Though I knew there was some risk of making matters worse, I had reluctantly decided that the best solution was a patch, executed in a "neat and workmanlike manner." The goal was to match the color and figure well enough that, at worst, it would blend into the surrounding material. At best, it would be "invisible." Accordingly, I had selected the most likely candidate from three or four blanks I'd prepared in the shop, and I proceeded to chop out the mortise to accept the patch.

The work was fairly straightforward. My blank had been prepared to match the width of the chisel I was using. And with the use of a sharp, finely set block plane (and a couple of jigs to guide my tools), I obtained a tight fit of the ever-so-slightly wedge-shaped patch in the mortise. I then continued to do some additional cleanup work in the area while the glue dried, then carved the patch down to match the surrounding profile and finished sanding the area. I was pleased to discover that I'd been extraordinarily lucky in finding a scrap that matched the figure, color and chatoyance (the gleam) of the surrounding material almost perfectly. The patch all but disappeared.

An Act of Madness

At that point, I went back out to the van for additional tools and supplies. When I returned, I was taken aback to find the painter kneeling on the stairs and peering intently at the handrail. Startled, he looked up somewhat sheepishly and said, with a bit of wonderment in his voice:

"Where is it? I can't find it."

Now, this painter worked around accomplished finish carpenters every day. So he was accustomed to seeing high- quality woodwork being carried out. Yet, he was shocked and astonished by this simple, straightforward bit of work. Why?

I believe the primary reason was that the work he typically observed was carried out almost exclusively with power tools and machinery. And, based on that experience, he shared an assumption that is common on construction sites (and in woodworking circles), that critical and quality work cannot be effectively accomplished using hand tools. For him to see someone deliberately drive a chisel into a completely installed and all but completed, curved, custom handrail, must have seemed an act of madness.

Hostility and Camaraderie

In a way, I was not surprised by his reaction. Typically, when I show up on a job site with my carving tools, a roll of chisels, a plane or two and possibly a small backsaw, I can tell that my presence creates a stir. There are a variety of reactions.

Sometimes it's mild hostility ("Hey, don't you know they've invented routers?"), most often from those in other woodworking trades. Sometimes it's simple curiosity. And sometimes it's instant camaraderie with other tradespeople whom I've never met before. These latter, I've observed, are often accomplished in an unusual trade, and may also feel anomalous on many job sites.

My purpose in relating this anecdote is to illustrate the widely shared perception that exclusive use of power tools and machinery is the only sensible route to take in woodworking. To offset this, advocates of using at least some traditional hand tools often argue that hand tools are safer, quieter, less polluting and less expensive. Additionally, there is often the (sometimes implied) message that it's easier than it looks.

While these arguments have a good deal of validity, I think they fail to address the fact that many power-tool woodworkers (vocational or avocational) do not consider hand tools to be safe, easy or effective.

They may have, in fact, attempted to use hand tools at one point or another, only to be utterly frustrated. Or, worse yet, they've spoiled the work.

This could be for any number of reasons, including an inadequately sharpened or tuned tool, an inappropriate tool for the job, and/or lack of experience, skill and knowledge needed for success. Whatever the reason, for these woodworkers, the safe course of action seems that of continuing along the path they're already on.

Risky but Rewarding

Truth is, there is risk involved in deciding to use hand tools. Risk, if nothing else, in the form of a real, and sometimes steep, learning curve. There will be failures and frustrations. It takes time and effort to learn about the tools, how to sharpen them, and when, where and how to use them, along with the equipment and appliances needed to use them effectively. Without the appropriate sharp chisel and the necessary skill, I would have been mad to use hand tools on the handrail.

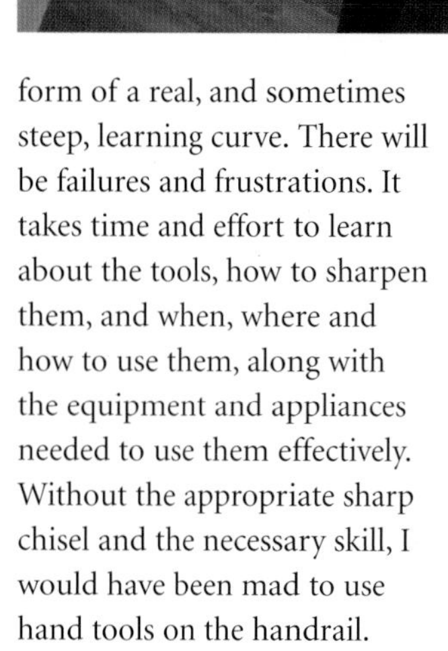

PHOTO AT LEFT Handsaws might seem like an antiquated way to size lumber, but a straight and sharp saw is highly effective (and a joy to use).

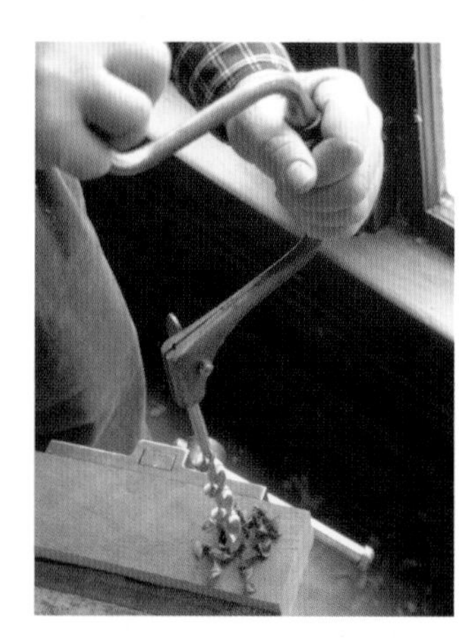

PHOTO ABOVE The brace and bit produces immense amounts of torque that your cordless drill could only dream about. Plus, many models (not the one shown here) have a ratcheting feature that allows them to be used in corners and right up against wall moulding.

Despite this, I believe valid reasons exist to consider the possibility of making some use of hand tools. For example, you may have some historic interest in what it was like to work in some bygone era. Or you might simply desire to explore some design and construction details that don't readily lend themselves to a machine-only approach to woodworking.

It is not the purpose of this chapter to convince every woodworker to use hand tools. Rather, it is to encourage those with such an interest to live dangerously and begin, or advance, along the lines of that interest. In a sense, the existence of this chapter is based on the presumption that many woodworkers have such an interest. Though, in today's woodworking climate, they may not have acknowledged that interest, even to themselves.

The good news is that the knowledge, skills and techniques are eminently learnable by anyone with average motor skills and abilities. And it is the primary purpose of this chapter to help that learning process by discussing the tools, trade techniques and applications in a manner that I hope will be informative and provocative.

Learn to properly tune up a plane, and you'll be hooked. Planes are capable of a great variety of tasks, from producing crown moulding to preparing lumber for its final finish.

CHOOSING A PROPER BENCH FOR WOODWORKING

A suitable workbench is key to satisfactory hand-tool woodworking. While you can best determine the most suitable bench for your own needs, I thought it might be useful to outline a few basic considerations.

Fundamentally, the purpose of a workbench is to support and/or immobilize the wood in a comfortable and accessible position for whatever work is being done.

Height, length, weight and rigidity are general characteristics that play a role in meeting this purpose.

Not surprisingly, the height of a bench depends on the woodworker as well as the nature of the work. For example, a bench that is low enough for heavy planing will be too low for extended periods of carving. This can be addressed with the use of more than one bench, but most woodworkers settle for a compromise if they are not specializing.

There are various methods to determine this compromise — the aim being to account for the person's height and arm length. One method is to hold your straightened arms downward, at a slight forward angle, allowing you to comfortably stretch your hands forward with level palms. The height of the palms determines the bench height.

A bench length of 6' is a generally accepted minimum for most work, though more length can be useful if the shop space allows. A bench width of approximately 2' (often including a 6" to 8" tool tray at the rear) is usually adequate. You can reach only so far over the bench, in any event, and additional width can limit access from the off side.

The benchtop needs to be thick enough to resist deflection under planing pressure as well as undue vibration from hammer or mallet blows. This tends to depend on the material used, but it can be about 1$^1/_2$" to 2", minimum, for the moderately hard woods, such as beech, birch and maple, which have traditionally been preferred bench woods.

The undercarriage of the bench needs to be rigid enough to resist racking pressures from planing. The illustrations show two of the traditional approaches used to achieve this. The joiner's bench is easier to construct in the absence of a suitable workbench, though the upper skirt can sometimes become an obstacle.

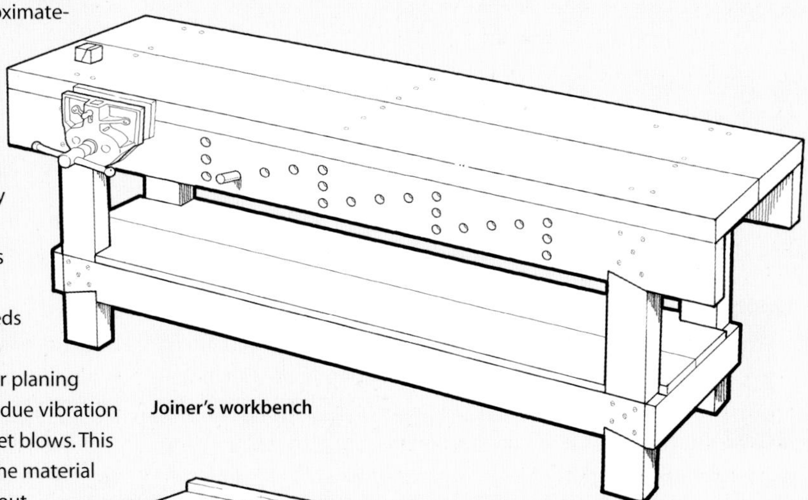

Joiner's workbench

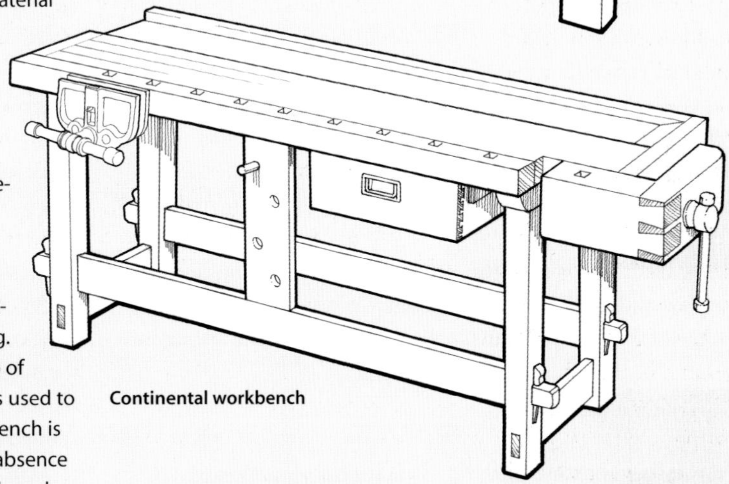

Continental workbench

Finally, there is the question of holding the work itself. Surprisingly, this can be accomplished with a few clamps and battens, though this can require inordinate setup time. For that reason, a face vise, planing stop and possibly a holdfast could be considered a minimum arrangement. The continental-style cabinetmakers bench, with its face vise, tail vise, bench dogs, etc., adds a great deal of convenience.

Much additional information is available, and it's worth consulting if you are considering building or buying a workbench. It can become very confusing, though, so having a grasp of some fundamentals, and a realization that no single bench is ideal for every purpose, can help sort things out.

More Information on Workbenches

Two excellent books on workbenches are *Making Workbenches* (Sterling Publications) by Sam Allen and *The Workbench Book* (Taunton Press) by Scott Landis. While both books offer a dose of history, plans and construction information, Allen's book focuses more on step-by-step instruction while the Landis book has more information about history and use. Both books are worth owning as you decide what kind of bench you need for your woodworking.

Another excellent resource is the Internet. I like two sites in particular.

BUILDING A TRADITIONAL WORKBENCH:
http://pages.friendlycity.net/~krucker/Bench/index.htm
Keith Rucker walks you through the process of building a continental-style workbench. The site includes construction drawings, a cutting list and step-by-step photos of the entire process. You can even download the bench plan in PDF format that is printer-friendly. Rucker covers the topic thoroughly with more than 60 pages of information.

BOB'S BENCH PAGES:
www.terraclavis.com/bws/benches.htm
Bob Key's Web site is another essential waypoint as you design your own bench. Key's site includes plans for a basic beginner's bench and an advanced model. Plus, there's lots of good information about all the accessories that help your work at the bench: bench hooks, bench slaves, shooting boards and the like. Key also keeps an eye on other workbench-related sites on the Internet and has a list of good links for you to explore.

CHAPTER 22

jigsaws

BY THE EDITORS OF *POPULAR WOODWORKING* MAGAZINE

If you're starting woodworking with just a few tools, the jigsaw should be at the top of your list. It is capable of cutting curves and straight lines. Plus, it can work on large pieces that cannot be cut on a band saw.

Getting Ready

Jigsaws require little setup when you buy them. Just make sure the blade is square to the base plate and set the saw for the type of work you're planning to do. Here are the basics:

- Blade speed: Most jigsaws have variable speed with a dial on or near the trigger that will allow you to limit the saw's top speed. In general, use slower speeds for dense materials, faster speeds for soft woods.
- Orbital action: Turn the orbital action off when working in hard materials such as metal, or when using reverse-tooth or carbide blades. The lowest orbital setting is generally for getting a fine cut in soft woods. The middle setting is for hard woods or particleboard. And the highest setting is for ripping through softwoods really quickly.
- Base plate: If you're concerned about marring your workpiece, most jigsaws can be fitted with a plastic shoe that slips over the metal base plate.

Making the Cut

The teeth of a jigsaw blade point upward. As a result, the cleanest cut will be on the underside. So, when laying out your cut, make your marks on the back side of your wood so the front will have the least splintering.

When making the cut, some people prefer to cut to one side of the line and then clean up the sawn edge to the line. Try this once or twice: When making your cut, try cutting right on the line. Some people find it easier to follow the line this way.

Never force the saw during a cut. Use minimal forward pressure; let the saw do most of the work. The motor should not bog down during the cut.

BEFORE YOU BUY

- **TOP-HANDLE VS. BARREL-GRIP.** In this country, top-handle saws are the norm. Too bad. We really like the extra control you get from a barrel grip. Check one out before you buy.
- **AMPS.** Unless you cut ironwood or ipe for a living, the 4- or 5-amp tools will handle most workaday tasks. So don't sweat the amperage; it's not an accurate measure of power anyway.
- **STROKE.** Simply put, the stroke is how far up and down the blade moves. Longer strokes (1" and up) cut faster and cleaner. Bargain jigsaws have shorter stokes, 5/8" to 3/4".
- **ORBITAL ACTION.** If your saw has this function, it can make the blade move slightly forward on the upstroke and back on the downstroke. The more aggressive the orbital action, the rougher (but faster) the cut.
- **BLADE CHANGING.** The ease of changing blades is all over the map, from needing a screwdriver to simply pulling a lever and the blade falling from the tool. We like toolless blade changing, but check out the saw before you buy; some toolless blade systems are as finicky as those needing screwdrivers.
- **BLADE TYPES.** A few jigsaws take only a proprietary blade, which can be a pain. Others take T-style blades (also called bayonet or Bosch-style). These blades have tangs that the tool's blade vise can grip — the best system in our opinion. Universal blades are held in place using friction or screws. Some jigsaws take both T-style and universal blades, though these tend to use only friction to grip the blade.

RECOMMENDATIONS

Occasional User

- **FREUD FJ85.** Freud's top-of-the-line jigsaw has features found on expensive saws: electronic feedback, a big stroke and orbital action.
- **GRIZZLY G8994Z.** This jigsaw is similar to Bosch's older jigsaws. For the occasional user, it's hard to beat.

Serious Home Woodworker

- **BOSCH 1584AVS, 1587AVS.** These two tools are identical except the 1584AVS is a barrel-grip and the 1587AVS is a top-handle tool. Bosch's jigsaws are what all others are measured against.
- **MILWAUKEE 6276-21.** The best toolless blade-changing mechanism on the market and a solid performer.

Advanced Woodworker or Professional

The two tools above are also excellent choices for the professional.

- **METABO STE105 PLUS, STEB105 PLUS.** Metabo's line of jigsaws are rock-solid performers that give Bosch a real run for its money. A shop favorite.

THESE TOOLS HAVE BEEN TESTED OR USED BY THE EDITORS OF *POPULAR WOODWORKING* MAGAZINE AND HAVE EARNED THEIR RECOMMENDATION. ALL SUPPLIES AND EQUIPMENT WERE CURRENT AT THE TIME OF ORIGINAL PUBLICATION AND ARE SUBJECT TO CHANGE.

Orbital action moves the blade forward during the cut. Here you can see the blade in an aggressive orbit.

STATS

MODEL	BODY TYPE	BLADE MOUNT TYPE	BLADE GUIDE	STROKE LENGTH (IN.)	CUTS PER MINUTE	AMPS	DUST CONTROL	WEIGHT (LBS.)
Black & Decker JS200	TH	U	Y	1	800–3,200	3.2	NA	3.6
Black & Decker JS300K	TH	U*	Y	1	800–3,200	3.5	CB	5
Black & Decker JS350	TH	U*	Y	1	800–3,200	4	CB, VP	5
Bosch 1581AVSK	TH	T	Y	1	500–3,100**	5	CB	5.5
■ Bosch 1584AVS	BG	T*	Y	1	500–3,100**	5	CB, Opt.VP	5.5
Bosch 1584AVSK	BG	T*	Y	1	500–3,100**	5	CB, Opt.VP	5.5
■ Bosch 1587AVS	TH	T*	Y	1	500–3,100**	5	CB, Opt.VP	5.5
Bosch 1587AVSK	TH	T*	Y	1	500–3,100**	5	CB, Opt.VP	5.5
Bosch 1587 AVSP	TH	T*	Y	1	500–3,100**	5	CB, Opt. VP	5.5
Craftsman 17228	TH	U	Y	3/4	0–3,000**	4	CB, VP	4.5
Craftsman 17240	TH	T,U*	Y	5/8	3,250	3.5	CB	3.5
Craftsman 17241	TH	T,U	Y	5/8	3,250	3.9	CB	3.7
Craftsman 17242	TH	T,U	Y	13/16	3,200	5	CB, VP	6.8
Craftsman 27719	TH	T, U*	Y	1	500–3,000**	5	CB, Opt. VP	7
DeWalt DW313	TH	U	Y	1	500–3,100**	4.5	NA	6.2
DeWalt DW318G	TH	T	Y	1	0–3,100***	4.5	NA	6.2
DeWalt DW318K	TH	U	Y	1	0–3,100**	4.5	NA	6.2
DeWalt DW321K	TH	T, U*	Y	1	500–3,100**	5.8	CB	6.4
DeWalt DW323K	BG	T,U*	Y	1	500–3,100**	5.8	CB, VP	6.4
DeWalt DW933K	TH	T,U*	Y	1	0–2,000**	18v cordless	CB	8.1
Fein Aste 638	BG	U	N	13/16	1,050–2,600	3.9	VP	4.8
Festool PS2E	BG	T	Y	1	1,200–3,100**	3.75	CB, VP	4.9
Freud FJ65	TH	T, U	Y	3/4	0–3,000**	3.2	VP	3.4
■ Freud FJ85	TH	T, U*	Y	1	0–3,000**	4.8	VP	5.4
■ Grizzly G8994Z	TH	T	Y	1	0–3100**	5	CB	5.5
Hitachi CJ65V2K	TH	T,U	Y	1	700–3,200**	5.2	CB	5.5
Makita 4304	TH	T, U	Y	1	500–3,000**	5.5	VP	5.1
Makita 4304T	TH	T, U*	Y	1	500–3,000**	5.5	VP	5.3
Makita 4323	TH	T	Y	11/16	500–3,100	3.7	VP	4
Makita 4324	TH	T	Y	11/16	500–3,100**	3.7	VP	4
Makita 4300DW	TH	Special	Y	9/16	2,700	9.6v cordless	NA	3.3
Makita 4331DWD	TH	T, U	Y	1	500–2,800**	12v cordless	VP	5.7
Makita 4333DWD	TH	T, U	Y	1	500–2,800**	14v cordless	VP	6.3
Makita 4334DWD	TH	T, U*	Y	1	500–2,800**	18v cordless	VP	7.3
Makita 4340T	TH	T, U*	Y	1	2,800	6.3	VP	5.3
Makita 4340CT	TH	T, U*	Y	1	800–2,800	6.3	VP	5.3
Makita 4340FCT	TH	T, U*	Y	1	800–2,800	6.3	VP	5.3
Makita 4341FCT	BG	T, U*	Y	1	800–2,800	6.3	VP	5.3
Metabo STE70	TH	T, U	Y	3/4	1,000–3,000**	4.8	CB	4.9
■ Metabo STE105Plus	BG	T, U*	Y	1	1,000–3,000**	6	CB, VP	5.5
■ Metabo STEB105Plus	TH	T,U*	Y	1	1,000–3,000**	6	CB, VP	5.7
Milwaukee 6256-6	TH	U	Y	1	0–3,100	3.8	CB	5.8
Milwaukee 6266-22	TH	T*	Y	1	500–3,000**	5.7	CB, VP	6.2
Milwaukee 6267-21	BG	T*	Y	1	1,700**	12v cordless	VP	5.8
■ Milwaukee 6276-21	BG	T*	Y	1	500–3,000**	5.7	CB, VP	6.2
Porter-Cable 548	TH	U	Y	7/16	0–4,500**	3.5	-	6.5
Porter-Cable 9543	TH	T*	Y	1	500–3,100**	6	CB, VP	6.5
Porter-Cable 97549	TH	U	Y	1	500–3,200**	4.8	CB	6.5
Porter-Cable 643	TH	T*	Y	1	0–2,200**	19.2v cordless	CB, VP	5.25
Skil 4240	TH	T, U	Y	5/8	3,250	3.3	CB	3.5
Skil 4280	TH	T, U	Y	5/8	800–3,250	3.5	CB	3.5
Skil 4380	TH	T, U*	Y	5/8	800–3,250**	3.7	CB	3.7
Skil 4445	TH	U*	N	5/8	800–3,250**	4	CB	4
Skil 4470	TH	U*	N	5/8	800–3,200**	4	CB, VP	4.1
Skil 4470-44	TH	U*	N	5/8	800–3,200**	4	CB, VP	4.1
Skil 4480	TH	T, U	Y	13/16	800–3,200**	5	CB, VP	5
Skil 4540	TH	T, U	Y	13/16	800–3,200	4.5	CB, VP	5
Skil 4580	TH	T, U	Y	13/16	800–3,200**	5	CB, VP	5

key

CB = chip blower
VP = vacuum port
TH = top handle
BG = barrel grip
T=T-style blade
U = universal blade
*Toolless blade changing
**Has orbital action
NA = not available
■ *PW* Recommends

ALL SUPPLIES AND EQUIPMENT WERE CURRENT AT THE TIME OF ORIGINAL PUBLICATION AND ARE SUBJECT TO CHANGE.

jointers

BY THE EDITORS OF *POPULAR WOODWORKING* MAGAZINE

Marketing and misconceptions have led a lot of woodworkers to think that as long as they own a planer, they don't need a jointer. Nothing is farther from the truth. In fact, if you own a planer, you should definitely own a jointer.

While a planer is great for smoothing a board and reducing the thickness, you really need to start with a board that's flat and square to allow the planer to produce the results you want. And that's what jointers are all about.

Boards Aren't Flat?

In a woodworker's fantasy, every board bought from the lumberyard is perfectly flat and straight and at least 12" wide. Reality is quite different. Wood is often crooked, bowed, twisted and cupped; see the drawing on the next page. If you're lucky, that's only one board in your stack! To build something with those boards, they need some time on a jointer.

BEFORE YOU BUY

- **BENCHTOP VS. STATIONARY.** Benchtop jointers are recommended only if your shop is small or you build only chairs or small boxes. Many are powered by universal motors, limiting their performance, and most have shorter beds than needed for adequately flattening boards. If you must go benchtop, go 6" and look for a decent motor size. Floor models range from 6" on up, but we don't recommend anything larger than a 12" jointer unless you're running a good-size production shop. In general, an 8" jointer is a great option for most home woodworkers. A 6" will suffice but limits you somewhat.
- **HANDWHEELS VS. LEVERS.** The infeed table on a jointer can be adjusted by either a handwheel or a lever. Handwheels are more precise, with each turn or quarter turn producing a measurable height adjustment. While levers are more subjective, all jointers offer a scale to measure the height change, and it can be argued that jointers aren't used to remove exact amounts of material very often. Chalk it up to personal preference.
- **KNIVES.** Knives will number two, three or four, depending on the size of the machine. Two knives are exclusive to benchtop machines. Four blades will usually occur on only the largest of jointers. The more knives that cut the wood, the better the finish. So three is better than two. Stock jointer knives are almost exclusively high-speed steel, and only production shops are likely to spend the money to replace them with carbide knives. This is more for durability, as steel knives still offer a better cut, but will dull and nick more easily. Currently, few jointers use two-sided or disposable knives, but the trend that is sweeping planers may hit the jointers soon.
- **SETTING KNIVES.** Setting jointer knives is accomplished with either a magnetic knife-setting jig (using a magnet to lift the knife out of the cutterhead to the proper height), or jackscrew adjustment (lifting the knives to proper height by adjusting a set of jackscrews under the blade). Both methods are accurate, though we find jackscrews to be easier to adjust.
- **FENCES** The longer the fence, the better. More importantly, the flatter the better. Due to internal stresses in cast iron, jointer fences can arrive warped or twisted. Whenever possible, check the fence prior to purchasing to make sure it is flat and straight. If you don't have the option to check it before it's delivered, make sure it is the first thing you do check. If it's not correct, contact the company and make arrangements to have it replaced. Fence movement is also important. It should slide easily across the table, and you should be able to move the fence to an angled setting with a minimum of fuss. Some jointers offer a rack-and-pinion mechanism for moving the fence, making it easier to quickly adjust the fence location.

Start with Some Face Time

The face of a board (as opposed to the edge) is the first part to run over a jointer. But first let's make sure things are set up correctly.

If you've followed the jointer's directions, the outfeed table (the one to the left of the machine as you face it) and the knives are set at exactly the same height. In most cases, this is how the jointer arrives from the factory. For the first rough pass, the infeed table should be set about 1⁄16" lower than the outfeed table.

The fence should be set square to the tables, and slid over the tables enough to expose about 1" more than the width of the board. This keeps the knives covered by the board during the cut.

Inspect your board. Most likely it will be bowed to one face or the other. If not, you're in pretty good shape and won't have to remove much material to prepare the board for the planer. If it is bowed, the concave side should be run over the jointer.

Use the photos on the next page to learn the optimal stance to use when feeding a board over the jointer. These steps are repeated until the majority of the board's face is clean and flat.

Once one face is flat, repeat the basic steps to square one edge of the board to the now-flat face. You will need to run the recently jointed face against the fence for this step. The stance and motions are similar.

Overall, flattening a face, then squaring an edge to that face is what a jointer does, and it does it well. The flat face allows your planer to then reduce the thickness of the board while still maintaining the flatness of the board. Without the jointer work, a planer will just make a thinner bowed or twisted board. Jointing the edge gives you a straight surface so you can rip the board to width on your table saw and fence.

A jointer can be used for a couple of other things, rabbeting being an efficient option on almost all machines. By removing the guard and setting the infeed table height and fence depth to the proper dimensions, you can rabbet a board easily in one or two passes with little difficulty.

Other jointer operations include tapering a board lengthwise, and by setting the fence at an angle, you can cut bevels on the edges of boards. If you have a smaller-width jointer than your material, don't fret. With a simple tip in the chapter on planers, you can safely flatten stock that's nearly twice the width of your jointer's maximum capacity. See "Planing 8"-Wide Boards with a 6" Jointer" on page 112.

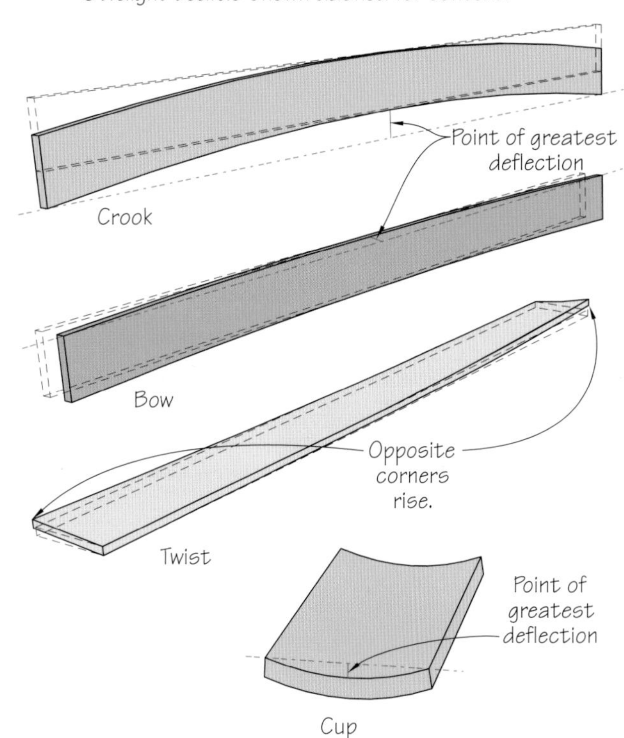

Some Safety Tips

Jointers are safe machines to operate if all the guidelines are followed. If you get sloppy on this machine, it can bite you in a hurry with a kickback or a slipped finger. Here are some basic guidelines that will help you operate your jointer in a safe manner:

- Prior to running the face or edge, check your board for knots or defects that could separate from the board and cause the board to jump during planing.
- Always use a push block when jointing a thin piece of stock, or when face jointing.
- Never run stock shorter than 12" in length over the jointer.
- The safety guard should always be in place unless you are cutting rabbets or face jointing stock wider than the capacity of the machine.

RECOMMENDATIONS

Occasional User

- **GRIZZLY 1182HW.** For a few dollars more than the price of a benchtop jointer, we recommend the 1182HW with handwheel bed adjustment.

Serious Home Woodworker

- **JET JJ-6CSX.** This 6" jointer is a proven bargain.
- **DELTA 37-195.** The convenience of the rack-and-pinion fence and top-mounted switch strongly recommend this 6" model.
- **DELTA 37-380.** The 8" version of the 37-195 is also a recommended machine.
- **JET JJ-8CS.** This 8" jointer offers a magnetic switch, handwheel adjustment and a long bed.
- **GRIZZLY G1018.** Without sacrificing features, this Grizzly 8" is a significant bargain.

Advanced Woodworker or Professional

- **POWERMATIC 60.** This 8" Powermatic is a pro-quality, accurate and reliable machine that will likely be handed down to your children.
- **BRIDGEWOOD BW-12J.** If you want to move up to a 12" machine without emptying your wallet, check out this strong performer.

THESE TOOLS HAVE BEEN TESTED OR USED BY THE EDITORS OF *POPULAR WOODWORKING* MAGAZINE AND HAVE EARNED THEIR RECOMMENDATION. ALL SUPPLIES AND EQUIPMENT WERE CURRENT AT THE TIME OF ORIGINAL PUBLICATION AND ARE SUBJECT TO CHANGE.

FACE JOINTING: HOW TO DO IT

Rock the board on the jointer table across its width to find the flattest area, then maintain this plane as you begin the cut. Stand near the back of the board and do not use any downward pressure on the board. Use your left hand to keep the board against the fence and your right hand to move the board forward and in the correct plane. Let the force of the cutterhead in the wood keep the board down on the outfeed table. Keep your body positioned as shown until the board is supported on the jointer tables.

1

With the board supported, move toward the cutterhead by taking shuffling steps with your feet. Again, the left hand keeps the board against the fence and applies only enough downward force to control the stock. Use a shuffling motion to move your hands, and always keep one hand on the board. When your left hand is about 18" from the cutterhead, pause, and while keeping firm control of the stock, reach for the push block with your right hand, then position it on the end of the board. Now continue moving the board forward.

2

To complete the cut, continue forward progress until the end of the board and push block have cleared the cutterhead and the safety guard has closed to the fence. Remember to keep firm downward pressure during the final phase of the cut if you have a long board extending off the end of the outfeed table.

3

STATS

MODEL	WIDTH × LENGTH (IN.)	# OF KNIVES × RPM	HP	VOLTS	TYPE OF HEIGHT ADJ.	DUST PORT	WEIGHT (LB)	COMMENTS & FEATURES
BENCHTOP								
Grizzly H2801	4 × 23	2 × 8,000	1/2	110	K	Y	28	
Craftsman 21788	6 1/8 × 29	2 × 8,000	1 1/2	115	K	Y	68	
Delta JT160	6 3/16 × 30	2 × 6k-11k	10 amp	120	K	Y	35	2-speed
Hitachi P12RA	6 5/8 × 12 1/4	2 × 10,400	15 amp	115	K	Y	83.5	jointer/planer

MODEL	WIDTH × LENGTH (IN.)	#/KNIVES × RPM	HP	VOLTS	TYPE OF HEIGHT ADJ.	DUST PORT	JACK SCREWS	WEIGHT (LB)	COMMENTS & FEATURES
FLOOR									
Bridgewood BW-6R	6 × 45 1/2	3 × 4,500	1	110/220	W	Y	Y	210	enclosed stand
Delta JT360	6 × 46	3 × 4,800	3/4	115/230	L	Y	Y	210	open stand
■ Grizzly G1182HW	6 × 47	3 × 5,000	1	110/220	W	OPT	Y	215	
Grizzly G1182Z	6 × 47	3 × 5,000	1	110/220	L	Y	Y	225	
Grizzly G1182ZHW	6 × 47	3 × 5,000	1	110/220	W	Y	Y	225	handwheel
Grizzly G1182ZX	6 × 47	3 × 5,000	1	110/220	L	Y	Y	235	R&P fence, top switch
Jet JJ-60S	6 × 46	3 × 4,800	3/4	115/230	W	Y	Y	192	
■ Jet JJ-6CSX	6 × 46	3 × 4,800	1	115/230	W	Y	Y	258	
Lobo JT-2206	6 × 42 1/2	3 × 5,000	1	115/230	W	Y	NA	194	
North State	6 × 42	3 × 5,000	1	110/220	W	Y	N	250	
Powermatic 54A	6 × 66	3 × 4,500	1	115/230	L	Y	Y	287	quick & fine adjust
Shop Fox W1679	6 × 47	3 × 5,000	1	115	W	Y	Y	255	magnetic top switch
Star WJ6	6 × 43	3 × 4,600	3/4	115	L	NA	NA	218	open stand
Woodtek 924-028	6 × 46	3 × 3,450	3/4	115/230	L/W	Y	Y	210	
Yorkcraft YC-6J	6 × 46	3 × 4,800	1	110/220	L	Y	Y	214	R&P fence
Craftsman 21706	6 1/8 × 46	3 × 5,000	1	115/230	L	Y	Y	230	enclosed base
■ Delta 37-195	6 1/8 × 46	3 × 4,800	1	115/230	L	Y	Y	225	R&P fence
Ridgid JP0610	6 1/8 × 45	3 × 5,000	1	115/230	W	Y	Y	213	dual bevel fence
Sunhill CT-60L	7 × 52	3 × 4,500	1	110/220	W	N	N	220	
Transpower JT700	7 × 46	3 × 4,500	1	115	W	Y	NA	170	
General 80-100M1	7 1/4 × 45 1/4	3 × 4,800	1	115/230	W	Y	Y	275	
General 80-100LM1	7 1/4 × 55 1/4	3 × 4,800	1	115/230	W	Y	Y	297	
General 80-150LM1	7 1/4 × 55 1/4	3 × 4,800	1	115/230	L	Y	Y	297	
Bridgewood BW-8J	8 × 66	4 × 4,500	1 1/2	110/220	W	Y	Y	412	USA motor
Craftsman 20651	8 × 66	3 × 3,450	1 1/2	230	W	Y	NA	420	2 speed
■ Delta 37-380	8 × 72	3 × 5,600	1 1/2	115/230	L	Y	Y	414	R&P fence
Delta DJ-20	8 × 76 1/2	3 × 5,500	1 1/2	115/230	L	Y	Y	480	
General 480-1-M2	8 × 64	3 × 4,500	1 1/2	230	W	Y	Y	440	
■ Grizzly G1018	8 × 65	3 × 5,000	1 1/2	220	L	Y	Y	440	
Grizzly G1018HW	8 × 65	3 × 5,000	1 1/2	220	W	Y	Y	440	handwheel
■ Jet JJ-8CS	8 × 66 1/2	3 × 5,500	2	230	W	Y	Y	398	magnetic controls
North State CT 200	8 × 68	3 × 4,500	2	115/230	NA	Y	NA	500	magnetic controls
■ Powermatic 60	8 × 72	3 × 7,000	1 1/2	115/230	L/W	Y	Y	584	quick & fine adjust
Seco SK-0008JT	8 × 66	3 × 4,500	2	220	W	Y	NA	397	
Shop Fox W1684	8 × 70 3/4	3 × 5,500	2	220	W	Y	Y	400	magnetic top switch
Star WJ8	8 × 66	3 × 4,500	1 1/2	220	L	Y	Y	430	
Sunhill CT-204L	8 × 72	4 × 4,500	2	220	W	N	N	510	
Woodtek 907-064	8 × 67	3 × 4,500	1 1/2	115/230	W	Y	NA	455	
Yorkcraft YC-8J	8 × 72	3 × 4,800	1 1/2	110/220	L	Y	Y	406	R&P fence
Grizzly G9859	8 1/2 × 73 3/8	3 × 5,900	3	220	W	Y	Y	900	single phase
Lobo JT-1008	8 1/2 × 66	3 × 5,200	2	230	W	OPT	NA	400	
Transpower JT980	9 × 67	4 × 4,500	2	220	W	Y	NA	430	
■ Bridgewood BW-12J	13 × 85	4 × 5,000	3 or 5	220	W	Y	Y	980	jackscrews, USA motor
Delta DJ-30 37-360	12 × 84	3 × 5,000	3	230/460	L	Y	Y	706	
General 80-300 HC M1	12 × 80	hel. × 5,000	3	230	W	Y	Y	1,080	Helical cutterhead
Grizzly G4178	12 × 76	3 × 5,200	2	220	W	Y	Y	840	R&P fence
Lobo JT-0012	12 × 72	3 × 5,250	3	230	W	Y	NA	836	
North State CCA512	12 × 87	3 × 5,200	3	230	W	Y	NA	1,450	
Powermatic 1285	12 × 84	3 × 5,000	3	230	L	Y	Y	880	
Sunhill J-127L	12 × 84	3 × 4,500	3	230	L	Y	NA	900	avail. w/spiral cttrhed
Grizzly G9860	12 1/2 × 80	3 × 5,900	3	220	W	Y	Y	1,080	avail. w/helical head

key

K = knob
W = wheel
L = lever
L/W = both lever and wheel
Y = yes, N = no
NA = not available,
■ = *PW* Recommends

ALL SUPPLIES AND EQUIPMENT WERE CURRENT AT THE TIME OF ORIGINAL PUBLICATION AND ARE SUBJECT TO CHANGE.

miter saws

BY THE EDITORS OF *POPULAR WOODWORKING* MAGAZINE

We've been hearing a lot of discussions about the value of expensive aftermarket miter gauges for your table saw to ensure accurate and simple crosscuts. Then just the other day we all realized we tend to use our miter saws for crosscuts, hardly even setting up our miter gauges; they're that accurate and simple to use.

Many woodworkers use miter saws in place of a radial-arm saw for rough-cutting lumber, as well. There are lots of good reasons to include a miter saw in your shop.

Miter saws aren't difficult to use, but you can do a few things to get better use out of them. Let's start with outboard supports for long pieces of wood.

Most of the work done on a miter saw is crosscutting long, and often thin, pieces. The base of the saw is usually not big enough to adequately support the work. Most manufacturers include outrigger supports of some type that add another foot or so of support to either side of the tool.

Our suggestion is to go one better and either use roller stands to one side of the saw to support the material, or build a stand that will do the same job.

Setting Up for the Cut

Before making your first cut, it's a good idea to check a few things on the saw to ensure accuracy.

Start by checking the fence. Check it for both squareness to the saw table, and also for flatness across the width of the entire fence. Unfortunately, if everything isn't right, usually the only option is to send the tool (or just the fence) back. The fence may be able to be shimmed to improve the squareness to the table. Even if you can't fix it, you'll know it's a problem and be able to compensate for it.

Next, check the blade's angle to the table; it should be a 90° angle. If it's not, check your manual for changing the set screw (usually set to 0° on the scale) on a compound miter saw. Also check the 45° setting while you're at it. If you're using a straight miter saw with no beveling adjustment, the blade may not have an obvious adjustment, but check the manual to be sure.

One last setting to check is the depth of cut. This is usually set at the factory, but on many saws it's adjustable to best

BEFORE YOU BUY

- **MITER, COMPOUND OR SLIDING?.** In increasingly more pricey categories, you can purchase a miter saw (capable of straight and miter cuts up to 45°), a compound miter saw (to cut straight, miter and compound angles) and a sliding compound saw (all the above capabilities, with increased capacity). But what do you need, realistically? Most woodworkers don't need the capacity of a sliding miter saw, and a 12" compound saw can cost hundreds of dollars less.
- **MOTORS.** While the range of amperage varies for the universal motors used to power all the miter saws on the market, you'll be within 12 and 15 amps in most cases, and that will be plenty of power to handle your needs. More importantly, look for replaceable brushes, indicating anticipated longevity on the motor.
- **THE BASE.** Important features to consider are the clarity and adjustability of the miter settings on the base, as well as the smoothness of operation and how well the miter setting locks in place. This is where many of the differences between manufacturers can be found. The height and convenience of the fence are important, as well. A higher fence offers better support, but on compound saws it should be able to easily move out of the way for bevel cuts.
- **THE HANDLE.** Manufacturers are now offering a few different handle styles: horizontal, vertical or pistol style. Sears Craftsman even offers a miter saw with a handle that can be changed for your preference. It's a personal choice, but look at the options before you decide.
- **BLADES.** Simple. Don't buy it unless it's carbide.
- **DUST COLLECTION.** In most cases, the provided dust bag does an adequate job for quick work. But if you'll be using the saw often, hook it to a shop vacuum and it'll stay clean.

match your needs. In fact, some saws can be set to cut dadoes.

Making the Cut

On 98 percent of the miter saws on the market, you're going to use the blade itself to gauge where the cut will happen. A couple of manufacturers (and some aftermarket companies) have started adding laser indicators to their saws. These are useful, but they take a little getting used to. In any case, chances are you'll be using the blade to set up your cut.

Make a mark on the piece of wood where you want to make the cut. Without turning on the saw, lower the blade assembly until the guard retracts and the carbide teeth touch the wood. Adjust your piece so the blade aligns with the waste side of your pencil line. Raise the blade until the guard is again in place, while firmly holding (or clamping) the workpiece in place. Start the saw and lower the blade into the wood.

When the cut is complete, it's safest to leave the blade in the lowered position and release the switch to stop the blade. When it is stopped, raise the blade out of the way. This is safest because the waste piece can come in contact with the rising, still spinning blade and be kicked into harm's way or destroyed.

Mitered cuts use the same process, but beveled cuts (with the blade beveled to one side) will need to be more carefully aligned with your pencil mark. And make sure your fence is clear of the blade when making bevel cuts. Saw manufacturers sell more replacement fences that way!

If you're using a sliding miter saw, the process is basically the same, though when using the sliding feature, the blade should be pulled, fully extended toward you, before starting the saw. Then slowly push the blade assembly toward the rear, through the cut.

One other crosscut worth talking about is used for fitting pieces. You may make a cut at what you expect to be the correct length, then find out it's still a little long. The easy way to take off a little at a time to get the right fit is to lower the stopped blade all the way to the table, then slide the piece against the left side of the blade. This will tell you where the cut will occur, and you can either lift the blade and scoot the piece over a bit, or you can push against the blade a bit (there's usually just enough give in the blade to equal about $\frac{1}{32}$") then raise the blade and make your cut.

A quick word about choosing blades is appropriate here, as well. Depending on the brand and model saw you purchase, the equipped blade could be great, or just good enough to get you through your first project.

For use in a miter saw, your blade should be carbide-tipped for extended life and sharpness. A 60-tooth blade will provide a smooth, clean crosscut edge. For sliding miter saws, buy a blade with the teeth ground with a negative 5° hook angle; this will prevent overfeeding and climb-cutting during slide cuts.

RECOMMENDATIONS

Occasional User

- **DELTA MS275.** Not the cheapest miter saw, but it has great features and power.
- **HITACHI C10FCB.** Hitachi has a great reputation in miter saws and this well-priced 10" saw is a great basic choice.
- **CRAFTSMAN 21250.** This 10" miter saw with laser sighting is hard to keep in the stores. It's a solid saw with a nice extra feature for a good price.

Serious Home Woodworker

- **BOSCH 3912.** For increased capacity, we recommend moving to a 12" saw, and this model from Bosch is a good choice.
- **DEWALT DW705S.** Another 12" model that's proven itself durable on many job sites.

Advanced Woodworker or Professional

- **MAKITA LS1011N OR LS1013.** When recommending a sliding compound saw, we think first of Makita. Both of these 10" models are reliable, accurate saws that are a pleasure to use. The LS1013's features have made it a favorite in our shop.
- **HITACHI C8FB2.** This $8\frac{1}{2}$" model is very popular at job sites. It's a lightweight portable tool, and its quality performance is only slightly offset by its reduced capacity.

THESE TOOLS HAVE BEEN TESTED OR USED BY THE EDITORS OF *POPULAR WOODWORKING* MAGAZINE AND HAVE EARNED THEIR RECOMMENDATION. ALL SUPPLIES AND EQUIPMENT WERE CURRENT AT THE TIME OF ORIGINAL PUBLICATION AND ARE SUBJECT TO CHANGE.

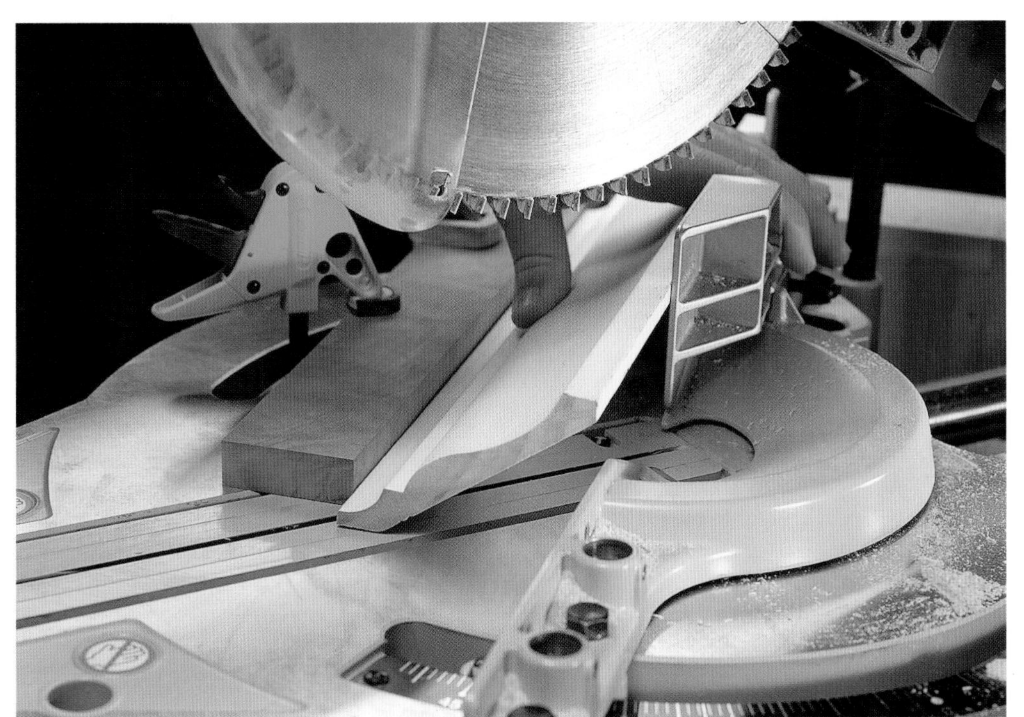

A high fence on a miter saw will cut crown moulding. With a compound miter saw, the blade can be set for miter and bevel and the piece can be cut flat on the table. But with a basic miter saw the setup at right will get you there with just the miter setting. The piece is positioned as it would be in place against the ceiling and wall, then held on the saw's table using a support board. Set the miter for 45° and you're on your way.

STATS

MODEL	BLADE DIA. (IN.)	MAX CROSSCUT T X W (IN.)	MITER RANGE (L, R)	BEVEL RANGE (L,R)	DEPTH STOP	AMPS	DUST COLLECTION	WEIGHT (LBS)	COMMENTS
STRAIGHT MITER									
Black & Decker BT1000	10	2×6	47, 47	N/A	N	15	VP	28	
Craftsman 21240	10	$2\frac{5}{8} \times 5\frac{3}{4}$	45, 45	N/A	Y	13	DB/VP	31	
Delta MS210	10	$2\frac{1}{4} \times 5\frac{3}{4}$	48, 50	N/A	N	13	VP	28	5 miter stops
Hitachi C10FM	10	$3\frac{1}{8} \times 4\frac{1}{4}$	47, 47	N/A	Y	13	DB/VP	27	9 miter stops
Makita LS1030N	10	$2\frac{3}{4} \times 5\frac{1}{8}$	45, 52	N/A	N	15	DB/VP	24	9 miter stops
Milwaukee 6490-6	10	$2\frac{1}{2} \times 5\frac{9}{16}$	51, 59	N/A	Y	15	DB/VP	32	steel blade
Ryobi TS1301DX	10	$3\frac{9}{16} \times 5\frac{9}{16}$	46, 46	N/A	Y	14	DB/VP	34	electric brake
Tradesman 8323	10	$2\frac{5}{8} \times 5\frac{3}{4}$	45, 45	N/A	Y	13	DB	32	electric brake
Makita LS1440	14	$4\frac{3}{4} \times 6$	45, 45	N/A	N	12	DB/VP	66	
Hitachi C15FB	15	$4\frac{3}{4} \times 7\frac{9}{32}$	52, 52	N/A	Y	15	DB/VP	55	table extensions
COMPOUND									
Craftsman 21218	$8\frac{1}{4}$	2×6	45, 45	0, 45	N	NA	DB/VP	21	18v cordless
Delta MS150	$8\frac{1}{4}$	$2\frac{1}{8} \times 5\frac{1}{8}$	45, 45	N/A	N	9	DB/VP	16	9 miter stops
Tradesman 8326	$8\frac{1}{2}$	$2\frac{1}{8} \times 5\frac{1}{4}$	45, 45	0, 45	Y	9	DB/VP	28	electric brake
Black & Decker BT1500	10	2×6	47, 47	-2, 47	N	15	DB/VP	30	
Bosch 3924	10	$3\frac{1}{2} \times 5\frac{1}{2}$	45, 45	-2, 47	Y	24v	DB/VP	30	w/2 batteries
Craftsman 21200	10	$2\frac{5}{8} \times 5\frac{1}{2}$	45, 45	0, 45	Y	15	DB/VP	29	
Craftsman 21213	10	$2\frac{5}{8} \times 5\frac{3}{4}$	45, 45	45, 0	Y	15	VP	34	sliding fence
■ Craftsman 21250	10	$2\frac{5}{8} \times 5\frac{3}{4}$	45, 45	45, 0	Y	15	VP	34	laser guided
Delta MS250	10	$2\frac{3}{8} \times 5\frac{3}{4}$	47, 47	48, -3	N	13	DB/VP	28	5 miter stops
Delta MS350	10	$2\frac{3}{8} \times 5\frac{3}{4}$	47, 47	48, -3	N	15	DB/VP	34	
■ Delta MS275	10	$2\frac{3}{4} \times 5\frac{5}{8}$	47, 47	48, -3	N	15	DB/VP	33	table extensions
DeWalt DW703	10	2×6	50, 50	0, 48	N	15	DB/VP	33	11 miter stops
■ Hitachi C10FCB	10	$2\frac{5}{8} \times 5\frac{3}{4}$	60, 45	45, 0	Y	15	DB/VP	31	pivoting fence
Hitachi C10FCD	10	$2\frac{27}{32} \times 5\frac{5}{8}$	45, 45	45, 45	Y	13	DB	33	10 miter stops
Makita LS1040	10	$2\frac{3}{4} \times 5\frac{1}{8}$	45, 52	45, 0	N	15	DB/VP	24	pivoting fence
Milwaukee 6494-6	10	$2\frac{1}{2} \times 5\frac{9}{16}$	51, 59	50, 3	Y	15	DB/VP	38	tall flip fence
Ridgid MS1060	10	$2\frac{1}{2} \times 5\frac{5}{8}$	48, 48	-3, 48	Y	15	DB/VP	34	extensions, stop block
Ryobi TS1350DX	10	2×6	47, 47	-2, 47	N	15	DB/VP	30	
Tradesman 8329N	10	$2\frac{5}{8} \times 5\frac{3}{4}$	45, 45	0, 45	Y	13	DB/VP	38	electric brake
Wilton 99164	10	$2\frac{3}{4} \times 5\frac{1}{8}$	0, 45	0, 45	Y	13	DB/VP	38	
■ Bosch 3912	12	$3\frac{7}{8} \times 7\frac{5}{8}$	52, 52	47, -3	Y	15	DB/VP	43	sliding fence
Craftsman 21224	12	$5\frac{7}{8} \times 7\frac{7}{8}$	45, 45	45, 0	Y	15	DB/VP	41	laser guided
Delta 36-255	12	$2\frac{1}{2} \times 8$	47, 47	48, -3	N	15	DB/VP	63	
Delta 36-255L	12	$2\frac{1}{2} \times 8$	47, 47	48, -3	N	15	DB/VP	65	twin laser guided
■ DeWalt DW705S	12	2×8	48, 48	0, 48	N	15	DB/VP	40	tall sliding fence
DeWalt DW706	12	2×8	50, 50	48, 48	N	15	DB/VP	44	double bevel
Hitachi C12FSA	12	$4\frac{7}{32} \times 12$	57, 57	45, 45	Y	12	DB	55	
Makita LS1220	12	$3\frac{7}{8} \times 6$	48, 48	45, 0	N	15	DB/VP	38	soft start
Porter-Cable 3802	12	$2\frac{1}{2} \times 8$	48, 48	47, 2	N	15	DB/VP	63	
Ridgid MS1250LS	12	$2\frac{3}{4} \times 7$	48, 48	3, 48	Y	15	DB/VP	45	includes leg stand
Ryobi TS1550DX	12	2×8	47, 47	0, 45	N	15	DB/VP	51	
SLIDING COMPOUND									
Makita LS0711Z	$7\frac{1}{2}$	$2 \times 7\frac{1}{8}$	47, 57	45, 0	Y	10	DB/VP	23	
Makita LS711DWBEK	$7\frac{1}{2}$	$2 \times 7\frac{1}{8}$	47, 57	45, 0		18 v	DB/VP	23	w/2 batteries
■ Hitachi C8FB2	$8\frac{1}{2}$	$2\frac{9}{16} \times 12$	45, 57	47, 0	Y	9.5	DB/VP	39	3 bevel stops
Tradesman 8336	$8\frac{1}{2}$	$2\frac{9}{16} \times 12$	45, 60	45, 0	Y	10	DB/VP	50	extension wings
Bosch 3915	10	$3\frac{1}{2} \times 12$	52, 62	47, -2	Y	13	DB/VP	47	table extension
Delta 36-240	10	$3\frac{5}{8} \times 11\frac{1}{2}$	57, 47	45, 0	Y	15	DB/VP	51	work clamp
Delta 36-250	10	$3\frac{5}{8} \times 11\frac{1}{2}$	57, 47	45, 0	Y	15	DB/VP	56	folding stand
Hitachi C10FS	10	$3\frac{17}{32} \times 12\frac{9}{32}$	45, 60	45, 45	Y	12	DB/VP	44	soft start
■ Makita LS1011N	10	$2\frac{5}{16} \times 12$	45, 57	45, 0	Y	13	DB/VP	35	single pole
■ Makita LS1013	10	$3\frac{5}{8} \times 12$	47, 52	45, 45	Y	13	DB/VP	47	dual pole
Milwaukee 6496-6	10	$3\frac{1}{2} \times 12$	51, 59	48, 3	Y	15	DB/VP	52	dual pole
Milwaukee 6497-6	10	$3\frac{1}{2} \times 12$	51, 59	48, 3	Y	15	DB/VP	56	table extensions
Porter-Cable 3807	10	$3\frac{5}{8} \times 11\frac{1}{2}$	57, 47	45, 0	Y	15	DB/VP	57	dual pole
Bosch 4412	12	4×12	50, 60	47, 47	Y	15	DB/VP	59	up front controls
Craftsman 21292	12	$4 \times 12\frac{5}{8}$	45, 45	NA	Y	15	DB/VP	74	2 dust ports
DeWalt DW708	12	$4\frac{1}{2} \times 12$	50, 60	48, 48	Y	15	DB/VP	57	tall sliding fences
Makita LS1212	12	$3\frac{7}{8} \times 12\frac{1}{4}$	47, 60	45, 45	Y	15	DB/VP	49	dual pole
Ridgid MS1290	12	$3 \times 13\frac{1}{2}$	60, 60	47, 47	Y	15	DB/VP	64	11 miter stops

key

NA = not available
DB = dust bag
VP = vacuum port
DB/VP = both
■ *PW* Recommends

ALL SUPPLIES AND EQUIPMENT WERE CURRENT AT THE TIME OF ORIGINAL PUBLICATION AND ARE SUBJECT TO CHANGE.

mortisers

BY THE EDITORS OF *POPULAR WOODWORKING* MAGAZINE

Mortisers seem like simple machines to use. Heck, they're just a drill press with an extra bushing that holds a square chisel, right? Well, if they were so simple, we wouldn't hear about all the problems readers have setting up and using them without stalling, burning and cutting mismatched joints.

Mortisers require a little finesse. But once you know the tricks, you'll blaze through your work.

Start with the Chisel

Mortiser tooling comes in two parts: a square, hollow chisel and a round auger bit that spins in the center of the chisel. Before you install the chisel in the mortiser, check to see if it's square by measuring its width both ways using a dial caliper. Choose the dimension that is closest to the dimension the chisel is supposed to be and use those two sides to determine the thickness of your mortise. Mark the chisel so you always install it this way.

To install the tooling with the proper amount of space between the chisel and bit, first put the chisel in place and let it drop down 1/8" from the bushing and secure it in place. Thread the auger through the chisel and into the chuck. Push its tip up against the chisel and tighten the chuck. Now loosen the screw that holds the chisel in place and push it all the way up to the bushing. You now have a 1/8" gap between the chisel and the bit. This is a good place to start. If you reduce this gap to 1/16", you'll make smaller chips, which are less likely to stall a slow-speed mortiser. Different woods require different gaps, so don't be afraid to experiment a bit with gaps.

Set the Table and Fence

Most people assume that their table is a perfect 90° to the chisel. Don't make this mistake. Check this angle using a square and then shim the

BEFORE YOU BUY

- **MOTOR.** We've used every benchtop machine on the market. With the smaller motor, the fast-speed mortisers are best. There's less stalling and we found little heat buildup if the chisel and auger bit were set up correctly. With the floor-model mortisers, the bigger motor works well at slow speeds.
- **HOLD-DOWNS.** Next to stalling, the No. 1 complaint of most benchtop mortiser users is that the hold-down slips during use. On the floor-model mortisers, the hold-downs are generally excellent and have a sliding table to boot.
- **CHISELS.** We've heard complaints that the chisels that come with the machines are of lesser quality. We haven't found this to be the case. If you sharpen your tooling and take care of it, it will serve you well for years to come.
- **CAPACITY.** Many people overlook two important statistics with mortisers: the maximum height under the chisel and the maximum distance between the fence and chisel. A significant difference here can be the difference between a simple setup and getting out your mortising chisel to cut a few that your machine just can't reach.

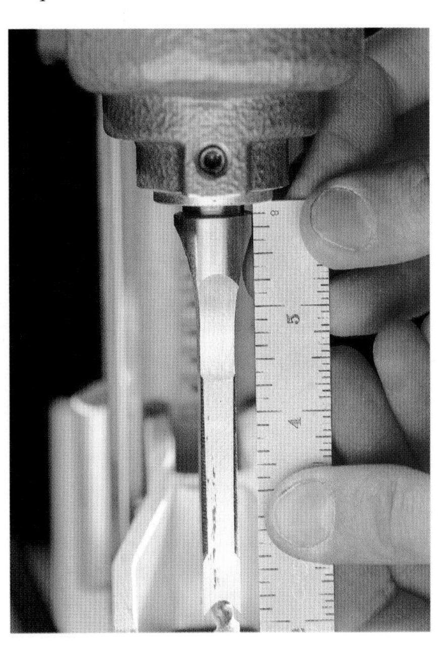

You can control precisely how much clearance there is between the auger bit and chisel bit by first mounting the chisel bit and backing it out of the bushing by the amount of clearance you want. Next, install the auger bit pushed all the way up into the chisel bit. Then loosen the screw in the chisel bit and push it all the way into the bushing.

The secret to cleaning out the bottom of your mortise is to go back over your work once you've cut the shape of the entire mortise. I repeatedly raise and lower the head of the mortiser about $\frac{1}{2}$" while moving the workpiece in small increments side to side.

Cut one hole, skip a space, then cut another. If you cut one right next to the other, you are heading for a bad bend or break in the chisel or auger bit.

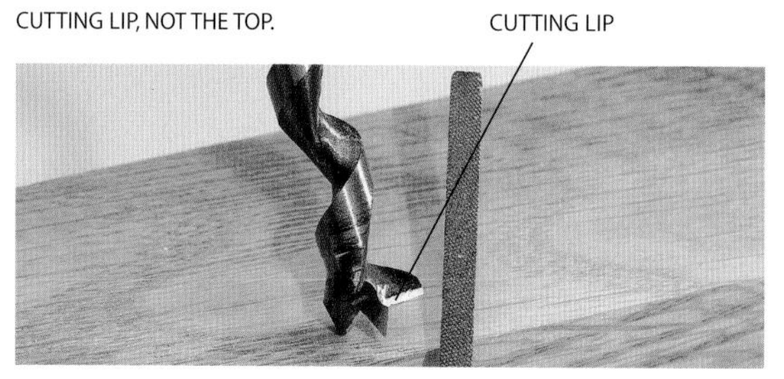

When you sharpen the cutting spur of your auger bit, try not to touch the cutting lip (above). When you sharpen the cutting lip, stroke the file upward into the bit and try not to change the cutting angle.

RECOMMENDATIONS

Occasional User

The occasional user can get by with using an inexpensive mortising attachment on a drill press, chain drilling or using a router to cut mortises.

Serious Home Woodworker

- **BRIDGEWOOD HM-11.** Low on frills, but its motor grinds through anything.
- **GRIZZLY G3183.** Virtually the same as the Bridgewood, the G3183 is inexpensive and powerful.
- **SHOP FOX W1671.** This machine has the capacity of a floor-model mortiser. It's hard to beat.

Advanced Woodworker or Professional

- **MULTICO PM-12.** The top-of-the-line benchtop machine. The holddown is the best of all the benchtops and the motor is gutsy.
- **POWERMATIC 719A.** This floor-model mortiser has sliding tables and a front-mounted clamp to hold your work securely. We use this machine in our shop, and it's now a common sight in small professional shops.

THESE TOOLS HAVE BEEN TESTED OR USED BY THE EDITORS OF *POPULAR WOODWORKING* MAGAZINE AND HAVE EARNED THEIR RECOMMENDATION. ALL SUPPLIES AND EQUIPMENT WERE CURRENT AT THE TIME OF ORIGINAL PUBLICATION AND ARE SUBJECT TO CHANGE.

MODEL	MOTOR HORSE POWER	SPEED/ RPM	LENGTH	HEIGHT	FENCE MAX." FENCE TO CHISEL*	FENCE MAX DEPTH UNDER HOLDDOWN	MIN. DEPTH UNDER HOLDDOWN	MAX SPINDLE TRAVEL	CHISEL BUSHINGS INCLUDED	CHISELS INCLUDED
BENCHTOP MACHINES										
■ Bridgewood HM-11	1/2	3,400	13 3/4	1 9/16	2 5/8	3 1/4	1 5/8	4 5/16	5/8, 3/4	none
Craftsman 21906	1/2	1,725	13 5/8	1 5/8	2 3/8	4 3/4	1 3/4	3 7/8	5/8	3/8"
Delta MM300	1/2	1,725	13 3/4	1 9/16	2 1/8	3 3/4***	1 15/16	3 5/8	5/8	1/4", 5/16", 3/8", 1/2"
Delta 14-651	1/2	1,725	13 5/8	2 15/16	2 1/8†	3 3/4†	1 15/16†	5†	5/8	1/4", 5/16", 3/8", 1/2"
Fisch BTM99-44252	1/2	1,725	13 9/16	1 5/8	2 9/16	3 1/4	1 5/8	3 3/4	5/8	1/4", 3/8", 1/2"
General 75-050 M1	1/2	1,720	11 1/16	2	3 1/8	5 1/4	1	5 1/4	5/8, 3/4	1/4", 5/16", 3/8", 1/2"
■ Grizzly G3183	1/2	3,450	13 3/4	1 9/16	2 5/8	3 1/4	1 5/8	4 5/16	5/8, 3/4	none
Jet JBM-5	1/2	1,725	14	1 9/16	2 5/8	3 5/8	1 3/4	4 5/16	5/8, 3/4	1/4", 3/8", 1/2"
■ Multico PM12	1/2	3,470	13 3/4	1 9/16	3 1/2	3 3/8	1 1/2	4	5/8	3/8"
Record RPM75	1/2	3,400	6	1	3 3/4†	6†	1	3 1/8	none	none
■ Shop Fox W1671	3/4	3,450	16	2 1/8	2 1/4	8 1/16	2 1/8	9 1/4	5/8, 3/4	1/2"
Woodtek 876-775	1/2	1,725	13 3/4	1 9/16	2 5/8	3 1/4	1 5/8	4 3/4	5/8, 3/4	none
Woodtek 900-881	1	1,725	18 3/4	1 9/16	3 3/4†	4 1/4	1 5/8	5 1/4†	5/8, 3/4, 1 1/8	none
FLOOR MODEL MACHINES										
Bridgewood MS-10	1	3,600	20	3 5/8	3 1/4†	NA	NA	5 1/4†	5/8, 3/4	none
Fisch FM99-66252	1	1,140	26	3 5/8	2 7/8†	6	3 5/8	7 1/2†	1/4, 5/8, 3/4, 1	1/4", 5/16", 3/8", 1/2"
General 75-075 M1	1	1,720	19	3 1/2	3†	NA	NA	6†	5/8, 3/4	1/4", 3/8", 1/2", 3/4"
Grizzly G8620	1	3,450	20 1/2	3 3/4	NA	NA	NA	5†	NA	none
Grizzly G4814	2	1,725/3,450	21 1/4	2 7/8	4 5/8	10 1/2	1	4	5/8, 3/4	1/4", 3/8", 1/2"
■ Powermatic 719A	1	1,720	20	4 1/4	3 7/8	NA	NA	7 1/4	5/8, 3/4, 1 1/8	none
Woodtek 924-020	1	1,725	20 5/8	8 3/4	3 1/2†	NA	NA	5†	5/8, 3/4, 1 1/8	none

STATS

key

*All measurements were taken with a 3/8" chisel and bit installed, which is why these measurements will sometimes disagree with those supplied by the manufacturer.

†= as reported by manufacturer.

***Add Delta's 14-611 height adjuster to this machine and it will increase the capacity to 5 3/4".

NA = not applicable or not available.

■ = *PW* Recommends

underside of the table using masking tape until you get a perfect 90°. This will prevent all sorts of problems.

Now set your chisel so it is parallel to your fence. You'll have to rotate the chisel slightly, make a test cut and readjust your chisel until you get it right. Once the chisel is square to the fence, make a sample cut in some scrap and set it aside. That scrap will help you set up your mortiser even faster next time.

Set the Depth

The depth of the mortise shouldn't be the length of the tenon. It should be a little deeper. About 1/16" or so will be fine. The deeper mortise prevents your tenons from ever hitting the bottom of your mortise. It also gives any excess glue in your joint a place to collect — instead of squeezing out.

Use Your Machine Correctly

Many beginning mortiser users will break a chisel in tough woods or after a long session of mortising. Usually this is a problem with their technique.

Here's how to avoid this problem: When making a hole with your mortiser, make your first plunge cut, then move your work (or your sliding table) so that you skip a space that's nearly equal to the width of the chisel. Then make another plunge. Now go back and clean up the waste between the holes.

If you make one hole right after another, the chisel will tend to bend toward one side. After a certain amount of stress, your tooling will break.

After you've completed a mortise, you want to go back and clean up the gunk at the bottom.

Sharpening Your Tooling

Dull tooling is another source of woe. A simple auger bit file is the best tool to touch up the auger bit. Always remove as little metal as possible and try to keep the cutting angles the same.

To sharpen the chisel, you can use a conical sharpening stone. Touch up the inside four edges and then remove the resulting burr on the outside with one pass on a fine-grit sharpening stone. Again, remove as little metal as possible to avoid changing the width of your chisel.

thickness planers

BY THE EDITORS OF *POPULAR WOODWORKING* MAGAZINE

Few machines are as magical as thickness planers. Put a rough-as-a-cob board in one end and something beautiful comes out the other. With prices on these machines dropping like a rock, they're a must-have machine in the home workshop. But before you start turning that cherry into chips, read this tutorial to ensure you get flat and flawless boards.

Planer Needs a Partner

One of the biggest mistakes beginners make is that they buy a planer and don't buy a jointer to go with it. By itself, a planer has a difficult time producing a dressed piece of wood that's true. That's because the planer is designed to make a finished surface that's parallel to the surface that runs against the bed of the machine. If the board is bowed on both sides when it goes in, it likely will be bowed when it comes out.

Another complication with planers is that the feed rollers that move the wood under the knives will press most wood flat for planing. Put a board with a cup or a twist through a planer, and the feed rollers will likely press it flat during the cut. But when the board comes out the other side, it will spring back to its original cupped or twisted shape. So you need one flat face on each board.

By first running one face of the board over the jointer (called face jointing), you'll remove the cup, bow or twist from one face. Then the planer will take it off the other side.

You can get around owning a jointer by feeding your wood on top of a piece of plywood and shimming the high spots to prevent the feed rollers from pressing the board flat. Do this a few times, and you'll want a jointer.

Setup is Simple

Planers are generally easy to set up, adjust and use. You want to make sure the cutterhead is parallel to the bed. Do this by checking the distance between the two using a dial indicator or even a plain old block of wood. Once you get the head

PLANING FIGURED STOCK

To overcome tear-out in figured wood, try this trick. Take a rag that is wet (but not dripping wet) with clean water. Thoroughly wipe the face of the board to be planed, adding more water to the rag as needed. Repeat, then give the water a minute to soak in and soften the wood fibers. I usually wet a board, then run another one while waiting. Each pass will require wetting. I've had excellent results using this technique.

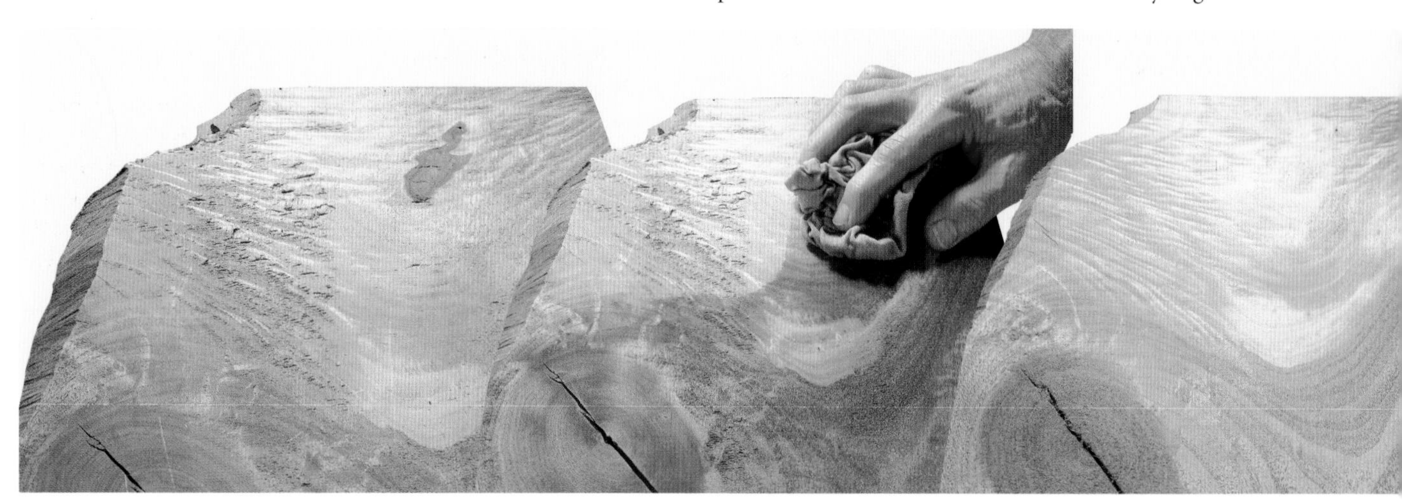

This piece of crotch walnut has great figure, but it also is almost impossible to surface without tear-out.

To help reduce tear-out, wipe the board with a wet rag before planing and allow the water to soak into the fibers.

With any luck, your next pass will result in a board that is virtually free of tear-out.

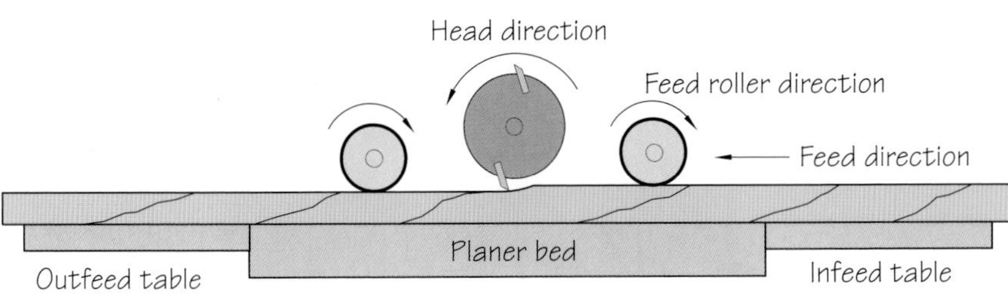

parallel, plane a board and check the thickness on the left and right edges with a dial caliper. They should be the same thickness.

With portable planers, there's not much else to do: Adjust the infeed and outfeed tables so they are in the same plane as the bed and you're ready to go.

If you own a stationary machine, you likely will need to adjust the height of the feed rollers, the chip breaker, the bed rollers and the pressure bar. All these adjustments will be covered in your machine's manual. If you don't get all these elements working together, you'll find your wood stalling under the cutterhead, refusing to go into the planer or tearing out like a woodchuck has been feasting upon it.

One more suggestion before you get started: Buy a dust collector for your planer. Planers are the messiest machines on the planet. And without dust collection, the chips are also likely to get embedded in your work, adding to your sanding chores.

BEFORE YOU BUY

- **BENCHTOP VS. STATIONARY.** Most home woodworkers opt for a benchtop planer because they're inexpensive, don't take up a lot of space, and produce a finished surface that's equal to most stationary models. Stationary planers excel when it comes to dealing with rough lumber and when you need to plane for hours on end. In the end, buy as much raw power as you can afford.
- **KNIVES.** The most annoying maintenance chore on a planer is changing the knives. On many (but not all) portable planers, this operation is a snap. If you buy a portable planer, make sure the knives are easy to change. On stationary machines, changing the knives is as much fun as going to the dentist. We recommend machines that come with springs installed in the cutterhead or at least jackscrews.
- **ROLLERS.** On portable planers, the infeed and outfeed rollers are generally rubber, so there's not much choice here. On stationary models, insist on a machine with a serrated steel infeed roller. Adjustable bed rollers will help you move rough stock through the machine more easily.
- **SNIPE.** Don't get worked up about snipe. All planers snipe to some degree. (Snipe is when the ends of the board are planed slightly thinner.) And most models can be adjusted to produce boards with acceptable snipe.
- **SPEEDS.** If you can afford a machine that has two feed speeds, get it. This handy feature slows down the feed rate to get a better finished surface. This means less sanding.

Tricks to Better Boards

Jointing and planing your wood are the first critical steps in any project. Any problems you have there will multiply as you proceed into the job. Follow these simple procedures and you'll produce flat boards that need little sanding.

After jointing one face, get ready to feed the boards through the planer. You want to take light cuts, usually about $^{1}/_{16}$" or less with a portable planer. Be sure to stand to one side of the planer as you feed the boards — never directly in front. Kickbacks are rare, but they do happen.

Feed the boards through the planer with the grain on the edges running downhill. This is commonly known as cutting with the grain. See the illustration above for details. This will greatly reduce tear-out. If a board is tearing out, turn it around and try it the other way.

After a board is planed completely on one side, flip the board to plane the other face after each pass. You want to remove equal amounts of wood from each face of the board. This will keep you from introducing warp into the board as it is planed. You see, there are internal stresses in many pieces of wood (have you ever seen the kerf close on your table saw's blade?). If you remove material from only one side of a board, there's a chance it will bow during planing.

If your stock is long or you

RECOMMENDATIONS

Occasional User

- **DELTA TP400LS.** This $12^{1}/_{2}$" portable planer has a good price and knife-changing is easy.
- **DEWALT DW733.** Rugged and powerful, this 12" planer is an excellent machine.
- **RIDGID TP1300LS.** This well-made machine has many refinements and a lifetime warranty to boot.
- **CRAFTSMAN 21743.** The first planer with on-board dust collection. The dust system works, and we're impressed.

Serious Home Woodworker

- **DELTA 22-580.** This new 13" benchtop machine has two feed speeds and a lot of high-end features.
- **YORKCRAFT YC-15P.** You'll be hard pressed to find another 15" planer with all these features, including two speeds, a cabinet base and bed rollers, for such a great price. Shipping is expensive out West.
- **GRIZZLY G1021Z.** This deluxe planer has all the features you want: steel rollers, two speeds and lots of power.
- **JET JPM-13 & 13CS.** These 13" induction-motor planers give you many features of floor-model planers and the ability to cut hundreds of moulding profiles.

Advanced Woodworker or Professional

- **GRIZZLY G1033.** Hands down the best deal in the 20" planer market. The G1033 has many of the features found on its competitors — except for the price.

THESE TOOLS HAVE BEEN TESTED OR USED BY THE EDITORS OF *POPULAR WOODWORKING* MAGAZINE AND HAVE EARNED THEIR RECOMMENDATION.

are working alone, use a roller stand or some other outfeed table to support the stock as it comes out of the machine. This will reduce snipe (as well as keep your boards from crashing to the ground).

Here are some other tips for special situations:

• Making legs: If you've got parts that are square (such as table legs), your best bet is to plane them to square instead of ripping them square on the table saw. This will produce the most consistent results.

• Planing panels: If you are planing down a glued-up slab, first remove all the glue that you can. Choose the face that seems flattest and run it face-down. Take light passes until the top face is flat. Then turn the slab over and plane the other side.

• Tricky boards: Wildly figured woods are tricky to plane without tear-out. Here are a couple of tricks to reduce your difficulties with problem woods. When you feed the stock through the planer, try feeding it at an angle, effectively creating a shearing cut. Through the power of geometry, this effectively lowers the cutting angle of your planer's knives, producing a cleaner cut.

Another trick is to wet the boards before feeding them through the planer. See the photos on page 110 for more details on this.

• Thin stock: If you need to plane stock down to $^1/_4$" thick or slightly less, you'll need to make a bed board for your planer — essentially an accessory planer bed. Planing thin stock can be tricky. If there's a slight bow, we've seen entire boards disappear into the cutterhead, never to be seen again (until we empty the dust collector, that is). So always make a little extra stock for this operation and make certain it is as flat as possible.

Once both sides of your board have all the rough milling marks removed, you need to flip the board every time it goes through the planer. The object is to remove equal amounts of wood from each side to reduce any warping in the board because of stresses being released in the wood as you plane. To keep the grain direction running the same way, here's how we flip a board: Hold the board in your left hand as if you are going to feed it that way into the planer. With your right hand, slap the front edge of the board downward. Allow the board to twirl in your left hand until the other face is facing up. Feed the board through the planer this way. This method allows you to work fast and reduces the effort needed to flip each board.

PLANING 8"-WIDE BOARDS WITH A 6" JOINTER

One of the thorniest problems in preparing stock is how to deal with boards that are too wide for your jointer to joint. This trick works with boards that are as wide as 8". A reader showed us this trick and it has become a shop favorite.

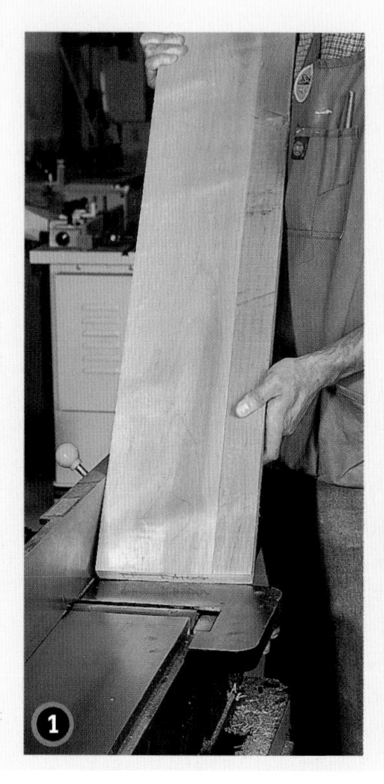

First, remove the guard from your jointer. Surface as much of one side of the board as you can. Make several passes and go to a depth of less than $^1/_4$".

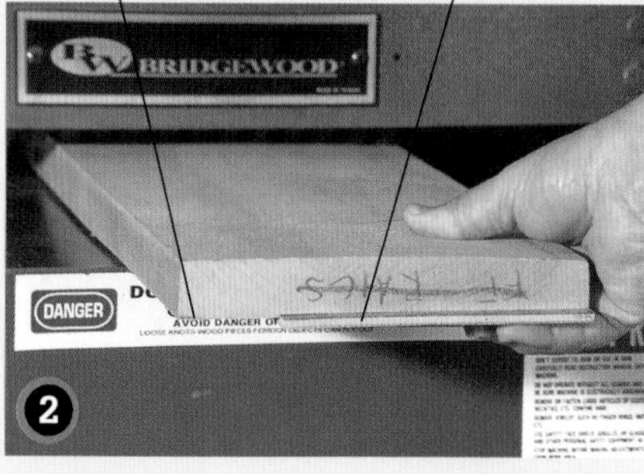

Now get a piece of $^1/_4$"-thick plywood that is as long as the board you are planing and 6" wide. Place the plywood in the notch you just jointed and run the two through the planer together with the plywood running against the bed of the planer. Make several passes until the face has been completely planed.

Now turn the board over and plane the opposite face. After the rough strip has been removed, continue planing normally until you get to your finished thickness.

STATS

BRAND/MODEL	MAX STOCK (T × W IN.)	MAX CUT DEPTH (IN.)	KNIVES # × RPM	BED MATERIAL	BED ROLLERS	FEED ROLLERS	HP	VOLTS	WEIGHT (LBS.)	COMMENTS
BENCHTOP										
Craftsman 21722	4 1/2 × 12	3/32	2 × 9,400	S	N	R	2 1/2	115	69	dust collector w/1/2 bag
Craftsman 21733	5 × 13	3/32	3 × 4,500	CI	N	R	2 1/2	115	135	planer/moulder
Delta TP300	6 × 12	3/16	2 × 8,000	S	N	R	15 amp	120	62	
Grizzly G1017	6 × 12	1/16	2 × 8,500	S	N	R	2	115	85	4 columns/ w/knife setting jig
Makita 2012NB	6 × 12	1/8	2 × 8,500	S	N	R	15 amp	115	62	reversible knives
Hitachi P12RA	6 5/8 × 12 1/4	3/32	2 × 10,400	S	N	R	2 2/5	115	83.5	jointer/planer
■ Delta TP400LS	6 × 12 1/2	1/8	2 × 8,000	S	N	R	15 amp	120	68	includes leg set
■ DeWalt DW733	6 × 12 1/2	1/8	2 × 10,000	S	N	R	3	115	80	resharpenable knives
Grizzly G8794	6 × 12 1/2	1/16	2 × 8,500	S	N	R	2	115	85	jackscrews, reversible knives
Jet JWP-12DX	6 × 12 1/2	3/32	2 × 8,000	CI	N	R	2	115	69	depth gauge, hed. lock, double-edged knives
Seco SK-0012WP	6 × 12 1/2	1/8	2 × 8,000	CI	Y	R	2	115	67	
Sunhill CT-345	6 × 12 1/2	1/8	2 × NA	NA	NA	NA	2	NA	67	
■ Craftsman 21743	6 × 13	3/32	2 × 8,000	S	N	R	2 1/2	115	105	dust collector w/1/2 bag
■ Delta 22-580	6 1/2 × 13	1/16	2 × 10,000	S	N	R	15 amp	120	97	two feed speeds
■ Ridgid TP1300LS	6 × 13	1/8	2 × 9,500	S	N	R	3	120	82	stand, chute, ex. knives inc.
Ryobi AP1300	6 × 13	1/8	2 × 8,000	S	N	R	NA	115	74	reversible knives
FLOOR										
Williams & Hussey	8 × 7	3/4	2 × 3,450	CI	N	U	2	110/220	200	moulder
Shopsmith Pro Planer	4 × 12	1/8	3 × 5,750	CI	N	S, R	1 3/4	115	151	variable speed
Belsaw 1120002	6 1/4 × 12 3/8	3/16	3 × 4,500	CI	N	R	5	220	350	moulder
Woodmaster 712	6 3/4 × 12 1/2	3/16	3 × 4,200	CI	N	R, S OPT	5	230	300	
General 30-100 M1	6 × 13	1/8	3 × 4,500	CI	N	R	1 1/2	230	275	
Grizzly G1037	6 × 13	1/8	3 × 5,000	CI	N	R	1 1/2	110/220	240	moulder
■ Jet JPM-13	6 × 13	1/16	3 × 4,500	CI	N	R	1 1/2	115/230	209	moulder
■ Jet JPM-13CS	6 × 13	1/16	3 × 4,500	CI	N	R	1 1/2	115/230	269	moulder
General 130-1	6 × 14	1/8	3 × 4,500	CI	Y	S	3	230	520	jackscrews
Grizzly G1021	6 1/8 × 14 7/8	1/8	3 × 5,000	CI	Y	S	2	220	440	roller extnsns
■ Grizzly G1021Z	6 1/8 × 14 7/8	1/8	3 × 5,000	CI	Y	S	3	220	540	closed stand
Jet JWP-15CS	6 × 15	1/8	3 × 4,500	CI	Y	S	3	230	502	closed stand
Powermatic 15	6 × 14 7/8	1/8	3 × 4,500	CI	Y	S	3	230	484	
Bridgewood BW-15P	6 × 15	1/8	3 × 4,500	CI	Y	S	3	220	465	jackscrews, closed stand
Craftsman 22615	6 × 15	1/8	3 × 5,000	CI	Y	S, R	3	230	560	2 speeds, roller extnsns
Lobo WP-0015	6 × 15	3/16	3 × 4,500	CI	Y	S, R	3	230	480	2 speeds
Seco SK-0015WP	6 × 15	1/8	3 × 4,500	CI	Y	R	3	230	480	
Star WPL15	6 × 15	1/8	3 × 5,000	CI	Y	S	3	220	480	
Sunhill CT-38B	6 × 15	1/4	3 × 5,000	CI	Y	S	3	220	500	
Sunhill CT-345	6 × 15	1/4	3 × 5,000	NA	NA	NA	3	NA	500	
Transpower AP900	6 × 15	1/4	3 × 5,600	CI	Y	S	3	220	485	
Woodtek 875-001	6 × 15	1/8	3 × 3,450	CI	Y	S	2	230	470	knife tool inc.
■ Yorkcraft YC-15P	6 × 15	1/8	3 × 5,000	CI	Y	S, R	3	230	427	jackscrews
Delta 22-680	6 1/2 × 15	1/8	3 × 5,000	CI	Y	S	3	230	340	jackscrews
North State 315	6 1/2 × 15	3/16	3 × 5,000	CI	Y	S	3	230	500	2 speeds
General 30-125 MI	7 × 15	1/8	3 × 5,000	CI	Y	S	3	230	539	
Sunhill CT-400D	6 × 16	1/4	3 × 5,000	CI	N	S, R	3	220	700	
Transpower AP800	8 × 16	1/4	3 × 5,600	CI	Y	S, R	3	220	485	
RBI 816	8 × 16 1/4	5/16	4 × 4,600	S	N	U	5	230	440	
Powermatic 180	6 × 18	1/4	3 × 4,800	CI	Y	S	5	230/460	1,523	quick change cttrhed, var. feed rate
Woodmaster 718	6 3/4 × 18 1/2	3/16	3 × 4,200	CI	N	R, S OPT	5	220	480	
Seco SK-820WP	6 × 20	3/8	3 × 5,400	CI	N	S	5	220	1,300	
Bridgewood BW-200P	6 1/2 × 20	1/4	3 × 5,000	CI	Y	S	5	230	780	jackscrews, USA motor
Seco SK-720-WP	6 1/2 × 20	1/4	3 × 5,200	CI	N	S	5	220	770	
Lobo WP-2000	7 × 20	1/4	3 × 5,500	CI	Y	S, R	3	230	850	
Woodtek 816-427	7 × 20	3/16	3 × 5,000	CI	Y	S	3	230	981	

BRAND/MODEL	MAX STOCK (T × W IN.)	MAX CUT DEPTH (IN.)	KNIVES # × RPM	BED MATERIAL	BED ROLLERS	FEED ROLLERS	HP	VOLTS	WEIGHT (LBS.)	COMMENTS
FLOOR (CONTINUED)										
Woodtek 816-434	7 × 20	3/16	3 × 6,000	CI	Y	S	5	230	981	3 phase
Grizzly G5850Z	7 3/4 × 20	1/8	4 × 5,200	CI	Y	S	5	220	900	17–26 ft. per min.
Lobo WP-1120	7 7/8 × 20	1/4	3 × 5,000	CI	Y	S, R	3	230	770	
Bridgewood BW-120P	8 × 20	1/4	3 × 5,200	CI	Y	S, U	5 or 7 1/2	220	1,320	jackscrews, spiral cttrhed
Craftsman 22622	8 × 20	1/8	4 × 5,000	CI	Y	S	3	230	792	2 speeds, extns rollers
General 30-300 MI	8 × 20	3/32	3 × 5,000	CI	Y	S	3	230	880	
General 330	8 × 20	1/8	4 × 4,000	CI	Y	S	5	230	2,100	
Lobo WP-0020	8 × 20	1/4	4 × 5,000	CI	Y	S, R	3	230	770	
North State CT-508	8 × 20	1/4	4 × 5,000	CI	Y	S	5	230	950	
Powermatic 208	8 × 20	3/32	4 × 5,000	CI	Y	S	3	230	640	opt. 5 hp, 3ph
Seco SK-0020WP	8 × 20	1/4	4 × 5,000	CI	Y	R	3	230	771	
Star WPL20	8 × 20	1/8	4 × 5,000	CI	Y	S	3	220	780	
Sunhill CT-508	8 × 20	1/4	4 × 5,000	CI	Y	S	3	220	925	
Sunhill P-20	8 × 20	1/4	3 × NA	NA	NA	NA	5	220	1,150	
Transpower AP200A	8 × 20	1/4	4 × 5,600	CI	Y	S, R	3	220	860	
Transpower AP720	8 × 20	1/4	3 × 5,200	CI	Y	S	7 1/2	230	891	
Woodtek 924-083	8 × 20	1/8	4 × 5,000	CI	Y	S	3	220	771	5" dust port
Grizzly G1033	8 5/8 × 20	1/8	4 × 4,833	CI	Y	S	3	220	785	2 speeds/16 & 20 FPM
Delta 22-450	8 5/8 × 20	3/16	3 × 5,000	CI	Y	S	5	220/440	840	controls in front
Grizzly G9740	9 × 20	5/16	4 × 5,000	CI	Y	S	7 1/2	220	1,700	3 phase
Grizzly G9967	9 × 20	5/16	4 × 5,000	CI	Y	S	5	220	1,678	1 phase, opt spiral cttrhed
Sunhill P-508V	11 × 20	1/4	4 × NA	NA	NA	NA	7 1/2	220	1,800	
Lobo WP-508	11 3/4 × 20	5/16	4 × 4,800	CI	Y	S	7 1/2	230	1,580	
■ Laguna P20	12 × 20	5/16	4 × 4,500	CI	Y	S	9	230	2,100	
RBI 820	8 × 20 1/4	5/16	4 × 4,600	S	N	U	5	230	500	
Mini Max SP-1	9 3/4 × 20 1/2	5/16	4 × 4,500	CI	Y	S	4.8/9	230/460	1,496	single or 3ph option
Powermatic 201	9 1/2 × 22	3/16	4 × 4,800	CI	Y	S	7 1/2	230	1,350	3ph, 2 speeds, adj. rollers
Seco SK-824WP	6 × 24	3/8	3 × 5,400	CI	N	S	7 1/2	220	1,390	
Bridgewood BW-240P	6 1/2 × 24	1/4	3 × 5,000	CI	Y	S	5 or 7 1/2	220	880	jackscrews
Seco SK-724WP	6 1/2 × 24	1/4	3 × 5,200	CI	N	S	7 1/2	220	990	
North State WJ-24	7 × 24	1/4	3 × 5,300	CI	Y	S	7 1/2	230	1,450	variable speed
Star WPL 24	7 × 24	3/8	3 × 5,400	CI	NA	NA	7 1/2	230	NA	
Bridgewood BW-124P	8 × 24	1/4	4 × 5,200	CI	Y	S, U	10	220	1,496	jackscrews, spiral cttrhed
General 30-460	8 × 24	5/16	3 × 5,000	CI	Y	S	10	220	1,015	
Transpower AP724	8 × 24	1/4	3 × 5,200	NA	NA	NA	5	NA	990	
Grizzly G5851Z	8 1/4 × 24	1/8	4 × 5,200	CI	Y	S	5	220	1,030	17–26 variable feed
Grizzly G7213Z	8 1/4 × 24	1/8	4 × 5,200	CI	Y	S	7 1/2	230	1,030	3 phase
Delta 22-470	8 5/8 × 24	1/4	3 × 5,000	CI	Y	S	7 1/2	230/460	980	2 speeds
Grizzly G9741	9 × 24	5/16	4 × 5,000	CI	Y	S	10	220	1,950	3 phase
Grizzly G9961	9 × 24	5/16	variable speed	CI	Y	S	10	220	1,950	spiral cttrhed
Delta 22-610	9 3/8 × 24	10 mm	4 × 5,000	CI	Y	S	10	220	1,675	3ph available
Laguna P24	12 × 24	5/16	4 × 4,500	CI	Y	S	12	230	2,000	
Woodmaster 725	6 3/4 x 25	3/16	3 × 4,200	CI	N	S	7 1/2	220	808	
Sunhill P-630	11 x 25	1/4	4 × NA	NA	NA	NA	10	220	2,025	

key

R = rubber

CI = cast iron

S = steel

U = urethane

OPT = optional

FPM = feet per minute

■ *PW* Recommends

ALL SUPPLIES AND EQUIPMENT WERE CURRENT AT THE TIME OF ORIGINAL PUBLICATION AND ARE SUBJECT TO CHANGE.

routers

BY THE EDITORS OF *POPULAR WOODWORKING* MAGAZINE

A router is a cool tool and is probably our favorite in the woodshop. You can do so many things with it: make grooves, dadoes, rabbets, tenons, large and small edge profiles, raised-panel doors; cut hinge mortises, cut circles. . . . The list goes on and on. And router technology keeps improving.

Router Satisfaction

Using a router is probably one of the more satisfying machining processes in woodworking. When you make the cut, whether a groove or profile, you've completed the task (except for all the sanding). Routers seem to bring the finesse and finish to a piece. Another satisfying feature is that by simply changing bits, it becomes a multifunction tool.

Setup

Setup on a router is simple. They're almost ready to use out of the box. But you should take a few minutes to familiarize yourself with all the features. Adjust the height up and down. Fiddle with the fine-height adjustment (if the tool has it) and put a bit in the collet. If it's an option, change the collets to get familiar with the tool.

Some routers have a self-releasing collet that is a benefit, but you might think something is wrong if you're not familiar with it. The self-releasing feature keeps bits from being jammed in the collet after use. When you release the nut on the collet, it will spin freely at first. But as you continue to loosen the nut it will again offer resistance. When you pass this point, the bit will release.

Once you've secured a bit in the router, you need to adjust the bit height. This can be a trial-and-error process, but it doesn't have to require a scrap piece. If you set the depth to be obviously less than the full cut, you can slowly creep the bit out, making short passes on your piece until the depth is just right.

Ready to Cut

With everything set, it's time to make some dust. But first you need to decide which direction you're going to rout. Because of the direction of the spinning bit (it's clockwise when handheld; counterclockwise when mounted in a router table) the router has to be moved through the cut in a certain direction to keep the tool from running out of your hands. Essentially, you want the feed direction to pull the tooling against the wood during the cut.

Here's how: When using a router in a handheld manner on the outside edge of a panel, you should move around the wood in a counterclockwise direction. When routing the

BEFORE YOU BUY

- **FIXED BASE.** Routers with a fixed base are available in two general sizes (6.5 and 15 amps). The height of the bit is adjusted by sliding or twisting the motor in the housing, then locking it in place for the cut. Useful for freehand and router table use.
- **PLUNGE BASE.** Routers with a plunge base are also available in two general sizes. The height of the bit is adjusted by sliding the motor up or down on spring-loaded posts, setting the depth, then locking the motor in place. Plunge routers excel at precision depth routing and making stopped cuts, such as mortises and stopped grooves. They can be used in router tables or freehand.
- **TRIM ROUTER.** These smaller (4 to 6 amp) routers offer great maneuverability and comfort in your hand for many small profile and detail routing tasks. They're limited to 1/4" shank bits, but they offer multiple bases for specialty applications.
- **MULTIBASE KITS.** Some manufacturers offer router motors sold with interchangeable plunge and fixed bases. These kits can be a great bargain.
- **VARIABLE SPEED.** Variable speed allows you to optimize the cutting performance of larger bits by slowing down the speed. As a side benefit, most variable-speed routers offer soft start, which keeps the router from jerking to full speed at start-up. Also, look for electronic feedback on these models, which maintains torque under load, again improving performance.
- **DEPTH CONTROLS.** Take a few minutes to investigate the variety of depth controls on routers. All are different, and some are significantly easier to use than others.
- **DUST COLLECTION.** Many routers do not offer integral or easily attached dust collection. While some systems are effective, most are better than nothing.

inside edge of a piece (such as the inside edge of a door), the direction is reversed. The pictures below explain this a little better, but even after years of woodworking, I have to stop and think about which way I'm headed before routing.

But now that I've told you to run the router the right direction, I'm going to tell you about the benefit of running it the wrong direction sometimes. It's a process called climb-cutting.

When climb-cutting, you're changing the angle of rake on the bit to the wood — making the bit scrape instead of cut. This is beneficial when routing highly figured wood or woods prone to splinter and tear-out. But climb-cutting should be done carefully and with very light passes. In fact, the best method is to remove most of the material by routing in the proper direction, then make a final finishing pass with a climb cut. Also, be aware that when climb-cutting, the bit is rotating in the direction you are moving the router, so keep a firm grip to prevent the router from running away from you.

Making the Cut

Before you make your cut, look at the bit you're using and decide whether you're taking too big a cut in one pass. While most small profiles can be cut in one pass, large roundovers and many cove cuts, grooves, rabbets or dadoes would be better made in one or two passes with increasing depths. As a rule, cutting any more than 1/4" is better done in multiple passes.

OK, the router is set correctly and you know which way you're going. To be safe, set the router in place on the wood before turning it on. Also, make sure that the bit isn't resting against the wood. Otherwise, when you turn the motor on, the bit can kick the router away from the work.

If you're routing a smaller piece, it should be clamped to a bench to keep it from moving during routing. With the router running, slowly move the router bit into the cut, then begin moving the router along the piece.

Two important comments here: Starting at the edge of a piece takes some practice. Knowing where the corner is without getting a face full of shavings is a learned skill, so the first few times you should start in from the corner and slowly climb-cut to the corner. Also, how fast you move the router is important. Move too fast and the cut will be poor, with chatter and ripple marks. A second pass usually fixes the problem. If you move too slowly, the bit can burn the wood's edge, and then you're in for a lot of sanding. About three seconds a foot is a safe speed. Gauge your speed by the sound of the motor. When the sound shifts from a high-pitched wine to a lower one as the bit goes into the cut, you've found the right speed.

Always wear eye and ear protection when using a router, and a dust mask is a good idea, too (especially if your router isn't hooked to a shop vacuum).

If you want more instruction on using routers, we recommend you check out Patrick Spielman's *The New Router Handbook* (Sterling Publications).

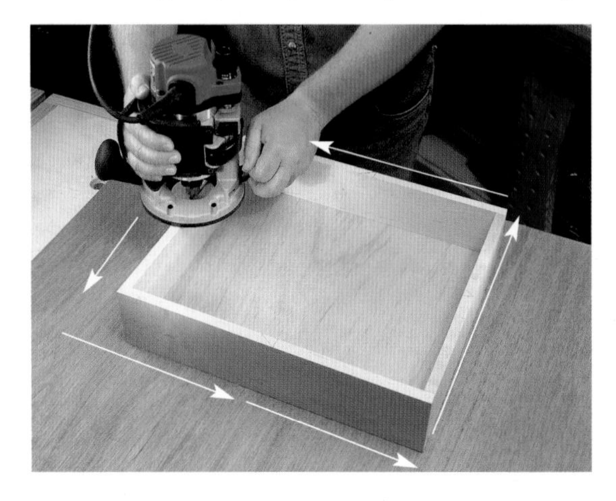

For most routing operations, counterclockwise is the correct direction. As shown here, that is with the bit on the outside of the box, following the arrows around the box. If this was a solid door or panel, instead of a drawer, the motion would still be the same — counterclockwise.

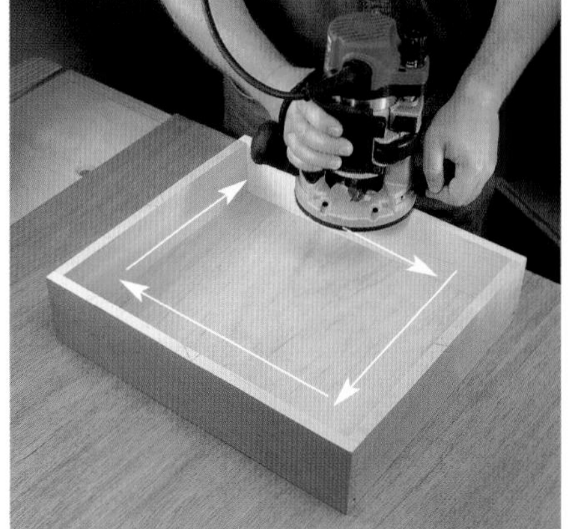

For an interior cut, whether on a drawer edge or on the inside of a door frame, the router direction is reversed to clockwise. The operation we're showing here is a good challenge of router control. It requires carefully balancing the router base on the edge. If not for illustrating router direction, it would probably be easier to make this cut with the router in a router table.

RECOMMENDATIONS

Occasional User

- **TWO-BASE KITS.** Four manufacturers now offer kits with a plunge and fixed base. These are great versatile first (or next) routers.
- **BOSCH 1617EVSPK**
- **DEWALT DW618PK**
- **MAKITA RF1101KIT**
- **PORTER-CABLE 693VSPK**

Serious Home Woodworker

- **MILWAUKEE 5615-20.** This fixed-base, single-speed router offers good power, good ergonomics and easy router-table operation.
- **MAKITA RD1101.** This 11-amp, variable-speed D-handled router offers quiet, powerful performance and easy height adjustment.
- **DEWALT DW621.** This is still our shop-favorite plunge router. It offers excellent dust collection and very good depth controls.

Advanced Woodworker or Professional

If you're looking for a beefy plunge router to use in a router table, or heavy-use situations, one of the following three will fit the bill nicely.

- **HITACHI M12V.** This large plunge is very popular in shops.
- **FEIN RT1800.** Priced higher than the Hitachi, but it's got a lot of power and it's built to last.
- **PORTER-CABLE 7539.** Used in cabinet shops for decades, this monster plunge is a deal.

If you've got all the routers you'll ever need, or have a special application, trim routers fill a luxury niche.

- **BOSCH 1609 AKX.** In our opinion this router is the best of the trim router kits, with four bases to offer lots of options.

THESE TOOLS HAVE BEEN TESTED OR USED BY THE EDITORS OF *POPULAR WOODWORKING* MAGAZINE AND HAVE EARNED THEIR RECOMMENDATION. ALL SUPPLIES AND EQUIPMENT WERE CURRENT AT THE TIME OF ORIGINAL PUBLICATION AND ARE SUBJECT TO CHANGE.

STATS

BRAND & MODEL	AMPS	SPEEDS (RPM)	SPINDLE LOCK	DEPTH ADJ. (IN)	DECIBEL RATING	WEIGHT (LB)	COMMENTS
TRIM ROUTERS							
Bosch1608	5.6	30,000	N	$\frac{1}{2}$	70	3.5	Four bases available
Bosch1608K	5.6	30,000	N	$\frac{1}{2}$	70	3.5	Std. base, dlxe. guide
■ Bosch1609 AKX	5.6	30,000	N	$\frac{1}{2}$	70	3.5	Installers kit, w/4 bases
Craftsman 27512	3.8	23,000	Y	$1\frac{1}{4}$	68	3	
DeWalt DW670	5.6	30,000	Y	$\frac{7}{8}$	70	3.7	4 bases available
DeWalt DW673K	5.6	30,000	Y	$\frac{7}{8}$	70	3.7	w/4 bases
Freud FT1000ET	7.5	20-30K	N	1	83	4.4	w/3 bases, soft start
Freud FT1000EK	7.5	20-30K	Y	$2\frac{1}{4}$	83	6.9	w/3 bases, soft start
Hitachi TR6	4	30,000	N	$1\frac{1}{16}$	68	3.4	Beveling base
Makita 3700B	3.3	28,000	N	$1\frac{5}{8}$	68	3.4	
Makita 3707FC	4.8	26,000	N	$1\frac{3}{8}$	NA	2.6	w/light
Makita 3708FC	4.8	26,000	N	$1\frac{3}{8}$	NA	2.9	Bevel base, w/light
Porter-Cable 309	3.8	28,000	N	1	70	3.3	
Porter-Cable 310	4	27,500	N	$\frac{7}{8}$	70	3.4	
Porter-Cable 7310	5.6	30,000	Y	1	72	3.4	Three bases available
Porter-Cable 7312	5.6	30,000	Y	1	72	4.25	Offset trimmer
Ryobi TR31	3.8	23,000	N	$1\frac{1}{8}$	68	3	w/2 bases

STATS

BRAND & MODEL	AMPS	SPEEDS (RPM/K)	COLLET SIZES (IN)	TRIGGER LOCATION	DEPTH ADJ. (IN)	DECIBEL RATING	WEIGHT (LB)	COMMENTS
FIXED ROUTERS								
Bosch 1617	11	25	$\frac{1}{4}$, $\frac{3}{8}$, $\frac{1}{2}$	B	$1\frac{7}{8}$	95	7.5	Best New Tool '98
Bosch 1618	11	25	$\frac{1}{4}$, $\frac{3}{8}$, $\frac{1}{2}$	H	$1\frac{7}{8}$	95	8	D-handle, Best New Tool '98
Bosch 1617EVS	12	8–25	$\frac{1}{4}$, $\frac{3}{8}$, $\frac{1}{2}$	B	$1\frac{7}{8}$	95	7.7	Soft start, Best New Tool '98
Bosch 1617EVSK	12	8–25	$\frac{1}{4}$, $\frac{3}{8}$, $\frac{1}{2}$	B	$1\frac{7}{8}$	95	7.7	w/case
Bosch 1618EVS	12	8–25	$\frac{1}{4}$, $\frac{3}{8}$, $\frac{1}{2}$	H	$1\frac{7}{8}$	95	8.2	D-handle, soft start, Best New Tool '98
Craftsman 17574	8	25	$\frac{1}{4}$	H	$1\frac{1}{2}$	98	7.5	Light, spindle lock, w/case, bit
Craftsman 17505	8.5	15–25	$\frac{1}{4}$	H	$1\frac{1}{2}$	NA	8.1	Light, spindle lock
Craftsman 17506	9	15–25	$\frac{1}{4}$	H	$1\frac{1}{2}$	98	8.6	Light, spindle lock
Craftsman 27500	9	25	$\frac{1}{4}$, $\frac{1}{2}$	H	$1\frac{1}{2}$	NA	9.3	Spindle lock
DeWalt DW616	11	24.5	$\frac{1}{4}$, $\frac{1}{2}$	B	$1\frac{5}{8}$	NA	7.1	Detachable cord
DeWalt DW616D	11	24.5	$\frac{1}{4}$, $\frac{1}{2}$	B/H	$1\frac{1}{2}$	NA	7.1	Detachable cord, D-handle
DeWalt DW618	12	8–24	$\frac{1}{4}$, $\frac{1}{2}$	B	$1\frac{5}{8}$	NA	7.21	Soft start, detachable cord
DeWalt DW618D	12	8–24	$\frac{1}{4}$, $\frac{1}{2}$	B/H	$1\frac{1}{2}$	NA	7.21	Soft start, detachable cord, D-handle
Makita 3606	7	30	$\frac{1}{4}$	B	3	81	5.5	
Makita RD1100	11	24	$\frac{1}{4}$, $\frac{1}{2}$	H	$2\frac{3}{8}$	81	7.9	D-handle; performance: 5 stars
Makita RF1100	11	24	$\frac{1}{4}$, $\frac{1}{2}$	B	$2\frac{3}{8}$	81	7.1	Performance: 5 stars
■ Makita RD1101	11	8–24	$\frac{1}{4}$, $\frac{1}{2}$	H	$2\frac{3}{8}$	81	7.9	D-handle, soft start
Makita RF1101	11	8–24	$\frac{1}{4}$, $\frac{1}{2}$	B	$2\frac{3}{8}$	81	7.1	Performance: 5 stars
Milwaukee 5660	10	24.5	$\frac{1}{4}$, $\frac{1}{2}$	B	$2\frac{1}{4}$	100	8.5	Depth-adj. ring
■ Milwaukee 5615-20	11	24	$\frac{1}{4}$, $\frac{1}{2}$	B	$1\frac{21}{32}$	87	8.2	Built-in table height adj.
Milwaukee 5619-20	11	24	$\frac{1}{4}$, $\frac{1}{2}$	B	$1\frac{21}{32}$	87	8.2	As above, with D-handle
Milwaukee 5680	12	26	$\frac{1}{2}$	B	$2\frac{1}{4}$	104	8.8	
Milwaukee 5682	12	26	$\frac{1}{4}$, $\frac{1}{2}$	B	$2\frac{1}{4}$	NA	8.8	
Porter-Cable 100	6.5	22	$\frac{1}{4}$	B	$1\frac{1}{2}$	NA	6.8	
Porter-Cable 690	10	23	$\frac{1}{4}$, $\frac{3}{8}$, $\frac{1}{2}$	B	$1\frac{1}{2}$	103	8	Optional bases avail.
Porter-Cable 690LR	10	23	$\frac{1}{4}$, $\frac{3}{8}$, $\frac{1}{2}$	B	$1\frac{1}{2}$	103	8	As above, with latch rls.
Porter-Cable 690LRVS	10	10–24	$\frac{1}{4}$, $\frac{3}{8}$, $\frac{1}{2}$	B	$1\frac{1}{2}$	103	8	Latch release, variable spd.
Porter-Cable 691	10	23	$\frac{1}{4}$, $\frac{3}{8}$, $\frac{1}{2}$	H	$1\frac{1}{2}$	103	9.3	D-handle
Porter-Cable 7518	15	10–21	$\frac{1}{4}$, $\frac{3}{8}$, $\frac{1}{2}$	B	$2\frac{1}{2}$	NA	14.5	Soft start
Porter-Cable 7519	15	21	$\frac{1}{4}$, $\frac{3}{8}$, $\frac{1}{2}$	B	$2\frac{1}{2}$	NA	15	Soft start
Porter-Cable 9290	19.2v	23	$\frac{1}{4}$, $\frac{1}{2}$	B	$1\frac{1}{2}$	NA	7.8	Cordless, opt. bases avail.
Ryobi R161K	8	25	$\frac{1}{4}$	H	$1\frac{1}{2}$	NA	7.5	For BT3000 table saw

STATS

BRAND & MODEL	AMPS	SPEEDS (RPM/K)	COLLET SIZES (IN)	TRIGGER LOCATION	DEPTH ADJ. (IN)	DECIBEL RATING	WEIGHT (LB)	COMMENTS
PLUNGE ROUTERS								
Black & Decker RP200	9.5	25	1/4	H	2	NA	NA	Soft start
Black & Decker RP400K	10	0–25	1/4	H	2	NA	NA	Soft start, dust collection
Bosch 1613AEVS	12	11–22	1/4, 1/2, 3/8	H	2 1/4	97	9.7	Soft start, precis. centering
Bosch 1613AEVSK	12	11–22	1/4, 1/2, 3/8	H	2 1/4	97	9.7	w/case
Bosch 1619EVS	15	8–21	1/4, 1/2, 3/8	H	2 9/16	99	13.2	Soft start, electronic feedback
Craftsman 17509	9	15–25	1/4	H	2	NA	7	Spindle lock
Craftsman 26835	15	10–22	1/4, 1/2	H	2 1/2	NA	13	Soft start
■ DeWalt DW621	10	8–24	1/4, 1/2	H	2 1/8	99	10	Dust collection, endurance tested
DeWalt DW625	15	8–22	1/4, 1/2	H	2 7/16	NA	11.3	Soft start, electronic feedback
■ Fein RT1800	15	8–22	1/2	H	3	100	12	Soft start, 1/4" collet opt.
Festool OF1000E	7.5	10–20	1/4	H	2 3/16	78	6	Soft start
Freud FT2000E	15	8–22	1/4, 1/2	B	2 3/4	NA	12.9	Soft start
Hitachi M8V	7.3	10–25	1/4	B	1 7/8	NA	6.4	Soft start
Hitachi TR12	12.2	22	1/4, 3/8, 1/2	B	2 7/16	104	11	Template guide includ.
■ Hitachi M12V	15	8–20	1/4, 3/8, 1/2	B	2 7/16	NA	11.7	Soft start, template guide includ.
Makita 3621	7.8	24	1/4	B	1 3/8	81	5.3	
Makita 3612	15	22	1/4, 1/2	B	2 3/8	102	13.2	Spindle lock
Makita 3612 C	15	9–23	1/4, 1/2	B	2 3/8	102	13.2	Spindle lock, electric brake
Makita RP1101	11	8-24	1/4, 1/2	B	2 19/32	81	9.3	Soft start, speed control
Porter-Cable 8529	12	10–23	1/4, 1/2	B	2 1/2	NA	11	Above the table bit adjustment knob avl.
Porter-Cable 7538	15	21	1/4, 3/8, 1/2	H	3	NA	17.3	Soft start
■ Porter-Cable 7539	15	10–21	1/4, 3/8, 1/2	H	3	NA	17.3	Soft start, 5 speeds
Ryobi RE175	9	15–25	1/4	H	2	106	9.4	Spindle lock
Ryobi RE180PL	10	15–23	1/2, 1/4	B	2	NA	8.4	
Skil 1823	8.5	25	1/4	H	2	100	7	
Skil 1840	9	25	1/4	H	2	97	7	
Skil 1845-02	10	8–25	1/4	H	2	97	7.3	Soft start, fine adjustment
Skil 1845-44	10	8–20	1/4	H	2	97	7.3	Soft start, fine adjustment
Triton TRC001	15	8–21	1/4, 1/2	H&B	2 21/32	NA	13.5	Through-base collet access
PLUNGE/FIXED BASE ROUTER KITS								
Bosch 1617PK	11	25	1/4, 1/2, 3/8	B	2	95	9	Precise cntring/quick clamp system
■ Bosch 1617EVSPK	12	8-25	1/4, 1/2, 3/8	B	2	95	9	Soft start, variable speed
DeWalt DW616PK	11	24.5	1/4, 1/2	B	2 1/4	NA	7.1	Detachable cord
■ DeWalt DW618PK	12	8–24	1/4, 1/2	B	2 1/4	NA	7.2	Detachable cord
■ Makita RF1101KIT	11	8–24	1/4, 1/2	B	2 19/32	81	9.3	Dust collection, edge guide
Porter-Cable 693 PK	10	23	1/4, 3/8, 1/2	B	2 1/2	103	11.5	
Porter-Cable 9690 VSK	10	10–24	1/4, 3/8, 1/2	B	2 1/2	103	9	Case, edge guide
Porter-Cable 693LR PK	10	23	1/4, 3/8, 1/2	B	2 1/2	103	11.5	Latch release
■ Porter-Cable 693VS PK	10	10–24	1/4, 3/8, 1/2	B	2 1/2	103	11.5	Variable speed

key

Y = yes

N = no

B = base

H = handle

NA = not available

■ = *PW* Recommends

ALL SUPPLIES AND EQUIPMENT WERE CURRENT AT THE TIME OF ORIGINAL PUBLICATION AND ARE SUBJECT TO CHANGE.

random-orbit sanders

BY THE EDITORS OF *POPULAR WOODWORKING* MAGAZINE

Throw away your old pad sanders and get yourself a random-orbit tool. For less than $50 you can reduce your sanding time dramatically with these high-tech wonders.

A Light Touch and Slow Hand

Many woodworkers are under the impression that if they work harder and faster, the work will get done more quickly. This is not so with random-orbit sanders. Don't use a lot of downward pressure when sanding. The engineers who design these tools say that this actually reduces the sanding effectiveness. Also, resist the urge to move the sander quickly over the surface of your wood. Slow and steady results in a more consistent scratch pattern. How slow? Aim for moving the sander about one foot every five seconds or so.

As you move the sander, don't use the same pattern again and again on the same workpiece. Sand horizontally across the work, then vertically, then at 45° to the grain (first one way, then the other). This will ensure you don't miss any spots. Most of all, sand all areas consistently.

Sometimes it's tempting to work in one area more than others or to lift one edge of the pad to sand some tear-out. Resist this as much as you can. It's easy to produce depressions that you can feel and (even worse) see after you've applied a finish. So keep the sander's pad flat to the work.

Changing Grits

Many woodworkers are also bemused at what sanding grits they should use when sanding projects. Here are some basic guidelines in our shop. With solid wood, begin with 100 grit, then go to 120, 150 and finish at 180. With plywood, begin with 150 and finish with 180.

If your project is going to get a clear finish, you usually can stop sanding at 150 grit because there will be no pigment to collect in the scratches. For outdoor furniture, you can usually stop sanding at 120 grit.

BEFORE YOU BUY

- **BODY STYLE.** Electric random-orbit sanders come in three body styles: palm grip, right angle and dual grip. The palm-grip sanders are inexpensive, easy to maneuver and are good for most woodworking tasks. The right-angle sanders are generally bulky, but powerful and well suited for large flat surfaces. The dual-grip sanders are somewhere in between. Most home woodworkers purchase the palm-grip variety.
- **POWER.** The aggressiveness of a random-orbit sander is determined by three things: the amperage (though this can be misleading), the orbits per minute and the offset (also called the orbit or pad movement). Essentially, the offset is the size of the sanding swirls left on the work. Big offsets remove material faster but leave more sanding scratches than tools with smaller offsets.
- **HOOK-AND-LOOP OR STICKY STUFF?** The sandpaper attaches to the tool's pad using one of two methods: hook-and-loop fasteners (essentially Velcro) or PSA (pressure-sensitive adhesive). We prefer the hook-and-loop fasteners because you can swap grits back and forth during a job. With the PSA sandpaper, once you remove it from the pad, it won't stick again. Many pros (who may have a sander for each grit) prefer the PSA.
- **DUST COLLECTION.** Except for quick jobs, it's a good idea to attach your sander to a dust collector. Not only is it healthier, but it will speed your sanding by removing dust between the paper and wood. Sanding the dust is no fun.

RECOMMENDATIONS

Occasional User

- **RYOBI RS240.** If money is tight, check out the Ryobi RS240. For a low price you get a machine that is powerful and versatile.

Serious Home Woodworker

- **MAKITA BO5010.** Among all the palm-grip sanders we use, this one feels the most aggressive. As an added bonus, the dust collection is superb.
- **MAKITA BO6030.** This professional 6" sander is tough and aggressive. It is our favorite dual-grip sander.
- **PORTER-CABLE 333.** This line of palm sanders is hard-working and available in two configurations.
- **BOSCH 1295D.** Bosch upgraded this sander with excellent dust collection. This is a good tool for the shop.

Advanced Woodworker or Professional

- **FEIN MSF 636-1.** In our book, the Fein MSF 636-1 is as good as a sander gets. It's aggressive as anything out there and is capable of great finesse. Add a Fein vacuum, and you will keep your shop dust-free. It's an excellent system.
- **MAKITA BO6040.** The Makita BO6040 is an excellent option. A high-quality sanding machine.

If you're a pro, you also should take a look at pneumatic sanders. You'll need a big compressor, but they are capable of many hours of continual use.

THESE TOOLS HAVE BEEN TESTED OR USED BY THE EDITORS OF *POPULAR WOODWORKING* MAGAZINE AND HAVE EARNED THEIR RECOMMENDATION. ALL SUPPLIES AND EQUIPMENT WERE CURRENT AT THE TIME OF ORIGINAL PUBLICATION AND ARE SUBJECT TO CHANGE.

BRAND & MODEL	PAD DIA. (IN.)	PAD TYPE	PAD BRAKE	ORBITS PER MINUTE	DUST COLLECTION	ORBIT/ OFFSET	AMPS	WEIGHT (LB.)
PALM GRIP								
Black & Decker RO100	5	HL	Y	12,000	DB	3/32	2	3.5
■ Bosch 1295D	5	HL	Y	12,000	DC	1/16	2	3.5
Bosch 1295DK	5	HL	Y	12,000	DC, VP	1/16	2	3.5
Bosch 1295DVS	5	HL	Y	7,000–12,000	DC, VP	1/16	2.2	3.5
Bosch 1295DVSK	5	HL	Y	7,000–12,000	DC, VP	1/16	2.2	3.5
Craftsman 11621	5	PSA	Y	12,500	DB	5/32	2.4	2.75
Craftsman 11636	5	PSA	Y	13,000	Box	5/32	3	3.5
Craftsman 27987	5	HL/PSA	NA	12,000	DB	3/32	2.6	3.6
Craftsman 27957	5	HL/PSA	Y	7,000–12,000	DB	5/32	3	3.8
DeWalt DW420	5	PSA	Y	12,000	–	3/32	2	3
DeWalt DW421	5	HL	Y	12,000	DB, VP	3/32	2	3
DeWalt DW423	5	HL	Y	7,000–12,000	DB, VP	3/32	2	3.2
Festool ES 125	5	NA	Y	6,000–13,000	DB, VP	3/16	2	2.4
■ Makita B05010	5	HL	Y	12,000	DB, VP	1/8	2	2.6
Makita BO5001	5	HL	N	10,000	VP	5/32	1.7	2.9
Makita BO5012	5	HL	Y	4,000–12,000	DB, VP	1/8	2	2.9
Milwaukee 6018-6	5	PSA	N	12,000	DB, VP	3/32	1.8	2.9
Milwaukee 6019-6	5	HL	N	12,000	DB, VP	3/32	1.8	2.9
Porter-Cable 332	5	PSA	Y	12,000	–	3/32	1.7	3.2
■ Porter-Cable 333	5	HL	Y	12,000	DC, VP	3/32	2.4	3.5
■ Porter-Cable 333VS	5	HL	Y	5,000–12,000	DC, VP	3/32	2.4	3.5
Porter-Cable 334	5	PSA	Y	12,000	DC, VP	3/32	2.4	3.5
Porter-Cable 335	6	PSA/HL	Y	9,000	DC,VP	3/32	1.7	3.5
■ Ryobi RS240	5	HL/PSA	Y	12,500	DB	5/32	2.4	2.75
Ryobi RS280VS	5	HL/PSA	Y	7,000–12,000	DB, VP	3/32	2.8	3.5
DUAL-GRIP SANDERS								
Black & Decker MS700K	5	HL	Y	10,500	DB, VP	2.2mm	1.4	5
Bosch 3107DVS	5	HL	Y	4,500–13,000	DB, VP	3/32	3.3	5
Bosch 3107DVSK	5	HL	Y	4,500–13,000	DB, VP	3/32	3.3	5
Bosch 3725DVS	5	HL	Y	4,500–12,000	DB, VP	3/32	3.3	5.1
Bosch 3727DVS	6	HL	Y	4,500–12,000	DB, VP	5/64	3.3	5.2
Festool ES 150/3 EQ	5	HL	Y	4,000–9,500	DB, VP	1/8	2.6	3.9
Festool ES 150/5 EQ	5	HL	Y	4,000–9,500	DB, VP	3/16	2.6	3.9
Grizzly G9910	5	HL	N	10,000	DB, VP	1/8	3	4.7
■ Makita BO6030	6	HL	Y	4,000–10,000	DB, VP	1/8	2.7	5.1
Makita BO5021K	5	HL	Y	4,000–12,000	DB, VP	1/8	2	3.1
Metabo SXE425	5	HL	Y	5,000–12,000	DB	3/16	3.6	5.2
Metabo SXE450	6	HL	Y	4,000–10,000	DB	1/8 or 1/4	3.8	6.5
RIGHT ANGLE								
Porter-Cable 7335	5	PSA	N	2,500–6,000	OPT	11/32	3.7	5.5
Bosch 1370DEVS	6	HL	Y	4,800–12,000	DB, VP	11/64	5	5
DeWalt DW443	6	HL	Y	4,300–6,800	DB, VP	3/16	4.3	5.7
■ Fein MSF 636-1	6	HL	Y	7,500	VP	5/16	4.7	3.7
Festool Rotex 150 E	6	HL	Y	4,000–11,200	VP	3/16	4.2	5
■ Makita BO6040	6	HL	Y	1,600–5,800	VP	7/32	6.6	5.9
Milwaukee 6125	5 or 6	PSA	N	10,000	NA	5/32	5.5	5
Porter-Cable 7336	6	PSA	N	2,500–6,000	OPT	11/32	3.7	5.75

STATS

key

HL = hook and loop
PSA = pressure-sensitive adhesive
DB = dust bag
VP = vacuum port
DC = dust canister
Y = yes
N = no
NA = not available
■ *PW* Recommends

ALL SUPPLIES AND EQUIPMENT WERE CURRENT AT THE TIME OF ORIGINAL PUBLICATION AND ARE SUBJECT TO CHANGE.

table saws

BY THE EDITORS OF *POPULAR WOODWORKING* MAGAZINE

Entire books have been written on how to use a table saw, and it's a good idea to get one if you've never used this machine. We recommend *Jim Tolpin's Table Saw Magic, 2nd Edition* (Popular Woodworking Books) and *The Table Saw Book* by Kelly Mehler (Taunton Press). Each brand of saw is a little different to set up, but the following tips will help you get your machine tuned for precision woodworking.

Everything Parallel

When you get your saw in place in your new shop, it's really tempting to fire it up and rip a few boards. Resist this temptation for a few minutes. Several critical adjustments should be checked to prevent your first cut from being a dangerous one.

The first thing to do is make sure the blade is parallel with at least one miter slot. You can check this with a ruler by measuring at the front of the blade and the back. If it's off by even a little, you're going to need to make this adjustment first. On contractor's saws you generally loosen the bolts that attach the trunnions to the top and knock the trunnions with a wooden block (your manual will show you how). On cabinet saws, you loosen three or

BEFORE YOU START

- **BENCHTOP VS. STATIONARY.** Unless your shop is in a closet, we don't recommend benchtop saws. Though the premium benchtop models get better each year, they're as expensive as entry-level contractor's saws — which are far more powerful and expandable. Start your hobby right by purchasing a contractor's or cabinet saw.
- **FENCE.** The heart of the table saw is its fence. We prefer front-locking fences such as the Biesemeyer, Unifence, Xacta and their clones. These commercial-style fences are stout and accurate. If you can't afford this premium fence, you can always upgrade later to one if you own a contractor's or cabinet saw. Most fences have 30"-long rails. If you have the room in your shop, spend the little extra and get the 50" rails.
- **MOTOR.** The motors on contractor's saws (generally 1½ or 2 horsepower) are fine for most day-to-day woodworking tasks. If you regularly rip 3" maple, you're going to need at least a 3-hp motor in a cabinet saw. TEFC (totally enclosed, fan-cooled) motors are preferable to standard motors.
- **WINGS AND WEIGHT.** The heavier a table saw, the smoother it is going to run. So heavy saws with cast iron wings (instead of stamped steel ones) are preferable.
- **ACCESSORIES.** Most table-saw users end up replacing the stock blade, throat plate and miter gauge. So don't be disappointed if these items seem less than perfect on the models you are considering buying.

four bolts and then shift the top (the trunnions are attached to the cabinet instead of the top). Take your time and get it right or your other adjustments will be more difficult.

If you have a contractor's saw, you'll want to ensure the pulley on the motor is lined up with the pulley on the arbor. Lay a straightedge across the two pulleys and check for gaps between the it and pulley. Adjust the pulley on the motor until the straightedge lies perfectly flat across the two pulleys. Tighten everything.

Next, you want to adjust the fence so it's parallel to your miter slots and the blade. You can measure it or go by feel. Lock the fence so it's flush to the edge of one of the miter slots and feel along the slot to see if the fence toes in or out.

Everything Else at 90°

Now get out your most accurate square and make sure your fence face is 90° to the table. If it's not, you're going to have zero luck cutting joints on your saw. Better fences allow you to make this adjustment by turning a screw or two. Other fences may need to be shimmed with tape between the fence and its rails.

Now get out your miter gauge and adjust it so it cuts at 90° to the blade. Make a cut and check it with your try square. Adjust the gauge and its stops when everything is perfect.

Other Adjustments

Attach the guard and splitter and fuss with those until the splitter is directly in line with the blade. Insert the throat plate and adjust the leveling screws until it is perfectly flush with your table. Finally, get out a straightedge and check your saw's wings and table board (on the right-hand side of many saws). Make sure these tables are as flush as possible with the top.

Now look at the motor. If you have a contractor's saw, you should be able to switch it between 220- and 110-volt power. If you have 220 service in your shop, we recommend you switch your saw to use this higher voltage. Though some electrical experts say it doesn't matter, we've found that with the wiring in home shops, 220 is the right choice to avoid voltage drops.

You're almost done. If you have a contractor's saw, you really should consider upgrading the V-belt that runs between the motor and arbor. We recommend PowerTwist belts (also called link belts), which are available from almost any woodworking supplier. These adjustable belts dramatically reduce vibration during operation.

Power On

You are ready to cut some wood. But as you reach for that switch, remember that saws with a circular blade (table saws, radial-arm saws and circular saws) are the No. 1 cause of injuries in workshops in this country. No. 2, by the way, is the jointer.

So the safety rules for saws are particularly important. Here's a list of the most important ones:

- Set the saw blade so it's 1/8" higher than the wood to be cut.
- Never stand directly behind the blade while cutting. Always stand slightly to one side.
- Keep your fingers clear of the throat plate. Consider this area the danger zone.
- Unplug the saw every time you change the blade.
- Use a push stick when ripping stock less than 4" wide.
- Keep your saw free of scraps and debris. Use a push stick or scrap to move them if the saw is running (or winding down).
- Always wear eye and ear protection when working.
- If you get into trouble during a cut, hold the stock down with one hand and turn off the saw or quickly lower the blade below the table with the other.
- Never crosscut narrow stock using your fence. Use your miter gauge. Never make a freehand cut without a miter gauge or the fence to guide the work.
- Never work on the saw without someone else within earshot.
- Roll up your sleeves. Take off any jewelry (watches, too). Pull back your hair if it's long.

Many first-time users are jittery about making their first rips and crosscuts. They mostly worry about where to put their hands and where to apply pressure.

Once you master these operations, you're ready to find out how versatile the table saw really is: You can cut tenons, rabbets, grooves, dadoes, cove moulding, you name it. For more table-saw tricks, you really should check out the wide variety of books available about this machine.

RECOMMENDATIONS

Occasional User

- **GRIZZLY 1022SM.** Why buy a premium benchtop saw when you can get this good entry-level contractor saw?
- **DELTA TS300**
- **JET JWTS-10JF**
- **BRIDGEWOOD TCS-10CL.** This bargain saw has a nice fence system and one cast wing.

Serious Home Woodworker

- **DELTA SERIES 2000 SAWS.** The contractor saw to beat, and the reputation is well-deserved.
- **JET JWTS-10CW2-PF.** A challenger to Delta's saws, this saw features a world-class fence.
- **POWERMATIC 64A.** Another serious contender, this left-tilt contractor saw also sports an excellent front-locking fence.
- **GRIZZLY 1022PROZ.** New to the Grizzly line, this saw has two solid cast wings, a 2 hp motor and an excellent front-locking fence.
- **GRIZZLY 1023S.** An excellent cabinet saw at a contractor saw price. We flat-out love this saw. The company also makes a 110-volt version and a left-tilt version that are worth checking out.

Advanced Woodworker or Professional

- **POWERMATIC 66.** The Cadillac of 10" saws that's famous for its three-point yoke and mirror finish.
- **GENERAL 50-200L M1.**
- **JET JTAS-10XL50-1.**
- **DELTA UNISAW 36-R31-BC50** or left-tilt version.

THESE TOOLS HAVE BEEN TESTED OR USED BY THE EDITORS OF *POPULAR WOODWORKING* MAGAZINE AND HAVE EARNED THEIR RECOMMENDATION. ALL SUPPLIES AND EQUIPMENT WERE CURRENT AT THE TIME OF ORIGINAL PUBLICATION AND ARE SUBJECT TO CHANGE.

One of the first steps in making sure your table saw is safe is to make sure the blade and fence are parallel to one another. (We'll assume you've already aligned the blade to the miter slot as instructed by your owner's manual.) Simply set the fence to any reasonable distance (9" in our photo) and check the distance between the fence and blade both at the front and rear of the blade. If the measurements are not equal, adjust your fence until correct. If this setup isn't done correctly, your material can become pinched between the fence and blade (or splitter guard) and either be violently kicked back at you, or make it too hard to push the piece all the way through. If you have to force a piece through a cut, you're doing something wrong. If the fence is out of parallel in the other direction, you may not get hurt, but you'll have a hard time making square cuts.

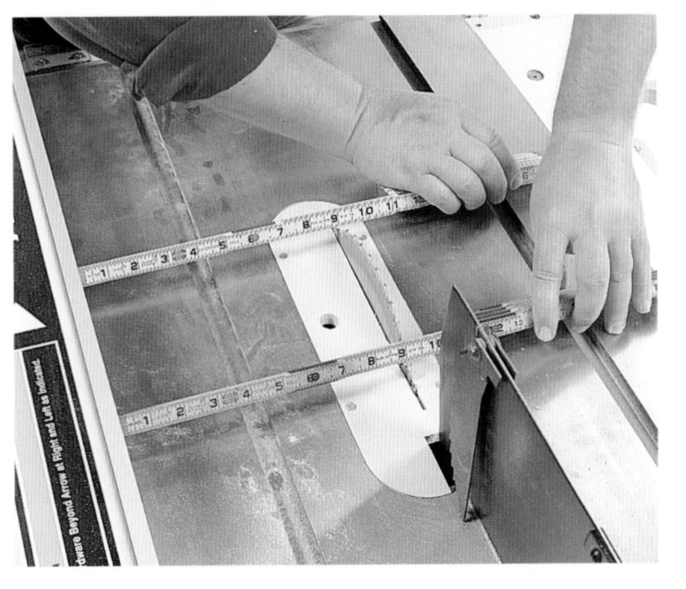

When crosscutting narrow pieces on the table saw, you will eventually encounter the situation where the falloff pieces are small enough to not move out of the way on each cut, and they will begin to accumulate to the outfeed side of the blade. This doesn't automatically create a dangerous situation, but one of the pieces could be pushed against the outfeed side of the blade and be thrown back at you. Even with the guard in place, a piece can be small enough to be kicked around between the guard and blade, or tossed back. Optimally, you should stop the saw and wait until the blade has stopped spinning, then remove the offending chunks. More likely than not, it will be inconvenient to keep turning off the saw. In that case, stand out of the kickback line of fire and use a scrap piece of wood or your push stick to nudge the pieces out of the way. Don't use your fingers! You can always make a new push stick.

MAKING TENONS WITH A DADO STACK

Set the height of your dado stack equal to the depth of your shoulder ($^3/_{16}$" in this case). Set the fence to equal the length of the tenon you want (1" here). The backup block reduces tear-out. Make the face cheek cuts first.

Cut the edge shoulders and cheeks in the same way. If you want a bigger shoulder, increase the height of the dado stack after cutting all the face cheeks and shoulders.

It's a good idea to check the fit of every tenon in a test mortise. The thickness of your tenon will vary slightly if you put less downward pressure on the tenon during the cut. If the tenon is a shade too thick, try making a couple more passes using more pressure.

MAKING TENONS WITH A CROSSCUT BLADE

First, define the shoulders on the face and cheek sides. Set the height of the blade to $^3/_{16}$" and the fence to the length of your tenon (don't forget to count the thickness of the blade).

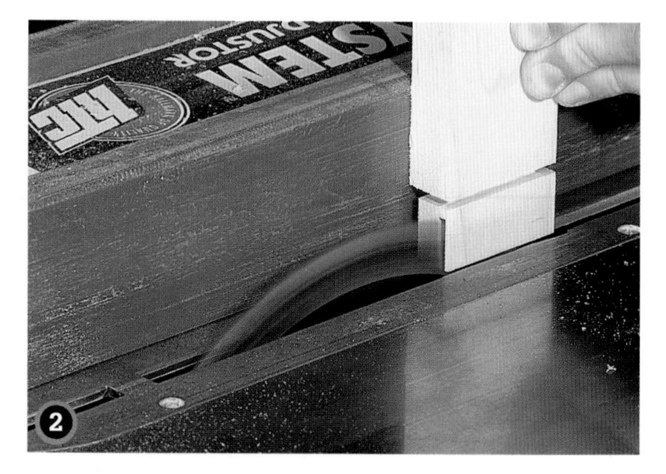

Now set your fence and blade height to remove the waste from the face cheeks. Be careful to keep the work tightly against the fence and your fingers away from the blade. Using a higher subfence is a good idea.

Using your miter gauge and a backing board for support, remove the waste from the edge cheeks. Keep your blade at the same height from the last step.

CUTTING WEDGES

Wedges are essential in every workshop. They shim machinery so it sits flat on the floor, will shim your cabinets as you install them in your house and even can be used to shim inset doors and drawers for the proper reveal. Making them on your table saw is easy with this simple jig.

The jig essentially is a push block. One layer of the push block has an angled notch cut into it. The top layer holds the work to the saw's table. The notch on the bottom layer measures 6" long and is $^1/_2$" deep at the back. This jig cuts wedges that have a 4° slope.

Cutting wedges is a ripping operation. Place your stock into the push block and run it through the blade. Use your left hand to support the stock on the left during the pass. After you cut one wedge, flip the board over and cut the next wedge from the other side. Continue this way until you run out of wood.

CROSSCUTTING WITH A STOP BLOCK

Making long crosscuts on your table saw is easy with your fence and a stop or gauge block. First, clamp the block to the fence of your saw. We use a 3"-wide stop block. Wider is better. If something goes awry during the cut, you don't want the work to get wedged between your blade and the fence. Be sure to clamp your block back far enough so that your work will clear the block before entering the cut. This removes a lot of potential kickback problems.

Set your fence to the length of the crosscut you want to make (don't forget to add the width of your stop block). Put the work against your miter gauge between the fence and blade. Push the work forward into the blade. When your work clears the blade, shift it right an inch or so before lifting it off the saw's table.

BRAND	BLADE DIAMETER (IN.)	MAX CUT DEPTH (IN.)	MAX RIP (IN.)	TABLE SIZE (IN.)	TABLE MATERIAL	DRIVE TYPE	VOLTS	AMPS	DUST PORT	WEIGHT
BENCHTOP										
Makita 2702	8 1/4	2 11/16	12	27 × 22	AL	D	115	15	Y	40
Bosch 4000	10	3 1/8	25	29 × 21 1/2	AL	D	120	15	Y	60
Craftsman 21825	10	3	24	26 7/64 × 19 3/32	AL	D	120	15	N	44
Craftsman 24810	10	3	24	26 7/64 × 19 3/32	AL	D	120	15	N	50
Craftsman 21810	10	3	24	26 7/64 × 19 3/32	AL	D	120	15	N	40
Craftsman 24888	10	3	24 1/12	22 7/64 × 19 3/32	AL	D	120	15	Y	80
Craftsman 21830	10	3 1/8	24 1/12	24 × 21	AL	G	120	15	Y	110
Delta TS200	10	3	9 7/8	17 1/4 × 26	AL	D	115	13	N	40
Delta TS220LS	10	3	20	17 1/2 × 34	AL	D	115	15	N	60
Delta TS300LS	10	3	9 7/8	17 1/4 × 26	AL	D	115	13	N	50
DeWalt DW744S	10	3 1/8	24 1/2	26 1/2 × 19 1/4	AL	D	115	13	Y	64
Hitachi C10RA2	10	3	15 3/4	34 × 19 5/8	AL	D	115	15	Y	56
Makita 2703	10	3 9/16	12	27 × 22	AL	D	115	15	Y	40
Porter-Cable 3812	10	3 1/8	24 1/2	26 × 20	AL	D	115	15	Y	60
Ridgid TS2400LS	10	3 1/8	25	39 1/2 × 21	AL	D	120	15	Y	75
Ryobi BTS10	10	3	9 1/2	16 × 25 3/4	AL	D	115	13	N	40
Ryobi BT3100	10	3 9/16	31	27 × 40	AL	B	115	15	Y	107
Skil 3400	10	3	12	26 5/8 × 17 5/8	AL	D	120	15	Y	38
Skil 3400-08	10	3	12	26 5/8 × 17 5/8	AL	D	120	15	Y	38
Tradesman 8032	10	3 1/8	9 7/8	26 1/2 × 17 1/2	AL	D	115	13	N	56
Wilton 99168	10	3	13	17 × 26	AL	D	120	13	Y	46

BRAND	BLADE DIAMETER (IN.)	MAX CUT DEPTH (IN.)	MAX RIP (IN.)	TABLE SIZE (IN.)	TABLE MATERIAL	FENCE TYPE	DRIVE TYPE	VOLTS	HP-AMPS	DUST PORT	WEIGHT
CONTRACTOR											
■ Bridgewood TSC-10CL	10	3 1/8	30	30 × 27	CI	Front lock	B	110/220	1.5/16-8	Y	297
Craftsman 22839	10	3 7/16	24	44 × 27	CI/S	F & R	B	120	1.5–13	OPT	218
Craftsman 24820	10	3 3/8	24	44 × 27	CI/S	F & R	B	120	1.5/13	OPT	254
Craftsman 22849	10	3 3/8	24	44 × 27	CI	F & R	B	120/240	1.5–6.5	OPT	236
Craftsman 22859	10	3 3/8	30	54 × 27	CI	F & R	B	120/240	1.5–13	Y	265
■ Delta TS300	10	3 1/8	27	22 1/4 × 38 3/8	CI	F & R	B	115	NA	NA	145
■ Delta 36-445†	10	3 1/8	30	62 × 27	CI	Front lock	B	115/230	1.5–12.8/6.4	N	248
■ Delta 36-460††	10	3 1/8	28	76 × 27	CI	Front lock	B	115/230	1.5–12.8/6.4	N	267
■ Delta 36-426†††	10	3 1/8	30	62 × 27	CI	Front lock	B	115/230	1.5–12.8/6.4	N	295
■ Delta 36-650	10	3 1/8	30	40 1/2 × 27	CI	F & R	B	115/230	1.5–12.8/6.4	N	234
DeWalt DW746	10	3 1/8	30	27 × 40 3/4	CI	F & R	B	120/240	1.75–15/7.5	Y	254
General 50-175	10	3 1/8	52	27 × 40 1/2	CI	Front lock	B	115/230	2–18/9	N	300
General 50-185	10	3 1/8	52	27 × 40 1/2	CI	Front lock	B	115/230	2–18/9	N	300
■ Grizzly G1022SM	10	3 1/8	24	40 5/8 × 27 1/8	CI	F & R	B	110/220	1.5–16/8	OPT	220
Grizzly G1022Z	10	3 1/8	24	40 5/8 × 27 1/8	CI	F & R	B	110/220	1.5–16/8	OPT	250
Grizzly G1022PRO	10	3 1/8	25	27 1/8 × 40 5/8	CI	Front lock	B	110/220	2–26/13	Y	325
■ Grizzly G1022PROZ	10	3 1/8	25	27 1/8 × 40 1/8	CI	Front lock	B	110/220	2–26/13	Y	345
Grizzly G1022ZF	10	3 1/8	25	40 5/8 × 27 1/8	CI	F & R	B	115/230	1.5–18/9	Y	290
Grizzly G1022zfx	10	3 1/8	25	40 5/8 × 27 1/8	CI	F & R	B	110/220	2–26/13	Y	290
■ Jet JWTS-10JF	10	3 1/8	30	40 × 27	CI/S	Front lock	B	115/230	1.5–18/9	Y	279
Jet JWTS-10CW2-JF	10	3 1/8	30	40 × 27	CI	Front lock	B	115/230	1.5–18/9	Y	317
Jet JWSS-10PF	10	3 1/8	32	41 3/4 × 27	CI	F & R	B	115/230	1 3/4–6/12	Y	320
■ Jet JWTS-10CW2-PF	10	3 1/8	30	40 × 27	CI	Front lock	B	115/230	1.5–18/9	Y	375
Jet JWTS-10CW2-PFX	10	3 1/8	52	40 × 27	CI	Front lock	B	115/230	1.5–18/9	Y	397
Lobo TS-0010	10	3 1/8	30	40 1/4 × 27	CI	F & R	B	115/230	1.5–20/10	OPT	245
North State TSL-10L	10	3 1/4	30	27 × 40 1/2	CI	Front lock	B	115/230	2/NA	N	310
■ Powermatic 64A	10	3 1/8	50	40 × 27	CI	Front lock	B	115/230	1.5–18/9	Y	400
Ridgid TS2412	10	3 3/8	24	44 × 27	CI	F & R	B	120	1.5–13	OPT	217
Ridgid TS3612	10	3 3/8	36	44 × 27	CI	F & R	B	120/240	1.5–13/6.5	OPT	242
Star WTS10	10	3 1/8	25	40 × 27	CI	F & R	B	115	1.5–16/8	Y	225
Transpower MS10	10	3	30	40 × 27	CI	F & R	B	115/230	2–24/12	N	260

STATS

BRAND	BLADE DIAMETER	MAX CUT DEPTH	MAX RIP	TABLE SIZE	TABLE MATERIAL	DRIVE TYPE	VOLTS	HP-AMPS	DUST PORT	WEIGHT	FENCE TYPE	COMMENTS
CABINET												
Bridgewood BW-10TS	10	3 1/4	50	27 × 40	CI	B	230	3–18	Y	409	Front lock	
Bridgewood BW-10LTS	10	3 1/8	50	77 × 47	CI	NA	230	NA	Y	473	Front lock	left tilt, boxed trunnion
Craftsman 22694	10	3	50	36 × 27	CI	B	230	3–17	Y	537	Front lock	
Delta 36-R31-U52	10	3 1/8	52	76 × 27	CI	B	230	3–17	Y	450	Front lock	left or right tilt
■ Delta 36-R31-BC50	10	3 1/8	50	76 × 27	CI	B	230	3–12.4	Y	457	Front lock,	also in left tilt
Delta 36-R-31-U30	10	3 1/8	30	76 × 27	CI	B	230	3–17	Y	450	Front lock	
General 50-200 MI	10	3 1/8	30	27 × 40	CI	B	115/230	2–24/12	Y	360	Front lock	dual voltage
■ General 50-200L MI	10	3 1/8	52	27 × 40	CI	B	115/230	2–24/12	Y	375	Front lock	dual voltage
General 50-250 MI	10	3	50	40 1/2 × 27	CI	B	220	4–12/7	Y	409	Front lock	right tilt
General 50-260 MI	10	3	50	40 1/2 × 27	CI	B	220	3–12/7	Y	409	Front lock	left tilt
General 350	10	3 1/8	52	28 × 36	CI	B	220	3–18	Y	540	Front lock	right tilt
General 650	10	3 1/8	52	28 × 36	CI	B	220	3–18	Y	540	Front lock	left tilt
■ Grizzly G1023S	10	3 1/8	25	40 1/8 × 27 1/8	CI	B	220	3–18	OPT	360	Front lock	
Grizzly G1023S110	10	3 1/8	25	40 1/8 × 27 1/8	CI	B	110	2–24	Y	360	Front lock	
Grizzly G1023SL	10	3	26	40 1/8 × 27	CI	B	220	3–18	Y	430	Front lock	left tilt
Grizzly G1023Z	10	3 1/8	25	36 3/4 × 27	CI	B	220	3–18	Y	460	F & R	
Grizzly G1023ZX	10	3 1/8	25	36 3/4 × 27	CI	B	220	5–25	Y	475	F & R	
Grizzly G1023ZX3	10	3 1/8	25	36 3/4 × 27	CI	B	220/3ph	5–15	Y	475	Front lock	
Jet JTAS-10X50-1	10	3 1/8	50	40 × 27	CI	B	230	3–17	Y	574	Front lock	
■ Jet JTAS-10XL50-1	10	3 1/8	50	40 × 27	CI	B	230	3–17	Y	594	Front lock	
Jet JTAS-10X50-1D	10	3 1/8	50	40 × 27	CI	B	230	3–17	Y	578	F & R	
Jet JTAS-10XL50-1D	10	3 1/8	50	40 × 27	CI	B	230	3–17	Y	598	F & R	
Lobo TS-1010	10	3	49	36 × 27	CI	B	230	3–36/18	Y	410	F & R	
Mini Max SC-2	10	3	51	22 × 33	CI	B	230	3–3/5–14	Y	616	NA	
North State TSC-10HK	10	3 1/4	50	40 1/2 × 27	CI	B	230	3–16	Y	450	Front lock	left or right tilt
■ Powermatic 66	10	3 1/8	50	38 × 28	CI	B	230	3–17	Y	605	Front lock	left tilt
Powermatic 66-5	10	3 1/8	50	38 × 28	CI	B	230	5–24	Y	605	Front lock	left tilt
Robland XZ	10	3 1/4	50	36 × 48	CI	B	230	3–25	Y	600	Front lock	
Seco SK-1010TS	10	3	49	36 × 27	CI	B	230	3–NA	Y	410	F & R	
Shop Fox W1677	10	3	26	40 1/8 × 27	CI	B	220	3–17	Y	500	Front lock	left tilt
Shop Fox W1677Ext1	10	3	54	40 1/8 × 27	CI	B	220	3–17	Y	600	Front lock	left tilt
Shop Fox W1677Ext2	10	3	50	40 1/8 × 27	CI	B	220	3–17	Y	575	F&R	left tilt
Star S3202	10	3	36	36 × 27	CI	B	230	3–15	Y	425	NA	
Star S3204	10	3	36	36 × 27	CI	B	230	5–35	Y	425	NA	
Transpower TSC-10HK	10	3	48	27 × 40	CI	B	220	3–NA	Y	360	F & R	
Transpower MBS-250	10	3	25	36 × 27	CI	B	220	3–18	Y	407	NA	
Bridgewood BW-12LTS	10	4	50	29 × 44	CI	B	230	3–18	Y	460	Front lock	left tilt
Craftsman 22692	12	4	50	48 × 30	CI	B	230	3–15	Y	717	Front lock	
General 50-375	12	4	50	48 × 30	CI	B	230	3–12	Y	690	Front lock	
Grizzly G5959	12	4	50	30 1/4 × 48	CI	B	220	5–27	Y	615	Front lock	
Grizzly G9957	12	4	50	30 1/4 × 48	CI	B	220/3ph	7 1/2–27	Y	615	Front lock	
Laguna TS	12	NA	48	NA	CI	B	220	NA	Y	NA	NA	
Laguna TSS	12	NA	48	NA	CI	B	220	NA	Y	NA	NA	
Lobo HTS-0012	10 & 12	4 1/8	30	27 × 37	CI	B	230	3–36/18	Y	330	F & R	
Lobo TS-1212	12	4	49	48 × 30	CI	B	230	5–19.6	Y	572	F & R	
Mini Max SC3W	12	4	50	34 × 23	CI	B	230	4.8–NA	Y	649	F & R	
Mini Max SC4W	12	4	50	34 × 23	CI	B	230	4.8–NA	Y	950	F & R	
Mini Max S315WS	12	4	50	34 × 23	CI	B	230	4.8–NA	Y	1,500	F & R	
North State MBS-300	12	4	50	30 × 48	CI	B	230	5–NA	Y	750	Front lock	
Seco SK-1212TS	12	4	78	48 × 30	CI	B	230	5–25	Y	570	F & R	
Star WTST10	12	4	36	40 × 29	CI	B	230	5–35	Y	600	NA	
Sunhill TAS-12	12	3 3/4	NA	40 × 30	CI	B	220	3/5–17/14	Y	570	F & R	
Sunhill TAS-16	12–16	4–6	NA	48 × 38	CI	B	230	7.5–23	Y	1,150	F & R	
Transpower MBS-300	12	4	38	30 × 48	CI	NA	220	5–NA	NA	572	NA	
Transpower TSC-12HK	12	4	30	40 × 27	CI	B	230	3–18	Y	410	Front lock	
Grizzly G7209	14	5	50 3/4	48 1/2 × 38	CI	B	220	5–26	Y	825	NA	
Grizzly G7210	14	5	50 3/4	48 × 38	CI	B	220/3ph	7.5–26	Y	825	Front lock	

key

AL = aluminum, CI = cast iron, S = steel,
B = belt, D = direct drive,
F & R = front and rear locking
† Avail. w/52" fence system
†† Avail.w/basic fence system
††† Available w/Biesemeyer fence system
■ *PW* Recommends

ALL SUPPLIES AND EQUIPMENT WERE CURRENT AT THE TIME OF ORIGINAL PUBLICATION AND ARE SUBJECT TO CHANGE.

CHAPTER 30

biscuit joinery

BY CHRISTOPHER SCHWARZ

My first woodworking class years ago was all about hand-cut joints. We cut mortises, tenons, dovetails, half-laps, bridle joints, you name it. All with hand tools. It's a lucky thing a coping saw doesn't make much noise because while cleaning out my 114th dovetail pin I overheard a classmate talking about biscuits.

Biscuits, he told us in hushed tones, are a faster and easier way to join wood. But some people, and he looked up at that moment to see if our instructor was looking, think that biscuits are cheating. Well, that was enough for me. I had to find out what all the fuss was about.

As it turns out, biscuit joinery is, in actuality, cheating — the same kind of way that nuclear weapons are cheating. Like 'em or not, they get the job done faster than anything else out there. Biscuits aren't right for every situation (chairs come quickly to mind), but for many projects, biscuit joints are

Biscuit joiners cut a semicircular slot that's the perfect size for a biscuit — essentially a manufactured loose tenon. To illustrate how the machine works, we cut a slot in some Lexan, a tough polycarbonate plastic. Though this isn't a common application for the tool, it handled the job with surprising ease.

WHERE DO BISCUITS COME FROM?

As important as the tool itself is the lowly biscuit. These football-shaped pieces of wood are a bit of an engineering marvel. Out of the box, biscuits are about 0.15" thick, and they fit into a slot that's about 0.16". When the biscuit comes in contact with the water in your glue, it swells up, locking the joint in place. To ensure the joint is strong, the grain direction on biscuits runs diagonally. This prevents your joint from splitting and gives you, in the worst case, a cross-grained joint.

Hermann Steiner, inventor of the Lamello joining system.

But just where do these little suckers come from? Kathleen Oberleiter, the dealer sales manager for Lamello, says her company has one plant in Switzerland that produces biscuits for Europe and the United States. In addition to producing biscuits under its own name, she says Lamello also makes the same quality biscuits for Makita and Black & Decker (and Black & Decker's sister company, DeWalt).

Lamello employs two people whose job is to find the perfect European beech trees for making biscuits. They look for trees that are at a particular stage of growth and choose those for harvesting. The trees are debarked, cut into thin panels and kiln-dried. When the panels are dry. the biscuits are stamped and compressed from those panels. Lamello brags that all its biscuits are within one-tenth of a millimeter in thickness and with a moisture content between 8 and 10 percent.

Here in the United States, Porter-Cable started making its own biscuits in Jackson, Tennessee, in the mid-1980s, according to company officials. Then the company concluded it would be better to have another company make the biscuits using Porter-Cable's tooling and equipment. Now Hill Wood Products of Cook, Minnesota, makes all of Porter-Cable's biscuits. The company also makes Ryobi's face-frame biscuits. In fact, Hill Wood's plant is the only major producer of biscuits in this country and makes between 60 percent and 70 percent of the biscuits sold in the United States, says Hill Wood President Steve Hill.

Since his company started making biscuits for Porter-Cable, Hill says his company has upgraded the original equipment three or four times and can now easily make 1 million biscuits a day.

Instead of beech, Hill Wood makes biscuits using Northern white birch from Minnesota, most of which comes from within a 150-mile radius of the plant. The trees are sawn using special equipment and then dried to a moisture content between 6 percent and 8 percent. Then the strips of birch are transformed into biscuits by the company's machinery.

Interestingly, Hill says Hill Wood does not compress the wood for its biscuits and relies on the moisture in the glue to swell the biscuit and lock the joint tight. The company's equipment is capable of compressing the biscuits, but Hill says he's found that wood can compress unevenly, resulting in biscuits of different thicknesses. Hill Wood cuts its biscuits within five-thousandths of the optimum thickness.

So how does birch compare to the European beech? Hill says beech is actually a little harder and the grain is a bit tighter than in birch, but that it's real close. "The glue or the wood is more likely to fail than the biscuit," he says.

Freud Tools, a major player in the biscuit market, has its biscuits made by a Spanish firm that makes biscuits for many other firms, according to Jim Brewer, vice president of operations. Freud's biscuits are made of beech and are compressed, he says.

Biscuits sold by Ryobi are manufactured in Minnesota from beech and are compressed, company officials say.

Kaiser biscuits, which are made in Austria from beech, have been distributed in the United States for the last five or six years by Practical Products Co. of Cincinnati, Ohio, according to Donald Baltzer, company president. Kaisers are well thought of in Europe and are compressed during manufacturing.

BISCUITING A PARTITION IN THE MIDDLE OF A PANEL

The best way to biscuit a partition into the middle of a panel is to use the partition itself as a fence for your biscuit joiner. Here's how: Mark on the panel where you want the partition to be placed.

Lay the partition flat on the panel and against the line you marked. Clamp the partition and panel to your bench. Mark on the partition where you want your biscuit slots to go. There is no need to mark the panel beneath it.

Now remove the fence from your biscuit joiner. Place it flat on the panel and cut the slots in the partition.

Now turn the biscuit joiner on its head and cut the slots in the panel. Use the layout lines on the partition and the center line on the bottom of the tool to properly line up the biscuit joiner.

just the thing.

First, they're strong. Lamello, the inventor of biscuit joinery, has done extensive stress tests on the joints. In one of these tests the scientists joined two pieces of beech, end grain to end grain, using a #20 biscuit. This is just about the weakest joint I could imagine. Then they had a machine grab each end and pull the thing apart. It took an average of 972 pounds of force to destroy the joint. Not bad for a little wafer of beech or birch.

Second, they're fast joints to make. We checked the amount of time it took to make several common joints for face frames. The winner was the pocket screw, but that's because there's no clamping time. Take the clamping time out, and biscuits and pocket screws are a tie for the fastest method.

Finally, they're safe and easy to use. It's difficult to hurt yourself with the machine, and injuries are rare. In fact, I know of only two ways an injury can occur. First, the tool slips or kicks out of a cut and your left hand gets chewed up before the blade retracts. Or second, you plunge the biscuit joiner before you turn it on. The tool walks into your hand that's holding the piece and up your arm.

If you've never used a biscuit joiner, it probably will take you about five minutes to learn the basics. That said, a few tricks ensure that all of your joints are perfectly lined up. Because the tool is so fast, it's easy to get lazy and a little sloppy.

The Basic Basics

Biscuits can add strength to a joint, such as when you join a table apron to a leg. Or they can be used as an alignment aid, such as when you glue up a slab using several boards or you need to glue together veneered panels. The biscuits won't add strength here, but they will keep your parts in line as you clamp. In a solid-wood panel, the biscuits reduce the amount of time you spend leveling your joints. In veneered panels, biscuits keep your parts in line so you don't end up sanding through the veneer.

When making a biscuit joint, first put the two parts together and decide how many biscuits you need for that joint. A basic rule of thumb is to place your first biscuit 2" from the edge and then every 5" to 7" or so, though the spacing is really up to you. Draw a line across the joint at each spot where you want a biscuit. Set the fence on your biscuit joiner so the biscuit will be buried approximately in the middle of your material (for example, if you're working with $^{3}/_{4}$"-thick wood, set your biscuit joiner for a $^{3}/_{8}$"-deep cut. Don't worry about being dead-on in the middle. If you cut all your joints on one side, say, the face side, every-

One of my favorite tricks with a biscuit joiner is using it to cut the slots for tabletop fasteners. Set the fence for $^{1}/_{2}$" (you want the slot to start $^{7}/_{16}$" down from the top of the apron) and make your cuts on the inside of the apron (you can do this after the table is assembled). The Z-shaped fasteners now slip into the slots and can be screwed to your tabletop.

thing will line up). Select the size biscuit you want to use and dial that into your tool. Use the biggest size you can.

Clamp one of your parts to your bench. Line up the line on the tool's fence or face plate with the line on your work. Turn on the tool and allow it to get up to full speed. Plunge the tool into the wood and then out. Repeat this process for the other side of the joint.

Now glue up your joint. There are at least two ways of doing this. You can put glue in the slots and then insert the biscuit, or you can put glue on the biscuit and insert it in the slot.

For small projects, paint half the biscuit with glue and insert it into one of the slots. Then paint the other half of the biscuit and clamp your pieces together. This method produces clean joints with minimal squeeze-out, but it's a bit slow.

When assembling big projects, I like to put the glue in the slots first, using a bottle designed for this task. Squirt a dab of glue in all your slots and use a spare biscuit, piece of scrap or brush to paint the edges. Put the biscuits in the slots and clamp up. The downside to this method is it's easy to use too much glue, and you're liable to get more squeeze-out.

No matter which method you use, be sure to go easy on the clamping pressure. It's easy to distort a frame made with biscuits. If you're using a regular yellow glue, clamp the project for at least 30 to 45 minutes before taking it out of the clamps.

Where to Use Biscuits

Making the biscuit slot is easy. The tricky part is knowing when to use biscuits and how many to use. Here are some situations when you should be careful:

Long-grain joints: Many people use biscuits to join several narrow pieces into a panel, such as a tabletop. Biscuits help align the boards so they don't slip as much when you clamp them. However, don't let anyone tell you that the biscuits make the joint stronger. In long-grain to long-grain joints, the glue is stronger than the wood itself. So biscuits here are only an alignment tool. Also, be careful to place the biscuits where they won't show after you trim your part to finished size. Once I raised the panel on a door and exposed half a biscuit. That panel had to go in the trash.

Face frames: Biscuits are just right for face frames as long as your stock isn't too narrow. A #0 biscuit will work only with stock as narrow as $2\frac{7}{8}$". Any narrower and the biscuit will poke out the sides. To join narrow stock, you need a biscuit joiner that can use a smaller cutter (such as the Porter-Cable 557 or Lamello Top 20S) or a tool that cuts slots for mini biscuits from Ryobi or Craftsman.

Continuous-stress joints: Biscuits are strong, but I wouldn't build a kitchen chair with them. The joints in chairs, especially where the seat meets the back, are subject to enormous amounts of stress. Call me old-fashioned, but I'd use a mortise-and-tenon joint.

With polyurethane adhesives: We like poly glue quite a bit, but you must remember that biscuits swell and lock your joint in place by wicking up the water in your white or yellow glue. Poly glues have no moisture in them. In fact, these glues need moisture to cure. If you want to use poly glue with biscuits, dip your biscuits in water before inserting them into the slot. The water swells

BISCUITING AN APRON TO A LEG

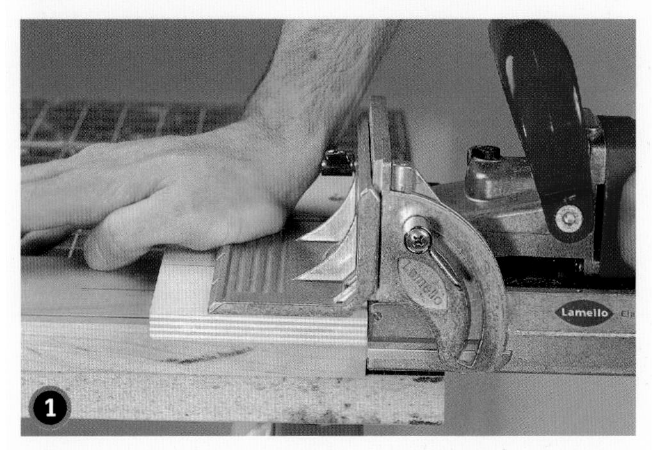

If you're going to use biscuits to attach a leg to a table apron, then you really should use two biscuits stacked on top of one another. This joint, according to experts and scientists, is nearly as strong as a mortise-and-tenon joint. The other challenge with this joint is you are going to want to offset the apron so it joins the middle of the leg. Here's the best way to do this. First, determine what your offset is. I wanted my aprons to sit $\frac{1}{2}$" back from the legs. Get a scrap piece of wood that is the same thickness as the offset. Put this block of wood on top of your apron and set the fence on your biscuit joiner to make the first cut. Make the cut on the apron.

Now cut the biscuit slot on the leg without the spacer. When that's done, go back to your apron and adjust the fence to make the second biscuit slot.

Finally, cut the second row of slots on the leg without the spacer. When you're done, you've got a double helping of biscuits ready for some glue.

BISCUITING MITERS

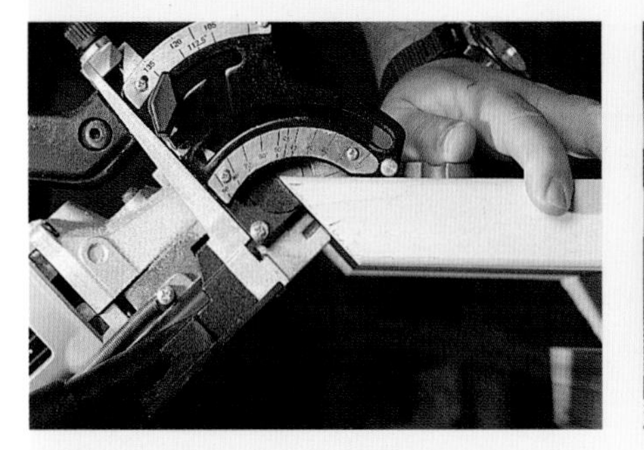

The fence on the Porter-Cable 557 allows you to biscuit your miters with the fence on the outside of the joint — a nice feature.

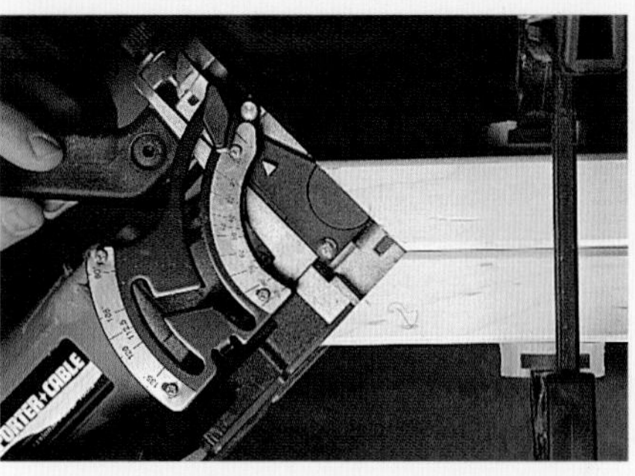

You can biscuit miters without using your fence by clamping the two joints together.

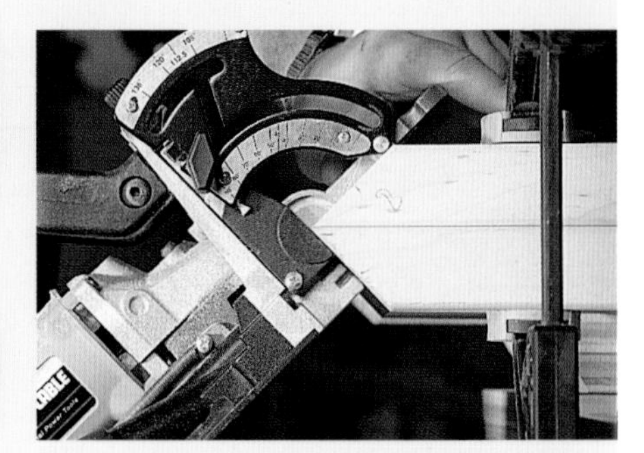

Or if you have a fixed 90° fence on your tool, you can clamp them together this way to cut your slots.

the biscuit and activates the poly glue.

Building tables: If you're going to build a table using your biscuit joiner, use two stacked biscuits to attach the aprons and stretchers to the legs. This might mean making your aprons 7/8" thick. See the photos for an easy way to get the apron in the right place and two biscuits into your joint. In fact, whenever you're joining thick stock it's a good idea to add an extra biscuit.

With 1/2" plywood: When using a biscuit joiner to join pieces of 1/2"-thick plywood, you might have trouble with the biscuits "telegraphing" their shape into the surface of your material. Use #0 or #10 biscuits with 1/2"-thick material and go a little easy on the glue.

Fence or No Fence?

Some woodworkers always rest the tool's fence on the work to control how deep the cut is; others prefer to take the fence off and let the tool's base ride on their bench or a table. Each approach has advantages. When you take the fence off and use your bench as the reference surface, you have a large flat area for your tool to rest against and sniped boards won't throw off your joiner. However, you have to watch for sawdust on your bench and work with all your parts facedown on your bench. Advocates of the fence approach say it's easier and more accurate to work with your parts faceup on your bench. But you have to ensure your biscuit joiner is square to your work. If you lift up or press down on the tool during the cut, it could throw off your joint. Try each method and see what works best for you.

Quick Jig Speeds Your Work

Your biscuit joiner doesn't need a lot of jigs and fixtures. However, building this jig will make the tool easier and safer to use. When I first started using biscuit joiners, I held the wood with my left hand and the tool with my right. After my grip failed me a couple of times, I became an advocate of clamping your work in place.

But clamping takes time. This jig makes clamping quick and easy. The quick-release clamps allow you to fix your work in place in a second or two (with almost 300 pounds of clamping pressure), and it gives your biscuit joiner a bed to ride on.

Why is that important? You see, if you retract or remove the fence on your tool, the tool is designed to cut a slot in the middle of a 3/4"-thick board when resting on a flat surface. So with this jig you don't need to set your fence. You simply clamp your wood in place, mark where you want the slot, put your tool on the bed and plunge.

This jig also makes your cuts more accurate because it ignores snipe on the ends of your stock. If you use the fence on your biscuit joiner when building face frames, you can get in trouble when the end of the board is sniped. Because of the snipe, your tool won't cut the slot in the right place and your joints won't be flush.

With this jig, all you have to do is remember to put all your pieces face-side down on the jig and keep it free of sawdust. Because the tool rides on the jig and not the work, your slot is going to be exactly where you need it.

I also made an attachment for this jig that guides the biscuit joiner when cutting slots in miters. This attachment keeps your tool on target and prevents it from kicking left as you plunge.

Building the jig takes less than 30 minutes. The most important part is the bed itself. You want it to be as flat as possible. Glue two pieces of 3/4"-thick plywood together and check the sandwich for flatness with a straightedge. Then nail another piece of plywood on the bottom of the jig's front edge so the jig hooks over your bench.

Nail and glue two strips of 1/2"-thick plywood in the locations shown in the diagram on the next page. Then screw the clamps in place. Let the glue dry before you go to work; engaging the clamps at this point can tear your jig apart.

Troubleshooting

Not much goes wrong with biscuit joinery, but here are some of the troubles we've run into and how to remedy them.

Sometimes when you get in a hurry, your biscuit slots aren't aligned. The joint will either be whopper-jawed or impossible to clamp shut. Using a ruler, figure out which of the slots is off (it might be both). Glue a biscuit into the botched slot and let the glue dry. Then trim the biscuit flush to your material and cut your joint again.

When your biscuit joiner bogs down and burns the wood, it's trying to tell you something. Usually your blade

BISCUIT JIG

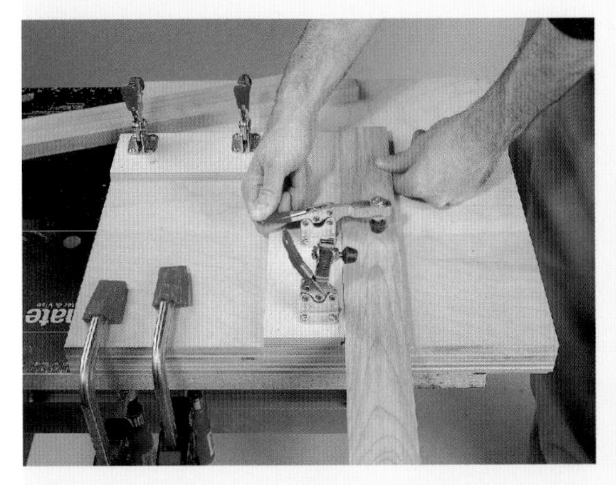

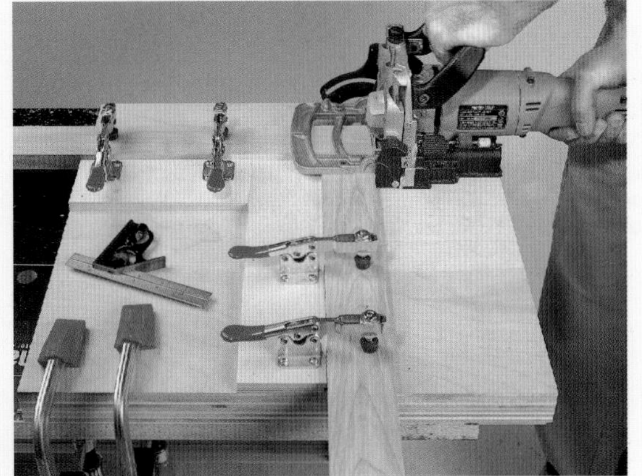

The beauty of this jig is that it holds both a rail and stile in place for cutting. You can cut one right after the other if you please, or cut them one at a time.

This jig is useful for two reasons. First, it will make your tool more accurate. You use the plywood base to guide your tool. That way if there's any snipe on the end of the board, your biscuit will still end up in exactly the right spot. Second, it will make your work a whole lot faster. The quick-release clamps on this jig (which supply hundreds of pounds of clamping force) will keep you from clamping each piece to your bench, which slows you down. If you're one of those people who holds your face-frame parts down with your hand as you cut them, you'll find this jig is just as fast as that method, and your work is a lot less prone to slipping.

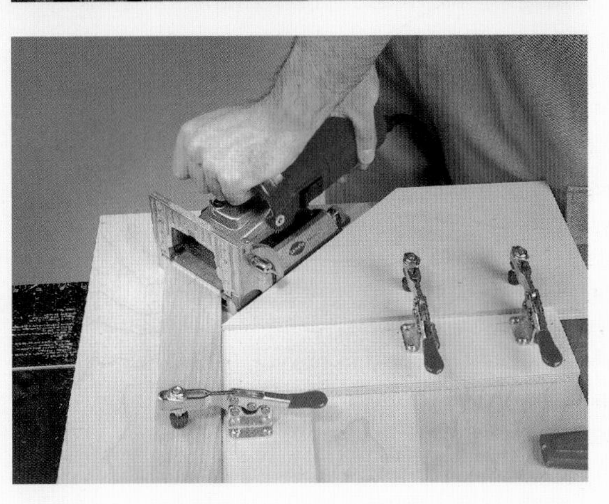

If you cut biscuits to join a mitered frame, this jig is quite useful when you add the 45° spacer shown in the photo above. The spacer helps guide the tool and prevents it from kicking to the left, something the biscuit joiners are prone to do in narrow stock.

is gummed up with resin or it's dull. Remove the blade and spray it with an oven cleaner. If that doesn't help, replace the blade.

Probably the weakest feature on most biscuit joiners is the dust collection. Typically, the tool tries to shoot the chips out a small port and into a cloth bag. This usually works for about half a dozen biscuits, then the port gets clogged and dust sprays everywhere when you make a slot. Sometimes this is a sign that your bag is getting old and frayed. The frayed ends cling together and the chips back up into the port and then get clogged. If your bag is old, first try turning it inside out. If that doesn't help, just get an adapter to connect your tool to a shop vacuum. That will solve your problem.

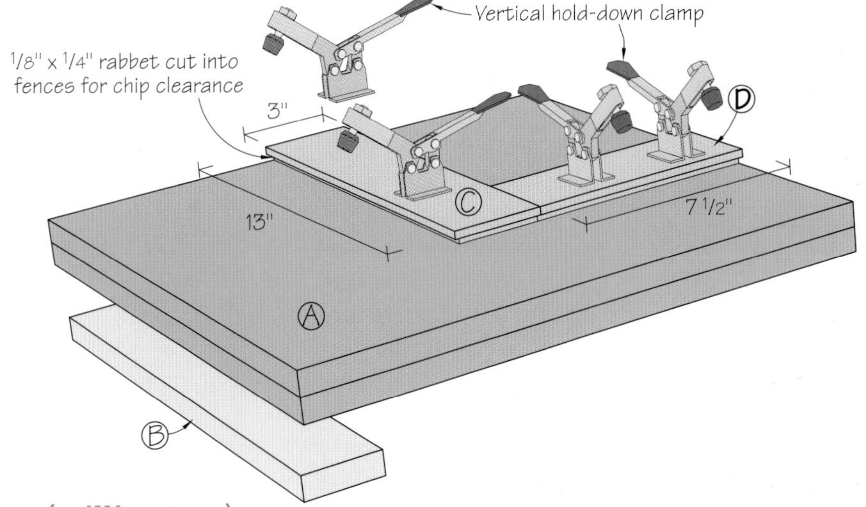

inches (millimeters)

REFERENCE	QUANTITY	PART	STOCK	THICKNESS	(mm)	WIDTH	(mm)	LENGTH	(mm)
A	2	bed	plywood	3/4	(19)	18 1/2	(470)	18 1/2	(470)
B	1	cleat	plywood	3/4	(19)	2 1/2	(64)	18 1/2	(470)
C	1	fence for stiles	plywood	1/2	(13)	3	(76)	13	(330)
D	1	fence for rails	plywood	1/2	(13)	3	(76)	7 1/2	(191)
E	1	mitering guide	plywood	3/4	(19)	8	(203)	15	(381)

cope-and-stick joinery

BY JIM STUARD

Cope-and-stick joinery today is all about tungsten carbide. But the origins of this important door-joinery method are rooted in the world of moulding planes, chisels and backsaws. A little history is in order as to the origin of the terms *cope* and *stick*. According to Graham Blackburn, a noted author on woodworking and its history, frame-and-panel construction came into its own back in the 14th and 15th centuries. Different methods evolved for joining a rail and a stile together and capturing a panel. The object is, of course, to circumvent wood movement and make stable panels and doors for furniture.

Cutting the stick

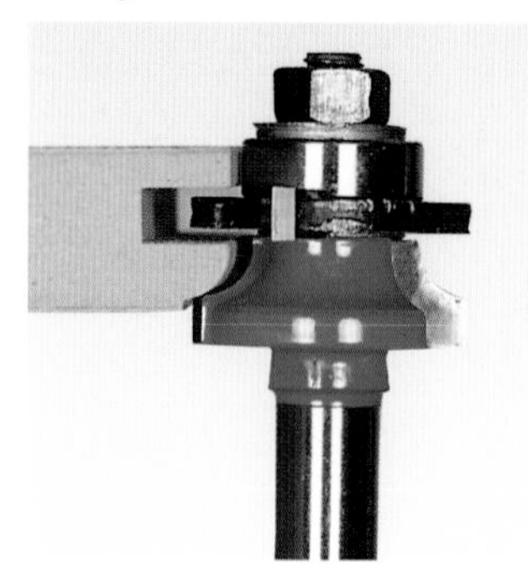
Cutting the cope

When the frame required a profile on the inside, it was made with moulding planes. This is referred to as a stuck moulding. As in, it's not an applied moulding, it's stuck on or made on the existing edge. Hence the term *stick*. The rail and stile were joined using a mortise-and-tenon joint with a miter on the moulded edge, where the rail and stile met. This is commonly referred to as a mason's miter. Coping comes from its actual definition: "to deal with a problem." In the case of rail-and-stile joinery, the problem was dealing with the stuck edge. The solution was to make an opposite of the stuck profile that fit over the edge, filling the profile.

With the advent of mechanization in the 19th century, different, faster methods had to be devised to join those pesky rails and stiles. Enter high-speed cutting tools. They could be set up to make thousands of feet of stuck moulding and then the opposite of the cutter could be made to cut the cope on the rail ends.

Which Bit Is Right for Me?

You can still make cope-and-stick doors using moulding planes, but most people use a router in a router table. Router bit catalogs are filled with cope-and-stick bits that are priced anywhere from about $50 to $150. Essentially there are three types of bits to choose from. The least expensive is what is called a reversible cope-and-stick cutter. This single bit has two cutters, a bearing and shims to adjust it. You cut the stick part of the moulding, then you disassemble the bit and stack the pieces in a different order to cut the cope. These are decent entry-level bits, but keep in mind that disassembling the bit can be a hassle, and you have to remember exactly how many shims go between each part or your joints won't fit. Also, wear on the cutter is doubled, necessitating resharpening more often.

The other single-shank solution is the nonadjustable combination bit. This one-piece bit is basically a chunk of metal on a ½" shank. It has a bearing on top and bottom. You cut the stick part of the moulding with the top section of the bit, then you raise the bit to cut the cope. The only drawback to these bits is they are a little long and will exaggerate any runout problems you might have with your router.

Last but not least expensive is the matched set. In a matched set, each bit has a fixed cutter close to the shank, a bearing and another matched cutter. These bit sets have advantages over the other sets. When they're sharpened, it's just a matter of proper shimming to get them back to an airtight fit. There's two separate sets of cutters, giving them longer life between sharpenings. They're relatively shorter than combination bits, so they'll be more stable in a router. And once you get them set up, you won't have to take them apart until they're resharpened. The only real drawback is that they are usually the most expensive solution.

Which bit is right for you? If you make an occasional door, use a single-shank solution. It's cheaper and you won't be sharpening the bit anytime soon. If there are a lot of doors in your future or you just want a setup that will last a long time, a real time-saver is having two bits in two tables and running all your stock at once. The price difference between one-bit and two-bit sets is around $20 to $50 dollars, depending on the manufacturer and quality.

SET YOUR FENCE
Setting up and using a cope-and-stick set of bits is relatively easy after the shimming is done. First, make sure the bearing on the bit is flush with the fence on the router table. Flushing the bearings makes sure that the profiles will match up. Use a straightedge that spans the two fences and tap the fence flush to the bearing. If possible, close the fence faces so there's about ⅛" clearance on both sides of the cutter.

Above are the three types of cope-and-stick bits. A is a matched set of cutters: one bit for the stick, another for the cope. B is a nonadjustable combination bit. You change from cope to stick by changing the height of the router. C is a reversible bit. After cutting the stick profile, you disassemble the bit and rearrange the pieces to cut the cope.

A. FREUD 99-260 • $111.50

B. CMT 891.521 • $127.50

C. MLCS 8852 • $65

Cut the stick profile. Using fingerboards to keep your stock in place, press the stock into the fence and down onto the router table. Which profile you cut first isn't critical. Use test cuts to get your bits in the ballpark. I cut the stick first. For door construction, you can cut your stock to finish length, but I prefer to leave the stiles a little long for trimming later.

Cut the cope. Next, cut the cope profile on the ends of the rails. Make sure to use a backing piece (sometimes called a cope block) of scrap. Because of the usual narrow width of a rail and the force of a router, the rail can easily be pulled into the bit. Hold the rail tightly to the cope block to avoid this. It's not necessary to push the entire setup through the cutter, just the rail ends. Once the front of the push block is touching the outfeed fence, gently pivot it away from the fence from the outfeed side.

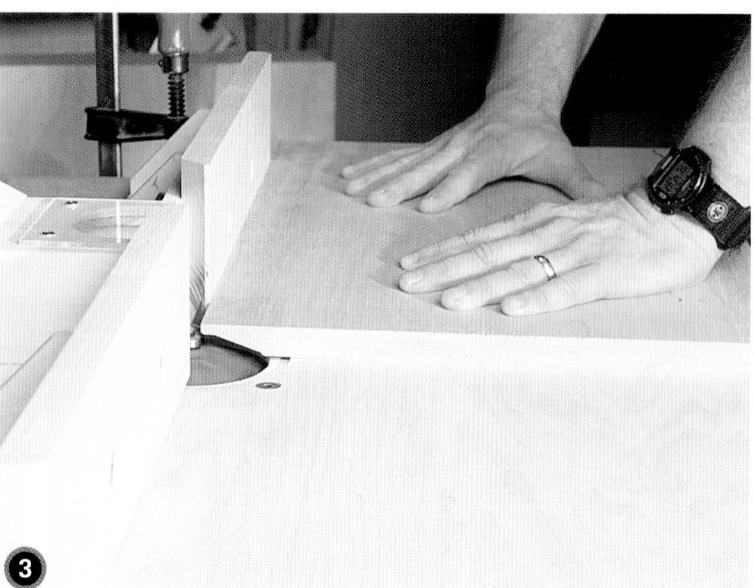

Cut the panel. Once you've got rails and stiles that are sized properly, fit the parts using light clamp pressure and take the measurements for the panel. Leave a $^1/_8$" gap all around to allow for seasonal expansion. Run the panel on the router by pressing it flat to the table. Cut the end-grain sides first, then the long-grain sides. Make the cut in several passes, adjusting the height of the panel cutter after each pass. If you're using a big panel cutter such as the one shown here, you'll probably want to slow the bit's speed (if you have an adjustable-speed router).

THE EASIEST WAY TO SET UP A TWO-BIT SET

If you're one of those people who plunked down your hard-earned dollars on a two-piece bit set, you may test it out and find that the joint isn't tight or aligned. Some sets require some fine-tuning upon arrival. Here's how it's done:

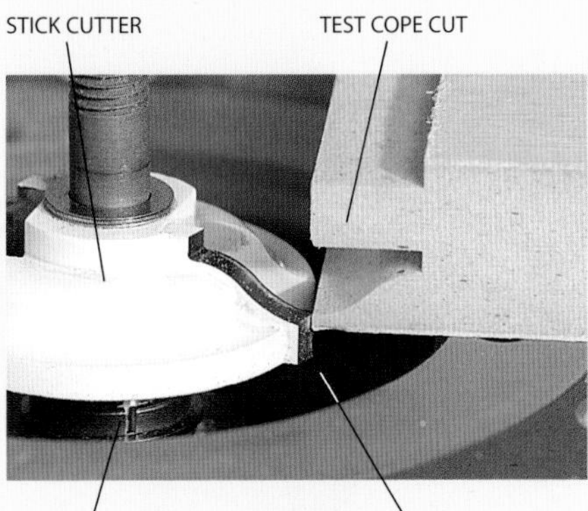

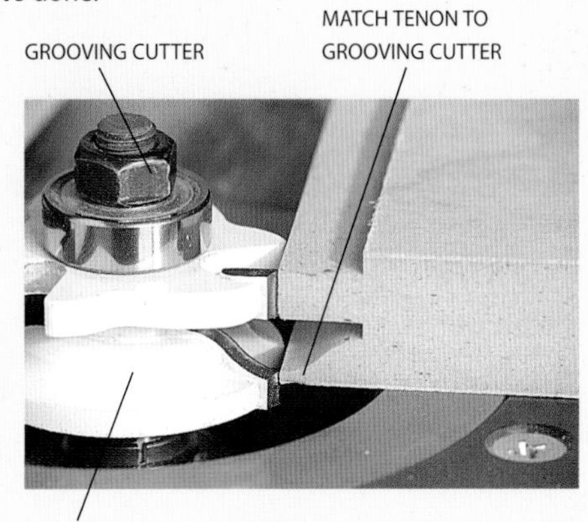

Get Familiar with the Parts

Many two-bit sets work great right out of the box; others make joints that are too loose or too tight. You can fix the problem, but you're going to have to disassemble the bits to adjust the cutters. Plan on this taking an hour or two of your time. It's a pain, but remember you won't have to do this again until you get your bits resharpened.

The easiest way to take these bits apart is to chuck them into a router. Use a wrench on top of the bit to loosen the cutters as you hold the bit in place with one of the router wrenches on the collet. Two-bit sets have a fixed bottom cutter, a bearing and a grooving cutter that are separated by thin shims. To get your two-bit set (or your reversible set) working, you're going to have to figure out which shims go where for a perfect fit.

Step One: Align the Shoulders

Start by chucking the cope cutter in a router and making a test cut on a piece of scrap. I use MDF for setup because it is made up of small particles that have no grain direction. This gives accurate, highly visible test cuts. Cut the cope, leaving about $^{1}/_{16}$" on what will be the top shoulder of the cut. Next, chuck the stick cutter into the router and remove the grooving cutter, bearing and shims. Start the alignment process by placing the shoulder cut of the sample cope cut up against the fixed cutter in the stick bit and matching shoulder heights by raising or lowering the router (see the photo above).

Result: Flush Shoulders

At this point the joint made by these cutters would be pretty sloppy, as shown in the photo below. You can see, however, that the cut is flush on the shoulder (bottom) of the joint, which is the point of this important first step.

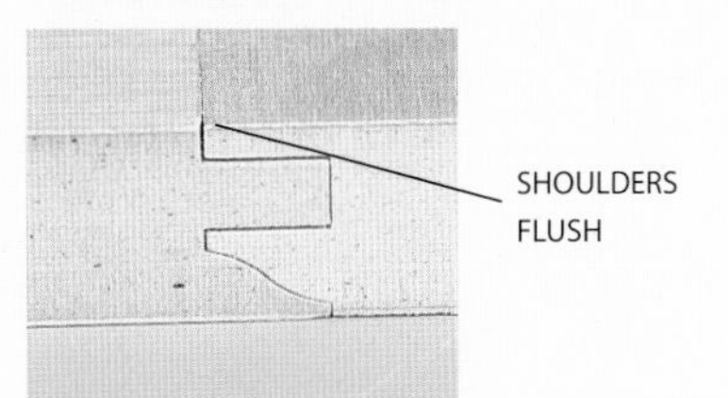

Step Two: Tighten the Top of the Tenon

The next step is to tighten up the joint between the tenon and the cope. Using your test cope piece as a guide, mount the grooving cutter and shim it as best as you can to match the tenon on the test cope piece.

Result: Top of Tenon is Perfect

After properly shimming the grooving cutter, you'll get a tight fit on the cope and the top of the tenon. Keep a test cut from the stick cutter. This is the finished, shimmed setup for the stick cutter.

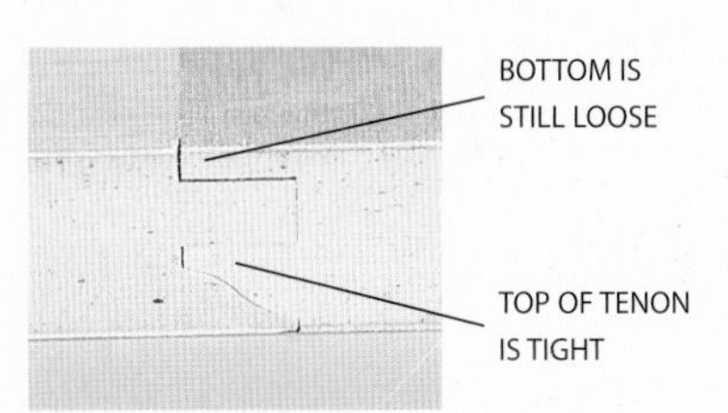

Step Three: Shim the Cope Cutter

Remove the stick cutter from the router and chuck up the cope cutter. It also has a grooving cutter on top that needs to be shimmed to get the bottom of the tenon to fit snugly. Disassemble the bit and shim the grooving cutter so it is flush with the bottom of the tenon on the stick test piece. Now your joints should be tight.

crosscutting

BY DAVID THIEL

Crosscutting Lumber

When crosscutting a board, the substantially narrower width of the piece (and not enough width to ride adequately against the fence) causes us to use a miter gauge rather than the fence. You may note the gauge in our photos is not standard equipment. We recommend either adding a backing board at least 24" long to your miter gauge or purchasing an aftermarket gauge.

1

Start by ensuring your miter gauge is square to the blade. Then align your cut and pull the board against the gauge. Put one hand on the gauge's handle and the other stretched across the piece to hold your work tightly against the gauge's fence. If your piece is too wide to reach across, clamp the piece against the gauge during the cut.

2

Guide the board into and past the blade.

3

Once the board is cut through, allow the fall-off piece (on the left in the photo) to lie in place. With your left hand, push the board away from the blade, sliding it along the gauge. Turn the saw off. Once the blade stops spinning, pull the falloff piece away from the blade.

Crosscutting Plywood

Crosscutting plywood on a contractor's saw is safely accomplished by the use of roller stands. Though plywood is bulky, don't worry as much about the board pinching the blade in the cut because plywood doesn't have the internal stresses of solid wood.

1

Here you see one stand positioned to one side of the table saw and another positioned at the outfeed side. When using the rip fence, do not crosscut a piece less than 18" wide or more than 48" long. There is too much chance of the board shifting and becoming pinched. Start the crosscut by standing in the center of the board to support the length. Keep your eye on the fence and keep the board tight against it. Arrows indicate the direction my hands are applying pressure.

2

Maintain the center position as you push the board through the blade. Keep your eye on the fence!

3

Once the keeper piece has cleared the blade, let the falloff piece lie where it is. Carefully push the piece between the fence and blade past the blade and onto the roller stand. Keep the piece flush against the fence until it's clear and then lift it out of the way.

dado joints

BY BILL HYLTON

In casework of any size, using natural or manufactured materials (or both), the dado is prime-choice joinery. It follows that hoary adage of woodworking: "Use the simplest joint that will work."

It certainly works. The dado joint is traditional, with a centuries-long history of use in cabinetmaking.

It definitely is simple. All dado joint variations derive from the cut itself. A dado is a flat-bottomed channel cut across the grain of the wood. (When it runs with the grain, the channel is called a groove.) You cut a dado or groove into one board, and the mating board fits into it. One well-placed, properly sized cut with the proper tool makes the joint. And with today's power tools, it's a cut that is almost trivial to make — if you know how.

The dado does not have to be deep to create a strong joint. In solid wood, 1/8" is deep enough, and 1/4" in plywood, medium-density fiberboard (MDF) or particleboard. The shallow channel helps align the parts during assembly, and the ledge it creates is enough to support the weight of a shelf and everything loaded on it. The dado also prevents the shelf from cupping.

The one stress it doesn't resist effectively is tension. In other words, it doesn't prevent the shelf from pulling out of the side. Only glue or fasteners can do that. Because all the gluing surfaces involve end grain, the glue strength is limited.

Different Kinds of Dadoes

When the dado extends from edge to edge, it's called a through-dado. It's easy to cut. The most common objection to it is that it shows. However, you can conceal the joint using a face frame or trim.

A dado or groove doesn't have to be through, of course. It can begin at one edge and end before it reaches the other (stopped), or it can begin and end shy of either edge (blind). These versions are a little trickier to cut.

To make a stopped or blind dado, the corners of the mating board must be notched, creating a projection that fits in the dado. Sizing the notches so you have a little play from end to end makes it easier to align the edges of the parts. But it does sacrifice a bit of the strength that the narrow shoulder imparts.

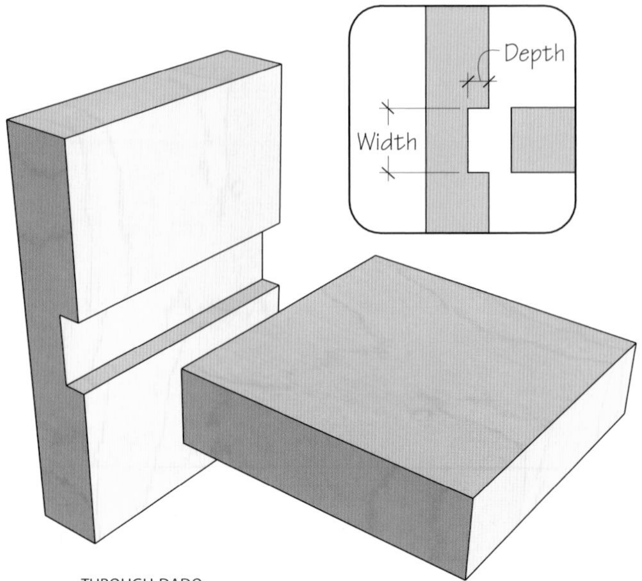

THROUGH-DADO

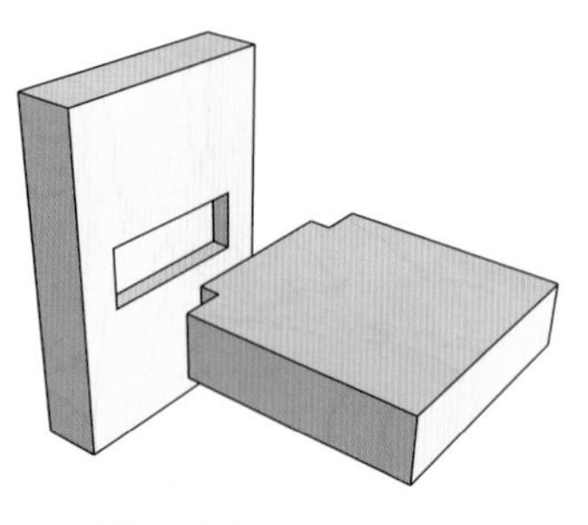
BLIND DADO

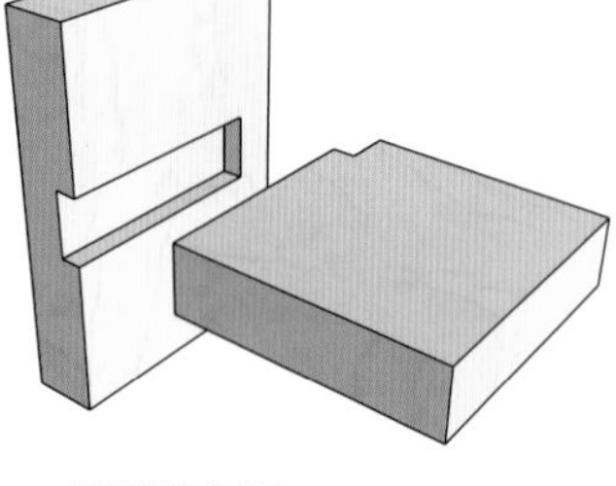
STOPPED DADO

Cutting Dadoes

Some other joints begin with dadoes, but before I even mention them, let's deal with the basic joinery cut. There are scads of ways to cut a dado successfully.

Keep a couple of criteria in mind as you tackle the dado cut. To end up with a strong joint, you need to make a cut of the correct width. The bottom needs to be smooth and flat, the sides perpendicular. If the cut is too wide, glue isn't going to compensate; the joint will be weak. Get the fit right.

The two most obvious power tools for cutting dadoes are the table saw and the router. But there are other options.

You can do dadoes with a radial-arm saw. If you are comfortable with this machine, you probably can recite the advantages. Fitted with a dado head, the radial-arm saw hogs through dadoes quickly. The workpiece is faceup, so you can see what you're doing. Layout marks are visible, and you can line up each cut quickly. When a stopped dado is needed, you can cut to a mark. The work isn't moved during the cut, so the piece is less likely to twist or shift out of position. This is especially helpful on angled cuts, whether a miter or a bevel (or both).

I have cut dadoes on narrow workpieces using a sliding compound miter saw. Most such saws have a cut-depth adjuster; you set the cut depth (with some trial and error), then waste each dado with kerf after kerf.

It's one of those operations you do once, just to try it. And once was enough for me. I prefer to stick with my table saw and my router for cutting dadoes.

A dado stack set consists of separate blades, chippers and washer-like shims. You fit the elements onto the saw's arbor, one by one.

An accurate, shop-made cutoff box is the best guide accessory to use for dadoing on the table saw. Set the cutoff box on the sled base, tight against the fence. The work won't shimmy or shift out of position as you slide the box across the dado cutter.

Table-Saw Dadoes

Let's look at the table saw first. It's powerful and equipped with accessories — a rip fence and a miter gauge — useful in positioning cuts. Like a lot of other woodworkers, I use a shop-made cutoff box (instead of the miter gauge) for crosscutting; it also works for dadoes. To use the saw effectively for dadoing, you need a dado cutter, either a stack set or a wobbler.

You can waste a narrow dado pretty quickly with whatever blade is on the saw. If you've got a manageable workpiece and just one or two dadoes to cut, you make five to seven kerfs to form each one. But to cut a cabinet's worth of dadoes, use a dado cutter.

If you're making cabinetry assembled with through-dado joints, you can knock out a lot of consistently sized and placed cuts in short order. What isn't necessarily quick and easy is achieving the precise width of cut you want. Stack sets, which give the cleanest cut, consist of separate blades and chippers. You have to select the combination needed to produce the approximate width of cut desired. To tune the cut to a precise width, you insert shims between the blades. It's got more trial and error in the setup than I like.

Some woodworkers (those with too much time on their hands, I think) make a chart or a cut sample with notes on the combinations of blades, chippers and specific shims needed to produce common-width dadoes. If you have the patience for this endeavor, my hat is off to you. Go for it.

But the woodworkers most likely to use the table saw for dadoing are those who are looking at a lot of cuts and not a lot of time to make them. Often, these folks adopt work-arounds to avoid protracted setups. They'll shoot for an

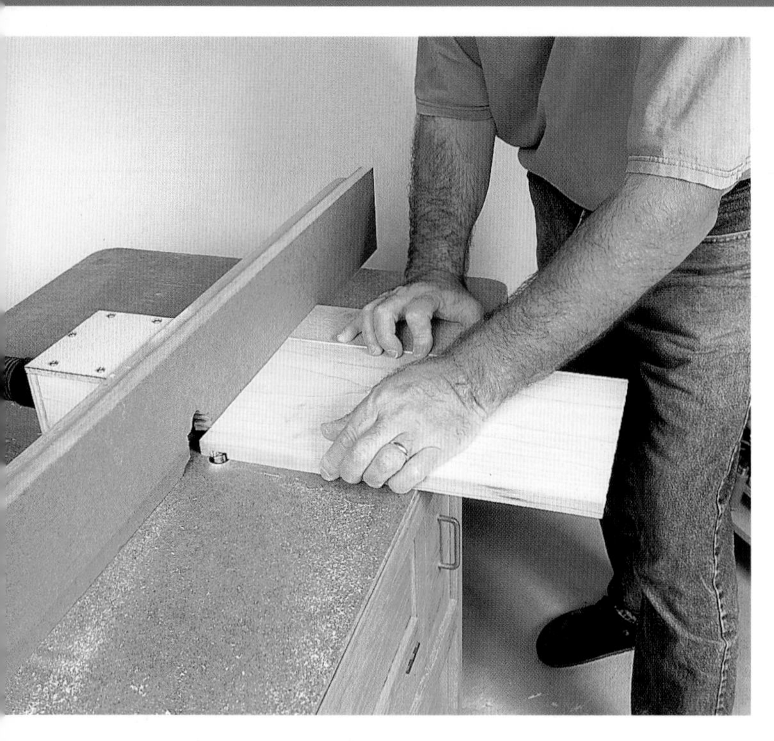

The typical router table setup works for dadoing parts like drawer sides. A push block — just a square scrap — stabilizes the work and backs up the cut, preventing tear-out as the bit emerges from the cut.

Dado large workpieces on a router table with a cutoff box-like sled. A stop clamped to the sled's fence locates the cut and immobilizes the work. Slides on the underside reference the edges of the tabletop to guide the sled.

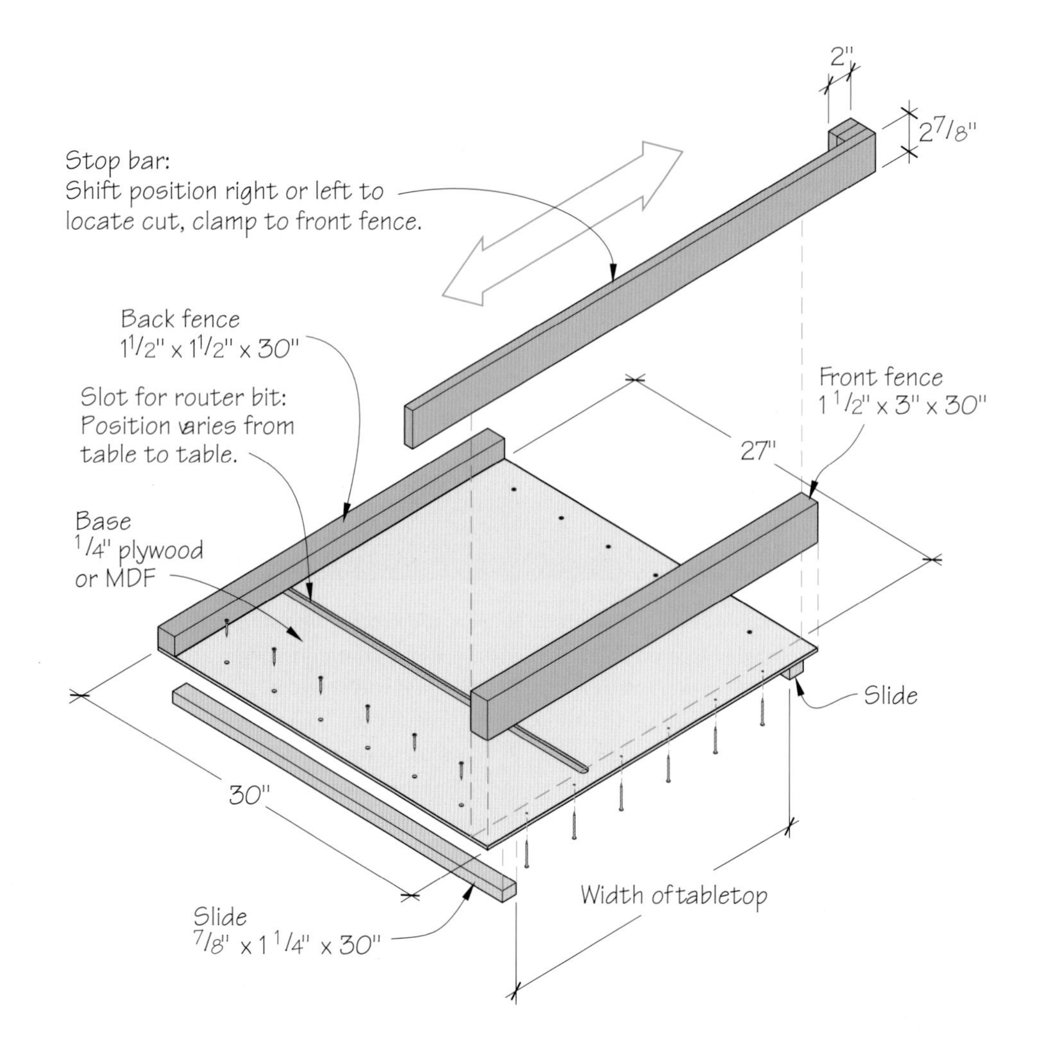

undersize dado, and then plane or sand the part to be housed in it to fit. Or they'll use the dado-and-rabbet joint: The mating part is rabbeted to form a tongue that fits whatever dado has been cut.

How do you locate and guide the cut? The rip fence is seductive, because it allows you to locate a cut consistently on both sides of a cabinet or bookcase. It eliminates the need for layout. But it isn't a crosscutting guide, and dadoes are crosscuts.

Of the two crosscutting guides, I prefer the cutoff box. It's built specifically for right-angle cuts and rides in both miter-gauge slots (instead of just one). In addition, it effectively immobilizes the workpiece, because the box is what moves, carrying the stationary workpiece with it. The work doesn't squirm or twist as you push it into the cutter. Fit the box with a stop so you can accurately and consistently locate a cut on multiples without individual layouts.

Stopped cuts can be problematic, and blind cuts can be downright hazardous. Because the work conceals the cutter, and because the cutoff box conceals most of the saw table, it's tricky to determine where to stop the cut. One good option is to clamp a stick to the outfeed table that stops your cutoff box at just the right spot.

A blind cut would require you to drop the work onto the spinning dado cutter — not a routine that I'd recommend.

Any stopped cut done with a dado head will ramp from the bottom of the cut to the surface. You can leave it and simply enlarge the notch in the mating piece, but in so doing, you sacrifice the strength in the joint that comes from a tightly fitted shoulder. Better to chisel out the ramp.

A crossbar attached at right angles to a plywood straightedge makes an easy-to-align T-square guide for dadoing with a router. Clamp it securely to the work and the benchtop at each end.

Routing Dadoes

The router's often touted as the most versatile tool in the shop, and it certainly is useful for dadoing. The cutters offer convenient sizing: Want a 1/2"-wide dado? Use a 1/2" bit. Want a dado for 3/4" plywood, which is typically under thickness? Use a 23/32" bit. Changing bits is quick and easy.

The tool also offers options on approach. If you have your router hung in a table, dadoing with it is much like table-saw dadoing. But the router gives you the option of moving the tool on a stationary workpiece, and in many situations, this turns out to be the better approach.

On the Router Table

For a long time, my mantra has been that you can rout grooves on a router table more easily than you can dadoes. Consider the typical router-table setup. It's small in comparison to the typical table-saw setup, with its expansive infeed and outfeed tables. So I'd say, limit yourself to dadoing small parts only, things such as drawer sides.

Guided by the fence alone, you can easily rout grooves. The grain runs along a workpiece's long dimension, so a groove is easy to locate and cut guided by the fence.

But try guiding the workpiece's short dimension edge along the fence. Or locating a dado 16" from that edge. Or 24" or 30". Maneuvering a 6'-long bookcase side or a 24" × 36" base cabinet side on a router-table top is a Keystone Kops routine. But a drawer side — where the piece is small and the dado (for the drawer back) is close to the end — can be routed pretty easily. You use a square-ended push block to keep the work square to the fence as you feed it and to back up the cut. Large case parts are best done on the table saw or with a handheld router.

Recently, however, I made a cutoff box-like accessory for my big router table. I don't like miter gauges (or the slots they require) on a router table, so the dadoing box I made is guided by the tabletop's edges. I've dadoed some pretty large workpieces with it. The setup was simple, the operation downright easy and the results were clean and precise.

This accessory is changing my attitude, I must say. It offers all the advantages of the table-saw cutoff box setup, but eliminates the trial and error with the stack set.

You do need to use a stop to position the work, because the stop also prevents the bit from moving the work. The bit in a table-mounted router is spinning counterclockwise, and it will pull work to the right. You

The gap between the fence bases on my dadoing jig represents the cut width. Pinch scraps of the work material between them to set the jig.

Position the jig by setting the fence base edge directly on your layout line. The crossbars ensure it will be perpendicular to the reference edge.

Cutting a dado is foolproof. The router is trapped between fences and can't veer off course, regardless of your feed direction. Reference the left fence as you push the router away, then reference the right one as you pull it back, completing the cut.

put the stop on the right to counteract that dynamic. (It's the equivalent of positioning the fence on the right.)

With a Handheld Router

I'm not ready to entirely abandon the router as a handheld tool, however. It remains a prime choice for dadoing large workpieces, such as sides for a tall bookcase or base cabinet. It seems easier and safer to move a relatively small tool on top of a cumbersome workpiece than the other way around.

The big question is how you will guide the router for the cut. A shop-made T-square fits the bill, as does a manufactured straight-edge clamp such as the Tru-Grip. An accurate T-square doesn't need to be squared on the work, as a Tru-Grip-type clamp does, but positioning it accurately can be a trick.

A setup gauge is helpful here. Cut a scrap to match the distance between the edge of the router base plate and the near cutting edge of the bit. Align one edge of the gauge on the shoulder of the desired cut and locate the T-square (or other guide) against the opposite edge. Bingo. The guide is set.

Though more elaborate to construct, my favorite dadoing jig is easy to position on simple layout marks, and it adjusts easily to cut the exact width of dado you need. You size the jig to suit your needs.

The jig has two ½" plywood fences, each laminated to a ¼" plywood or MDF base strip. Both are matched to a particular router and bit by running that router along the fence, and trimming the thin base with the straight bit. One fence is then screwed to two hardwood crossbars.

The bars must be perpendicular to the fence, of course. The second fence is mounted so it can be adjusted toward or away from the fixed fence, as shown in the photos.

Obviously, you cannot produce a dado narrower than the cutting diameter of the router bit, but you can do a wider one easily. Because the router is trapped between two fences, the feed direction is less of an issue and miscuts are unlikely.

The bases make it easy to adjust the cut width and to position the jig on simple layout marks. To do the former, use a scrap or two of the stock to be housed in the cut as gauges. Set them against the fixed-fence base, slide the adjustable fence into position and lock it down. To do the latter, align the fixed fence directly on one of the marks, with a crossbar tight against the work's edge. Secure the jig to the work with two clamps.

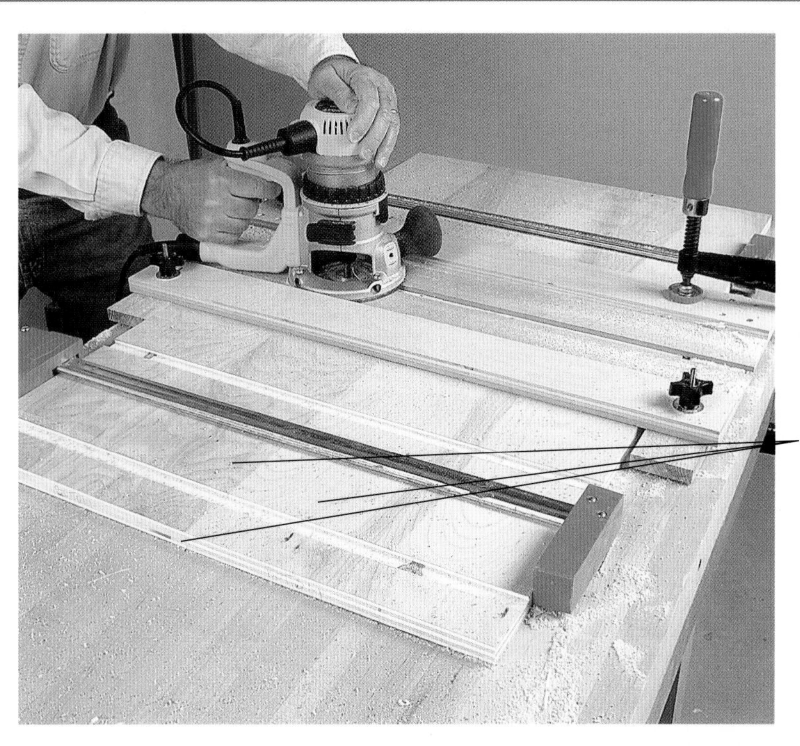

Dadoing cabinet sides? Clamp them edge to edge and rout both at the same time for cuts that line up perfectly.

For stopped or blind dadoes, clamp stop blocks to the jig (rather than the work). Move the jig, and the stops move with it. Using the plunge base eases beginning and ending these cuts.

dovetail jig

BY JIM STUARD

Years ago when I first learned to cut dovetails, my first joints weren't things of beauty. Sometimes there were more shims than pins. Over time, my work got better and faster. But despite the improvement in my skills, I still had trouble cutting tails or pins consistently, especially if I got out of practice.

This jig allows you to make great dovetails on your first day. The idea came to me when I was building a Shaker step stool using hand-cut dovetails. I made a jig that fit over the end of a board to guide my saw through the cut and provide a perfect tail. The jig didn't cut pins and worked only on $^3/_4$"-thick boards. I guess I wasn't thinking big that day.

A few weeks later it came to me: Why not build a jig that cuts both tails and pins and is adjustable to a variety of thicknesses? So I made this jig. From the first joint I cut using it, I got airtight joints. It was very cool.

This jig uses a 9° cutting angle. Woodworking books say that 9° is intended more for softwoods than hardwoods (which use a 7° angle) but I thought it a good compromise. You can build this jig entirely by hand, but I cheated and used a table saw for a couple of the precise angle cuts. Let your

Begin by sandwiching three pieces of wood. This part is made from two pieces of 3/4" × 6" × 36" plywood with a piece of 1" × 1" × 36" solid wood centered between. Use a spacer to index the center precisely in the middle of the larger panels. Glue and nail the sandwich together.

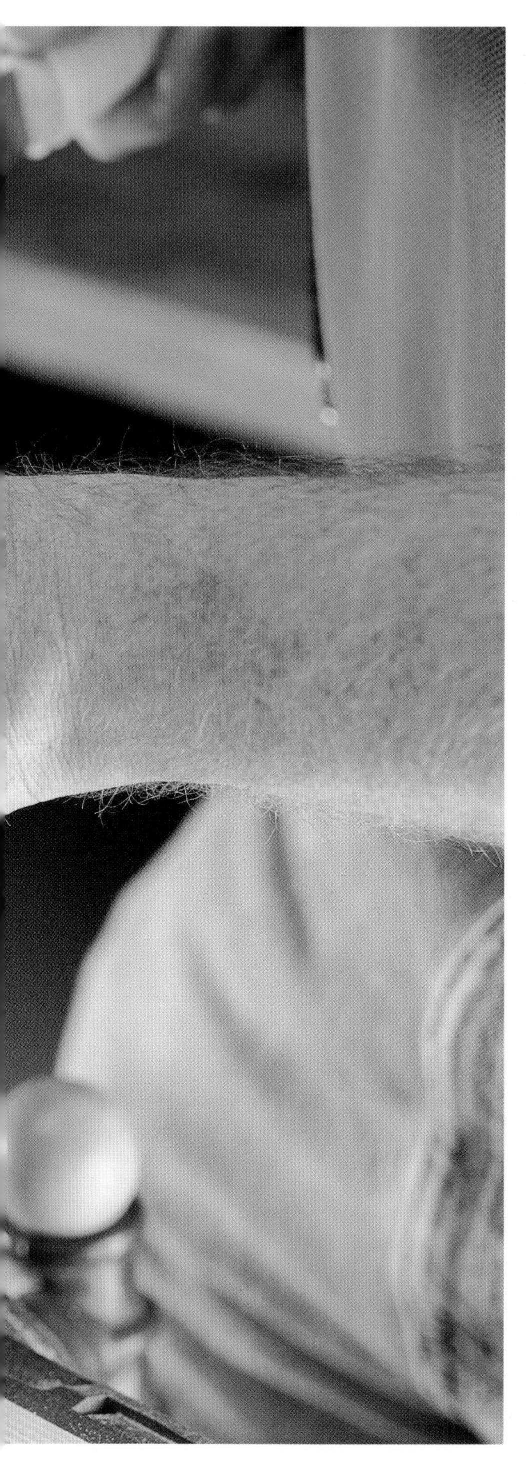

Set your saw's blade to 9° and crosscut the end of the sandwich while it's flat on the saw. Next, tilt the blade back to square and set the miter gauge to 9° as shown above. You can use the angled end of the sandwich to set your miter gauge. Lay out a center line down the middle of the sandwich and mark from the end of the line about 3 1/2". Use a sliding T-bevel to transfer the angle to the flat side. This yields a jig that will let you cut dovetails in material as narrow as 3" wide. Any narrower and you'll have to shorten the jig. Lay the extrusion flat on the saw table and cut to the line. The jig will be a little narrower on the other side, but that's OK.

conscience be your guide.

One of this jig's peculiarities is that you'll sometimes have to cut right on the pencil line. As designed, this jig works best with Japanese-style ryoba saws on material from 3/8" to 3/4" thick. Use the saw's ripping teeth when making your cuts. You could modify this jig to accommodate Western saws, but you'd have to take a lot of the set out of the teeth so as not to tear up the faces of the jig. The set of a saw's teeth basically allows you to steer a blade through a cut. This jig does all the steering. You just have to press the gas.

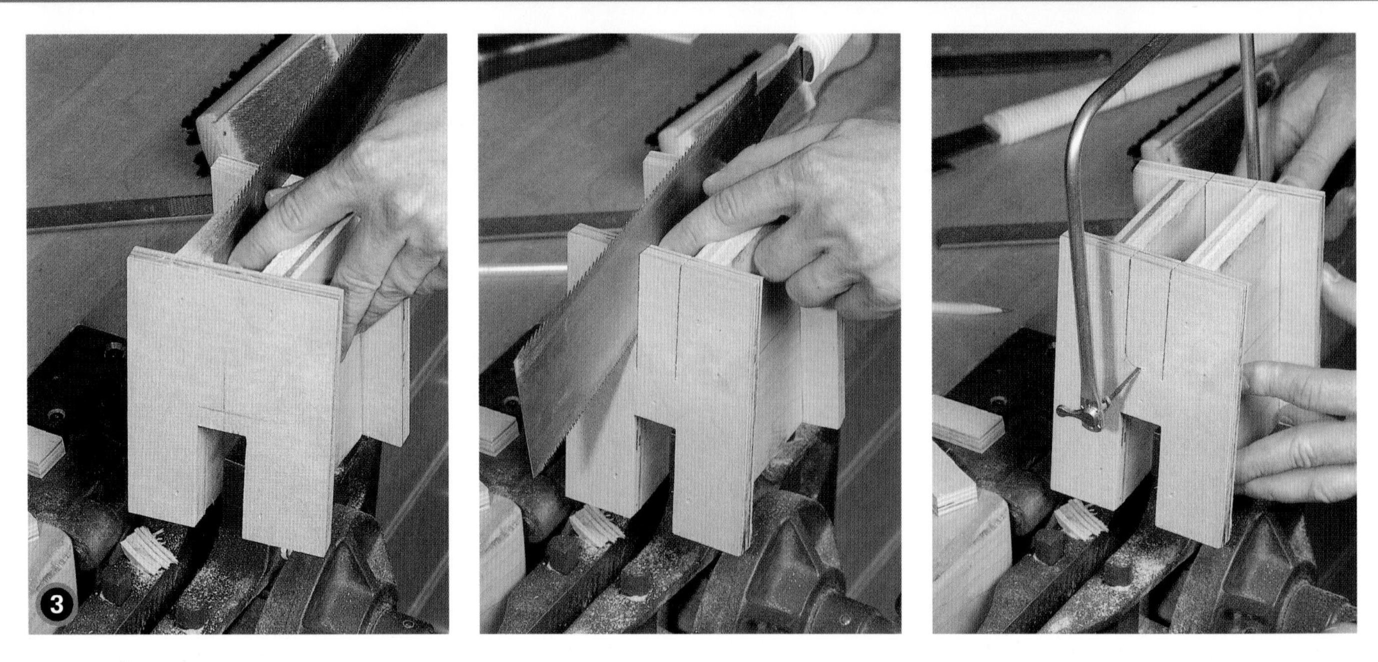

Attach the $1/2" \times 4^1/4" \times 6"$ faces to the ends of the jig with nails and glue. Use a ryoba saw to start the cuts to open up the channels in the jig. Use a coping saw to cut out the part of the ends that cover the little channels in the sandwich. Note, the blade is perpendicular to prevent binding on the jig itself. Clean up with a rasp and sandpaper.

Lay out and drill 5/16" holes as shown in the diagram. These accommodate the flanged insert nuts for the thumbscrews. Attach the flanged inserts using a hex key.

Using contact cement, attach 120-grit sandpaper to the same side of the inside channel, on both sides of the jig.

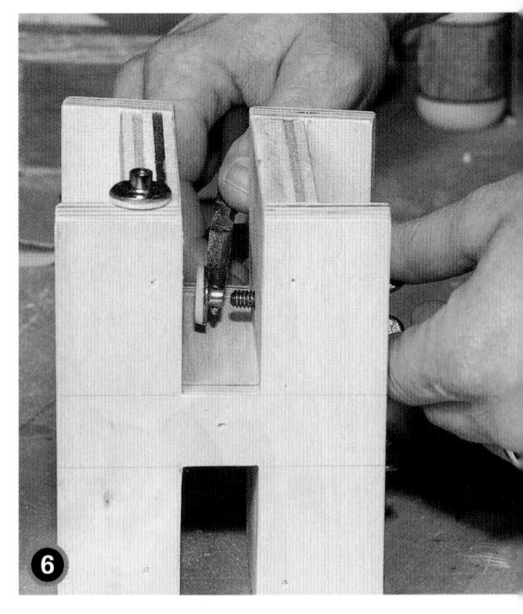

Doctor up a couple of 1/4"–20 T-nuts by pounding over the set tines and grinding off a little of the threaded barrels. With some two-part epoxy, attach some 1/8"-thick wooden pads to the face of the T-nuts. When the epoxy is set, sand the pads to fit the T-nuts. Run your thumbscrews through the flanged inserts and attach the T-nut/pads to the thumbscrews with some thread-locking compound (available at any automotive parts store). Finish the jig by attaching something slick to the faces. I used some UHMW (ultra-high molecular weight) plastic self-stick sheeting. It's 1/16" thick, and if you wear out the material on a face, you just peel off the old material and stick on some new. You could just as easily use some wax on the wood faces. You'll just have to sand them flat, eventually.

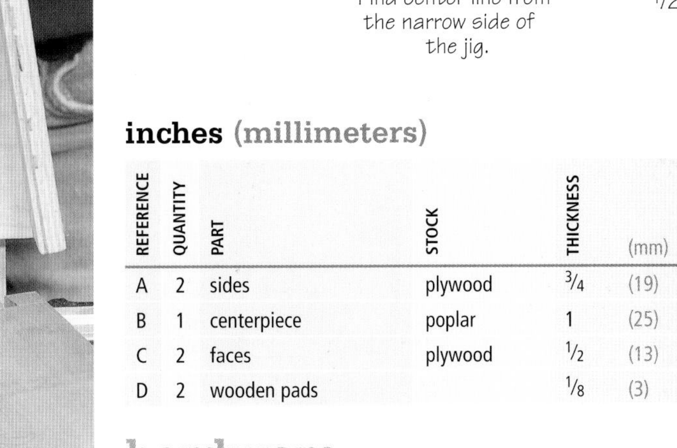

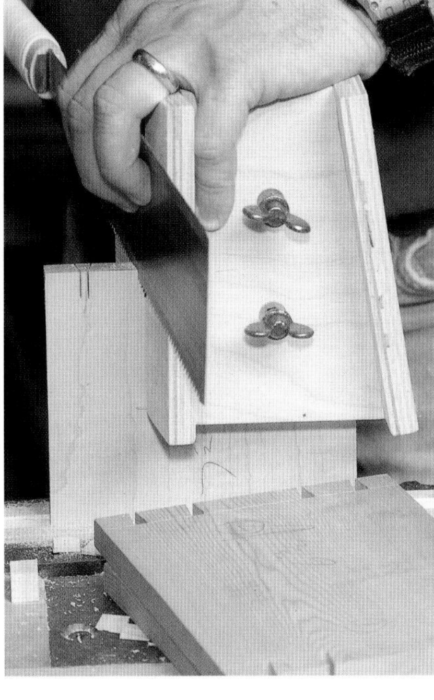

inches (millimeters)

REFERENCE	QUANTITY	PART	STOCK	THICKNESS	(mm)	WIDTH	(mm)	LENGTH	(mm)
A	2	sides	plywood	$^3/_4$	(19)	6	(152)	36	(914)
B	1	centerpiece	poplar	1	(25)	1	(25)	36	(914)
C	2	faces	plywood	$^1/_2$	(13)	$4^1/_4$	(108)	6	(152)
D	2	wooden pads		$^1/_8$	(3)				

hardware

2	13mm flanged insert nuts
2	$^1/_4$"–20 (6mm–20) thumbscrews
	3"-wide (76mm-wide) UHMW self-stick tape
2	$^1/_4$"–20 (6mm–20) T-nuts

Using the jig couldn't be simpler. I cut tails first. That's a personal choice, but this jig will work well whether you're cutting tails or pins first. The layout is a little simpler than freehand. All you do is mark the depth of the cut with a cutting gauge and lay out the spacing for the tails on the end of the board. Use the pencil marks to cut out the tails, and when you get the waste cleaned out, use the tail end of the board to lay out the pins. Use a sharp pencil for marking, then cut out the pins. Check the fit of the pins to the tails, using a piece of scrap as a hammer block across the whole joint. If they're a little big, do some fitting with a four-in-hand rasp. The joint should be snug, but not so tight that it cracks the tail board when hammering the joint together.

edge jointing

BY STEVE SHANESY

Edge jointing is easier than face jointing because you have less surface to run over the cutterhead, and you have a flattened surface to press against the jointer fence. Before starting, make sure your jointer fence is square to the jointer tables. Holding your board's jointed face flat against a squared fence will ensure you produce a jointed edge that's square to the jointed face. Also, examine your board's edges by sighting along them to determine which edge is straighter. The straighter edge is the one to joint.

If the edge is severely bowed, set your infeed table to take a deeper cut, say 1/8". You also can make multiple passes over the ends of the boards before taking a full pass along its length. Remember, if the jointed leading edge of your board runs off the end of your outfeed table before the cutterhead joints the trailing edge, you will produce a curved edge instead of a straight one.

See the photos for step-by-step instructions for edge jointing a board. Be aware of the importance of keeping the face-jointed surface flat against the fence. It's easy, especially on larger and heavier boards, to allow the board to simply rest on the edge being jointed. This, of course, will not result in an edge that's perpendicular to the face-jointed edge and will lead to problems later in your project construction.

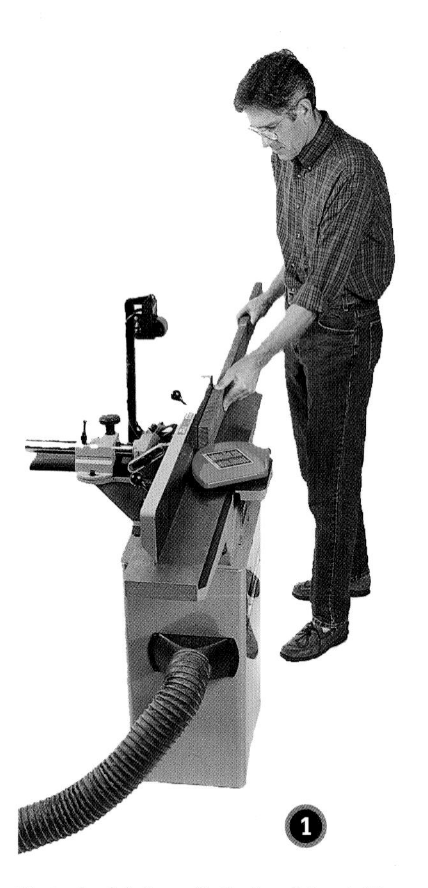

1 Start edge jointing with the face-jointed side pressed to the fence with your left hand. Your right hand supports the board off the table. Stand well behind the cutterhead with your hips and shoulders about 30° to the jointer tables.

2 When the board is supported by the tables, take a shuffling step forward. While keeping the jointed face flat to the fence, move your left hand to the outfeed side and maintain downward pressure. Alternate hand pressure as you move the board.

3 At the completion of the cut, move your right hand on top of the board over the cutterhead, making sure the board remains flat on the outfeed table. Note the high position of my hand. On narrow stock, use a push stick.

CHAPTER 36

face frames

BY STEVE SHANESY

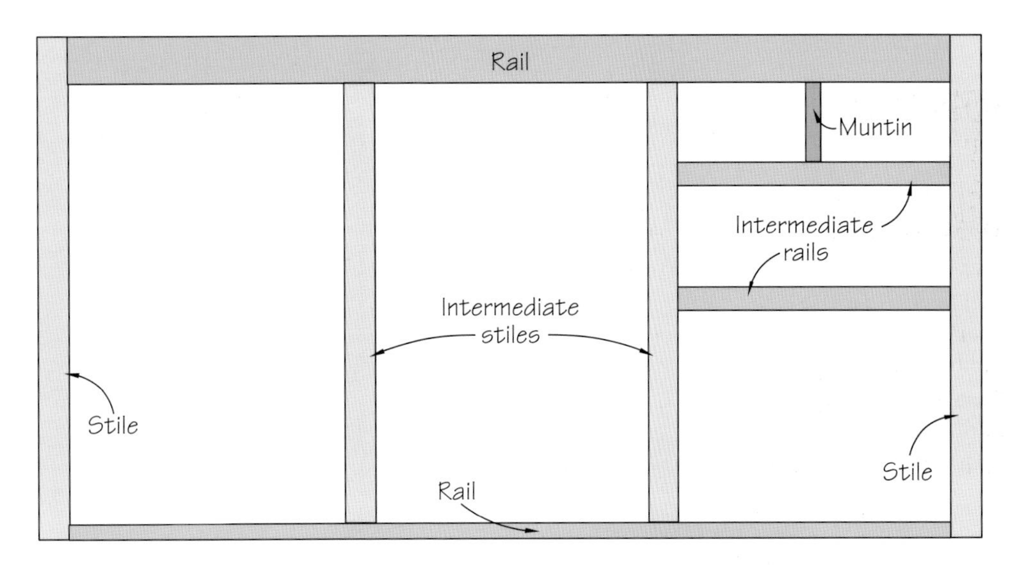

Today, many woodworkers move freely between building frameless cabinets and those with face frames, viewing one style or the other as a design consideration only. But to do so and disregard the engineering advantages and disadvantages of each method is a significant oversight.

The assembled components of any cabinet that lacks a face frame or back have an enormous propensity to shift from side to side with only a slight bit of force. Add a face frame to the cabinet and the structure has integrity. Take away the face frame but add a sturdy ½" or ¾" back, and the frameless case is structurally sound.

So now we know that face frames add structural integrity and suggest a certain style (albeit still generic) cabinet. But there's more. The face frame also provides openings with square corners that make fitting doors and drawers a predictable task. Nothing is more aggravating than tediously fitting a door in an opening that's out of square.

Lastly, face frames cover the front edges of the cabinet's sides and partitions, which are often made from plywood or particleboard.

Face-Frame Components

Face-frame parts have specific names and orientations within the frame. Stiles always run vertically; rails are always horizontal. Stiles always run through, and rails always run between stiles. Intermediate stiles (sometimes called muntins) and intermediate rails are always located within the main frame surrounding the cabinet. An intermediate stile will run between a top and bottom rail, and intermediate rails will always run between stiles.

These arrangement of parts help provide a rigid structure that gives the case parts strength. To derive this structural integrity, face-frame components need to be of a certain size. You'll find that most face-frame base cabinets (the kind you would find in kitchens) have 2"-wide stiles, 3¼"-wide top rails, ⅝"-wide bottom rails and 1½"-wide intermediate rails.

Smaller cabinets can have somewhat narrower parts, but functionality suffers with stiles less than 1½" and rails less than 1¼".

Face frames are attached to cases in several ways, and the method used has often been one of the important factors in determining the quality grade of the cabinet work. Face frames with mitered end stiles glued to mitered cabinet sides are a premium grade. Frames that overlay the sides and are only glued and clamped would be the next best grade. Lower grades would include frames glued and nailed on and frames only nailed on.

The following pages show you four common ways to join rails and stiles and compare the ease and expense of each method. All four methods are used in commercial shops and are appropriate for face-frame construction at home.

MORTISE AND TENON

This traditional and tough joint is time-consuming to make.

Lay out a practice mortise. First, mark a center line down the edge of the part getting mortised. Place the part into the mortiser and line up the point of the bit in the mortising chisel on the line. Always do a practice cut on scrap and use that to check the tenons you'll make on the saw.

Cut a practice mortise. Be sure your work is clamped down well. Mortising bits are prone to stick and require serious pressure to keep the piece in place. After making the first hole, the drilling gets easier. Use a hole-skipping technique. That's drilling one hole, then skipping over one chisel width and making another hole.

Cut the tenon cheeks. Using a dado head in a table saw is easy. Set a 3/4"-wide dado stack to the height of the shoulder on the mortise. Set the saw fence to the length of the tenon (in this case, 1"). Always do a test cut, using the test mortise from the mortise setup. Cut the shoulder first. This keeps tear-out on the shoulder to a minimum. Cut the rest of the tenon and check the fit with the mortise. Next, set the dado stack to 1/2" high for cutting the top and bottom shoulders. Cut the shoulder first, then finish the cut. Check the fit. It should be snug without being tight.

Lay out the mortise. Take the tenon you've cut and lay it right on the stile that requires the mortise. Use the tenon like a ruler to mark the stopping and starting points of the mortise. Now cut your mortise in the same way you cut the practice mortise.

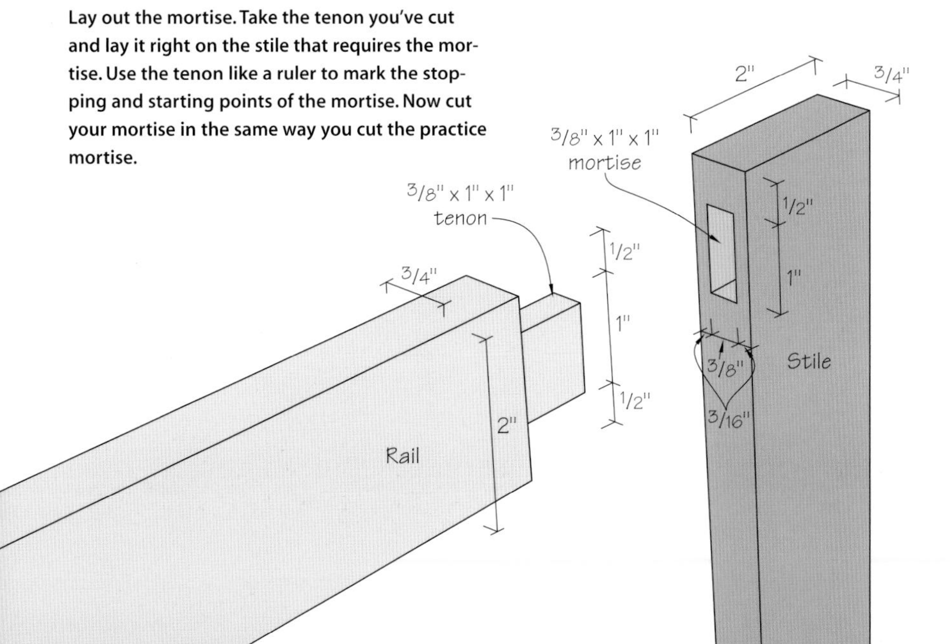

pros

- **MORE WOOD-TO-WOOD CONTACT MAKES IT A STRONGER JOINT:** If you actually measure the wood-to-wood contact that takes place in a mortise-and-tenon joint, the area of contact here is greater than any other joinery style.
- **CAN BE MADE ENTIRELY WITH HAND TOOLS:** If necessary, this joint can be made with only a layout tool, a saw and a couple of chisels. That makes it one of the cheapest joints to make. However, it is also the most labor- and skill-intensive method.
- **APPROPRIATE FOR REPRODUCTION FURNITURE:** Mortise-and-tenon joinery shows up in the coffins of Egyptian mummies that are thousands of years old. It was used extensively and almost exclusively on furniture made from the Middle Ages up to around the 1850s.
- **EASY GLUE-UP:** There's no chance of your parts bowing under simple clamping pressure. The tenon provides a solid backbone to the joint.
- **NO MATERIAL SIZE CONSTRAINTS:** You can make any size joint that you want. The tenons on some wider materials will have to be split up, however, to keep wood movement down.

cons

- **HIGHEST SKILL LEVEL REQUIRED:** Cutting one of these joints by hand requires a great deal of time and talent before it can be done with any kind of regular accuracy.
- **CAN BE THE MOST EXPENSIVE METHOD:** The machine method shown is accurate and easy to learn, but add up the cost of a table saw, mortiser and tooling for both and you can easily go over $1,000.
- **THE SLOWEST METHOD:** Either by hand or machine, the layout and setup time required to do mortise-and-tenon joinery is the longest of all the techniques.
- **UNNECESSARY AMOUNT OF STRENGTH FOR A FACE-FRAME CABINET:** Mortise-and-tenon joinery was necessary back in the days of hide glue and no screws, dowels or biscuits. These days, modern fasteners and glues make this an unnecessary joinery style for face frames. Do it if you like, but there's a time consideration to be paid for all that historical accuracy.

POCKET SCREWS

Say farewell to your clamps with this high-tech method.

The instructions for the Kreg pocket hole jig are simple and few. There just isn't that much to learn. All you really have to do is line up the center on the back side of the part being drilled between the best spacing of the three holes on the jig. To do this, mark a center line down the middle of the part to be machined.

Place the rail in the jig and with the bit set for the proper frame thickness, drill the angled hole. The bit makes a stepped clearance hole for the special screws used to attach the frame together. The screws drill their own pilot holes into the stile.

Different types of screws are available. Screws with coarse threads are for softwoods such as pine. Fine-thread screws are used for hardwoods. A third type of screw works for both. All three types drill their own pilot holes thanks to a milled notch in the shank that works like a drill bit.

THE TALE OF THE INDESTRUCTIBLE FACE FRAME

Contributing editor Troy Sexton is a connoisseur of pocket screws and contends they are a fast and strong way to keep his commercial shop humming.

One day when we were up at his shop in Sunbury, Ohio, he handed us a face frame for a small wall cabinet.

"Here," he says, "try and break it."

Troy had made the face frame with pocket screws and glue (Titebond to be exact) but then realized the frame was the wrong size or something, so he backed out the screws to use them again.

However, no matter how we twisted, pushed or pulled, we couldn't break the frame apart. Of course, we didn't drop it off a building. We concluded two things: First, glue technology has come a long way. And two, pocket screws give you amazing clamping pressure.

pros

- **FEW WIDTH RESTRICTIONS:** The only width restriction you'll possibly face is a rail that's too small for one hole (about $^3/_4$"). If you're using rails the same thickness as the cabinet sides, you might as well nail the parts on and call it a frameless cabinet.
- **NO CLAMPING REQUIRED:** Outside of using the supplied locking pliers to align the joint for assembly, if the parts are cut square and the correct screws are used, you don't need clamps.
- **FASTEST JOINT FROM LAYOUT TO FINISHED PRODUCT:** I timed every operation using this jig; without a doubt, it makes a ready-to-apply frame in the shortest time. I came up with less than a minute for each joint. The learning curve is almost nonexistent for this method. It's very easy to pick up.
- **SELF-CONTAINED SYSTEM — EXCEPT FOR THE DRILL:** The Kreg 2000 kit that we used came with everything you need to get started, except for a corded drill. The kit's price put it in the midrange for equipment costs when compared to other joinery methods.

cons

- **COST PER JOINT IS HIGH:** If you don't want to plug your screw holes, each joint is going to cost you about 8 cents (less if you buy your screws in bulk). If you want to plug your holes, the cost goes up to about 36 cents a joint. Biscuits and dowels cost between 2 and 3 cents. If you're in a big hurry, saving at least 30 minutes of time when clamping up your face frame can be worth it.
- **VISIBLE JOINT ON THE INTERIOR OF THE CABINET:** Requires special (and expensive) plugs if you want to conceal the screw holes.

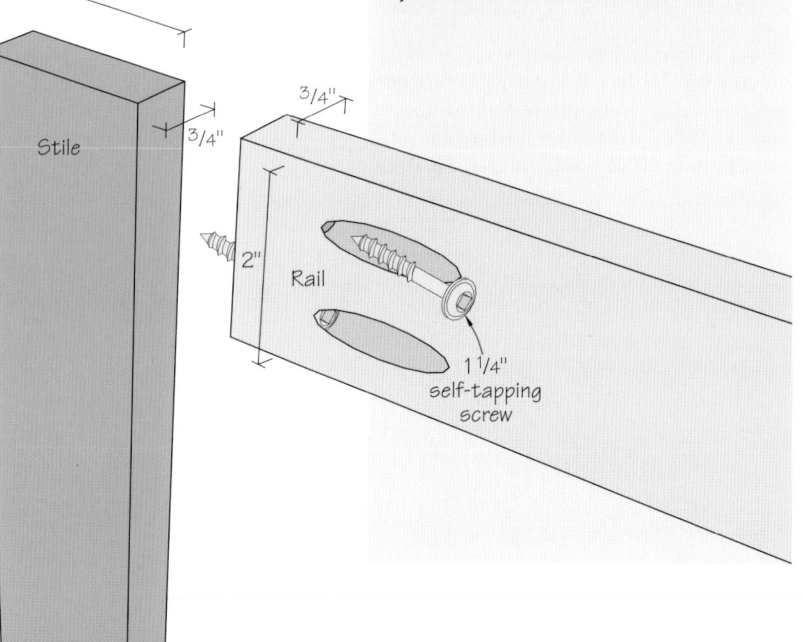

BISCUITS

Like pocket screws, biscuits are quick, accurate and easy.

Mark the joint. When marking the joint for the biscuit slot, butt the pieces together and measure over roughly half the width of the rail and mark a line across the joint. A combination square holds everything square for an accurate mark. Mark your parts all face up or face down so your slots will align.

Set the joiner. Most biscuit joiners have a scale that shows you where the center of the blade is. Some, such as this one, even have a setting for the center of a 3/4"-thick part. Set the joiner and make a test cut on some scrap to make sure you aren't cutting past the width of the end of a rail.

Make the cut. If you use Porter-Cable's face-frame biscuit cutter in the Porter-Cable 557, be sure to use a clamp to hold the parts in place. Place gentle pressure on the fence to make sure the joiner remains square to the part.

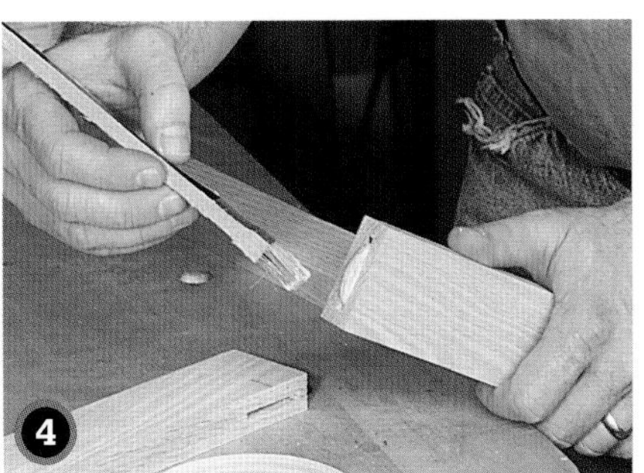

Glue up. One of the many uses I've found for plastic lids is as small glue pans. I cut up a disposable cardboard-handled paint brush for applying the glue. Use a small brush with somewhat stiff bristles to spread the glue. This gives you more control of the glue during application. Paint glue on half of the biscuit and press it into one slot of the joint. Then paint glue on the exposed part of the biscuit and assemble the joint. Clamp up your work and measure across the corners to check for square.

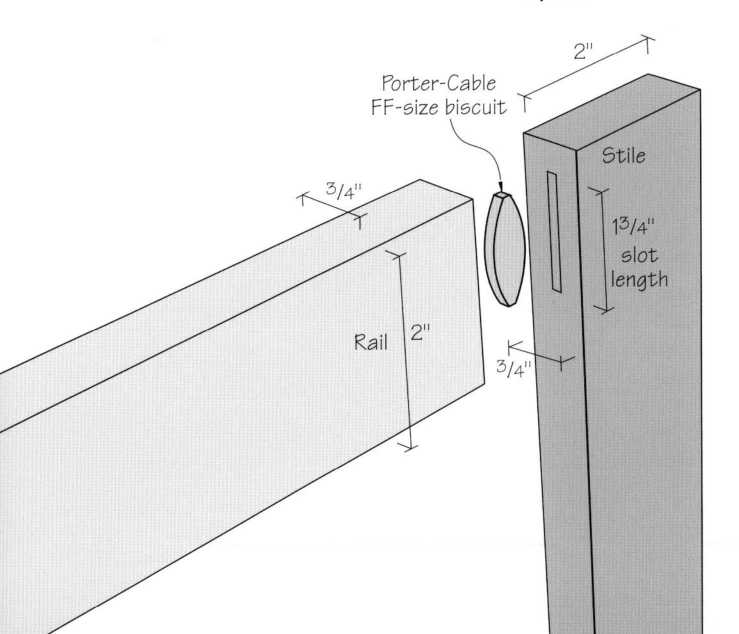

pros

- **FAST JOINT:** With the exception of the pocket hole jig, biscuit joinery is the fastest method. All you do is mark a center line on a rail and stile, set the joiner and you're off to the races. This was the first time I'd used the face-frame blade in the Porter-Cable 557 joiner, and I had some problems with the parts moving around. A clamp helped.
- **MOST FORGIVING TECHNIQUE:** Pocket screws aside, this is the most forgiving technique. The slots are bigger than the biscuits, so you routinely get almost 1/4" of slop in the joint for alignment.
- **LEARNING CURVE IS LOW:** It takes little time to learn how to make one of these joints. While it's been a while since I learned how to use a biscuit joiner, I'm always amazed at how easy these tools are to use.

cons

- **BISCUITS CAN TELEGRAPH THROUGH THE JOINT:** A biscuit is like a sponge and will wick up moisture in glue. If a biscuit is installed too close to the surface of a joint, it can expand and create a bump in the surface, which you can flush up. When the biscuit dries, it takes the surface of the joint with it, creating a hollow. Avoid this problem by cutting your slots in the middle of the thickness of the parts.
- **STOCK DIMENSIONS HAVE LIMITATIONS:** You are limited on the smallest width of rail you can use. With the Porter-Cable face-frame biscuits I could make a rail only about 1 5/8" wide before cutting through the sides of the rail. You can get smaller dimensions using Ryobi's Mini Biscuit Joiner. Here are the maximum widths of the rails for common biscuit sizes.

BISCUIT #	WIDTH
Ryobi R1	1"
Ryobi R2	1 3/16"
Ryobi R3	1 3/8"
Porter-Cable FF	1 5/8"
#0	2 3/8"
#10	2 1/2"
#20	2 3/4"

- **BISCUITS ARE HIGH-MAINTENANCE FASTENERS:** Store them in a dry environment, such as a resealable jar or airtight bag. Try microwaving biscuits that won't fit in their slots.
- **WATCH FOR BENDING:** If you use too much clamping pressure, it's possible to bow the parts. Ease off on the pressure and compensate by placing clamps on both the front and back sides of the frame.

DOWELS

This joint replaced the mortise and tenon and is still a favorite method of some.

Improve the jig. Most doweling jigs have marks that are obviously meant to be seen only under a microscope or by a test pilot with 20/15 vision. Improve the visibility of your jig by painting a contrasting paint on the increments. This self-centering jig had a black painted finish so I used white paint. Make a brush from a pine splinter whittled to suit the job.

Mark the joint. Use the same technique for marking dowel joints as you would use for biscuits. You have to be pretty accurate. Mark in about 1/2" from both sides. On a joint that's wider than 3", put a third dowel in the center.

Drill the stile. Use 3/8" dowels in 3/4"-thick material. Clamp the stile so that enough of the edge protrudes from the clamp to attach the doweling jig. Line up the 3/8" hole on the layout mark. You want the hole depth to be 1/16" deeper than the dowel will go. Use a brad-point drill with a stop collar. You'll find that you get better results when you use a corded drill with its higher speed and torque than you will with a cordless drill.

Drill the rail. Clamp the rail so its end is sticking straight up in the air. This is when it can get dicey. You have to make sure the jig is clamped to the end of the rail and square with the part. If not, you'll get a hole that's out of parallel with the holes on the stile. You might have to transfer the layout marks to the other side of the part and turn the jig around to get the jig to stay put.

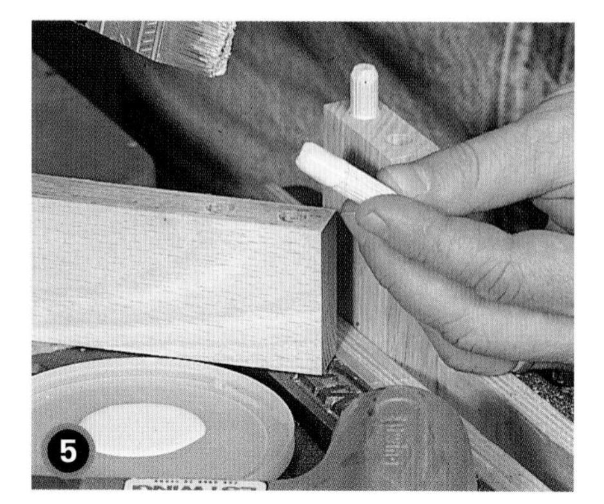

Glue up. Dowels are made with small splines that discourage the joint from going hydraulic. What this means is that a dowel without splines (or a spiral cut in the side) can act like a piston when clamped. The dowel effectively plugs the hole, and the resulting back pressure can actually keep a joint from clamping together (or at least make it very difficult to clamp). Put just a small amount of glue in the hole and be sure to apply glue to the dowel, as well.

pros

- **NO MATERIAL SIZE RESTRICTION:** Like the pocket hole jig, you can use almost any width of stock for your rails.
- Modest equipment costs: All you need is a jig, some dowels and a drill.
- **GOOD SOLID JOINT FOR FACE FRAMES:** With the extra gluing area (more than a biscuit but less than the mortise and tenon) this is a strong joint that is just right for face frames.
- **EASIER THAN MORTISE AND TENON TO LEARN:** The only critical skills are the ability to lay out the joint correctly and holding the jig square with the parts.

cons

- **TRICKY TO ALIGN:** If you botch the alignment of the holes even the slightest bit, the joint will be difficult or impossible to assemble. Always double-check the jig's position on your work.
- **YOU NEED GOOD EQUIPMENT:** A good jig and stop collars are paramount to getting good results. Dowl-it and Stanley both make good jigs.
- **DOWELS MUST STAY DRY:** If they get any moisture on them, they're subject to the same problems as biscuits in getting them into a hole.

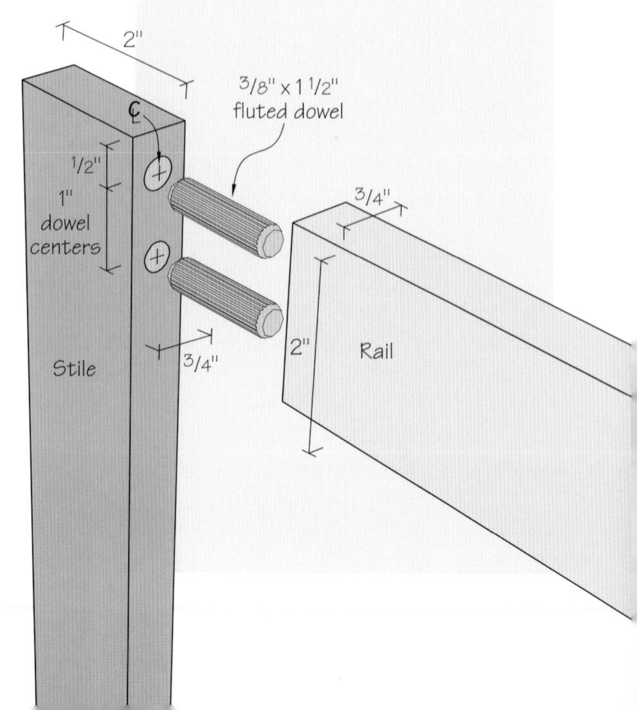

face jointing

BY STEVE SHANESY

The jointer's primary function is to flatten rough stock by removing cups, warps and twists on the wide dimension (or face) of the lumber and to straighten an edge by removing any warp or bow. Starting a project with lumber that is straight and flat with consistent thickness is fundamental to building furniture.

When selecting the face to joint on any rough board, look for cups, warps and twists. For cupped or warped boards, joint the face so that the cupped or warped side (concave) is down. This reduces the chance the board will rock on the infeed or outfeed table as it moves over the cutterhead. The flat surface you create on the first jointer pass must remain on the same plane during every pass to achieve a truly flat board.

Before turning on the machine, set the fence for a width that's slightly more than your widest board. Don't bother squaring the fence to the table. Then set the infeed table so it's about 1/16" below the high point of the knife in the cutterhead and lock it in place. To determine which way the board should go through the jointer, read its grain direction.

See the photos on the next page for step-by-step instructions. Note that with boards more than 3' long you'll need to change foot position during each pass. Because you are standing with your right foot nearly perpendicular to the table and your left foot skewed slightly outward, foot movement should be in a shuffling motion. Never take steps by crossing your legs.

Some boards require only one pass before they are ready to plane; others need several. The objective of face jointing is not to smooth the entire bottom surface, but to flatten it to the point where it can maintain a parallel plane relative to the planer's cutterhead knives in the next operation. The board is ready for the planer when there is enough flattened surface along the width and length of the board to prevent the planer's feed rollers from pushing the face-jointed surface out of parallel with the planer knives.

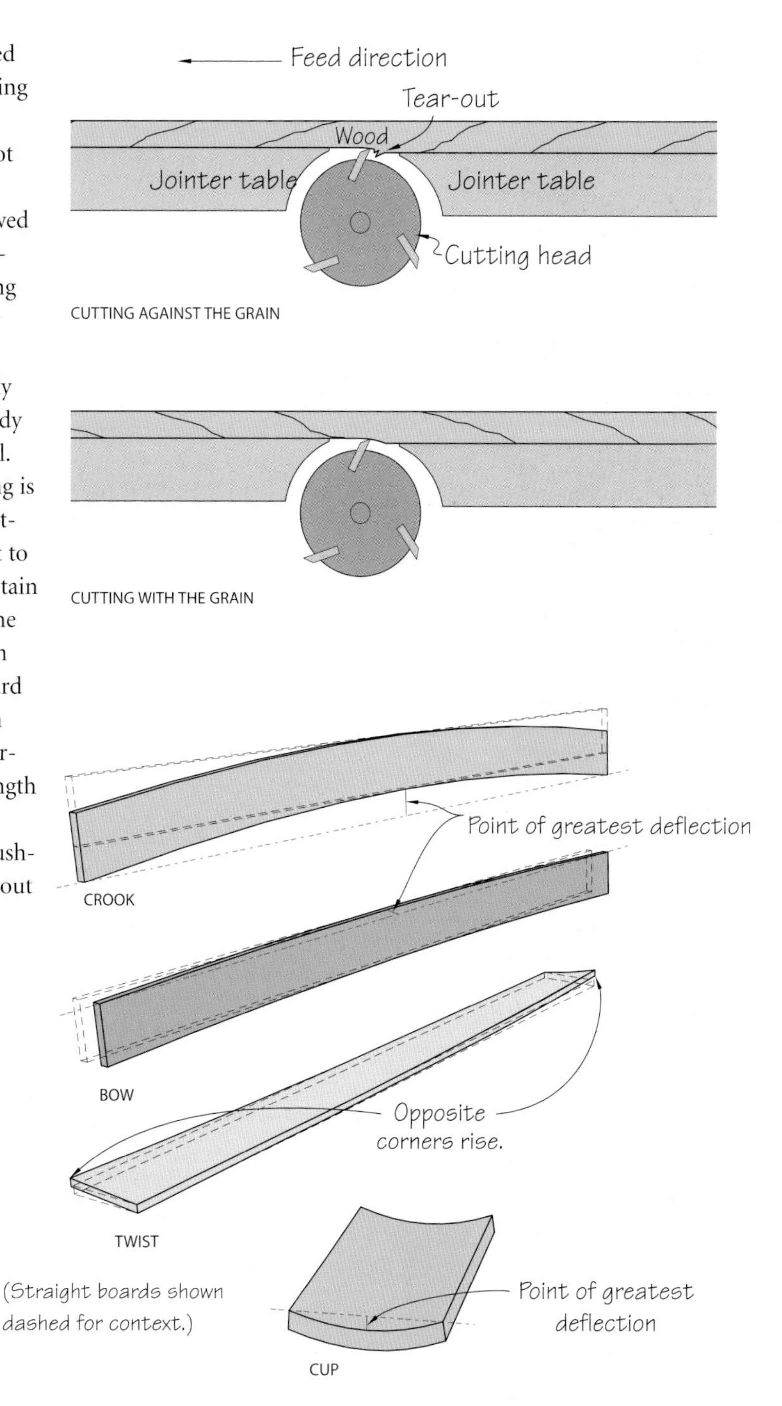

Rock the board on the jointer table across its width to find the flattest area, then maintain this plane as you begin the cut. Stand near the back of the board and do not use any downward pressure on the board. Use your left hand to keep the board against the fence and use your right hand to move the board forward and in the correct plane. Let the force of the cutterhead in the wood keep the board down on the outfeed table. Keep your body positioned as shown until the board is fully supported on the jointer tables.

With the board supported, move toward the cutterhead by taking shuffling steps with your feet. Again, your left hand keeps the board to the fence and applies only enough downward force to control the stock. Use a shuffling motion to move your hands, and always keep one hand on the board. When your left hand is about 18" from the cutterhead, pause, and while keeping firm control of the stock, reach for the push block with your right hand, then position it on the end of the board. Now continue moving the board forward.

To complete the cut, continue forward progress until the end of the board and push block have cleared the cutterhead, and the safety guard has closed to the fence. Remember to keep firm downward pressure during the final phase of the cut if you have a long board extending off the end of the outfeed table.

make accurate half-lap joints

BY BILL HYLTON

A half-lap joint is strong, versatile and easy to cut. You simply cut recesses in both mating pieces, then nest them together, forming an X, L or T.

Half-laps can be used for all sorts of flat frames: doors, for example, but also face frames, web frames and picture frames. An intermediate rail half-lapped to the stiles looks right because it visually abuts the stile (the way a mortise-and-tenon joint would) rather than crossing it (the way a bridle joint would). On the other hand, a rectangle of end grain is exposed in assembled end laps and T-laps that can be regarded as unsightly.

The half-lap can be used in post-and-rail constructions to join rails or aprons to legs. You usually see this joint in worktables rather than fine furniture. But even in the most traditional table construction, the half-lap is used where stretchers cross (a cross lap).

From a practical perspective, the half-lap enjoys an advantage over the mortise-and-tenon joint in that one tool setup can suffice for both parts of the joint. (There's more than one way to cut the joint, of course, and some do require two setups, as we'll see.) You can join parts at angles quite easily. The joint accommodates curved parts, too. You can join curved pieces, or you can shape the half-lapped frame after it's assembled.

Despite its simplicity, this joint is strong if properly made. The shoulders resist twisting, and there is plenty of gluing surface.

But be wary of using half-laps on wide boards. Wood movement can break the joint, so confine the joinery to members no more than 3" to 3½" wide.

You can cut half-laps using several different power tools. Let the job suggest the tool to use and the way to use it, too.

The half-lap is made by cutting dadoes of equal width and depth on two pieces of wood so that the face surfaces are flush when assembled. Each piece is trapped between the shoulders of the other, so it's a can't-fail joint. The wood will break first.

On the Router Table

Everyone has favorite approaches, and mine involves the router. I cut end laps on the router table using a lapping sled I originally made for tenoning. This shop-made device looks like a T-square on steroids. The stout fence is long enough to extend from the tabletop edge to well beyond the bit. The shoe rides along the edge of the tabletop. An adjustable stop clamps to the fence to control the length of the cut.

Construction is simple, but pay attention to the details. The fence must be square to the shoe. The edge of the fence must be perpendicular to the tabletop. The adjustable stop also needs to be square to the fence. If any of these is off, you won't get consistently sized, square-shouldered laps.

What bit to use? Well, a straight bit is the obvious choice, and it will work fine. I use what's variously called a planer, mortising or bottom-cleaning bit. The several bits I have range in diameter from ¾" to 1½", and the vertical-cutting edges range from 7⁄16" to ⅞". The bit is designed to clear a wide, smooth recess. Perfect for laps!

The first time you use the lapping sled you'll cut into the fence. This cut is what you use to position the stop for the length of lap you want. Measure from the shoulder of the cut (include the cut itself

Cutting a half-lap on the router table is fast and accurate using a lapping sled to guide the work and a large-diameter mortising bit to cut it. The guide references the edge of the tabletop, and a stop sets the length of the cut.

in the measurement, of course). The stop prevents you from making a cut that's too long.

Be mindful of the size of the cut and of the amount of material you will remove in a pass. You don't necessarily want to hog out a ³⁄₈"-deep cut in a single pass, especially if you are using a 1¼"- to 1½"-diameter bit.

You probably know two ways to moderate the bite: Reduce the depth of the cut or the width of the cut. Here, the most expeditious approach is the latter. Form the full cut in small steps. The first pass should be about ⅛" wide, produced by holding the workpiece well clear of the stop, so only ⅛" of the workpiece extends over the bit. Make pass after pass, shifting the workpiece closer and closer to the stop. One last pass with the workpiece dead against the stop and your lap is complete.

This approach works well for end laps, but not for laps midway between the ends of the workpiece. For a cross or a T-lap, the router table accessory to use is a dadoing sled. You need to use a stop with this sled to keep the work from moving as the bit cuts it, and that helps you place the cut, as well. Set the stop to position the final cut, and use a spacer between the stop and the work to position the first cut.

Personally, I think it's fussy to do Ts and crosses accurately on the router table. Given my druthers, I'd do them with a handheld router and a job-specific (and thus disposable) jig, such as the lapping platform.

Handheld Router

When cutting this joint with a handheld router, I prefer a fixed-base router, rather than a plunge. I use the same planer

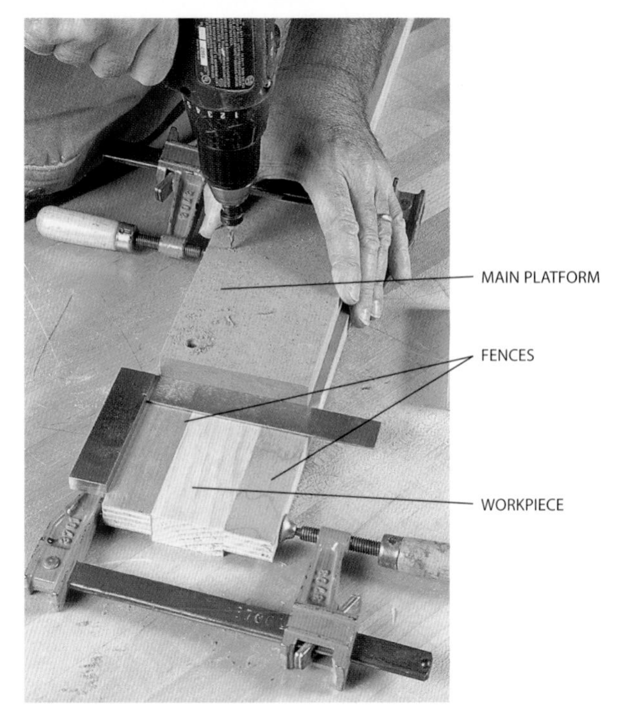

To assemble a lapping platform, capture a workpiece between the fences and align the primary platform on them. The edge of the platform must be square to the work. You can build the simple version of this jig for cross laps as shown in the photo or add a work stop as shown in the illustration to also cut end laps.

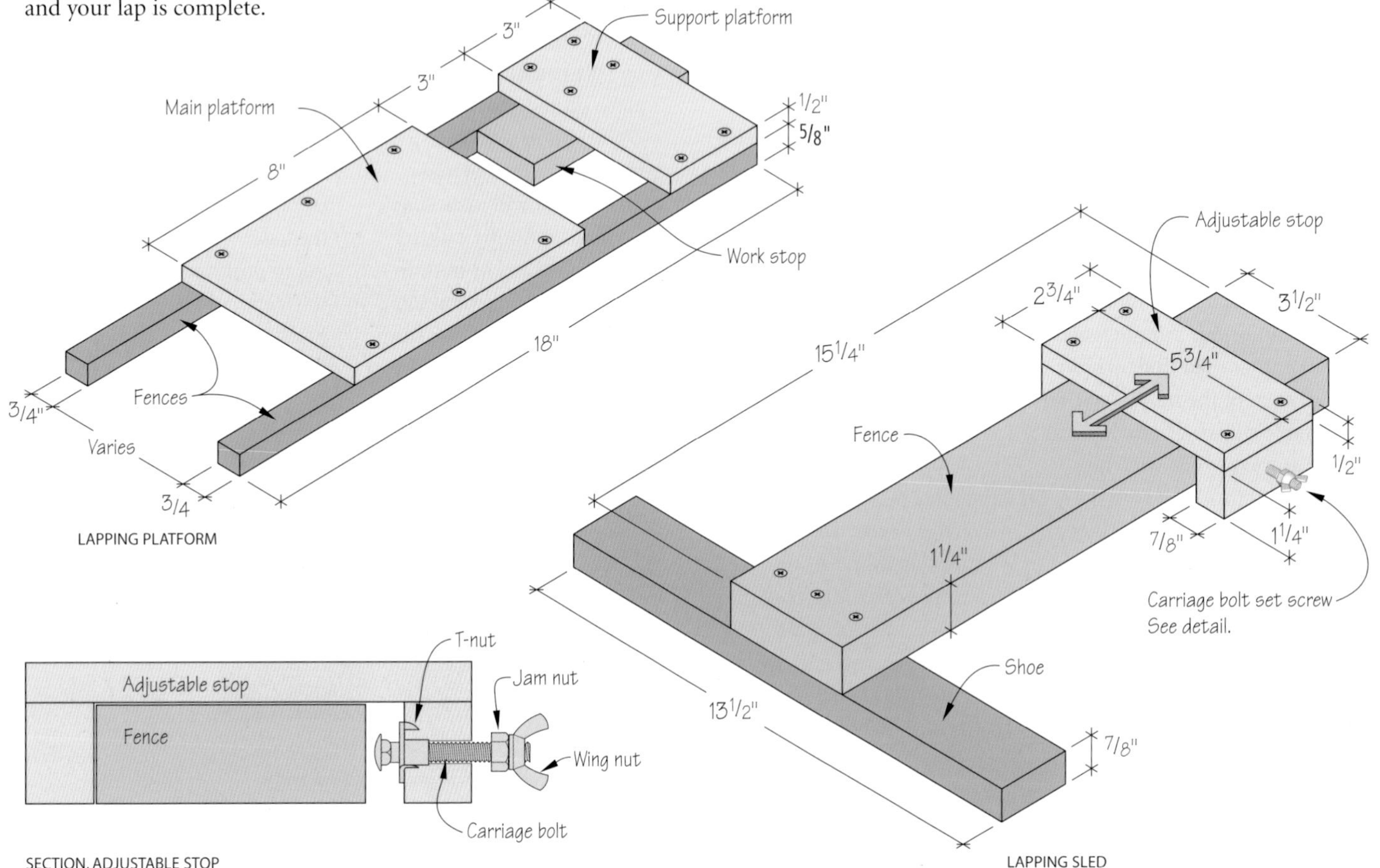

Use the mating workpiece as a spacer to position and align the support platform. Screw the support platform to the fences and you're ready to get to work.

Make the cut with a mortising bit with a shank-mounted pilot bearing. Trapped between the platforms, the bit produces a smooth, square-shouldered cut that perfectly matches the width of the workpiece.

mortising bit, but I mount a pilot bearing on the shank of the bit. The lapping platform I make from four scraps and a dozen drywall screws. I use the actual workpieces to scale it.

Begin by clamping the jig's two fences to the edges of a workpiece. These fences need to be a bit less than the thickness of the workpieces, and their edges need to be straight and parallel for the jig to work well.

Next, set the main platform on the workpiece and the fences. I usually use some ¾" medium-density fiberboard for this, but plywood is OK for this application. Square it on the jig, then screw it to the fences.

Finally, lay your mating workpiece across the first, tight against the platform's guiding edge. Set the support platform in place and clamp it tight against the second workpiece. Screw it to the fences.

The gap between the platforms is the width of the lap. It is easy to position: You just set

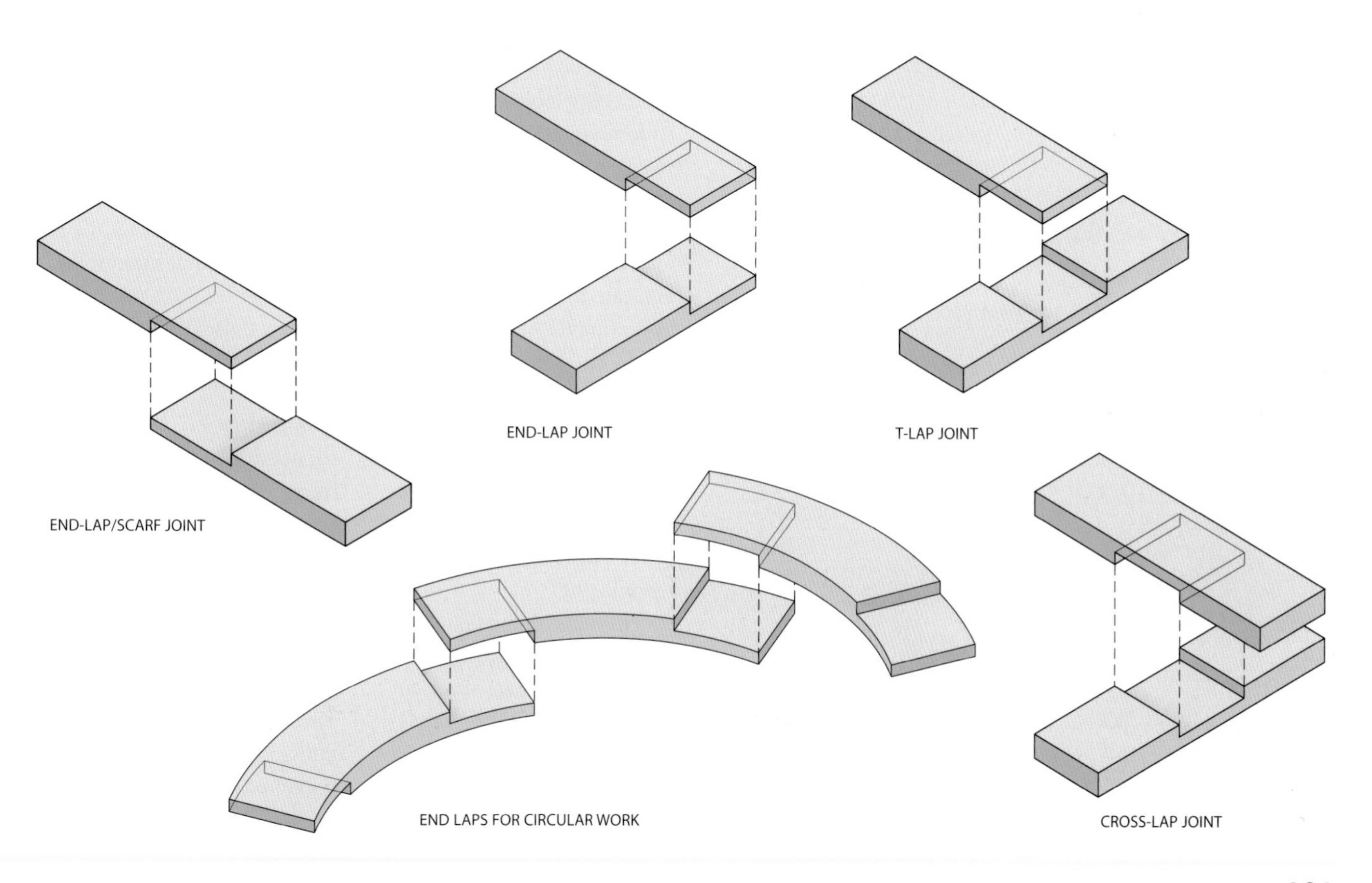

Set the height of the blade to half the stock thickness and cut the half-lap shoulders.

Cut the cheeks using a tenoning jig; this one is shopmade. For the cut, adjust the blade to match the width of the stock. Position the jig and the work so the waste falls to the outside of the blade.

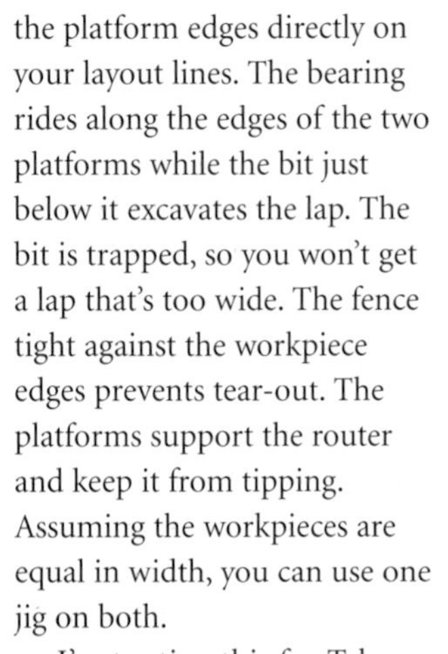

the platform edges directly on your layout lines. The bearing rides along the edges of the two platforms while the bit just below it excavates the lap. The bit is trapped, so you won't get a lap that's too wide. The fence tight against the workpiece edges prevents tear-out. The platforms support the router and keep it from tipping. Assuming the workpieces are equal in width, you can use one jig on both.

I'm touting this for T-laps and cross laps, but you can use it as well for end laps. For this use, add a fifth scrap as a work stop. Attach it to the underside of the support platform so the workpiece end can butt against it.

Sawing Half-Laps

Not everyone is as enamored of router woodworking as I am, of course. Saws such as the band saw, the table saw, the radial-arm saw, the sliding compound miter saw and, yes, even the carpenter's workhorse — the circular saw — all can be used.

Doing the job with a circular saw or miter saw is a wasting process. You adjust the saw's cut depth to half the stock thickness, carefully kerf the margins, then waste the material between the margins with lots and lots of kerfs. Typically, you get a ragged cheek. It has to be smoothed somehow to glue well. But if you're using a circular saw, you are probably doing something rough, where nails or screws work as well as glue.

Gluing up a half-lapped frame requires the usual complement of pipe or bar clamps to pull the shoulders of the joints tight. Each joint also requires a C-clamp or spring clamp to pinch its cheeks tight together.

The band saw roughs out end laps very quickly, but it leaves you with a rough surface that needs to be flattened and smoothed to glue well. Some woodworkers opt to rough out half laps on the band saw, then finish them with a router. To me, that's extra setups and extra work. Besides, you'll be hard-pressed to effectively band-saw a lap that isn't at the end of a workpiece.

The radial-arm saw can be an effective tool for half-laps. A dado head in a well-tuned radial-arm saw will cut end and cross laps quickly and cleanly. You can see your layout lines, so locating the cut precisely is easy. You can do angled laps easily; just swing the arm right or left for the cut. You can set stops to expedite production jobs.

The table saw gives you some options. You can use your everyday saw blade or a dado head. Guide the work with the miter gauge, a cutoff box or a tenoning jig.

I'm sure you can figure out how to use the dado head with either a miter gauge or the cutoff box. This is the fast, single-setup approach on the table saw.

But if you don't have a dado head or you don't want to switch from blade to dado set, you can use the blade with a tenoning jig to cut the laps. The routine is to saw the shoulders using the miter gauge, then saw the cheeks using the tenoning jig.

The cut depth on the shoulder cut is critical, of course. If you cut too deeply, you will have a kerf that shows on the edges of the assembled frame. If you cut too shallow, it isn't ideal but you can correct this with the following cheek cut.

Use whatever tenoning jig you have for the cheek cut. Delta's block-of-iron model is great, but I don't think it works any better than the shop-made fence rider I use. Mount the jig on the saw and position it for the cut, adjust the blade height and saw those cheeks, one after the other.

Assembly

It's not difficult to assemble a frame joined with half-laps. You must apply clamps to the individual joints, however, in addition to using clamps that draw the assembly together. Use bar or pipe clamps to pull the joints tight at the shoulders. Then squeeze the cheeks of individual joints tight using C-clamps or spring clamps.

mortise-and-tenon joinery

BY THE EDITORS OF *POPULAR WOODWORKING* MAGAZINE

Mortise-and-tenon joinery requires a little more finesse than, say, biscuits or pocket screws, but for many woodworkers, the strength it provides is well worth the effort. It's a strong, hard-wearing joint that can suffer age, racking and even sudden stresses better than other joints.

Of the many variations, the most common is the blind mortise and tenon, in which the mortise stops in the work without passing all the way through your leg or stile. When the tenon is inserted, the joint is hidden. Less common is the through mortise and tenon, in which the mortise passes all the way through your work so the end of the tenon is visible. It's a nice way to show off your craftsmanship — and your mistakes.

Dozens of variantions on the mortise and tenon exist, but it's best to start simple.

The Basics: Backwards Is Better

Conventional wisdom says you should cut your mortises first and then fit your tenons. We don't go along with that. You can save yourself a lot of layout hassle by cutting your tenons first and then using them to lay out the mortises on your project. Before you grumble, give it a try.

First, cut a test mortise in some scrap wood. A hollow-chisel mortiser does the job best. A Forstner bit in a drill press or a mortising chisel can do a nice job, too. You will use this test mortise to size all your tenons.

The pictures on the next page show a mortise being made on a drill press using a ¾"-diameter Forstner bit and a fence. You can make amazingly clean mortises this way.

To make your test mortise, first select a piece of scrap. As a rule of thumb, mortises should be half the thickness of your tenon's stock. For example, if your project's tenon stock is ¾" thick, the mortises need to be ⅜" thick. It's also a good idea to make your mortises about 1⁄16" deeper than the tenons are long. This will keep the tenons from bottoming out in the mortises.

After you've made your test mortise, it's time to cut the tenons. Many different methods exist for cutting tenons, but a dado stack and a table saw require only one saw setup. It's a good method for a beginner. When doing it this way, the fence determines the length of the tenon; the height of the dado blades determines the measurement of the tenon's shoulders. Set each accordingly.

Next, hold the piece to be tenoned about 1⁄16" from the fence and push it through the blade, using your miter gauge. Then hold the piece directly against the fence and, using your miter gauge, push it through the blade again. Repeat this same procedure for the other edges of the tenon. Once you've defined all the edges, check your work using the test mortise you cut earlier. If the fit is firm and smooth, you can go ahead and cut all your project's tenons.

Once all your tenons are cut, use them to mark out the mortise locations on your

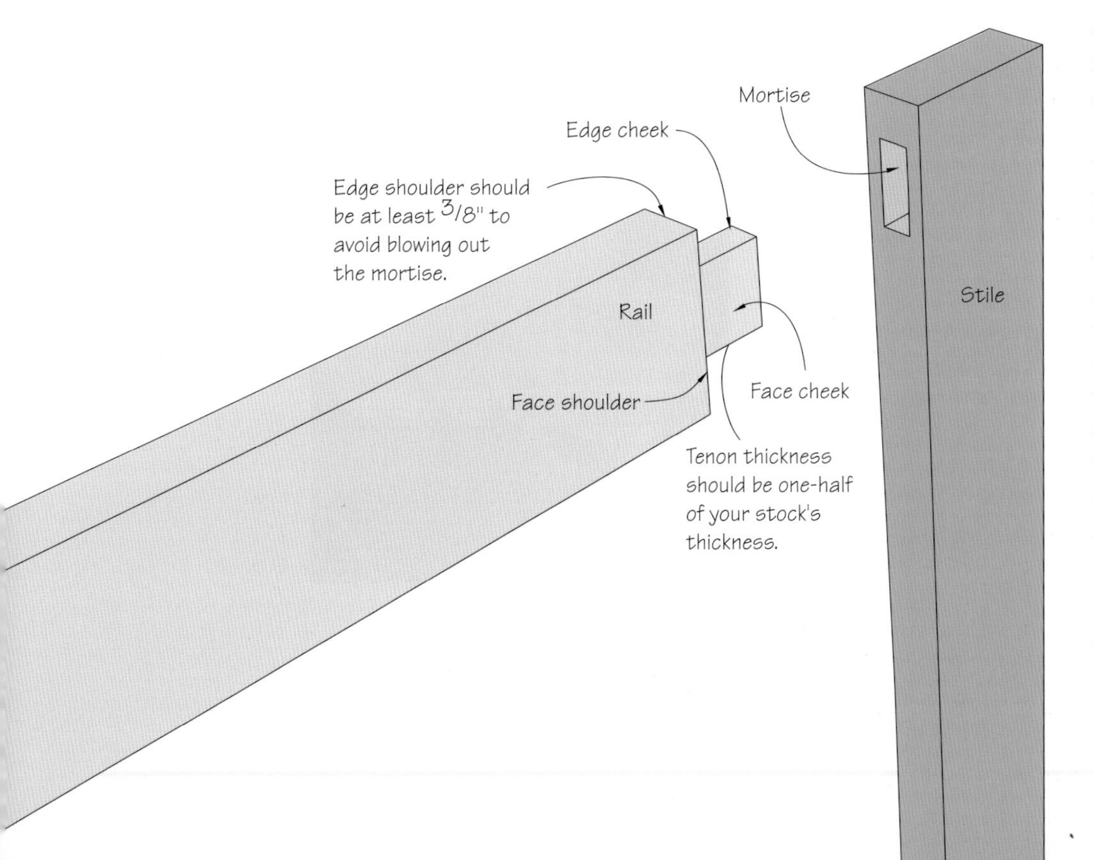

The easiest way to make clean mortises using your drill press is to first drill a series of overlapping holes (top photo). Then go back and clean up the waste between these holes several times until the bit can slide left to right in the mortise without stopping (directly above). Then square up the ends with a chisel.

I cut my tenons using a dado stack as shown. I like this method because it requires only one saw setup to make all the cuts on a tenon. First, define the tenon's face cheeks and shoulders.

Then define the edge cheeks and shoulders.

Check your work using the test mortise you cut earlier.

work. You'll see how they act as a ruler to define where to start and stop each mortise — without measuring.

Be sure to cut each mortise a little over each measured line so that you are able to maneuver the tenoned pieces for perfect positioning during glue-up. When you glue this joint, place the glue in the mortise and spread it on the walls of the mortise with a piece of scrap. Putting glue on the tenon or on the shoulders will result in lots of messy squeeze-out.

Once you have basic mortise-and-tenon joinery under your belt, it's good to try your hand at some advanced through-tenons.

Wedged Through Mortise and Tenon

Wedged through-tenons create a splayed dovetail effect. Once the joint is assembled, it can't be withdrawn because the tenon expands inside the mortise, completely locking the two pieces of wood together. Your first step is to cut the tenons.

The tenons should be cut to size on the table saw; make them 1/4" longer than the thickness of the piece they'll be inserted into. After cutting the tenon, use your table saw to cut the slots to accept the wedges. Use a backing board on your miter gauge to help hold the boards upright.

Once your tenons are cut and cleaned up, lay out and cut the tapered through-mortises. The mortises are angled, or tapered, so that they can accommodate the wedged tenons. The mortises must be cut to fit right over the tenons.

Make the wedges. The wedges driven into the tenons

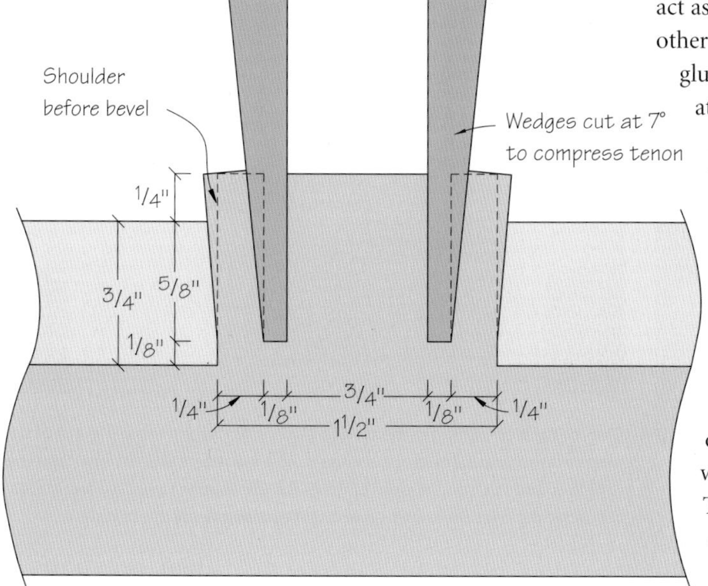

WEDGED THROUGH-MORTISE-AND-TENON DETAIL

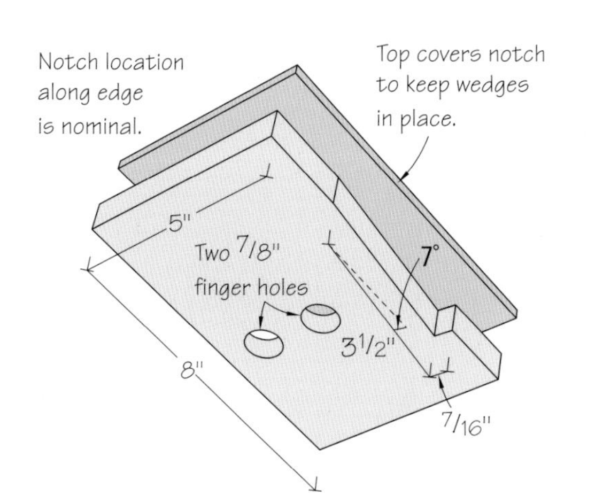

WEDGE-CUTTING JIG — SHOWN FROM BELOW

act as the clamps. In fact, no other clamps are needed during glue-up. The wedges are cut at an angle wider than the mortise because the wedge becomes compressed when driven into the tenon. This compression takes away some of the wedges' ability to spread the tenon. That's why you cut a slightly higher-degree taper on the wedges than the mortise. This yields a good spread on the tenon during assembly.

Once all is cut, test a set of wedges in a joint. Using no glue, assemble a joint by tapping in a couple of wedges to see if they completely spread a joint apart before bottoming out in the tenon slot. If they leave a little room, cut a little off of the wedge's narrow end and taper it to fit the top of the slot accordingly. This gives a little more play to spread the tenon apart.

Gently disassemble the dry-fit joint and proceed to glue up your project and drive home the wedges with glue on them. It helps to wait a bit to clean up the squeezed-out glue. This lets it get a skin that keeps the mess to a minimum. Clean up with a chisel and a damp rag.

Once everything is glued up, you must trim the tenons. First, cut the tenon a little proud. Next, mask off the tenon for sanding by taping around the entire tenon with two widths of masking tape. The tape keeps you from sanding a depression in the top around the tenon. Chisel and plane an angle on all four sides of the tenons and round them over with a sander.

Loose Wedged Mortise and Tenon

Sometimes you want to be able to knock a piece of furniture down to move it easily, and that's where this next joint comes in handy. A loose wedged mortise-and-tenon joint lacks the permanency of a wedged mortise-and-tenon joint, but it is still quite strong. A few good whacks to the wedges with a rubber mallet and the joint can easily be broken apart.

According to Albert Jackson and David Day's book *Good Wood Joints* (Popular Woodworking Books), the

When making the wedged through mortise and tenon, use your table saw to cut the tenons to the actual width. Set the blade to define the length of the tenons. Mark the depth with a gauge. Cut the waste out from between the tenons. Set the saw for cutting the slots that accept the wedges. Use a backing board on your miter gauge to hold the boards upright.

When you can press fit everything together, make a simple angle gauge to cut the angle on the narrow widths of the tapered through-mortises. The angle widens the top of the mortise. Before chiseling the angle, take a small saw and cut the sides of the mortises to the marks, reducing tear-out. Clamp the gauge in place and gently chisel out the angle on the mortise sides. The angle shouldn't go completely to the other side of the mortise. This leaves a softer bend for the tenon to make, thereby reducing cracking — something you have to be careful about in a brittle wood.

The wedges are cut on the table saw using a simple jig that holds the wedge stock while cutting on the saw.

One method of trimming the tenons flush is to make a template out of a thin piece of cardboard. The front and back of a magazine will do. Just tape them together and cut out a couple of holes for the tenons to come through. Lay the template over the tenons and cut them flush with the template.

length of the tenon in a loose wedged mortise-and-tenon joint must be at least three times the thickness of the piece it is passing through.

The first step is to cut a through-mortise-and-tenon joint with a sliding fit. Next, cut a through-mortise for the wedge in the tenon you just cut, as shown. Mark the taper on your wedges and cut the taper, using a band saw or a sander. You can clean up the wedges easily with a chisel. Finally, test fit the wedges, as shown.

The through-mortises for the loose wedged mortise-and-tenon joint are cut through the tenon. Here we're cutting them with a mortiser. You can see how the mortises are cut across the line to give the drawboring effect.

Most of the tapered part of the wedges should slide through each mortise. As the wedge gets wider, you will need a mallet and a block of wood to finish pounding them down to a uniform height.

CHAPTER 40

four good ways to cut rabbets

BY BILL HYLTON

The rabbet joint surely is one of the first ones tackled by new woodworkers. The rabbet is easy to cut, it helps locate the parts during assembly and it provides more of a mechanical connection than a butt joint.

I vaguely remember thinking, back when I was tackling my first home-improvement projects, that with practice I'd outgrow rabbet joints. Well, I'm still cutting rabbets because woodworkers never outgrow them.

The most common form is what I call the single-rabbet joint. Only one of the mating parts is rabbeted. The cut is proportioned so its width matches the thickness of its mating board, yielding a flush fit.

The depth of the rabbet for this joint should be one-half to two-thirds its width. When assembled, the rabbet conceals the end grain of the mating board. The deeper the rabbet, the less end grain that will be exposed in the assembled joint.

Depth = 1/2 to 2/3 of width

Width

In the double-rabbet joint, both of the mating pieces are rabbeted. The rabbets don't have to be the same, but typically they are.

The rabbet works as a case joint and as an edge joint. Case joints generally involve end grain, while edge joints involve only long grain. In casework, you often see rabbets used where the top and/or bottom join the sides (end grain to end grain), and where the back joins the assembled case (both end to end and end to long). In drawers, it's often used to join the front and sides.

Because end grain glues poorly, rabbet joints that involve it usually are fastened, either with brads, finish nails or screws concealed under plugs. (OK, in utilitarian constructions, we don't sweat the concealment.)

We don't necessarily think of the rabbet as an edge-to-edge joint, yet we all know of the shiplap joint. Rabbet the edges of the mating boards and nest them together. Voilá!

It's also a great right-angle edge joint. We see this in the case-side-and-back combination, but also in practical box section constructions such as hollow legs and pedestals. Long grain joins long grain in these structures. Because that glues well, you have a terrific and strong joint.

Saw a rabbet on the table saw in two steps. Set the blade elevation and fence position first to cut the shoulder (above photo), then adjust either or both as necessary to cut the bottom.

You can gussy up the joint's appearance by chamfering the edge of the rabbet before assembly. When the joint is assembled, the chamfer separates the face grain of one part from the edge grain of the other. Because the chamfer is at an angle to both faces, it won't look inappropriate even though its grain pattern is different.

One important variant is the rabbet-and-dado joint. This is a good rack-resistant joint that assembles easily because both boards are positively located. The dado or groove doesn't have to be big; often it's a single saw kerf, no deeper than one-third the board's thickness. Into it fits an offset tongue created on the mating board by the rabbet.

The rabbet-and-dado joint is a good choice for plywood casework because it's often difficult to scale a dado or groove to the inexact thickness of plywood. It's far easier to customize the width of a rabbet. So you cut a stock-width dado, then cut the mating rabbet to a custom dimension. An extra cutting operation is required, but the benefit — a big one — is a tight joint.

There are lots of good ways to cut rabbets. The table saw, radial-arm saw, jointer and router all come to mind. The most versatile techniques use the table saw and router.

SINGLE-RABBET JOINTS

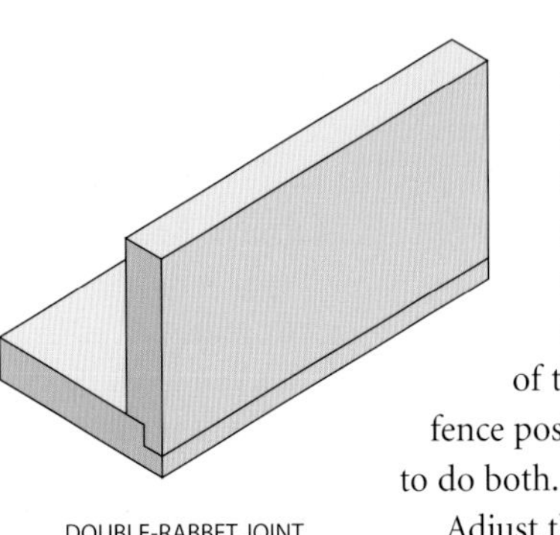

DOUBLE-RABBET JOINT

Rabbeting on the Table Saw

Rabbets can be cut at least two different ways on the table saw. Which method you choose may be influenced by the number of rabbets you have to cut, as well as the sizes and proportions of the workpieces.

It's quickest to cut the rabbets using whatever blade is in the saw. Two passes are all it takes. But if you have lots of rabbets to cut, or if the workpieces are too big to stand on edge safely, then use a dado cutter. (The latter is especially appropriate if your job entails dadoes as well as rabbets.) Let's look at the quick method first.

The first cut forms the shoulder. To set it up, adjust the blade height for the depth of the rabbet. You can use a variety of setup tools here, but it's always a good idea to make a test cut so you can measure the actual depth of the kerf.

That done, position the fence to locate the rabbet's shoulder. This establishes the rabbet width, so you measure from the face of the fence to the outside of the blade.

The cutting procedure is to lay the work flat on the saw's table, then run the edge along the fence and make the shoulder cut. If you are rabbeting the long edge of a board, use just the fence as the guide. When cutting a rabbet across the end of a piece, guide the work with your miter gauge and use the fence simply as a positioning device. It is easy to set up, and the miter gauge keeps the work from walking as it slides along the table saw's fence. Because no waste will be left between the blade and the fence, you can do this safely.

Nevertheless, if you feel uneasy about using the miter gauge and fence together, use a standoff block. Clamp a scrap (your standoff block) to the fence near the front edge of the saw's table. Lay the work in the miter gauge and slide it against the scrap. As you make the cut, the work is clear of the fence by the thickness of the scrap. (Try using a 1"-thick block to make setup easier.)

Having cut the shoulders of all the rabbets, you next adjust the setup to make the bottom cut. You may need to change the height of the blade or the fence position. You may need to do both.

Adjust the blade to match the width of the rabbet. Reposition the fence to cut the bottom of the rabbet, with the waste falling to the outside of the blade. Make that cut with the workpiece standing on edge, its kerfed face away from the fence.

When the workpieces are so large as to be cumbersome on edge — cabinet sides, for example — you want to cut the rabbets with a dado cutter. That way you can keep the work flat on the saw's table. Control the cut using a cutoff box or the fence. It's easy to set the width of the cut with this approach.

Where the proportions of the workpiece allow it, use the rip fence to guide the cut. Clamp a sacrificial facing to the fence. Don't fret about the width of the stack, so long as it exceeds the width of the rabbet you want. Part of the cutter is buried in the fence facing, and you just set the fence to expose the width of the cutter that's working. Guide the work along the fence.

Alternatively, use a cutoff box to support the work and

RABBET-AND-GROOVE (OR DADO) JOINTS

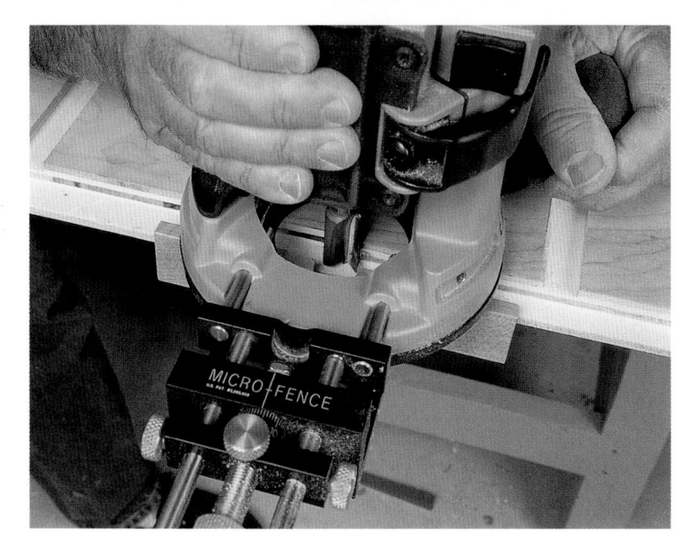

With an edge guide and straight bit, you can customize the rabbet's width, forming it in a series of passes.

guide the cut. You get the same advantages in rabbeting that you do with dadoing: The work really doesn't move; the box does. Use a stop block to position the work to yield the width of rabbet you want. On the other hand, it may be a little more difficult to get exactly the cut width you want.

Rabbeting with the Router

The router is an excellent tool for rabbeting, in part because you can deploy it as a hand tool. For some jobs, you just want to immobilize the workpiece to your bench and move the cutting tool over it. In those situations, the router is the tool to use.

Occasionally, you might want to cut a rabbet into an assembly — perhaps a frame for a door or lid. If you use a router, you can wait until the frame is glued up and sanded, then produce the rabbet for a pane of glass or a panel. You do have to square the corners, but that's simple with a chisel.

A major benefit of the handheld router approach is that you can see the cut as it is formed. On the table saw (and the router table), the work itself conceals the cut.

You can cut rabbets on the router table as well, of course. Cutting a rabbet on the router table is quite similar to doing it on the table saw with a dado head. But I want to focus on handheld approaches here.

A rabbeting bit is the commonly used cutter, but it is not the only one that will work. If you use an edge guide to control the cut, you can use a straight bit or a planer bit.

The rabbeting bit is piloted, and the typical bit makes a 3⁄8"-wide cut. Most manufacturers sell rabbeting sets, which bundle a stack of bearings with the cutter. Want to reduce the cut width? Switch to a larger bearing. The set I have yields six different widths from 1⁄2" to 1⁄8" (no 3⁄16"), and with the largest bearing, the bit can do flush trimming work.

The piloted bit enables you to rabbet curved edges. You can't do that on the table saw. Making a cut with a piloted rabbeting bit is pretty much a matter of setting the cut depth, switching on the router and diving in. Cut across the grain first, then with the grain. If you are routing only across the grain, either climb-cut in from the corner or clamp a backup scrap at the corner to prevent blowout as the bit exits the work.

The bit and the bearings do work well, but I'm often inclined to use an unpiloted bit with an edge guide for rabbeting. I get an infinitely variable cut width with this setup, rather than a few predetermined widths. In addition, I have better control over the tool and the cut.

With a piloted bit alone, the cutting edges begin their work before the bearing makes contact with the edge. All too often, you dip around the corner of the workpiece at one end of the cut or the other. That doesn't happen with an edge-guide-controlled cut because the guide surface extends well beyond the cutter both fore and aft.

Keep the guide in contact with the workpiece edge throughout the feed — beginning before the cut actually starts and continuing until the bit is clear of the work — and you won't run into trouble.

The latter is especially true if you elect to circumvent blowout by climb-cutting in from a corner. The guide gives you the good control needed for a climb cut.

The edge guide is a big help in beginning and ending stopped or blind cuts, as well. Brace the tip of the guide against the workpiece edge, shift the whole router as necessary to align the bit for the start of the cut, then pivot the router into the cut.

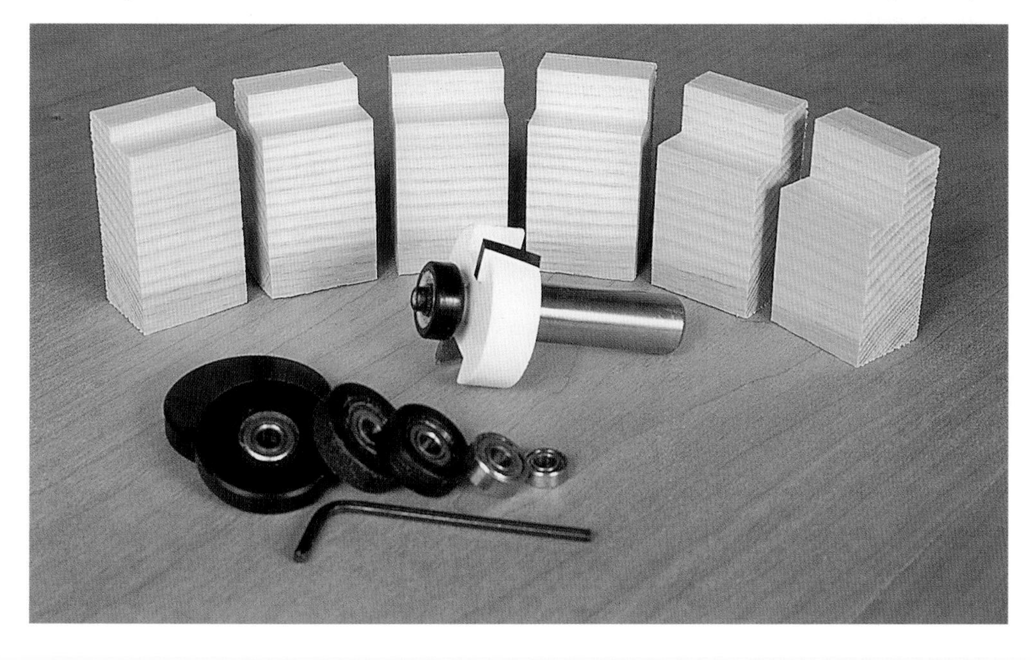

One bit with a selection of bearings enables you to cut rabbets of many different widths.

ripping

BY DAVID THIEL

Ripping Lumber

Ripping a piece of solid lumber is simpler than ripping plywood, but the potential for danger is greater because the stress in a solid-wood board can pinch the blade when it is ripped. Roller stands are recommended (you can't see mine in these photos) and should be positioned to support both pieces coming off the saw.

1

To start the cut, stand at the rear corner of the board, supporting the back end with your right hand. Your left hand (at the center of the board) provides pressure against the fence, keeping it flush. The arrows indicate the direction I'm applying pressure.

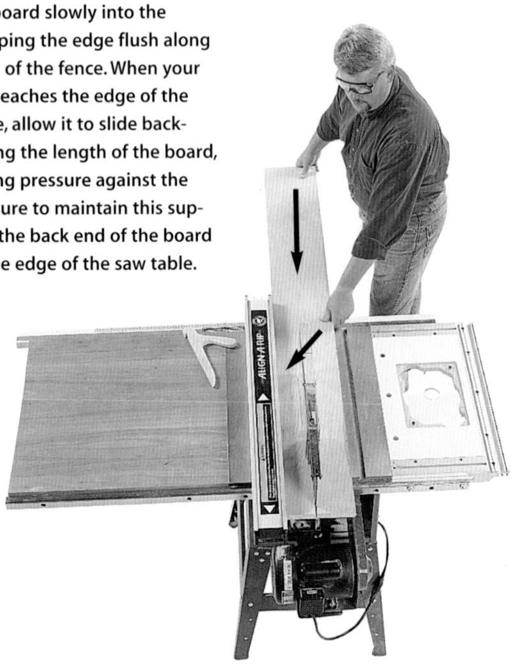

2

Walk the board slowly into the blade, keeping the edge flush along the length of the fence. When your left hand reaches the edge of the saw's table, allow it to slide backwards along the length of the board, maintaining pressure against the fence. Be sure to maintain this support until the back end of the board reaches the edge of the saw table.

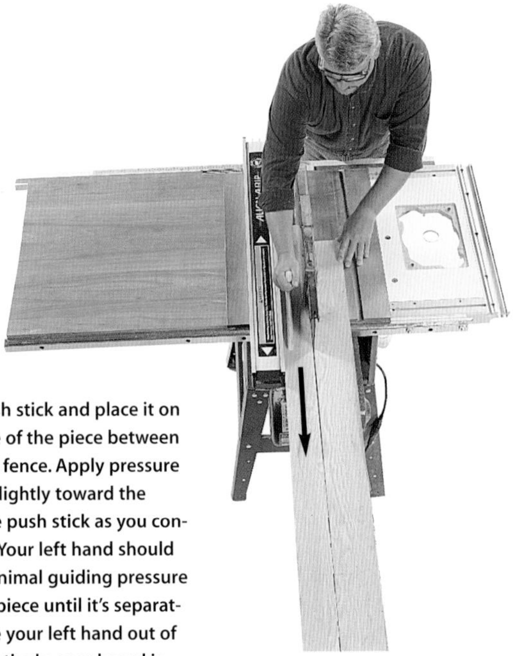

3

Grab your push stick and place it on the back edge of the piece between the blade and fence. Apply pressure forward and slightly toward the fence with the push stick as you continue the cut. Your left hand should apply only minimal guiding pressure on the falloff piece until it's separated, then move your left hand out of the way. Once the keeper board is clear of the blade and guard, push the falloff piece safely forward, again using the push stick.

Ripping Plywood

Ripping a 4' × 8' sheet of plywood on a contractor's saw is possible, but it's a cross between a waltz and a balancing act. Roller stands are a must, and they should be positioned to support the largest piece coming off the saw or, preferably, both pieces. (You can't see mine in these photos.)

1 To start the cut, stand near the rear corner of the sheet, supporting the back end of the sheet with your right hand while your left hand provides pressure against the fence and presses the sheet flush to the fence. With the piece pushed up nearly to the blade, check the fit against the fence, then slowly walk the sheet into the blade. The arrows indicate the direction I'm applying pressure.

2 As you move forward, keep your eyes on the fence to keep the sheet flush against it. As the balance of the weight of the sheet is transferred to the saw table you can shift your position to the rear of the sheet, supporting from the back but still maintaining pressure against the fence with your left hand. Continue to push the sheet forward. Pay attention to the point where the sheet contacts your roller stand (to make sure it's riding on the stand, not pushing it over), then continue the cut.

3 As you reach the end of the cut, allow the waste piece (under my left hand) to come to a rest and transfer your attention to the piece between the fence and blade. Push this piece clear of the blade, careful not to extend your reach over the blade. Once clear of the blade and guard, lift the piece up and over the fence and bring it to rest on the side of the fence opposite the blade. Don't drag the piece back toward you over the guard. With that piece safe, continue to push the waste piece forward and away from the blade until it clears the blade and guard.

wall and base cabinets

BY JIM STACK

When I first started in the furniture-making and cabinetmaking business, I worked in a shop that built anything the clients wanted. But our main source of revenue was building cabinets — cabinets for kitchens, bathrooms, dens, closets, hospitals, restaurants, banks. The list seemed never-ending.

A cabinet is a box with doors, drawers (which are just little boxes inside bigger boxes) and pullout shelves. I liken cabinetmaking to Hollywood, because all the focus is on the surface, but what is behind the finished piece is solid, hard work.

Most of the time, the cabinet boxes don't have to be works of art. They need to be sturdy and the right size and shape. Works of art are made by adding the doors, drawer fronts, false panels, face frames and mouldings.

When a woodworker is starting out, cabinetmaking is the best place to start learning. Once the basic techniques of cabinetmaking are learned, all other furniture making is easier.

The arrangements of base and wall cabinets are flexible. A kitchen is one specialized arrangement of cabinetry. The

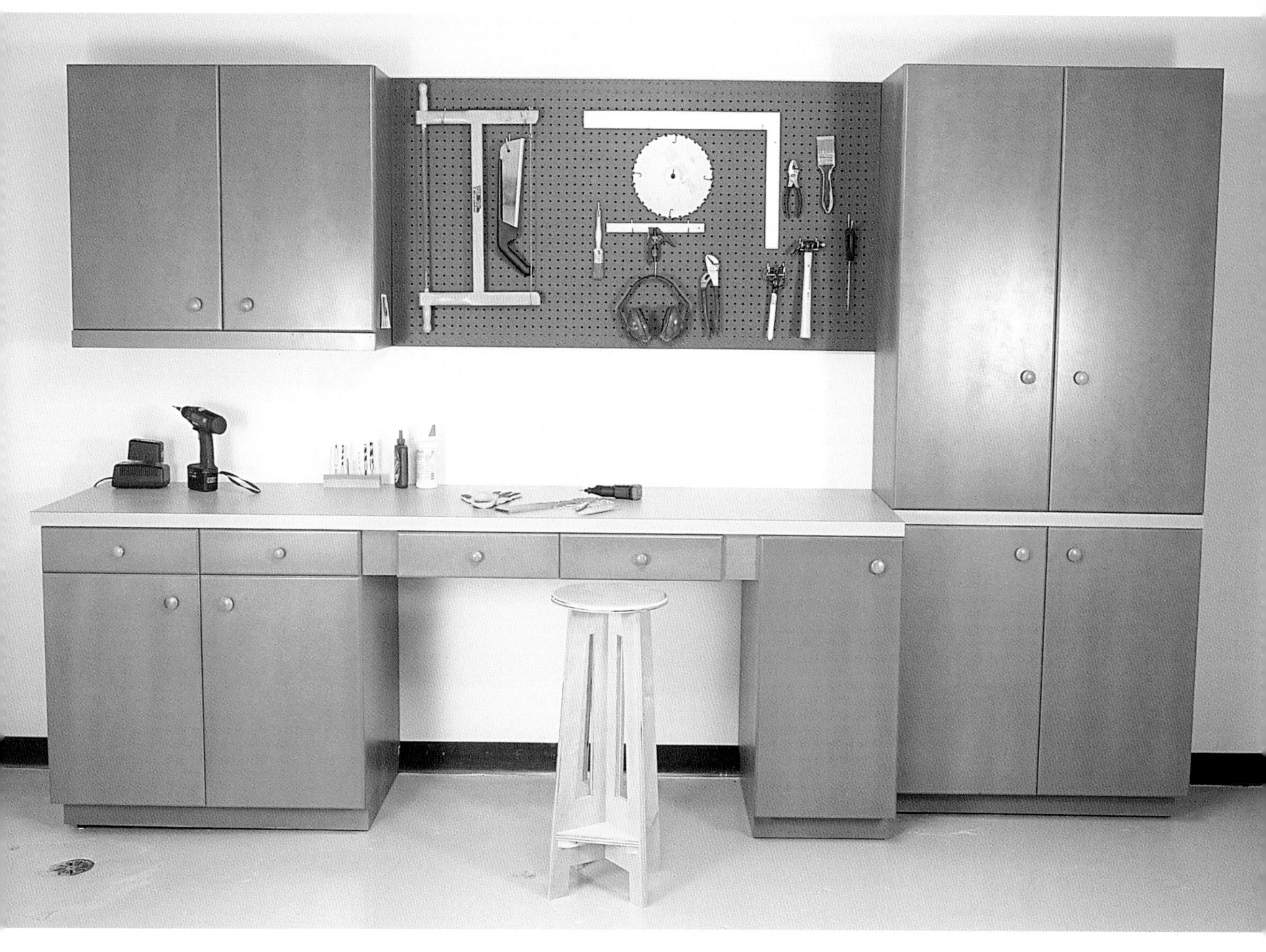

base cabinets serve as storage units and hold a worktop in place. The wall cabinets serve as storage units and can have lights mounted under them to illuminate the countertop. Also, if the wall cabinets don't finish out to the ceiling, their tops can be used to display things.

Cabinetry becomes part of a room. Kitchen and bathroom cabinetry is often attached to the walls, making it a permanent part of the house. Design elements that need to be considered when building cabinetry are the finish, types and styles of mouldings to be applied and how the piece will be used.

Base Cabinets

When cabinetry is mentioned, kitchens are usually what come to mind, so let's talk about them first.

When I was growing up, we spent a lot of time in the kitchen. It was a gathering place for the family, our friends and neighbors. Of course, food was prepared, but homework was done on the table, science projects were constructed and haircuts given, all in the kitchen.

In deciding how to arrange your kitchen, look at the room: Where are the windows and doors? What are the heights of the window sills? How high are the ceilings, and how much square footage does the room have? Do you cook a lot, or do you mostly fix prepackaged meals? Do you want to have a table and chairs in the kitchen? Do you entertain a lot? Do you have some special dishes you want to see on display? Do you like the look of wood, solid colors or laminate patterns (of which there are thousands)? All these questions need to be asked and answered completely before anything else can be done.

The drawings on the following pages show the basic dimensions and configurations of kitchen base and wall cabinets. If you use this information and nothing else, you won't go

This set of practical cabinets is made from medium-density fiberboard (MDF) and finished with clear lacquer. Basic cabinet construction is used and can be arranged in any configuration that is needed.

wrong. When designing, always start with the simplest idea first, then build on that.

Kitchen cabinets are built to certain standard dimensions. Design your kitchen layout using these various cabinet sizes in combinations that will work in your kitchen space. It's easier to use and remember these standard sizes.

Sometimes, though, you just can't get standard-size cabinets to fit in the space you have. For example, the space between the walls, a door or a window creates a problem. Use the standard cabinets where you can. Usually only one custom-size cabinet will be needed to fill in that space.

Base cabinets can have two pullout shelves (which I think are a great idea). One shelf is mounted at the bottom of the cabinet, and one is mounted halfway between the bottom of the cabinet and the bottom of the drawer at the top of the cabinet. Adjustable shelves, drawers, turntables for a lazy Susan and trash can holders can also be added to base cabinets.

Kitchen appliances mounted under kitchen cabinets are made to standard sizes. Of course, there are exceptions, but you should have no trouble finding what you want.

I don't think there is such a thing as a traditional kitchen anymore. There are wood cabinets with raised- and flat-panel doors, crown moulding trim that is stained or painted, flat doors and drawer fronts with laminate or wood veneers that are stained or painted; I even built a base cabinet that had 20-gauge stainless steel applied to the doors.

Cabinets can be built with face frames or no frames and with doors and drawer fronts that are mounted flush to the fronts of the cabinets or overlay the fronts. More cabinet combinations exist than can be listed here.

This Shaker wall cabinet (5"-deep by 20"-wide by 28"-tall) is perfect for a small room. The depth will hold bottles, combs and other personal items. It is a straight-line cabinet with a couple of design elements that make it more than just a box with a door. The frame and panel door with the raised panel and the flat crown moulding make this cabinet a visual treat. The wood selection also makes a strong statement!

One simple but effective way to finish the top of a wall cabinet is to add crown moulding. The moulding adds a flair to the top, and it gives the cabinet depth as you look up at it. Dentil moulding underneath the crown can add even more flair.

This is a detail photo of a face-frame mounted hinge. These hinges are adjustable up and down but not in and out or sideways. This is an overlay door that is cut to fit over the cabinet, opening a certain distance all around, so little or no adjustment is necessary.

It seems there is never enough storage room for your shop tools. This one-piece cabinet will hold a lot of tools! The doors are overlay and use European hinges. This is cabinetry at its most basic, but it still has style. This is a good project to construct if you want to learn the basics and gain some valuable shop storage at the same time!

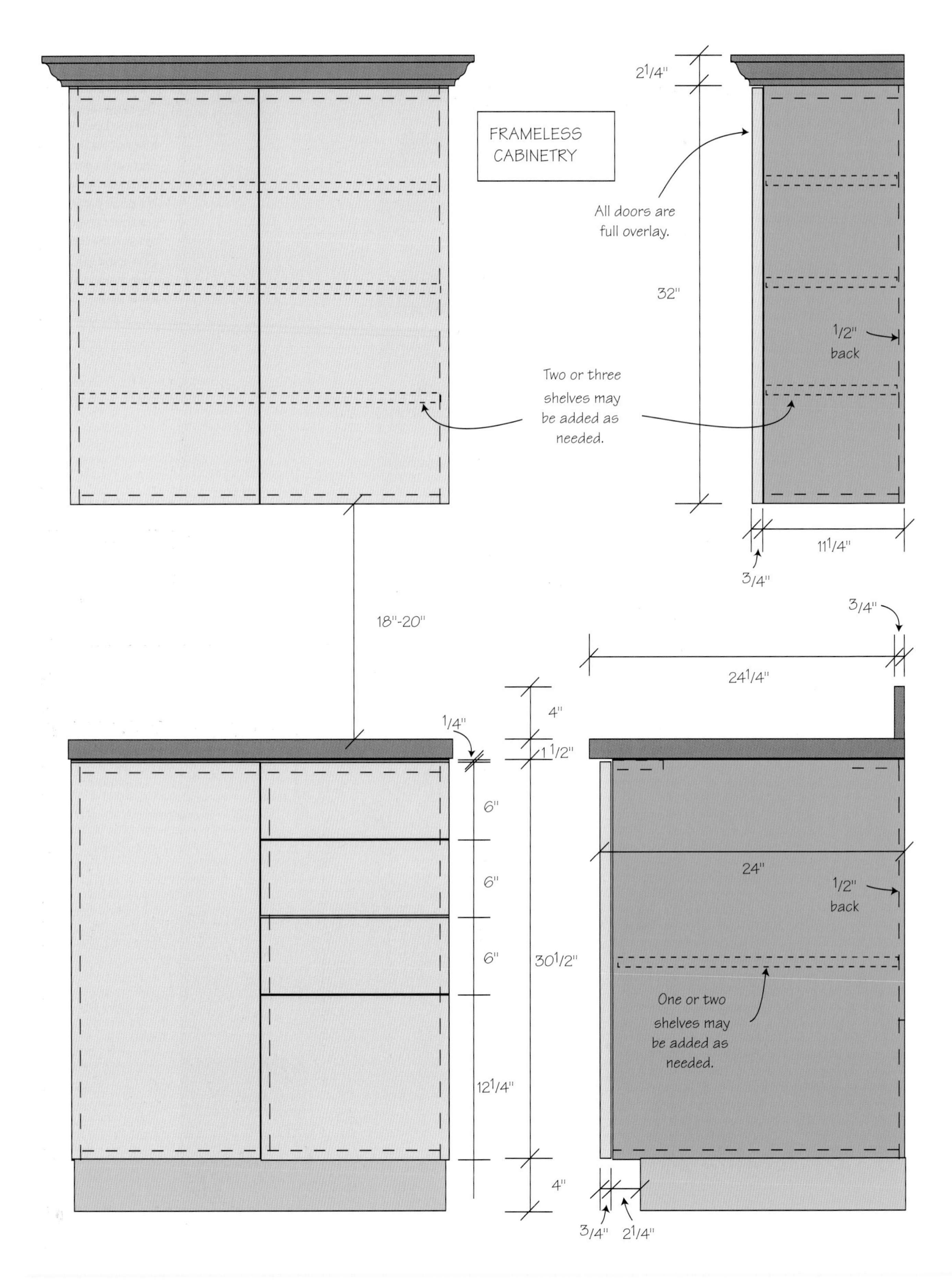

FRAMELESS CABINETRY
2 1/4"
All doors are full overlay.
32"
1/2" back
Two or three shelves may be added as needed.
11 1/4"
3/4"
18"-20"
3/4"
24 1/4"
4"
1/4"
1 1/2"
6"
6"
6"
30 1/2"
24"
1/2" back
One or two shelves may be added as needed.
12 1/4"
4"
3/4"
2 1/4"

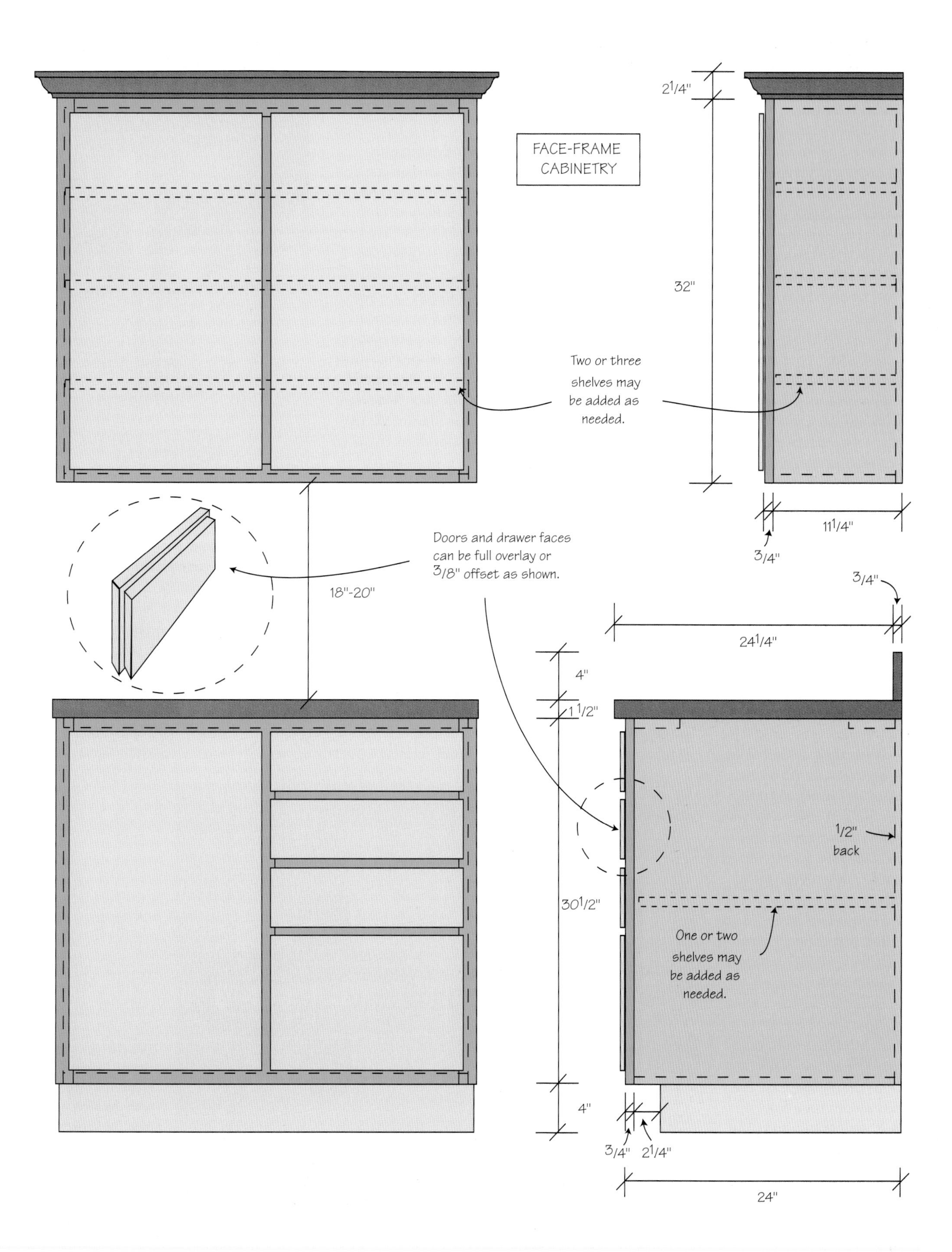

FACE-FRAME CABINETRY
2 1/4"
32"
Two or three shelves may be added as needed.
11 1/4"
3/4"
Doors and drawer faces can be full overlay or 3/8" offset as shown.
18"-20"
3/4"
24 1/4"
4"
1 1/2"
1/2" back
30 1/2"
One or two shelves may be added as needed.
4"
3/4"
2 1/4"
24"

THE EUROPEAN OR 32MM SYSTEM

For several decades, European cabinetmakers have used a system of cabinetmaking that is quick, flexible and efficient.

The cabinet parts are cut out, edge-banded, drilled as needed for hardware and finished. Then the drawer hardware and hinge plates are installed. One of the benefits of this system is that the cabinet parts can be shipped flat and delivered to the job site. The cabinets can then be assembled and installed.

It's called the 32mm system because the 5mm hardware mounting holes are drilled in a line 32mm on center. Two vertical rows of these 5mm holes are drilled on the inside of the cabinet side panels. The side panels have 8mm assembly holes drilled near the top and bottom edges. Matching 8mm holes are drilled into the edges of the bottom and top panels. The drawer boxes are predrilled for dowels or assembly screws.

All the necessary hardware for this construction system can be found at home-improvement centers. The door hinges come in two parts: the hinge and its mounting plate. The drawer slides also come in two parts: the main part of the slide, which is mounted on the inside of the cabinet, and the drawer box part, which is mounted on the drawer. Special, deep-thread comfirmat assembly screws are used to hold the cabinets together.

Adjustable leveling feet can be mounted on the bottom of the cabinet. These are used to level the cabinets when they are installed and are adjusted with a screwdriver from the inside of the cabinet through a small hole drilled in the bottom of the cabinet. After the cabinets have been leveled and set, these holes are plugged with plastic covers. The feet also have clips that will accept cleats mounted on the cabinet base fronts. The base is simply pushed and clipped into place after the cabinets have been installed.

Hardware is available for hanging and leveling the wall cabinets. A hanger rail is attached level on the wall, cleats are attached to the back of the wall cabinet and then the cabinet is hung by these cleats on the rail. If front-to-back or end-to-end leveling is needed, access holes drilled in the back of the cabinet allow adjustment of the hanging cleats with a screwdriver. These holes are then plugged with a plastic cover.

Face frames are sometimes used with the European system. The frames can be built and finished separately, then put on the cabinets at final assembly. They are attached with glue and dowels or biscuits.

The drawer-box face panels have 25mm-diameter by 13mm-deep holes drilled into their backs to accept adjustable hardware used to mount the drawer faces to the drawer boxes. A machine screw is inserted into this hardware through the drawer-box front. After the drawers are put into the cabinet, these screws are snugged up and the drawer faces can be adjusted as needed. When all adjustments have been completed, permanent screws are added to hold the faces in place.

The cabinet doors are drilled with 35mm-diameter by 13mm-deep holes for the hinges. The hinges are pressed or set into place with two screws. After the cabinets have been installed, the doors are hung by clipping the hinges into place on the hinge plates. The door hinges can be adjusted with a screwdriver to line up the doors on the cabinets.

The backs of the cabinets are attached with screws, nails or staples driven into rabbets in the back edges of the side panels. The sides, bottoms, tops, shelves, bases, top rails (used on the base cabinets), doors and drawer-box front panels are $^3/_4$" or 19mm thick. The back panels, drawer-box sides, fronts, backs and bottoms are $^1/_2$" or 13mm thick. Sometimes $^1/_4$"- or 6mm-thick material is used for drawer bottom panels.

Countertops are $1^1/_2$" or 38mm thick and 25" or 635mm deep and as long as necessary! Countertops can be made of butcher block, solid-surface materials, marble, colored concrete, stainless steel, ceramic tile set onto a plywood top, or particleboard or plywood covered with high-pressure laminate.

This is a typical self-closing European hinge. The hinge clips onto the plate, and the door can be removed without removing the hinge. A 35mm drill bit is used to cut the hole for the European hinges.

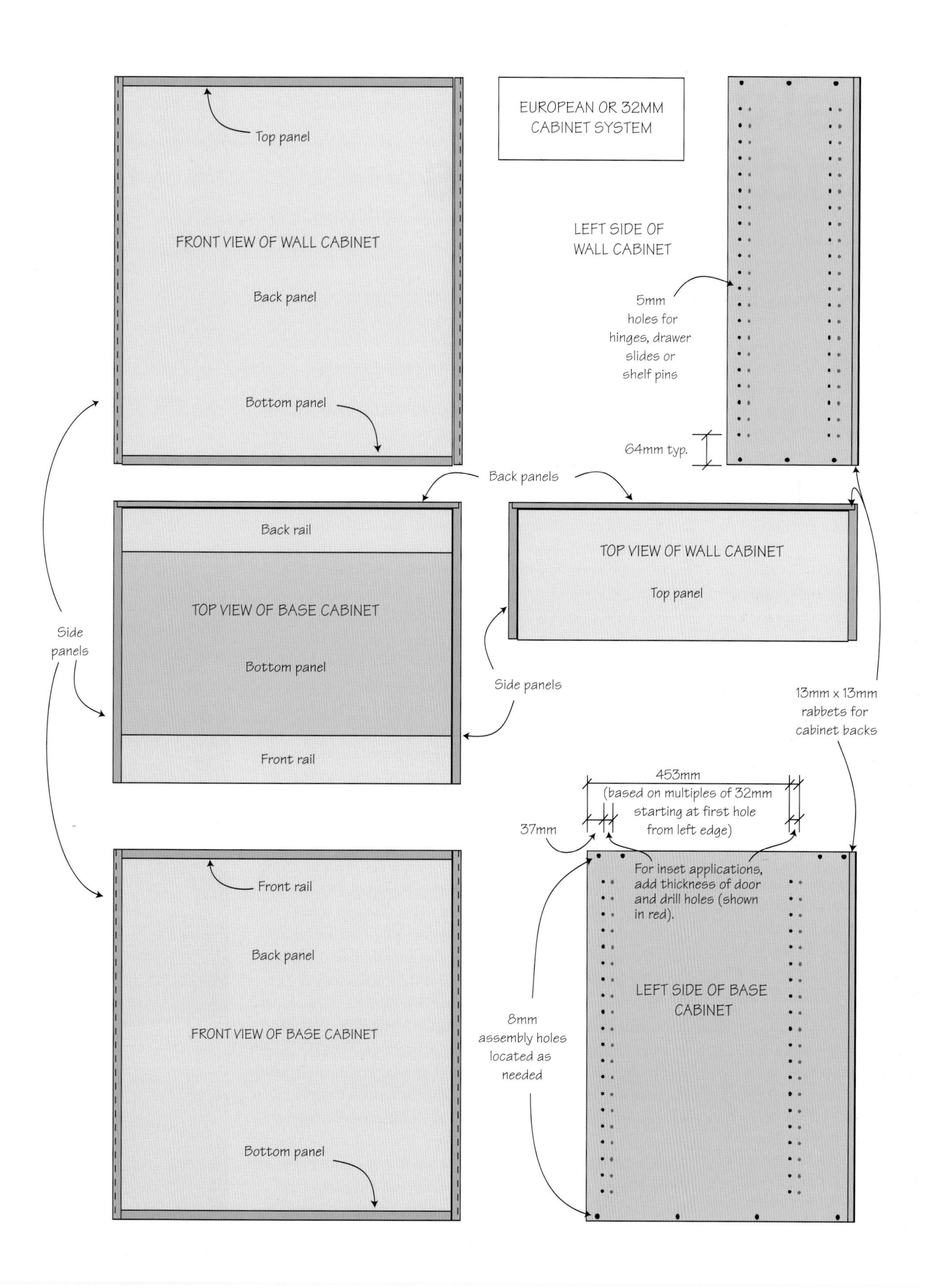
EUROPEAN OR 32MM CABINET SYSTEM
Top panel
FRONT VIEW OF WALL CABINET
Back panel
Bottom panel
LEFT SIDE OF WALL CABINET
5mm holes for hinges, drawer slides or shelf pins
64mm typ.
Back panels
Back rail
TOP VIEW OF BASE CABINET
Bottom panel
Front rail
TOP VIEW OF WALL CABINET
Top panel
Side panels
Side panels
13mm x 13mm rabbets for cabinet backs
453mm
(based on multiples of 32mm starting at first hole from left edge)
37mm
For inset applications, add thickness of door and drill holes (shown in red).
Front rail
Back panel
FRONT VIEW OF BASE CABINET
Bottom panel
LEFT SIDE OF BASE CABINET
8mm assembly holes located as needed

shelving fundamentals

BY TROY SEXTON

Building a set of shelves for muddy boots or a Chippendale secretary seems deceptively simple. First, you install a horizontal surface between two sides. Then you load up your newly built shelf with Wellingtons or glass kitty cats, stand back and admire your work.

One day you grow weary of the kitties and decide to put encyclopedias on your shelf. The shelf sags, the books don't fit under the shelf above, and the books' spines hang over the front edge. You wish you had used a more rigid material and adjustable shelf pins so you could change your shelves to fit your needs.

Shelves, as you might have guessed, are not as simple as they appear. That's not to say they're hard to build. It's just that a whole set of rules applies to properly designed bookshelves and display shelves, which ensures that they will hold a wide variety of common objects.

This shelving unit is the perfect tutorial for etching these rules into your brain. You'll see how I followed the rules to design this project, and you'll get a down-and-dirty lesson in how to build shelving units that are quick, easy, rock solid and good-looking.

Here are a couple of rules of thumb when you're putting your design on paper. It's accepted practice to build your cabinets in 3" increments. For example, the side units are 24" wide. If I wanted to make them wider, I'd jump to 27", then 30". Another rule of thumb is that whenever a cabinet is 42" or wider it needs a vertical support in the center. My cabinets are narrower than that, so that was no problem for me.

PERFECTLY FLUSH FACE FRAMES

When you mill out your parts, a couple of tricks will help you get the face frames perfectly flush to the cabinet without a lot of sanding. First, when ripping your stiles from wider stock, joint one edge on your jointer, then rip the stile 1/16" wider than your finished width. When you cut your mortises, make sure you cut them on the edge that you ran over your jointer — not the edge that has saw blade marks on it.

Then, after you attach your face frames to your case, use a router loaded with a flush trimming bit to trim the face frame flush to the plywood case.

The result: A face frame that is perfectly flush with no saw blade marks to sand out.

Where to Begin: Face First

This large wall unit is essentially six plywood boxes with solid-wood face frames on front. The part of the back that is visible behind the shelves is solid wood. The back behind the doors is plywood.

When building shelves, it's tempting to begin with the case because it goes together really fast. Resist this temptation. Begin your project by building the solid-wood face frames. Your entire project is based on your face frame, so if you have a problem with your design, or how you milled your parts, you're most likely to find out about it when you build the face frame. And I'd rather throw away a skinny piece of solid wood than a sheet of plywood.

I make my face frames using ¾" material and mortise-and-tenon construction. First, I cut my tenons on the rails, then I use those to lay out my mortises on my stiles. When working with ¾" material, I always make my tenons ⅜" thick and 1" long. Usually I cut a ½" shoulder on the width of the tenon, but if the stock is narrow (less than 3"), I'll use a ¼" shoulder. I cut my tenons on my table saw using a dado stack.

I now lay out my mortises using the tenons. Cut the mortises — I use a hollow-chisel mortiser — about 1¹⁄₁₆" deep so the tenon won't bottom out in the mortise. Put glue in the mortises, clamp and set the frames aside.

inches (millimeters)

REFERENCE	QUANTITY	PART	STOCK	THICKNESS	(mm)	WIDTH	(mm)	LENGTH	(mm)	COMMENTS
CENTER CASE, UPPER UNIT										
A	1	bottom rail	cherry	3/4	(19)	1 1/2	(38)	33	(838)	
B	1	top rail	cherry	3/4	(19)	4	(102)	33	(838)	
C	2	stiles	cherry	3/4	(19)	4 3/4	(121)	50	(1270)	
D	1	top	cherry ply	3/4	(19)	16 3/4	(426)	39 1/2	(1003)	
E	3	adjustable shelves	cherry ply	3/4	(19)	16	(406)	38 3/4	(984)	width includes dropped edge
F	1	bottom	cherry ply	3/4	(19)	16 3/4	(426)	39 1/2	(1003)	
G	2	sides	cherry ply	3/4	(19)	17 1/4	(438)	50	(1270)	
H	2	columns	cherry	1	(25)	3	(76)	50	(1270)	
J	1	back	cherry	1/2	(13)	39 1/2	(1004)	50	(1270)	
CENTER CASE, LOWER UNIT										
K	1	top rail	cherry	3/4	(19)	1 1/2	(38)	33	(838)	
L	1	bottom rail	cherry	3/4	(19)	5	(127)	33	(838)	
M	2	stiles	cherry	3/4	(19)	4 3/4	(121)	30	(762)	
N	1	bottom	cherry ply	3/4	(19)	16 3/4	(426)	39 1/2	(1003)	
P	1	adjustable shelf	cherry ply	3/4	(19)	16	(406)	38 3/4	(984)	width includes dropped edge
Q	1	top rail	cherry	3/4	(19)	1 1/2	(38)	39	(991)	
R	2	sides	cherry ply	3/4	(19)	17 1/4	(438)	30	(762)	
S	2	columns	cherry	1	(25)	3	(76)	30	(762)	
T	1	back	cherry ply	1/4	(6)	39 1/2	(1003)	26 1/4	(667)	
ONE CENTER UNIT DOOR										
U	2	rails	cherry	3/4	(19)	2 1/2	(64)	12 1/2	(318)	
V	2	stiles	cherry	3/4	(19)	2 1/2	(64)	23 1/2	(597)	
W	1	panel	cherry	5/8	(16)	11	(279)	19	(483)	
SIDE CASE, ONE UPPER UNIT										
X	1	bottom rail	cherry	3/4	(19)	1 1/2	(38)	21	(533)	
Y	1	top rail	cherry	3/4	(19)	4	(102)	21	(533)	
Z	1	interior stile	cherry	3/4	(19)	2 5/8	(67)	50	(1270)	
AA	1	exterior stile	cherry	3/4	(19)	2 1/2	(64)	50	(1270)	
BB	1	top	cherry ply	3/4	(19)	12 3/4	(324)	23	(584)	
CC	3	adjustable shelves	cherry ply	3/4	(19)	12	(305)	22 1/4	(565)	width includes dropped edge
DD	1	bottom	cherry ply	3/4	(19)	12 3/4	(324)	23	(584)	
EE	2	sides	cherry ply	3/4	(19)	13 1/4	(337)	50	(1270)	
FF	1	back	cherry	1/2	(13)	23	(584)	50	(1270)	
SIDE CASE, ONE LOWER UNIT										
GG	1	top rail	cherry	3/4	(19)	1 1/2	(38)	21	(533)	
HH	1	bottom rail	cherry	3/4	(19)	5	(127)	21	(533)	
JJ	1	interior stile	cherry	3/4	(19)	2 5/8	(67)	30	(762)	
KK	1	exterior stile	cherry	3/4	(19)	2 1/2	(64)	30	(762)	
LL	1	bottom	cherry ply	3/4	(19)	12 3/4	(324)	23	(584)	
MM	1	adjustable shelf	cherry ply	3/4	(19)	12	(305)	22 1/4	(565)	width includes dropped edge
NN	1	top rail	cherry	3/4	(19)	1 1/2	(38)	22 1/2	(572)	
PP	2	sides	cherry ply	3/4	(19)	13 1/4	(337)	30	(762)	
QQ	1	back	cherry ply	1/4	(6)	23	(584)	16 1/4	(413)	
ONE SIDE UNIT DOOR										
RR	2	rails	cherry	3/4	(19)	2 1/2	(64)	16	(406)	
SS	2	stiles	cherry	3/4	(19)	2 1/2	(64)	23 1/2	(597)	
TT	1	panel	cherry	5/8	(16)	14 1/2	(368)	19	(483)	

Plywood Boxes

Make the cases out of ¾" plywood. Cut ¾" × ¼"-deep dadoes on the sides to hold the bottom pieces. These should be flush to the top edge of the bottom rail. Cut ¾" × ¼" rabbets in the top edge of the side pieces to hold the top. This is also the time to cut the grooves in the sides of the center cabinet to line up all three cases. Read "Another Face-Frame Trick" for details. Now, cut rabbets on the sides to hold the back. The size of the rabbet is determined by whether it's a plywood back or a solid back.

Drill your adjustable shelf holes. I use a commercial jig, but you can make a template yourself from plywood. I drill my holes every 1" or 2" on center, which allows for a lot of adjustment. The standard is to drill them every 2" on center, or less, and within 6" of the top and bottom of the cabinet. For years I used shelf pins that required ¼" holes. Then I switched to metric 5mm because they're less conspicuous.

Sand the inside of your case pieces with 180-grit sandpaper to knock off the fuzz and splinters.

Go ahead and put your cases together. Put glue in the dadoes and rabbets, and nail through the outside of the cases into the top and bottom. Putty the nail holes. You don't need to clamp the case.

Attach your face frames using glue and nails. Trim the face frames flush (see "Perfectly Flush Face Frames" on page 180) and putty your nail holes. Now sand your face frames. I begin with 100-grit, then 120, 150 and finally 180. Sand the outside of the plywood case beginning with 120-grit and work up to 180.

Drill your shelf pin holes before you assemble your case. I like to put mine on 1" or 2" centers. Depending on what you're going to put on your shelves, you might not need that many holes.

ANOTHER FACE FRAME TRICK

Here's another great trick for dealing with face frames. One of the biggest pains when attaching multiple shelving units together is getting them to line up when one is set back from another. Here's the easy way. First, cut a ¾"-wide by ⅛"-deep groove in the plywood case of the larger unit, at the location where the two cases will meet. Then, when making the face frames for the smaller unit, rip one stile ⅛" wider and don't trim it flush to the case; let it hang over the edge. When you start attaching these cases, everything will line itself up as illustrated in this photo.

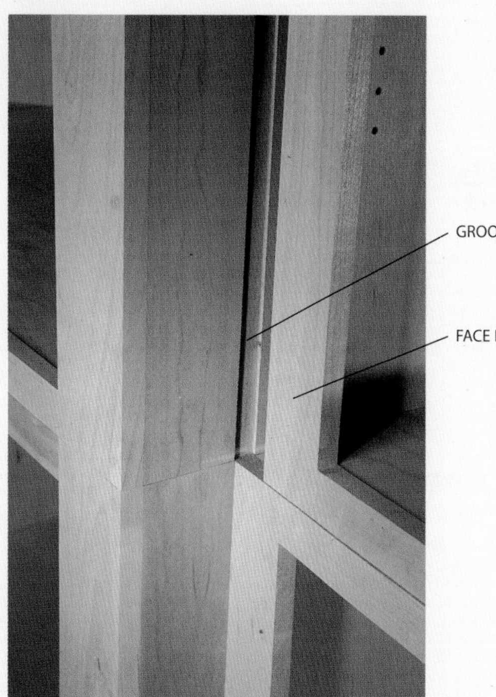

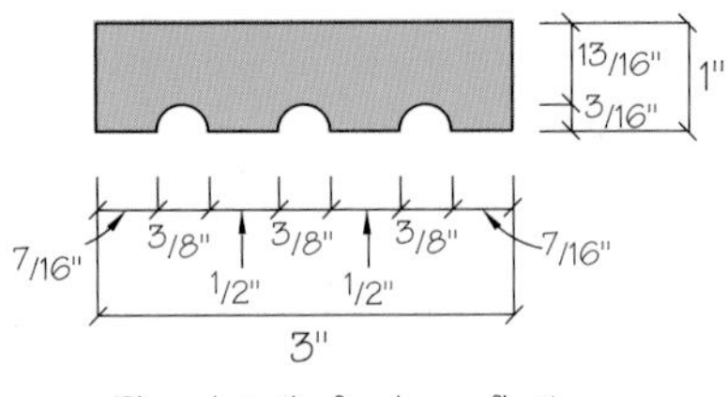

Plan detail of column fluting

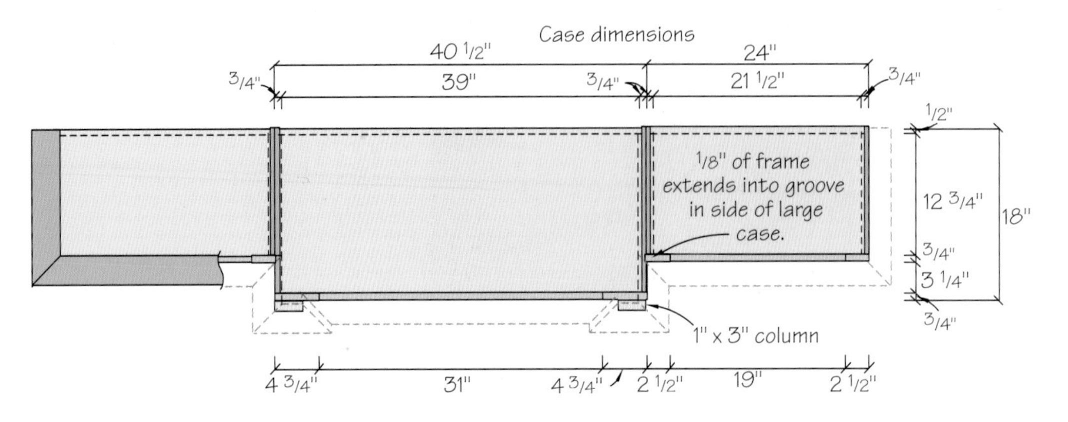

Face-frame dimensions

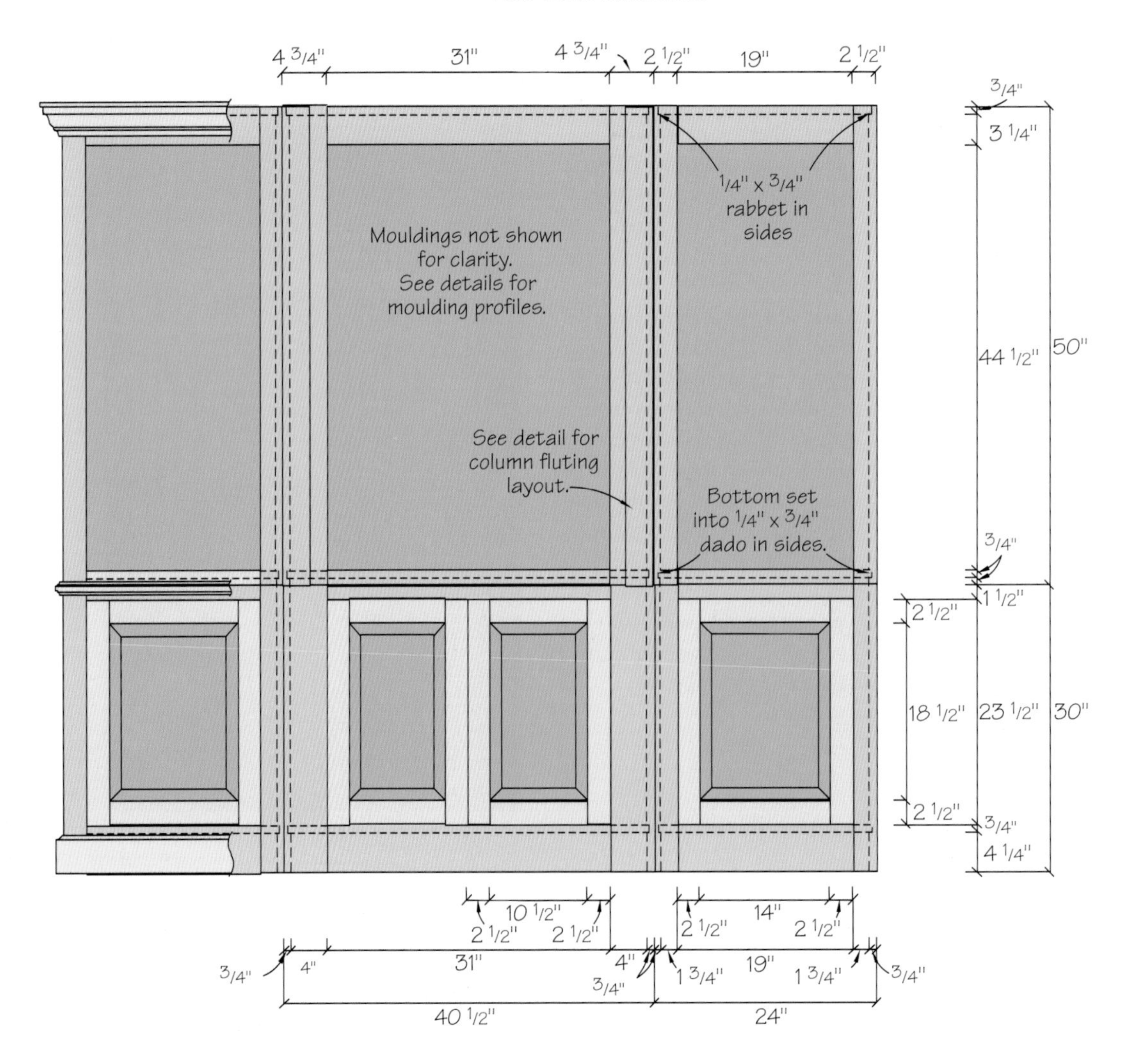

If you're going to add columns to your center case, cut the details using a fluting bit in your router and attach the columns to your face frame with glue.

Finally, screw all the top units together, then screw all the bottom units together. Now turn your attention to the moulding.

Many Mouldings

This unit has five types of moulding:

- The crown moulding: Buy it premade from a hardwood supplier.
- The ½" cap on top of the crown moulding: This is simply square stock with a ⅜" roundover cut on one edge.
- The waist moulding: This covers the seams between the upper and lower units. You can buy moulding like this off the rack, or you can make it. First, cut your stock to size, then use a beading bit to cut the center bead. Use a ½" cove cutter in your router to cut the coves on the top and bottom. Be wary as you make the second cove cut; the moulding won't be as steady.
- The base moulding: This is flat stock with a ½" cove cut on one edge.
- Shelf moulding: This goes on the front edge of the plywood shelves, which you'll make later. I used a rail-and-stile bit to make this moulding in two passes. You also could use a Roman ogee bit to get the same effect.

Hand sand all your moulding before applying it. Attach the moulding with glue and nails. Start from the center and work out. One word about the waist moulding: Position it so it sticks up ½" above the lower case and nail it to the lower case.

Get a friend to help you stack the cases on top of one another (left). Then use spring clamps at the back to hold everything together as you screw the upper cabinets together and the lower cabinets together. Be sure to screw right behind the face frame so the screw is less visible (below left).

which thickness should I use for that part?

This might seem obvious to veteran cabinetmakers, but some beginning and intermediate woodworkers might wonder what thickness of lumber should be used for different parts of your standard face frame cabinet.

Part	Thickness
Case parts (sides, tops, bottoms, dividers etc.)	¾"
Face frames	¾"
Backs (plywood)	¼"
Backs (solid)	½" to ⅝"
Drawer sides, backs subfronts	½"
Drawer bottoms	¼"
Drawer fronts	¾"

Doors

Build the doors the same way you built the face frames, with one exception. You'll need to cut a ⅜" × ⅜" groove on the rails and stiles for the solid-wood panel. That also means you'll need to cut haunches on your tenons to fit into the grooves.

With raised panels I allow a ⅛" gap on each side so the panel can expand and contract in the groove. To "raise" the panel, first cut the approximate angle on the panel's edge using your table saw. Then use an 8° raised-panel cutter in your router to raise the panel. This way you'll need to make only one pass on your router table. Sand the panel, assemble the doors, then sand the rest of the door. Peg the tenons, cut the pegs $\frac{1}{16}$" proud and sand them smooth but not flush to the doors.

Attach the pulls and fit your doors so there's a $\frac{1}{16}$" gap all around. I use Amerock

Moulding Details

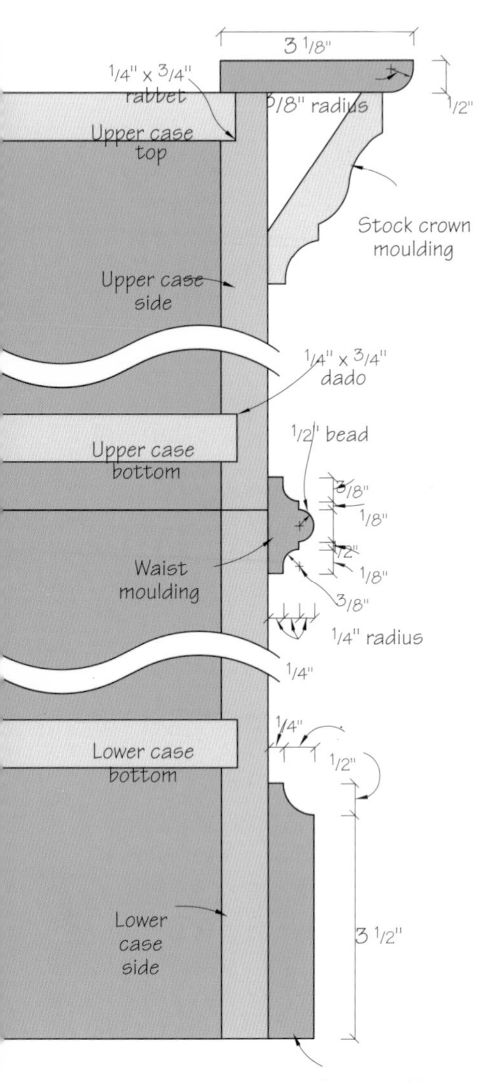

Attach the waist moulding using nails. Nail it to the lower case and allow the top edge to cover the seam between the upper and lower cases.

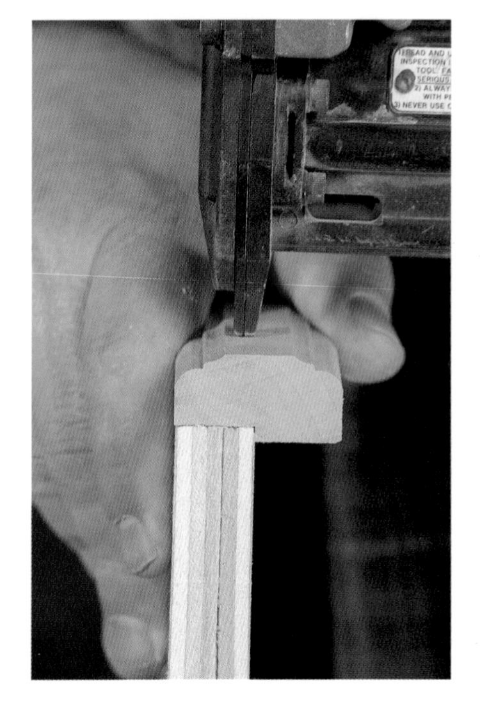

Here you can see what the shelf moulding looks like close up. Nail and glue the moulding to your plywood shelves.

keep your shelves from sagging

You don't want your shelves to sag, yet you don't want to waste materials by overbuilding them either. In general, here are the guidelines for how long shelves can be before they start to sag, according to the Architectural Woodwork Institute. Typical shelves vary from 8" deep to 12" deep.

MATERIAL	MAX SPAN (3/4" MAT.)	MAX SPAN (1 1/16" MAT.)
Solid wood	36"	48"
Veneer-core ply	36"	48"
Medium-density fiberboard	32"	42"

Of course, some woods and manufactured wood products are stronger than others. The following chart shows how much weight it takes to make a 12"-wide shelf bend 1/4" across a 36" span and a 48" span. As you can see below, solid wood makes the strongest shelves, followed by a manufactured shelf with a solid-wood edge that's wider than the plywood is thick (commonly referred to as a "dropped" edge). This is the shelf I used for the project.

SHELF MATERIAL	36" SPAN	48" SPAN
Yellow poplar	284 lbs.	117 lbs.
Hard maple & red oak	313	232
Birch	348	146
MDF	87	38
Birch veneer-core ply	129	54
Birch veneer MDF	109	46
MDF with 0.05"-thick laminate	205	87
MDF with 1/8" wood edge	79	33
MDF with 3/4" wood edge	90	38
MDF with 3/4" x 1 1/2" wood edge, dropped	241	107

SOURCE: ARCHITECTURAL WOODWORK INSTITUTE, DEPARTMENT OF WOOD SCIENCE, DIVISION OF FORESTRY AT WEST VIRGINIA UNIVERSITY

common sizes of stuff you put on a shelf

When building shelves for a specific purpose — say, for an entertainment center — you need to plan around the standard sizes of objects. Use these handy dimensions to figure out your shelf opening heights and depths.

OBJECT	DEPTH × HEIGHT
Paperbacks	4 1/4" × 6 7/8"
Hardbacks	7" × 9 1/2"
Textbooks	9" × 11"
Vinyl LPs	12 3/8" × 12 3/8"
Compact discs	5 1/2" × 5"
Cassettes	2 3/4" × 4 1/4"
DVDs	5 1/2" × 7 1/2"
VHS tapes	4 1/8" × 7 1/2"

adjustable nonmortise hinges. These hinges are pricey (about $3 each), but they are worth every penny because they are simple to install and are adjustable.

Back and Shelves

I used a shiplapped and beaded 1/2"-thick back on the top part of the case, and a plywood back on the lower section. Cut your 1/4" × 1/2" shiplaps, then cut the bead on the edge using a 1/4" beading bit in your router. Fit the back, being sure to leave space for seasonal expansion and contraction. Don't nail the back in place until after finishing. Cut your shelves from plywood, nail the moulding to it, then sand the shelves.

Finishing

I used a clear finish on this piece, sanding between coats with 3M sanding sponges (fine grit). Nothing gets into moulding and raised panels better. When everything's dry, nail your back pieces in place and hang your doors.

built-in basics

BY CHRISTOPHER SCHWARZ

Making built-in furniture isn't tough. I've seen lots of first-time woodworkers build passable bookshelves that fit in the nooks by their fireplace.

However, making built-ins that hug the wall, sit level and are anchored firmly to the house requires a little more know-how.

With a little planning and a few modifications to the plans of almost any cabinet, you can make it a built-in that will look great in your house. After trying several different systems for making built-ins, this is the one that I prefer. It's simple, rock solid and almost foolproof.

Cabinets in a Crooked House

If you've ever hung a cabinet or built in a few shelves, you've probably noticed that your rooms aren't square and your walls aren't plumb. This is usually the result of your house settling. It's also possible your framers or drywallers were, unfortunately, a little sloppy.

Either way, don't build your cabinets crooked to fit a catawampus corner or sloping wall. Always build your projects square and add a couple of features to allow them to fit in an irregular space. Two tricks to accommodating out-of-whack walls are oversize back rabbets and fitting strips.

Big Back Rabbets

All cabinets should have a back that rests in rabbets in the sides of the case. This ensures a tight fit between the back and sides. With freestanding furniture, if your back is $\frac{1}{2}$" thick, then the rabbets for that back should be $\frac{1}{2}$" wide. This is not the case with built-ins.

You need to cut a rabbet that is significantly wider. I make it between $1\frac{1}{4}$" and $1\frac{1}{2}$", depending on how out of kilter the wall is. This large rabbet creates two long tongues on the back of your cabinet that can be scribed to fit almost any wall.

What's scribing? That is when you cut the edge of the cabinet so it matches the shape of your wall and fits tightly against it. Scribing isn't difficult, and I'll show you how I go about it later.

Fitting Strips, Scribe Stiles

Two other weapons in your arsenal against the crooked wall and odd corner in your house are fitting strips and scribe stiles. They are a lot like the large rabbets on the back of your cabinet except they help fit the sides of your cabinet to a wall or an adjacent cabinet.

If you're building and installing a face-frame cabinet, your best bet is incorporating a scribe stile into your design. With this technique you make your face-frame stiles (the vertical pieces of the frame) wider so they extend over the sides of the cabinet by $\frac{3}{4}$". Cut a rabbet on the back side of the stiles.

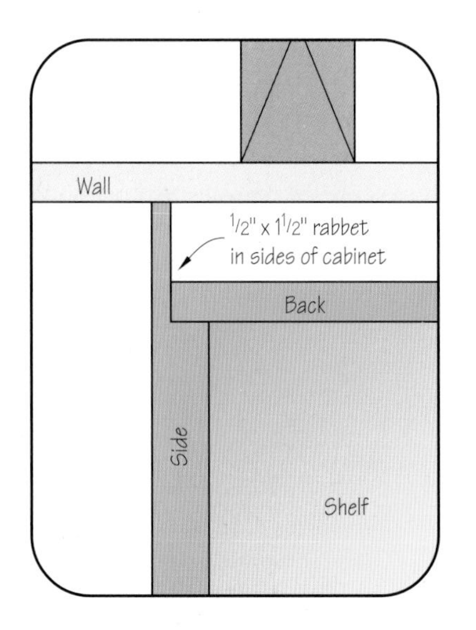

BACK RABBET DETAIL
PLAN VIEW

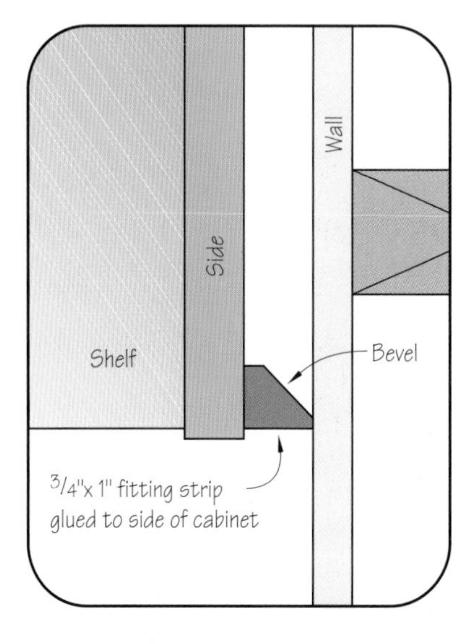

SIMPLE FITTING STRIP
PLAN VIEW

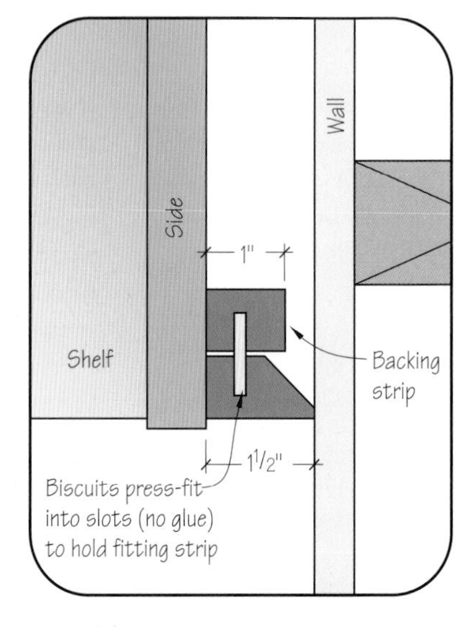

A COMPLEX FITTING STRIP
PLAN VIEW

You can buy a wide variety of cabinet levelers, but they all basically work the same way. Some are adjustable at both the foot and from above through an access hole you drill in the cabinet's bottom. This feature is a huge convenience when leveling your cabinet on an uneven floor.

Once the cabinet is level front to back as well as left to right, you can plug the holes you drilled to access the leveler hardware. Many brands of levelers come with their own plastic plugs, though a shop-made tapered wooden plug works just as well.

This makes them easier to scribe to fit. Then you have a seamless way of attaching your cabinets to walls or other cabinets.

If you are building a cabinet without a face frame, you should turn to the fitting strip. Fitting strips are attached to the cabinet sides and are cut to fit against a wall. Typically you cut a 45° angle on the back side of the $\frac{3}{4}$" × 1" fitting strip so that when you scribe it, a lot less material must be cut away. You can attach a fitting strip to a case in a variety of ways. Whatever method you use, avoid using metal fasteners because they could get in the way when you scribe and then trim the fitting strip to size.

If the case is small, simply glue the fitting strip to the side of the case. If the case is large, come up with an alternate plan. It's no fun turning a big case on its side, trimming a little more and then setting it back up over and over again.

One solution is to glue a backing board to the cabinet behind the fitting strip that is a little narrower. Then you attach the fitting strip to the backing board using several biscuits but no glue. This allows you to set the cabinet against the wall, mark your scribe, cut it and then put the cabinet in place. Then you fine-tune the fit by pulling the strip out for more trimming.

Attaching It to the Wall

Another issue when installing a built-in is how you actually attach it to the wall. You can do this in a number of ways. Some people simply run long screws through the back and into the studs. This works, but the screw heads are visible inside the cabinet, and you must use really long screws to reach into the studs across your big back rabbet.

Another idea is to install a hanging strip inside your cabinet. The hanging strip is usually a piece of ¾"-thick material that is about 3" wide, and it is nailed or biscuited between the sides — right beneath the top. With this system, you attach the cabinet to the wall through the hanging strip using countersunk screws. Then you can simply plug the screws to hide them.

I prefer using a French cleat. It sounds complicated at first, but once you get it straight in your head, you'll see it has some advantages.

The French cleat uses two cleats, each with one long edge beveled at 45°. One of the cleats is screwed to the wall and the other is screwed to the back of the cabinet. The two 45° angles nest together, locking the cabinet to the wall. This is a common way to hang kitchen wall cabinets, but I've found it's great for hanging cabinets that go to the floor, too. And I've come up with a method that makes it easy to do. But before you can install any cabinet, the first thing you have to do is get it sitting level on the floor.

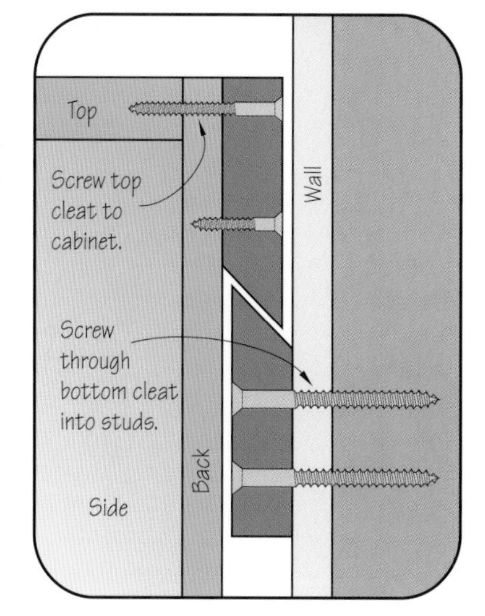

FRENCH CLEAT DETAIL
PROFILE VIEW

A Word about Cabinet Bases

When building large cabinets, it's best to build a separate base from the cabinet itself that is about 3" to 4" in height. You can then set the base in place and level it using wooden shims or leveler feet. Leveler feet are pieces of hardware that attach to the inside corners of your base. The feet screw up and down. You adjust the feet until the base is level and then set the cabinet on top of the base and move on to scribing.

With smaller cabinets, such as the bookcase shown here, you can skip the separate base and install the leveler feet under the bottom shelf or use shims to level the entire cabinet. Either way, get the cabinet level left to right and front to back before you begin scribing.

Scribing

Scribing isn't difficult, but it requires practice. The first thing to do is see if your cabinet is going in a corner. If so, you should entirely remove the big back rabbet that goes into the corner; it's only going to get in the way of scribing the other rabbet and the fitting strip (if you have one).

Push the cabinet back against the wall or walls until some part of the cabinet meets the wall. To mark a scribe line on your back rabbet, get a compass that allows you to lock the swinging arm. Using a ruler, find the biggest gap between your wall and cabinet. Set the distance between the pencil and the compass point to this distance.

Now, trace the shape of the wall onto the back edge of the cabinet. Use the point of the compass to follow the wall and let the pencil draw that shape onto the cabinet. Keep the compass level.

Once you've drawn your scribe line, trim the back rabbet to that line. You can use a jigsaw followed by a hand plane, a belt sander or even a handheld power planer. Test the fit of your scribe line to the wall and make any corrections.

Once the back is fit, scribe the fitting strip (if you have one) where the front of the cabinet meets the wall. Once everything fits snugly, attach the case to the wall using your French cleats.

Installing French Cleats

It's simple to get a perfect fit with these if you follow some basic steps. I like to use plywood or any tough hardwood such as maple for the cleats. First, rip your two cleats to about 3" wide and cut them to length so they're about 1" shorter than the width of the back of your cabinet. If your back piece is 23½" wide, then cut the cleats to 22½" long; this gives you some left-to-right play during installation.

First, install a cleat on the wall so it's level and about 2½" below where the top of the cabinet will touch the wall. Screw the

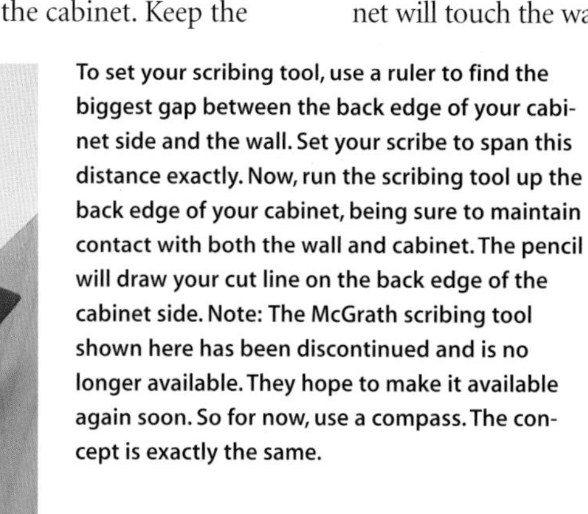

To set your scribing tool, use a ruler to find the biggest gap between the back edge of your cabinet side and the wall. Set your scribe to span this distance exactly. Now, run the scribing tool up the back edge of your cabinet, being sure to maintain contact with both the wall and cabinet. The pencil will draw your cut line on the back edge of the cabinet side. Note: The McGrath scribing tool shown here has been discontinued and is no longer available. They hope to make it available again soon. So for now, use a compass. The concept is exactly the same.

cleat to at least two studs in your wall using No. 10 × 3" screws.

Now, push the cabinet in place against the wall and use a stepladder so you can work on the top of the cabinet. Take the other cleat and drop it behind the cabinet with the bevel facing the back of the cabinet. It should drop into place with about ½" sticking above the top of the cabinet. Mark a line on the cleat where it intersects with the back. Lift the cleat out and rip it to width. Be sure to rip it exactly to your line.

Pull the cabinet away from the wall and screw the cleat to the back side of the cabinet so the top edge of the cleat is flush with the top of the cabinet.

With the help of an assistant, lift the cabinet a few inches and place it on the cleat. The cabinet should sit flush against the wall, flat on the floor and refuse to rock or move.

If the cabinet doesn't sit on the floor, remove one cleat and shave off a tad from the bevel with a hand plane or jointer. Or you can adjust the leveling feet. If the cabinet rocks a bit on the cleat, add a short strip or two of masking tape to the bevel on one cleat and that will tighten things.

Other Cleats

Some other other types of cleats are useful for hanging cabinets, some shop-made and some store-bought. Try this shop-made cleat: Instead of ripping a 45° bevel on each long edge, cut a rabbet on each. The rabbet should be exactly one-half the thickness of the cleat so the cleats nest together like a shiplap joint.

Install the first cleat against the wall. When you attach the second cleat to the cabinet, nudge it up ⅛" and then screw it in place. This will prevent the rabbets from bottoming out when they nest and will give you a little play when the cabinet rests on the floor.

If you don't want a wooden

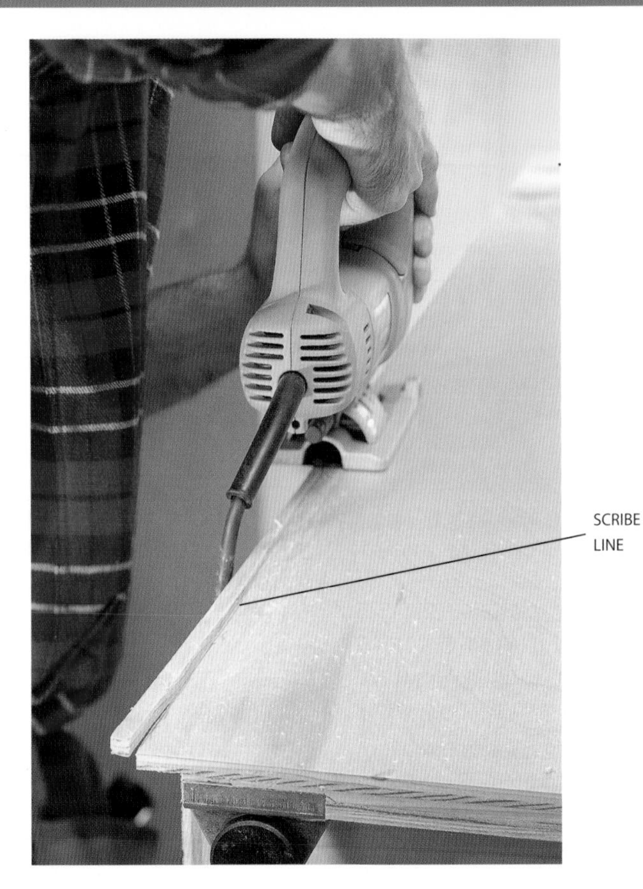

Many professionals use a belt sander to remove the material down to the scribe line. Belt sanders are a little too speedy for my tastes. I prefer to use a jigsaw to cut right up to the line (as seen here) and then clean up the cut with a block plane. It's still quick, and there's little chance of obliterating your scribe line.

Install the first French cleat to your wall using the longest screws available. These screws must anchor the cleat into the stud wall of your house or the cabinet could come toppling down if children ever attempt to climb it.

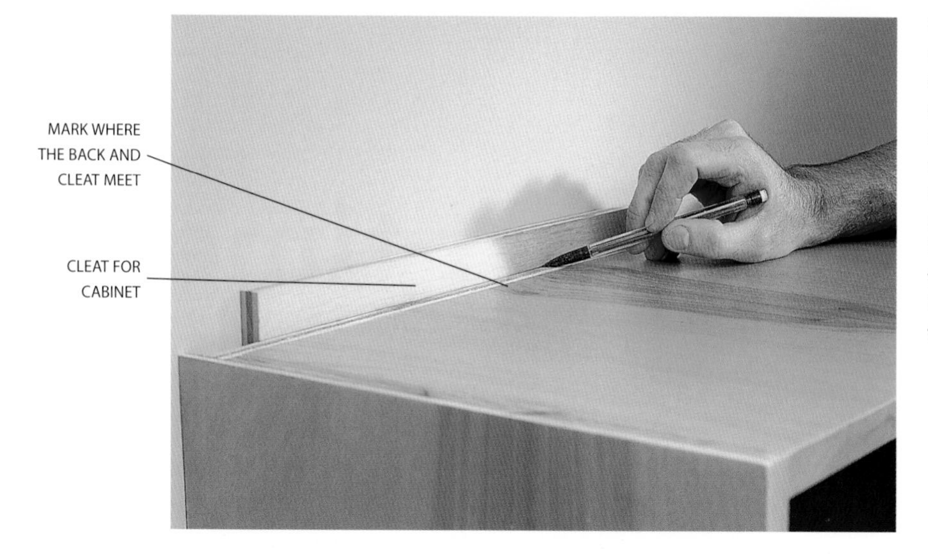

With the back rabbet scribed and a cleat screwed to the wall, push your cabinet in position and drop the second cleat in place behind the cabinet back. Using a sharp pencil (left), mark a line on the cleat where it meets with the cabinet back. Remove the cleat (below left) and rip it to width. If you had to scribe near the top of your cabinet, you might have to plane down your cleats a tad, too.

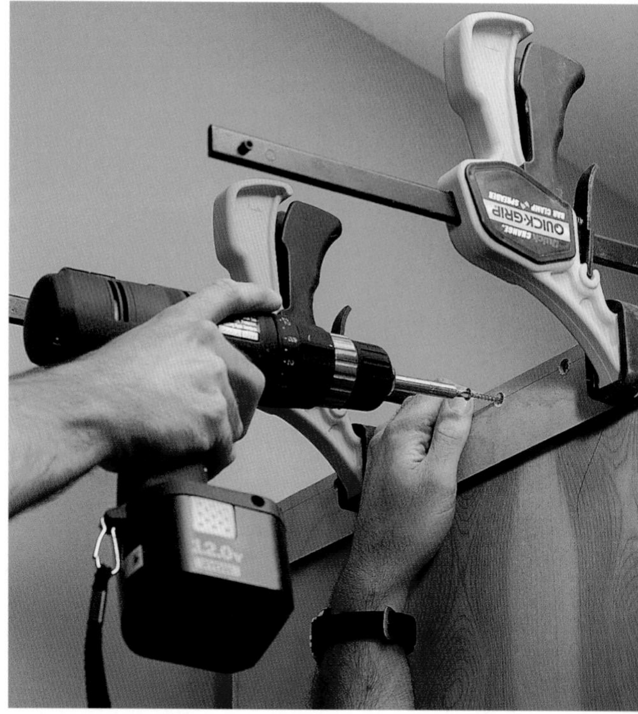

Clamp your cleat to the back of the cabinet with the top edges of the cleat and cabinet back perfectly flush. If they're out of kilter, you're going to make trouble for yourself, so take care. Screw the cleat to the cabinet using long screws that you countersink into the cleat.

cleat, steel and aluminum ones are available from woodworking suppliers. One common steel cleat, available from Rockler, has two nesting pieces that extend 7/16" off the back of your cabinet. The cleats come in a standard 18" length, but you can hacksaw them to any length you need. At about $5 a set, they're a pretty good bargain.

Aluminum ones are also available, some of which have bubble levels built-in to make securing the cleat as easy as possible.

Cleaning Up

With the cabinet in place, you might have to screw one of the side pieces to a wall to pull the cabinet tight against it.

Sometimes, depending on the weight of the cabinet, you might actually end up pulling the drywall out to the side of the cabinet with your screws. Either way, try to ensure that your case is square after this operation or your drawers and doors might not fit like they did when you built the cabinet in your shop.

The cabinet is now complete, except for any trim around the base and crown. To finish the run of cabinets shown at the beginning of the chapter, I still need to build and install another large unit with drawers and doors. Then comes the trim moulding. And then a cold beer.

finishing for first-timers

BY BOB FLEXNER

It's one thing to describe finishing steps to an experienced finisher. It's quite another to teach someone who has never applied stain or finish to anything. Describing finishing so a novice feels comfortable and experiences success the first time is not easy, but here's an attempt. The steps are (1) sanding the wood smooth, (2) deciding on the color and applying it and (3) deciding on the finish and applying it.

Sanding

Flaws in the wood, such as machine milling marks, scratches, gouges, etc., have to be sanded out before applying a stain or finish, or these flaws will be highlighted. To sand them out, always sand in the direction of the wood grain, beginning with a sandpaper grit coarse enough to remove the problems efficiently without creating greater problems. In most cases this means using 80-grit or 100-grit sandpaper. Then sand out coarse-grit scratches with increasingly finer-grit sandpaper up to 150 grit or 180 grit.

Unfortunately, knowing which grit sandpaper to begin with, when it's time to move to the next finer grit, and when the wood is ready to be stained or finished can be learned only from experience. You can look at the wood in a low-angle, raking light, and even wet the wood with mineral spirits (paint thinner) as an aid to spotting remaining flaws. But even these tricks don't always work.

Keep in mind that if you don't sand the wood well enough and the flaws still show after you've applied the stain or finish, you can always remove the stain or finish at any time using a paint-and-varnish remover (or simply paint thinner for stain alone) and start over. You don't need to remove or sand out all the color from a stain, just the binder — the stuff that makes the stain stick to the wood.

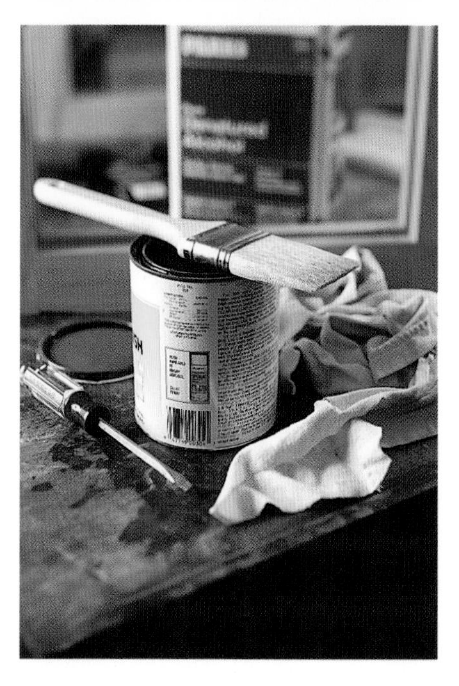

Staining

You can see what the wood will look like with only a finish applied by wetting the wood with a liquid, such as paint thinner. If the wetted wood isn't dark enough or the right color, you'll have to use a stain. Unless you are finishing a quality hardwood, such as oak, mahogany or walnut (not cherry, it blotches), you will be safest using a gel stain. Gel stains are thick and very effective at reducing blotching (uneven coloring due to inconsistent densities in the wood).

No matter which stain you use, the method of application is the same. Using any application tool (such as a brush or rag), apply a wet coat and wipe off the excess before it dries. Begin working on smaller surfaces such as legs and drawer fronts to get a feel for the drying time. If the stain dries too hard to wipe off, reliquefy it by applying more stain right away, then remove the excess immediately.

Apply the stain and remove the excess from one or more complete surfaces at a time. Don't overlap the stain onto a surface that has already been completed or the double application may cause a difference in color.

Finishing

A finish is necessary to protect the wood from water damage, dirt and stains. You can apply a finish either directly to the wood or over a stain after it has dried. It's always better — that is, more attractive and protective — to use a stain and finish packaged separately than a stain-and-finish combination, which is just a stain with a little more binder in it.

In my opinion, the two best finish choices for a first-timer are oil-based polyurethane in a satin sheen and wiping varnish. Wiping varnish is oil-based varnish or polyurethane thinned about half with paint thinner and usually sold as tung oil. You'll know the product is wiping varnish and not real tung oil if it's labeled tung oil and contains petroleum distillate. Real tung oil doesn't contain petroleum distillate. Wiping varnish is also sold as Waterlox, General Finishes Sealacell, Valspar Val-Oil and Daly's Profin.

Oil-based polyurethane and wiping varnish are easier to use than water-based finishes, which dry very fast, raise the grain and are difficult to use in combination with stains.

Oil-based polyurethane provides excellent durability with only two or three applications. Wiping varnish goes on with reduced brush marking and fewer dust nibs but requires many more applications to achieve the same durability. Polyurethane is best for surfaces that get a lot of wear. Wiping vanish is best when you want a thinner, more flawless finish.

Applying Polyurethane

Apply polyurethane using a bristle or foam brush about 2" wide. Foam works well and eliminates the chore of cleaning, because the brushes are cheap and thus disposable.

You can apply the first coat full strength or thinned up to half with paint thinner, making, in effect, a wiping varnish. (Use a separate can or jar.) Thinning leaves less actual finish on the wood, so the finish dries hard faster and is thus easier to sand sooner.

Always sand the first coat of finish smooth to the touch after it has cured (usually overnight in a warm room) using 280-grit or finer sandpaper. Remove the dust with a tack rag (a sticky cloth you can buy at paint stores) or a vacuum and apply a second coat full strength. Brush the polyurethane just like brushing paint. If bubbles appear, brush back over the finish lightly to make them pop out. Brush with the grain of the wood when possible.

On flat horizontal surfaces such as tabletops, spread the finish onto the wood, working from side to side (with the grain) and front to back. Stretch out the finish as thin as possible. After every 6" to 12" of surface covered from edge to edge, line up the brushstrokes. Do this by lightly bringing the brush down onto the surface near one edge in an airplane-like landing and moving the brush across and off the other side. Then do the same back the other way — back and forth until all the brushstrokes are lined up and the bubbles are almost gone. The remaining bubbles should pop out on their own.

Then apply the next 6" to 12" in the same manner, working the finish back into the last inch or so of the previous application. Continue until the surface is covered.

The trick to reducing problems, such as bubbles, runs and sags, is to work in a reflected natural or artificial light. This is the critical instruction that is rarely given. If you move your head so you can see your work in a reflected light while you're brushing, any problem that occurs will become quickly apparent, and the solution will be obvious. In most cases, it is to brush back over the area and stretch the finish out thin.

You should use as clean a brush as possible and work in as clean a room as you can, but you will still find dust nibs when the finish cures. Sand these out between each coat. When the finish looks good — after two or three (maybe four) coats — it's done. Leave the last coat unsanded.

Applying Wiping Varnish

You can apply wiping varnish exactly like polyurethane by brushing coat after coat onto the wood. Or you can wipe on, and then wipe off, most of the excess. The more excess you leave, the greater the build.

This second method is the easy one, and the way wiping varnish is usually applied. It's an almost foolproof finish when applied in this manner. Again, the trick to achieving good results is to check the finish for flaws in a reflected light as you're applying it.

reducing brush marks and orange peel

BY BOB FLEXNER

Brush marks and orange peel are the flaws created in a finish by the two most common application tools: brushes and spray guns. Unfortunately, there's no way to totally prevent these flaws and still use these tools, but the flaws can be reduced by controlling the viscosity of the finish and by using the tools properly.

Brush marks and orange peel can always be removed after they've occurred, of course, by sanding the hardened surface level, but that's a lot of work, and it can be reduced by keeping the problem to a minimum to begin with.

Brands of the various finishes (varnish, polyurethane, lacquer, water-based finish and so on) differ in how well they flatten out after application, but with any given finish or brand, brush marks and orange peel are worse when the finish is thick or dries fast. Specific to spraying, orange peel can also be made worse by holding the spray gun too close to the work, holding the gun too far away, by moving it too fast, or by not having the gun set right.

The key to determining if you may be creating a problem is to watch the finish in a reflected light while you're applying it. You'll see if the finish is going on smoothly and

Orange peel, a problem that occurs with spray systems, can be reduced by thinning and by adjusting the gun. This piece of closed-grained birch should have a flat, nearly flawless finish.

evenly or if it's brush-marking or orange-peeling more than you would expect or want.

(I've heard several people say that the way to eliminate brush marks is to use a more expensive brush, but I haven't been able to confirm this. As long as I'm using a decent-quality brush — meaning one that costs six dollars or more, has a chisel edge and is made from China bristles or some other good-quality natural or synthetic bristle that doesn't fall out — brush marks don't seem to vary noticeably among brushes.)

Thinning Helps

You know that thinner alone (mineral spirits, for example) will flatten out perfectly on a flat surface. Thus it's logical that the more thinner you add to a finish the better it will flatten out. In fact, this is the case with all finishes no matter how you apply them.

So, with any finish, you can reduce brush marks and orange peel by thinning it. This is exactly what manufacturers have produced for you in wiping-varnish products, which are commonly mislabeled tung oil, tung-oil finish or tung-oil varnish, or labeled with some nondescript name such as Waterlox, Sealacell or Val-Oil. The finish manufacturers have merely thinned some

Brush marks can be reduced by thinning your finish or slowing the drying time by using a retarder. Buying an expensive brush isn't going to help much.

varnish enough (usually by half or more) so it flattens out well.

The trade-off with this finish, or with any finish you thin yourself, is that you reduce the build. So you'll have to apply more coats to reach the same film thickness you would with fewer coats of unthinned finish.

One trick you might consider for overcoming the build problem is to apply several full-strength coats of finish. Sand the surface level and finish off with one or two coats thinned enough so they flatten well but are still thick enough to fill the sanding scratches and produce an even sheen.

Drying Time

Different types of finish dry at different rates. Finishes that dry fast, such as lacquer, shellac and water-based finish, may be drying too fast to flatten out well if the temperature in your shop or work area is high.

With lacquer and water-based finish, you can purchase retarders that will slow the drying process. In the case of lacquer, the retarder is usually marketed simply as lacquer retarder (you can use this also with shellac). In the case of water-based finishes, it's often called flow additive.

Because brands of retarder vary in strength, you'll need to experiment with how much to add to get the results you want. You don't want to add more than you need because you can slow the drying of the finish so much that it collects an unnecessarily large amount of dust, or you get an unnecessarily low build.

Spraying

Reducing orange peel when spraying is more complex than reducing brush marks simply because a spray gun and its air source are more complex. In other words, more factors than finish viscosity and drying time are involved.

To begin with, it should be obvious that if you hold the spray gun too close to your work, the air from the gun will create turbulence in the sprayed finish that will show up as orange peel. And if you hold the gun too far away from your work, or if you move the gun too fast over your work, you won't wet the surface well enough and this will result in orange peel.

This second cause of orange peel is very common, and both of these application errors are easy to avoid simply by watching what's happening during application in a reflected light and adjusting your distance and speed until you're laying down an even wet coat on your project.

One caveat: With water-based finishes, it's best to keep each coat as thin as possible while still wetting the surface well, even if the finish seems to be orange-peeling right after application. As the solvent comes out of the finish, it will relax and flatten out.

Optimizing a Spray Gun

The spray gun itself can also be optimized to reduce orange peel, and you do this by increasing or decreasing the amount of air (and in some cases, fluid material) to the gun.

If you're using a compressor with either a conventional or HVLP (high-volume, low-pressure) spray gun, open the controls on the gun all the way and turn off the air to the gun at the compressor's regulator. Then start opening the regulator in 5-psi increments while testing the spray in short bursts on brown paper, cardboard or scrap wood. When the pattern no longer improves (that is, the fan width doesn't increase), the gun is optimized for the viscosity of that material.

More pressure just produces an excessively foggy work environment as well as unnecessary bounce back and waste. To reduce orange peel from this point, you'll have to thin the material.

If you reduce the fan width to spray a narrow surface, you'll still be depositing the same amount of material into a smaller surface area, so you'll need to reduce this volume by screwing in the fluid-control knob. The gun will remain optimized for best performance.

If the transfer of material is slower than you would like, don't increase the air pressure or you'll just increase bounce back. Instead, increase the size of the needle/nozzle set and air cap, and reoptimize the gun.

If you're using a turbine with an HVLP spray gun, you don't have the same control of air to the gun as you do with compressed air. To reduce orange peel, you'll need to thin the material you're spraying until the orange peel comes closest to disappearing.

CHAPTER 47

caring for furniture

BY BOB FLEXNER

Furniture care is a subject you're probably not very interested in, but it's a sure bet that the people you give or sell your projects to find it interesting. In fact, "How do I care for it?" is probably the first question they ask you.

If you give them an intelligent answer, their respect for you grows, but if you fumble around and show you don't really understand the subject, they may lose some confidence in you. There's no reason for this to happen, because you need to know only two things: the causes of damage and how to avoid them, and which furniture polish to recommend.

Don't go looking for these furniture-care products on your next trip overseas. For the most part, the United States is the only country that uses them. Why? Water usually cleans just as well.

Causes of Damage

The two elements that cause the most damage to furniture, especially to the finish, are light and physical abuse. No one can keep furniture totally away from light, but furniture can be kept away from bright light near windows, which causes finishes to deteriorate faster than they would otherwise. To see what light does to finishes, compare the condition of an old finish protected from light under some hardware with the finish around it. (See the photo later on page 201.)

So the first instruction you should give is, "If you want the finish to stay in good shape for as long as possible, keep the furniture away from bright light, especially direct sunlight."

The second is, "Discipline your children and pets so they don't abuse the furniture, and use tablecloths, place mats and coasters to protect the finish from scratches and water rings."

Furniture-Care Products

More hype, myth and misinformation is spread about furniture polishes and waxes than about any other product related to furniture. Most of the problem is created by the suppliers themselves.

Here are the facts.

Furniture-care products do five things more or less well:

- Add shine to a dull surface.
- Add scratch resistance.
- Aid in dusting.
- Aid in cleaning.
- Add a pleasant scent to a room.

No furniture polish or wax replaces natural oil in the wood (only a few exotic woods ever had it in the first place), feeds or moisturizes the wood, feeds or moisturizes the finish, or builds up (unless, of course, the excess isn't wiped off). No furniture polish or wax does any harm to the wood or finish, either. Furniture polishes and waxes are totally inert.

In fact, furniture-care products don't really do much at all, and the United States and, to a lesser degree, Canada, are the only countries where these products are used to any great extent. Most people in Europe and Japan just wipe their furniture with a damp cloth when it gets dusty or dirty.

So you could simply advise your family member, friend or customer, "You don't need to do anything at all except keep the furniture clean by wiping it now and then with a damp cloth." But this probably won't work, because people are conditioned to want to use something, to do something good for their furniture.

The furniture polishes that clean best are emulsifications of water and petroleum-distillate solvent. These polishes are usually packaged in aerosol spray cans and are always milky-white in color.

So, to understand the differences in the furniture-care products they could use, let's look at the ingredients in them and see what each does.

Besides the added scent, which does nothing for the furniture but rewards people for their dusting effort by making their house smell nice, furniture-care products are composed of one or more of four basic ingredients: slow evaporating petroleum-distillate solvent, water, wax and silicone oil.

- Petroleum-distillate solvents used in furniture polishes are essentially slow-evaporating paint thinner. This liquid adds shine and scratch resistance only until it evaporates (usually within a few hours), helps pick up dust and cleans grease and wax. It has no cleaning effect on water-soluble dirt like sticky fingerprints or soft drink spills.

Most clear polishes on the market, those commonly sold as lemon or some other nice-smelling oil and packaged in clear plastic containers, are composed of this single ingredient.

- Water evaporates too rapidly to be effective at adding shine or scratch resistance, but it helps pick up dust, and it's a great cleaner for most types of dirt. In many liquid and so-called cream furniture polishes, and in some liquid and paste waxes, water is added to improve cleaning ability. You can recognize these products by their milky-white color (they are emulsifications, like milk is an emulsification of water and animal fat). Most are packaged in aerosol-spray containers.

- Wax is a solid substance at room temperature and is by far the most effective of the four ingredients at adding shine and scratch protection over a long period of time because it doesn't evaporate. But wax is hard to apply (because of the effort necessary to wipe off the excess) and there's no reason to apply it very often, so it's not effective for dusting, cleaning or adding scent.

Sometimes wax is added to liquid polishes, and you can identify these by the settling that occurs over time — polishes containing wax have to be shaken before use. Clearly, these polishes will be more effective at adding long-lasting shine and scratch protection than polishes that don't contain wax, but more effort will be required to remove the excess from the surface.

- Silicone oil is a synthetic oil similar to mineral oil in the sense that it is totally inert and doesn't evaporate, but silicone oil is slipperier and bends light better than mineral oil. The first quality makes furniture polishes that contain this oil extremely effective at reducing scratches, and the second makes finished wood appear richer and deeper.

Most aerosol-spray polishes contain silicone oil, though

Light is a prime cause of finish deterioration. Here you can see that the finish protected under the hardware is in near-perfect condition, while the finish exposed to light for many decades is badly crazed.

rarely is this admitted. Silicone oil has been given a bad reputation by furniture refinishers and museum conservators due to the added difficulty they have refinishing furniture treated with this oil. But consumers love silicone-oil polishes because they keep furniture looking good between polishings, better than anything except wax, and they're easy to use.

Most polishes that contain silicone oil also contain petroleum distillates and water, so they're good cleaners.

How to Choose

So how do you make sense of this for the recipients of your projects? Easy.

If they just want something for dusting, choose any liquid furniture polish.

If they want something that will clean in addition to picking up dust, choose any milky-white furniture polish — virtually all polishes in aerosol containers except Scott's Liquid Gold.

If they want maximum scratch resistance and richer depth without the work involved with using paste wax, choose a polish that contains silicone oil — virtually all polishes in aerosol-spray containers except Endust and Scott's Liquid Gold.

If they want to add shine and protect an old, deteriorated surface from abrasive damage, choose paste wax — because the other possibilities either evaporate too quickly (petroleum distillate) or highlight the cracks in the finish (silicone oil). Dusting and cleaning will have to be done separately with a damp cloth.

the challenge of cherry

BY BOB FLEXNER

Cherry has become popular with woodworkers in the last decade or so, at least in part because it's a beautiful wood that machines and tools easily, and it has a pleasant scent.

Compared to other woods, however, cherry is difficult to finish. You can put almost any stain or finish on oak or walnut, for example, and these woods look nice. But cherry becomes blotchy with stains, and it looks better with some finishes than others. So with the caution that much of the choice in stains and finishes is determined by one's own aesthetic tastes, here are some thoughts that may help you decide how to finish your next cherry projects.

Old cherry has a warm glow that new cherry simply cannot compete with. This antique table will continue to darken even more as the cherry is exposed to the light. Table is courtesy of Federation Antiques of Cincinnati, Ohio.

The Finish

In my opinion, tight-grained woods such as cherry, maple, birch and pine look too flat when finished with oil finishes.

(By oil finish I mean linseed oil, tung oil and any blend of oil and varnish, including polyurethane varnish. You can identify these finishes by their tendency to wrinkle badly when left to cure in puddles or around the lids of their containers and by their inability to cure hard.)

Cherry looks much better with a hard-curing, film-building finish — even if it isn't built up very much. This would include any varnish or wiping varnish (varnish thinned with paint thinner and often misleadingly labeled tung oil), polyurethane, shellac or lacquer, but it doesn't include water-based finish because this finish doesn't bring out cherry's rich color. Rather it leaves the wood looking washed out.

If you're thinking of using an oil finish anyway because applying it is so easy, or you like working with water-based finish because of its lack of odor, I suggest you finish a scrap board with one of these finishes when you start your project and live with it for a while. By the time you're ready for the finishing step, you'll have a good idea of whether you're going to be happy with the look.

Beyond appearance, you're making the choice of finish primarily on durability and whether or not you're using a spray gun, the same considerations you have for choosing a finish for any wood. Varnish, polyurethane and catalyzed lacquers are more durable than shellac and nitrocellulose lacquer; and spray guns are usually best for applying fast-drying finishes such as lacquer.

This year-old cherry piece was finished with orange shellac. Its color is starting to deepen, but give it another 100 years or so to become really beautiful.

The Stain

Staining is, of course, the big problem with cherry because cherry has resin pockets that get darker when any liquid is applied — and stain exaggerates the darkening. Not all cherry has these resin pockets, however, and if you choose your boards carefully, you may be able to avoid the blotching problem altogether no matter which stain you use. (To see if you're likely to get blotching, wet the wood with a liquid such as mineral spirits. Use blotchy boards in areas that won't show.)

The two basic ways to color wood are to apply a stain directly to it, or to seal or partially seal (condition) the wood and apply the color on top. Applying stain to the wood accentuates the figure and grain (which is what most people want to do), while applying the color on top of a sealed surface muddies the wood. Applying a stain to a partially sealed surface and then wiping off the excess doesn't add much color because there's so little penetration. Nor does applying a gel stain to unsealed wood — for the same reason.

Most factory-finished cherry has the color applied on top in the form of glazes or toners in order to avoid the blotching. This is the reason factory-finished cherry doesn't look as alive as does old cherry that has taken on its rich coloring naturally due to light and oxidation.

Imitating the look of old cherry, with its rust-red color and almost translucent depth, is not at all difficult. You can do it with either a dye stain or with lye — with the problem being, of course, that you will accentuate any natural blotching that exists in the wood. So, if you want to achieve this look, you're going to have to choose your wood carefully. Either it should be blotch-free, or it should have a blotch pattern that you find attractive (curly maple is a blotchy wood, after all).

You can use any brand of dye stain, but one that I find particularly effective at matching old cherry is Lockwood's water-soluble Natural Antique Cherry dye. You can buy this directly from W.D. Lockwood or from Woodworker's Supply, where it is sold under the J.E. Moser's name.

Lockwood water-soluble dyes are very forgiving and easy to use. Follow the directions for mixing, and then apply a wet coat to an entire surface and wipe off the excess before it dries. If the wood isn't dark enough while it's still damp, wait until it dries and apply another coat. If you get the wood too dark, or if you've caused streaks by overlapping onto already dry dye, wait until the wood dries and wipe it in the direction of the grain with a wet cloth. You'll redissolve the dye colorant and remove some of it from the wood, lightening and evening the color.

There's no way to avoid the potential blotching and achieve this color, however, so you should surely experiment on scrap wood first to see what you're going to get.

Lye is very unforgiving because you can't lighten it, and I don't recommend using it, because it's also dangerous. It will, however, produce the right color, so if you decide to use it, make sure you're fully clothed and your hands and eyes are protected.

After you apply the lye, you must neutralize its alkalinity by washing the project several times with half-and-half white vinegar and water. If you don't neutralize, any water that gets through your finish and into the wood later on will activate the lye and blister the finish (lye is a very effective stripper).

Both water-soluble dye and lye require putting water on the wood, so you should wet the wood with water before staining, let the wood dry, then sand off the raised grain so the wood feels smooth again. What little grain raising you get when you then stain the wood, you can sand off easily with fine (320-or-finer-grit) sandpaper without the risk of cutting through.

To avoid blotching altogether and to not muddy the wood, the best solution for coloring cherry is to let it age naturally, just as the old cherry did.

The color will change quite rapidly (just leave a sanded board out in your shop with lots of window or fluorescent light for a couple of days and see for yourself), but it will take a very long time to reach the color of 19th-century cherry.

the basics of coloring wood

BY BOB FLEXNER

So you've completed your project and now you want to color it so it matches another object, a color chip or a vision you have in your head. Achieving this match can be one of the most difficult tasks in wood finishing, but before you get into the actual mixing of colors, it helps to understand what's possible and know the tools you have at your disposal.

The Wood

Any color can be matched, but not any wood. You have to pay attention to how the wood or woods you're finishing compare to the sample you're trying to match.

The four large categories of woods are softwoods such as pine and fir; tight-grained hardwoods such as maple, birch and cherry; medium-grained hardwoods such as walnut and mahogany; and coarse-grained hardwoods such as oak and ash.

Within each of these categories, you can pretty successfully match any two woods using some combination of bleach and stain. But trying to match woods of two different categories has its limitations because of the large differences in grain and figure. You should take these limitations into account when you're choosing the wood for your project.

Types of Stain

The basic way to change a wood's color is to apply stain. In choosing a stain, you need to take into account the four ways in which they differ besides the obvious variances in color.

• Type of colorant: Two types of colorant are used in stains: pigment and dye. Pigment is finely ground natural or synthetic earth. Dye is a chemical that dissolves in a liquid. Everything that settles to the bottom of a container is pigment, and all the color that remains in the liquid after the pigment has settled is dye.

Pigment is better at highlighting grain if the excess is wiped off, and at obscuring the wood if the excess is left in any thickness on the surface. Dye is better at changing the color of wood without muddying it — especially dense woods such as maple. Some stains contain only dye, some contain only pigment, and some contain both.

• Amount of colorant: Stains differ in the ratio of colorant (pigment and dye) to liquid (thinner and binder). The higher the ratio of colorant in the first coat you apply, the darker the stain will make the wood. You can control how dark you color the wood in one application of stain by adding pigment or dye to increase the ratio or by thinning to decrease the ratio.

• Type of binder: Most stains contain a binder, which seals the pigment or dye into the wood or onto its surface. Binders are oil, alkyd, oil/alkyd or water-based finish. The biggest difference among binders is drying time; oil dries slowly, alkyd and water-based dry rapidly. But also important is water-based stain's characteristic of raising wood grain. Some dye stains, usually identified as non-grain-raising (or NGR), water-soluble

The same stain was applied to the left side of each of these woods — from the top down: oak, pine, mahogany, maple. Yet each still retains its' unique characteristics. There are limitations on what you can accomplish to make one wood look like another.

A green toner was applied to the right side of this mahogany to kill the red and turn it brown. Toners can be used to adjust color after the application of a stain.

A full-strength stain was applied to the left side of this oak. The same stain, thinned half with paint thinner, was applied to the right side. The ratio of colorant (pigment and dye) to liquid (thinner and binder) determines how dark the wood will be.

or alcohol-soluble don't contain a binder.

If a stain contains a binder, every coat after the first remains on top of the wood; it doesn't go into the wood. Pigment in these stains obscures the wood if some is left on the surface. Dye in these stains is fairly transparent. Dye without a binder continues to add color into the wood and darken it more with each coat.

If you apply a pigment or dye stain over a sealed surface and leave it, the stain is called a toner or shading stain.

• Thickness: Most stains come in liquid form for fast and easy application, but some are thick gels. Gel stains are useful for reducing blotching on woods such as pine and cherry, because gels don't penetrate into the wood.

Just as with liquid stains, the color in a gel stain can be adjusted by adding pigment to darken or tweak its color, or by adding a clear gel finish to lighten its color.

Gel stains are usually labeled as such, but manufacturers rarely provide much information about the type or amount of colorant or binder. To a large degree, you have to experiment and learn by trial and error, and this is the primary reason many people find staining so problematic.

Application Methods

The basic way to apply a stain is to wipe, brush or spray a wet coat onto the wood, then wipe off the excess before it dries. This will produce an even coloring as long as the wood isn't naturally blotchy and you have prepared it well.

Other ways to apply color include the following.

• Spray on a stain and leave it (called toning or shading). You can spray an entire surface to produce an even coloring, or you can limit the spray to parts (for example, just sapwood) to correct an uneven coloring in the wood or create special effects. You should thin the stain with four-or-more parts thinner to prevent lap marks.

You can also tone or shade using a brush, but it's difficult to keep the coloring even.

• Partially seal or washcoat the wood before applying a stain. A washcoat is any finish, sealer or white glue that is thinned to approximately 3 to 7 percent solids so it seals the wood just enough to prevent deep stain penetration and the resulting blotching on some woods.

Most finishes are 20 percent to 35 percent solids right out of the can, so thinning the finish 5-1 usually gets you in the ballpark.

When staining large or multiple objects, using a fast-drying, spray-on washcoat followed by a liquid stain is more efficient than using a gel stain, but experimentation and practice are necessary to learn the right amount of washcoat to apply. A gel stain is far more predictable.

Slow-drying washcoats, called stain controllers or wood conditioners, are designed for wipe and brush application, but they also take experience to use successfully.

• Seal the wood with a sanding sealer or first coat of finish and apply a glaze to create a special effect. A glaze is a pigmented stain thickened enough so it stays where you put it. You can use rags, brushes or specialized glazing tools to manipulate the glaze. Once you have the look you want, let the glaze dry, then coat over it to protect it from being scratched or rubbed off.

• Seal the wood with a sanding sealer or first coat of finish and spray on a toner or shading stain to change the color of the wood or highlight parts of it. Toners and shading stains (the terms are often used interchangeably) are very useful for tweaking a color to an exact match.

Remember that a pigmented toner obscures wood while a dye toner doesn't, and that over a sealed surface, toners and shading stains add color but don't bring out the wood's figure.

Conclusion

Every color-matching situation is different, and many are challenging. Once you've determined the degree the wood will allow you to be successful, achieving a good match involves choosing types of stains and methods of application in addition to choosing the right color.

colors to dye for

BY BOB FLEXNER

Just as in woodworking, where you choose among tools to accomplish the task you want, you can choose among types of stain to get the look you want. I'm not talking about the color of the stain, which also is important, but rather the effect the stain has on the wood. You can choose from three broad categories.

• Wiping stains are the most common stains and are available in every paint store and home-improvement center. These are liquid stains containing a binder — either oil- or water-based finish — that glues the colorant (pigment and/or dye) to the wood.

• Gel stains are also widely available and contain a binder, but these stains are thick like mayonnaise and are made with just a pigment colorant. They are most useful for avoiding blotching on tight-grained woods such as pine, cherry and birch, and for glazing (adding color) between coats of finish.

• Dye stains are not so widely available, but they're extremely useful for adding deep, rich and even coloration to wood no matter what the grain structure. These stains don't contain a binder, and this makes them more forgiving and easier to manipulate.

What Are Dyes?

Dyes are colorants that can be natural (coffee, tea, berries and so on) or synthetic, which means aniline dyes derived from coal tar or petroleum. Aniline dyes are, by far, the most widely used dyes in wood staining because they are more lightfast (resistant to fading) than natural dyes, and they're available in a much wider range of colors — all colors, in fact, except white.

The main difference between dye and pigment is that dye dissolves in a liquid and pigment doesn't, so dye soaks into the wood along with the liquid while pigment just lodges in pores and sanding scratches large enough to hold it. This means that dye will produce a much more even coloration on coarse-grained woods such as oak and ash, and a darker color on all woods without obscuring them. (Dye accentuates blotching, however, if the wood has a tendency toward it.)

Another difference is that dye, even aniline dye, fades more quickly than pigment, especially in direct sunlight. So you shouldn't use dye on outdoor projects or on projects that will sit next to a window.

Dye stains are available in a wide variety of colors and are easy to mix at home. Best of all, unlike pigment stains, you can easily add or remove color to your project using dyes.

Stains from Dye

Dye stains are available in powder and liquid form. Powder dyes dissolve in water, alcohol or petroleum distillate (paint thinner, naphtha, toluene or xylene); the label will tell you which. Liquid dyes are already dissolved in solvents and are ready to use, but the solvents evaporate quickly, which makes these dyes difficult to manipulate except by spraying and leaving the excess to dry.

If you intend to apply a dye stain by hand rather than spray, I recommend you use water-soluble dyes in powder form, because water is essentially free, it isn't toxic, and it dries slower than organic solvents, so you have more working time. Water-soluble dyes are also among the most lightfast of the dyes.

I also recommend you use Lockwood dyes because of the wonderful colors available. W.D. Lockwood, Inc., began supplying dyes to the furniture industry in 1895, and the colors that were popular then were early American and old English — the colors the wood had aged to after 100 years or more. These are the colors most woodworkers want for their projects, anyway, so the burden of mixing colors can be avoided.

To dissolve the dyes, simply stir the powder into water. The powder will dissolve faster in hot water, but cold water also will work. Distilled water is best because there's no metal residue that can influence the color, but I've never had problems with tap water. Dissolve enough dye in the water to achieve the color intensity you want. You can always add more water or dye powder later, or you can manipulate the color right on the wood. You can blend colors of any brand of dye as long as the dye dissolves in water.

The one drawback of water-soluble dyes is that water raises wood grain. Because sanding after you've applied the dye may remove some of the color, it's usually best to wet the wood prior to applying the dye, let the wood dry and then sand it smooth with fine-grit sandpaper. Very little grain will then be raised when you apply the stain.

Applying Dye Stains

You apply dyes just as you do liquid wiping stains — by getting the entire surface wet with stain using a rag, brush or spray gun, and then wiping off the excess stain before it dries. If you do this, you'll always get an even coloring as long as the wood is clean (meaning there's no glue seepage or finish remaining after stripping) and not naturally blotchy.

The great application advantage of water-soluble dyes over stains containing a binder is that you can lighten or darken the color after the stain has dried because there's no binder gluing the dye to the wood. You lighten the color by wiping the surface with a wet cloth to redissolve the dye and lift some from the surface, and you darken the color by applying more dye.

One of the disadvantages of a dye stain is that it doesn't get into the pores of open-grained wood, such as this piece of red oak.

You can correct that easily by sealing the wood and then wiping on a similar-colored wiping stain. When you wipe it all off, only the color in the pores will be darkened.

You can also move the color to the red, green or yellow side by applying one of these colored dyes, or reduce the intensity of the color by applying black dye — without muddying the wood. And you can bleach most of the color out of the wood by applying household bleach.

All of this gives you great control of the final color, but you might find it worthwhile to practice a few times on scrap wood if you've never used dyes. Too heavy a dose of black, for example, will be hard to correct.

Solving Problems

You may find that water-soluble dye doesn't get into the grain of coarse-grained woods such as oak. You can correct this easily by applying a similar colored, oil-based wiping stain over your first (sealer) coat and wiping off all the excess stain. The colorant will lodge in the grain and color it but won't affect the overall color.

Because water-soluble dye will redissolve when brought into contact with water, you shouldn't brush or wipe any water-based product over dye, because you'll drag the color and leave streaks. If you want to brush a water-based finish, apply a thin barrier coat of dewaxed shellac or thinned varnish first.

Also due to its lack of resistance to water, it's not wise to apply an oil finish over water-soluble dye, because this finish is too thin to offer much protection. If any water gets through the finish, it will cause a light spot, which will be difficult to fix.

Most manufacturers in the furniture industry and most skilled finishers use dye stains to advantage, and you can, too – with just a little practice.

Many professionals use dye stains, which give you brilliant colors without obscuring the grain. This piece by Glen Huey, a contributing editor to this magazine, was colored using a dye stain.

protecting exterior wood

BY BOB FLEXNER

Woodworkers have probably more misunderstanding about how to protect wood outdoors than about any other aspect of wood finishing. The need for a coating to protect exterior wood is much greater than for interior wood, because objects outdoors are subjected to the ravages of sun and rain. When sunlight or water come into frequent contact with wood, they cause the wood to lose its color, split, warp and often rot.

The best way to protect wood exposed to sun and rain is to apply a paint or finish that blocks sunlight and moisture and holds up to these destructive elements.

You must choose your exterior finishes wisely. This pine chair was treated with a non-UV-resistant polyurethane. After less than one season, the finish flaked off and the wood began to absorb moisture on its way to rotting.

Effects of the Sun

Light is the principal enemy of paints and finishes. Over time, ultraviolet (UV) rays, which are strongest from direct sunlight, break down paints. The dull and sometimes chalky result is visible on cars and buildings that have been exposed to the sun for many years. If you catch the problem before the paint is damaged all the way through, you often can rub off the dullness with abrasives (contained in many car polishes, for example) and expose paint that looks shiny and new.

UV rays also break down clear finishes, but most peel before dulling and chalking become problems. Clear finishes peel because the UV rays penetrate the film and destroy the lignin that glues the cellulose cells of wood fiber together. The surface cells separate, and the finish bonded to these cells peels.

The best sun-blocking agents, and thus the best protection for finishes applied outdoors, are pigments (contained in paints and stains). But pigments hide the wood, and many people would rather have it visible. The next best sun-blocking agents are UV absorbers, which are similar to sunscreen agents used in suntan lotions. They convert ultraviolet light energy to heat energy, which dissipates.

UV absorbers don't hide wood, and they are fairly effective at preventing wood deterioration underneath a finish. But they are expensive, and a significant amount — 1 to 3 percent by weight — has to be in the finish to be effective. It isn't enough to add just a few drops to a vat so it can be claimed, as many manufacturers do, that the product contains UV absorbers.

The most common finishes that contain sufficient UV absorbers are marine varnishes, which cost more than $50 a gallon and are difficult to find except at marinas.

Effects of Moisture

Moisture causes paints and finishes to peel when it gets between the coating and the wood. Paints resist moisture penetration well, but most clear finishes don't. Water repellents, which contain a low-surface-tension waxy substance (manufacturers use different types), cause water to bead but don't totally keep it out of the wood.

The best moisture-resistant, clear finishes are varnishes called spar or marine varnish that are made flexible so they can keep up with extreme wood movement. Varnishes made with phenolic resin and tung oil are best because they don't crack as quickly as those made with polyurethane resin.

How to Choose

The best way to protect wood outdoors is to paint it. Paint repels water and blocks UV rays effectively. The two major categories of paint are oil-based and water-based (latex). Oil-based paints are best for objects such as chairs and picnic tables because latex paints don't wear as well.

Oil-based primer is also best on wood that has been exposed to the weather for a month or more because it penetrates deeper than latex primers. (As mentioned, UV light breaks down the lignin near the wood's surface, making it difficult for paint to get a good hold.) If the wood is freshly milled or sanded, acrylic latex primers perform well.

Latex paint offers the best protection for wood siding because it allows moisture vapor, which is generated inside from cooking, showers, etc., to pass through better than oil-based paint. If the moisture vapor can't get through the paint, it builds up behind the paint and causes it to peel. A primer coat of oil-based paint is not thick enough to stop the penetration.

No clear finishes work as well as paint if exposed to bright light, but expensive marine varnishes come closest. Keep in mind, however, that these finishes are very glossy and relatively soft (for flexibility), and you need to apply eight or nine coats to reach maximum UV resistance. Because the UV absorbers don't prevent the finish itself from deteriorating, you need to sand off surface deterioration and apply a few additional coats whenever the finish begins to dull, which could be as often as once a year in southern exposures.

Commonly available spar varnishes that don't contain sufficient UV absorbers won't hold their bond to wood that is exposed to sunlight. Interior/exterior polyurethanes have an even shorter life.

Left unfinished, white oak and other weather-resistant woods will turn a silvery gray. This Adirondack chair has survived seven seasons outside with little deterioration.

Deck Finishes

Decks present a special case, because paints and clear finishes are so difficult to repair when they peel, which occurs fairly rapidly because water can get in so many places and work its way behind the coating. Most people who have applied paint or clear finish to a deck have regretted it.

Pressure-treated decks are resistant to rot, but they split when exposed to the elements. The best way to stop this is with a deck stain.

Unfortunately, there are no good alternatives. The best solution is to use high-quality redwood heartwood and leave it unfinished. The wood will turn gray in a few years, but it won't rot. Because it is cut on the radius (quarter-sawn), the boards are stable and resist splitting. Heartwood cedar performs almost as well as redwood.

Pressure-treated pine, hemlock and fir are the most widely used woods for decks because they are less expensive than redwood or cedar and even more resistant to rot. But pressure-treated wood is not cut on the radius, so it splits severely when exposed to sun and rain. Water repellents often claim to retard this deterioration, but none work well, because they don't block UV rays.

UV rays break down clear finishes, such as the polyurethane on this front door. Clear finishes peel because the UV rays penetrate the film and destroy the lignin that glues the cellulose cells of wood fiber together.

The best way to protect a deck made of pressure-treated wood, assuming you've ruled out paint, is to apply deck stain. Stains contain enough pigment to partially block UV rays and contain enough finish, which glues the pigment to the wood, to partially block water. But stains don't build (solvent-based stains less so than water-based stains), so they don't peel.

You can also apply a stain to redwood or cedar to help maintain or change the color, but no matter which wood you are coating, you should recoat whenever the stain begins wearing through.

the folly of food-safe finishes

BY BOB FLEXNER

It's a shame, but many woodworkers worry about which finish to use on objects that will come into contact with food or children's mouths. The reason for the worry is that woodworkers have been conditioned by several decades of articles in woodworking magazines to believe that ordinary finishes like boiled linseed oil, alkyd varnish and polyurethane varnish may leach poisonous ingredients like metallic driers. And other finishes, like lacquer, catalyzed (two-part) finishes, shellac and water-based finishes, may leach poisonous solvent.

The idea that some finishes are harmful is reinforced by a few manufacturers who label their finishes food- or salad-bowl-safe, which implies that other finishes are not.

A Nonissue

The shame for woodworkers is that a lot of energy is spent on the issue of food safeness when none is warranted. Food safeness is a nonissue because there's no evidence of any problem. So far as we know, all finishes are safe to eat off of,

Check out the label on your finishes. Likely it says something about how you shouldn't drink the product and to induce vomiting if you do. But does the label say anything about how it shouldn't be used on items that will come in contact with food? We haven't found a label that does.

and safe for children to chew on, once the finish has fully cured (the rule of thumb being 30 days).

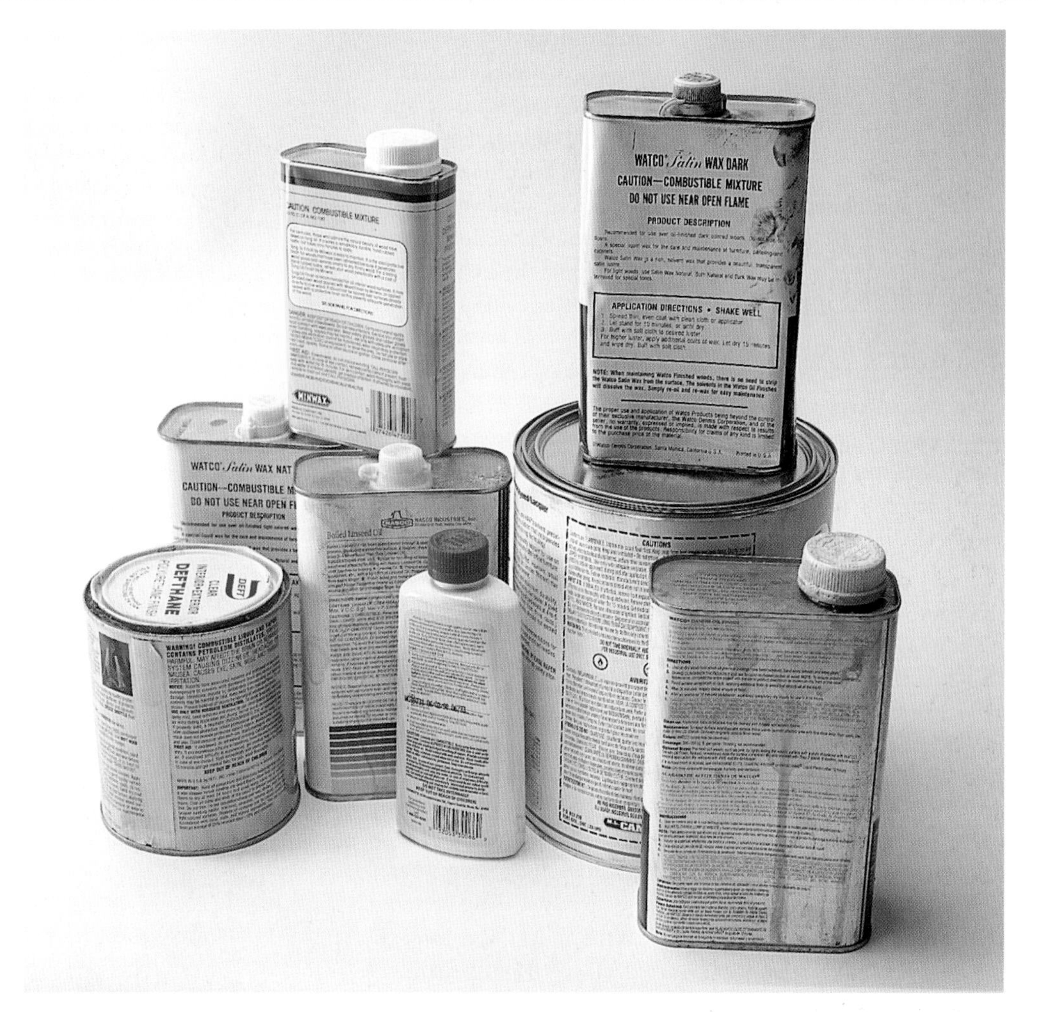

Think About It

• Have you ever heard or read of anyone, child or adult, being poisoned from contact with a cured, nonpigmented finish?

• Is it likely that any finish could be sold in paint stores or home centers without a warning if the finish were known to be dangerous for food or mouth contact? (Paint store clerks are rarely even aware that there might be an issue.)

• If any evidence exists that common wood finishes are unsafe for food or mouth contact, why is no mention made on the MSDS (material safety data sheets)? All unsafe uses of products are required by law to be listed on these forms, along with information about treatments for resulting health problems.

• Finally, does it make any sense that commonly available oils and varnishes that contain driers and solvents could be a health risk while the so-called food-safe oils and varnishes, which contain the same driers and solvents, aren't a problem? (These finishes wouldn't cure without the driers and would be too thick without the solvents.)

I want to make clear that I'm not saying that all finishes are food safe; we can't be absolutely sure about the safety of any curing finish. I'm saying that no evidence exists of any common wood finish being unsafe for food or mouth contact once it has fully cured, so a distinction between food-safe and non-food-safe is speculative.

For those who would then reply, "Well, there's no point in taking a chance," I would say that we take chances every day with almost everything we come in contact with. To rule out certain finishes when there's no evidence of a problem is unreasonable and arbitrary.

The FDA

A lot of the discussion about food safeness centers on what the Food and Drug Administration (FDA) allows. The FDA doesn't approve products, it regulates them. And it has published a set of regulations for establishing the food safeness of finishes. These regulations are contained in the Code of Federal Regulations, Title 21, Part 175, which you can find at larger public and university libraries and on the Internet at www.fda.gov.

There are two conditions for meeting FDA regulations.

• First, the finish must be made from among the raw materials listed on nine double-columned pages (additional ingredients can be added by a petition method). This list includes every oil, resin, drier and additive commonly used in wood finishes (polyurethane is covered in Part 177). It does not include lead or mercury. Because lead is no longer used in common wood finishes, and mercury never was, it can be assumed that all common wood finishes use only FDA-approved ingredients.

• Second, the finish must be formulated in such a way that it does not leach more than a specified amount of extractive when subjected to a variety of specified tests. The point of these tests is to show the finish cures properly. It's important to note that these tests must be done on every batch of finish to establish that no foreign substance has gotten into the finish (for example, from the finish having been made in a dirty vat), and that these tests are expensive.

No manufacturer providing finishes to the woodworking community puts their finishes through these tests. Thus, no manufacturer can legitimately claim they meet FDA regulations.

On the other hand, there's no evidence of problems, so manufacturers feel pretty safe in claiming food safeness anyway.

The Issue of Metallic Driers

Metallic driers are added to oil and varnish finishes to speed curing. Without driers, these finishes take many days or weeks to cure.

Lead driers were once commonly used in oil and varnish finishes, but in the 1970s it was learned that lead is highly toxic, especially to children. The problem was associated with the relatively large amount of lead contained in pigment and not with the tiny amount contained in clear finishes. Nevertheless, to be safe, lead was removed from all commonly available paints and finishes, including oils and varnishes. (Lead is still used in some specialty art and marine finishes, and labels are required to disclose its inclusion.)

Other metallic driers, including salts of cobalt, manganese, zirconium and zinc, continue to be used in all varnishes and curing-oil finishes except raw linseed oil and pure tung oil. Without these driers, these finishes cure extremely slowly.

There is no indication that these driers cause health problems. A very small amount is used, and it is well encased in the cured finish film so that if any is ingested, it passes through the body without causing harm.

Other Finishes

All other common wood finishes also are safe for food and child contact. In fact, commercially made wooden bowls, baby beds and children's toys are usually coated with one of these finishes.

The solvents, which cause some people to worry, evaporate out completely enough so they aren't a problem. And catalysts, which can be toxic in their liquid state, become so fully reacted with the finish that there is no evidence of a problem.

Conclusion

The issue of food safeness in finishes is a classic case of the concept of validation by repetition. Consistent, long-term repetition in woodworking magazines of a food-safeness issue, despite the complete lack of supporting evidence, has led to a widely held belief in the woodworking community that food safeness is an issue.

It shouldn't be. No other segment of society treats it as such. A more reasonable approach is as follows.

You can't be absolutely sure about the food safeness of any finish you put on wood. Even mineral oil and walnut oil could have problems that we just don't know of yet. Raw linseed oil, pure tung oil, wax, shellac and salad bowl finish could also have problems, because we don't know where these substances have been or what they might have come in contact with. None have met the regulations laid out by the FDA.

But, based on FDA regulations, the way finishes are made, the complete lack of any evidence to the contrary, and the countless other untested objects food and children come in contact with, no reasonable argument can be made for avoiding the use of any finish.

glazes and glazing techniques

BY BOB FLEXNER

Glazing is the act of applying and then manipulating color over a sealed surface. The color can come in many forms, including common stain, oil color, Japan color, universal-tinting color or a specially made product called glaze. A glaze is simply a stain that is thick so it stays where you put it, even on a vertical surface. Gel stain, for example, makes a good glaze.

Note that it's the position of the colorant in the order of finishing steps — over at least one coat of finish, but under a topcoat — that defines glazing. You don't have to be using a glaze to be glazing. On the other hand, even if you are using a glaze, you are staining, not glazing, if you apply it directly to bare wood.

Though it's easy to do, glazing is still a sophisticated decorating technique because of the many effects you can create. These include adding depth to three-dimensional surfaces such as raised panels and mouldings, faking the wear and dirt accumulation associated with age, adding definition to painted surfaces, adjusting color after the actual finishing has begun, and creating faux (fake) grain or other decorative patterns.

Besides its ease, glazing is also one of the most forgiving steps in finishing. You can actually practice on the wood you're finishing, and if you don't like the effect you get, you can remove the glaze and start over without damaging any of the finish.

Though the application of glaze is not difficult, skill is involved in knowing the look you want to create (having an artistic sense), and in maintaining consistency when glazing multiple objects, such as all the doors on a set of cabinets.

Glazing Products

The two types of glaze are oil-based and water-based. Oil-based glaze gives a deeper, richer appearance and is easier to control because of the longer working time. You can remove oil-based glaze for up to an hour or more by wiping with paint thinner or naphtha, neither of which will damage any paint or finish.

Water-based glaze is more difficult to work with because it dries so fast. But it has much less solvent smell, so it is less irritating to be around. Once you've applied a water-based glaze, you have only a few minutes to remove it using water before it dries too hard.

Oil-based glaze is best for cabinets and furniture when the finish is lacquer, varnish or shellac, and you're applying the glaze in a shop with good ventilation. Water-based glaze is best for faux finishing on large surfaces like panels and walls in buildings with little air movement, and on furniture and woodwork when you're topcoating with a water-based finish. To use a water-based finish successfully over an oil-based glaze, you have to let the glaze cure completely, which could take a week or more depending on the weather conditions.

By applying glaze between coats of finish, you can add the appearance of age to furniture. Here, I applied and left glaze in the recesses on the right side of a ball-and-claw foot.

Brands of glaze vary in thickness and drying time, but all brands produce good results. Some manufacturers provide glazes in a range of colors. Others provide only a clear glaze base to which you or the paint store add the pigment. Dark browns and whites (for pickling) are the colors most often used on furniture and cabinets.

If you need to thin a glaze to lighten its color, it's usually best to thin it with clear glaze base instead of common thinner so you don't lose the run-resistant quality. If you need to adjust the color of a glaze, you can do so easily by adding pigment ground in oil or Japan (which means varnish) to oil-based glaze, and pigment ground in glycol solvent or acrylic to water-based glaze.

You can use glaze to accentuate the three-dimensional construction of raised-panel cabinet doors. This door was stained and sealed before the glaze was applied and wiped off from the raised areas. Then the door was topcoated.

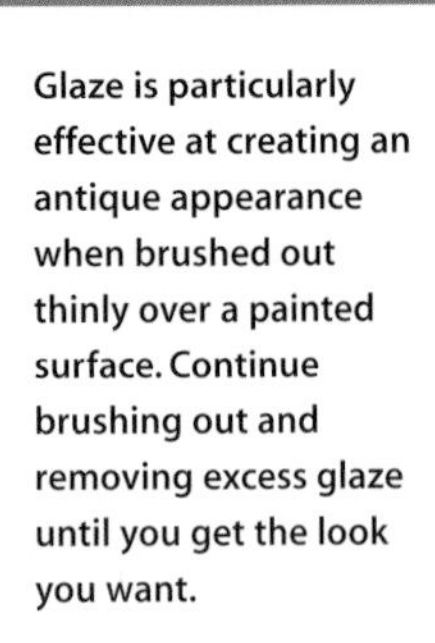

Glaze is particularly effective at creating an antique appearance when brushed out thinly over a painted surface. Continue brushing out and removing excess glaze until you get the look you want.

Applying Glaze

You can use any finish, sanding sealer or paint under the glaze. You can sand this first coat if you want to roughen the surface so the glaze can bond better to it. But sand lightly with fine sandpaper or steel wool so you don't sand through, or the glaze will become a stain and color the wood.

You can stain the wood under the sealed surface, leave the wood unstained or fill the pores of the wood. But in all cases, you should apply the glaze close enough to the wood so you can still apply one or more topcoats of finish to protect the glaze from being rubbed or scratched off without getting the overall finish build too thick.

Because there's no build with oil finishes or wax, you can't glaze successfully between coats of these finishes. You must use one of the film-building finishes.

To apply glaze, wipe, brush or spray an even coat onto the surface. Then manipulate the glaze with the following methods.

• Wipe off the unwanted glaze while it's still wet. In most cases, this means wiping the glaze off raised surface areas and leaving it in recesses on carvings, turnings, mouldings and raised panels. But it can also mean wiping off flat surfaces in a way that imitates grain or other decorative effects.

• Wipe off the unwanted glaze right after the thinner has flashed off and the glaze has become dull. This is the same as wiping off while still wet, but the glaze is usually a little easier to control at this point.

• Using fine steel wool, abrade off the unwanted glaze after it has dried. There is a risk that you might abrade through to the wood, but it's nice to know that you can always use steel wool to remove glaze if you don't get enough off with a cloth before the glaze gets too hard.

• Using an almost dry brush, spread the glaze out thinly to achieve the appearance you want. All this amounts to is continuing to remove glaze with a brush you keep fairly dry by wiping with a clean cloth until you achieve the effect you want.

• Adjust the color of the object you're finishing by brushing glaze out thinly and evenly over the surface. As long as you keep the glaze thin, you won't muddy the wood much. This is an excellent technique for creating a more perfect color match.

• Using tools such as rags, sponges, brushes, grainers and toothbrushes (to create a spatter effect), create a decorative faux pattern. Here, the techniques and colored patterns you can achieve are endless. Many books explain these techniques. Most are focused, however, on decorating walls rather than woodwork.

• Instead of manipulating glaze you've already applied, use a dry brush to apply the glaze to raised areas of carvings or turnings, or to flat surfaces to create the appearance of dirt accumulation. Begin with a totally dry brush and swirl it in some thick oil or Japan color you've applied to paper, cardboard or wood so that some of the color is transferred to the bristles without making them wet. Then brush lightly.

As long as you keep the glaze very thin, you can use it to adjust a color after you've sealed the wood without causing significant muddying. Here, I've added glaze to the left side of this cherry board to redden the color.

Glazing Problems

Most glazing problems occur because you've applied the glaze too thick or not allowed it to cure enough before applying the topcoat of finish. The two are related because a thick layer of glaze takes significantly longer to cure.

Too thick a layer of glaze (most common in crevices and recesses) weakens the bond of the finish to the wood because the glaze layer itself is not strong. The finish applied on top of the glaze could separate if knocked or abraded and this would pull some of the glaze with it and leave some attached to the surface underneath. This problem is even more likely to occur if the glaze hasn't thoroughly cured.

Not allowing the glaze to thoroughly cure can also lead to the topcoat wrinkling or cracking. If this happens, you'll have to strip the finish and start over.

CHAPTER 54

hvlp finishing

BY TROY SEXTON

Over the years I've used almost every variety of finishing technique from brushes and rags to high-pressure spraying systems. Whatever the style of furniture, I still get the best results from a spray-on finish. It's fast and quick-drying, provides a durable surface and looks great. I've used high-pressure finishing systems, but I now prefer a high-volume, low-pressure (HVLP) system. It wastes less finishing material, is safer and more environmentally friendly, creates less overspray and generally is less expensive.

High Pressure vs. HVLP

What's the difference between a conventional high-pressure system and a low-pressure system? In a nutshell, it's the speed of the air and the amount of finishing material you waste. HVLP systems produce no more than 10 pounds of air pressure per square inch (psi), and the amount of finishing material that lands on the workpiece (also called the transfer efficiency) is 65 percent or higher. Conventional high-pressure systems generally operate at around 35 psi and have a transfer efficiency of about 35 percent.

The two types of HVLP sys-

DE-'MISTIFYING' SPRAYING

I started to try to explain how a liquid finish is turned into a mist by a spray gun, but then I read Bob Flexner's description from his *Understanding Wood Finishing* (Reader's Digest) book, and I thought I'd let him do the talking.

"Spray guns shoot a stream of fluid that is broken up into a mist of tiny droplets by jets of air coming out of the air nozzle. The droplets hit the wood and flow together to make a smooth film. The breaking up of the finish into droplets is called atomization. It's important that the atomization be thorough, or the droplets won't flow together well.

"The trick to achieving proper atomization is getting the right amount of air striking the fluid as it comes out of the tip of the gun. If you have too little air, the atomization won't be great enough, and the finish won't flow together. It will cure looking like the surface of an orange; the effect is called orange peel. If you have too much air, the finish will dry before it hits the wood, producing a dusty look. This is called dry spray.

"The two air jets that direct the atomizing air have an additional function. Because they are placed 180° apart, in the horns of the air nozzle, they force the atomized air into an oval-shaped pattern called a fan. The fan is perpendicular to the line of the horns. By increasing the airflow through these jets, you widen the fan, so you can coat a wider area with each pass. By decreasing the airflow, you shrink the fan to a very small circular pattern, which you can use to fill in small defects. By rotating the air nozzle, you can change the angle of the fan relative to the gun."

The nozzle on either an HVLP or conventional spray gun works the same. It's just that the way the air is delivered to the jet nozzles is different. The photo above shows the nose of an HVLP gun. You can clearly see the jets described by Bob, as well as the fact that I've been using the gun and it's due for a cleaning.

By adjusting the fan on the air cap (or air nozzle), you can spray a wide fan either vertically or horizontally, adjust the width of the fan, spray a thin line, or even do a Morse code or a little graffiti. I'd recommend you set yourself up with a large piece of paper as soon as you get your gun and spend some time practicing. Try not only the different ways of adjusting the fan, but also overlapping the spray patterns and to get a feel for how fast or slow you need to move the gun to get an even coat without causing runs.

tems are conversion and turbine. Conversion guns are similar to a conventional high-pressure system, working with a compressor but using a regulator to step down the pressure of the air at the gun. Though this is a good system and it produces less waste and overspray, it requires a fairly large compressor, which is expensive. One advantage of a conversion system is it applies finishing material faster than a turbine system, making it a favorite choice for production shops.

Turbine units operate by producing air through a series of turbines (spinning fan blades, or a squirrel cage). The air produced is fed continuously to the gun at a lower pressure, but is capable of producing a high volume of air. This produces a gentle (but slower) application of finishing material to the project. Air flows from the turbine through the gun and into a plastic tube running to the cup to pressurize it enough to push the fluid into the fluid passageway of the gun. Unlike a conventional or conversion system, the air is not stored in a compressor's tank, but is a continuous stream. In bleeder-style guns, the air passes continuously through the nozzle, causing a constant hiss. Nonbleeder guns evacuate the unused air near the turbine, giving the gun a more conventional feel and reducing the chance of blowing dust around with the air stream.

When speaking of HVLP, most people are referring to a turbine system (as we will be here). For most readers a turbine system is the better choice because it's less expensive, more mobile and safer to use.

What Affects the Finish Quality?

No matter what spray system you're using, many of the same concerns exist to produce a good-quality finish: humidity, air temperature during spraying and keeping the system clean.

Spraying during periods of high humidity (over 40 percent) and high temperatures (over 70°F) can result in a poor-quality finish by causing the material to dry either too fast or too slow. By adjusting the material-to-carrier (lacquer-to-thinner) ratio, you can adapt to atmospheric conditions.

Many HVLP systems provide a viscosity cup to determine how much to thin the finishing material for optimal spraying conditions. First-time users should try the viscosity cup to get an idea of what thin is. Play with the mixture a little to get a feel for your gun's capabilities. Honestly, most furniture finishes (not paint, mind you) spray adequately through the standard nozzle provided with most guns without thinning. Eventually you'll put the cup away. I haven't used mine in years.

No matter how experienced you are at spraying a finish, if the fluid passageways in the cup and the gun (especially around the fluid nozzle) aren't clean, you're headed for trouble. The jet nozzles control the amount of air atomizing the fluid, as well as adjusting the

An HVLP gun has several critical adjustments. The fluid control knob regulates how much liquid is allowed into the airstream at the nozzle. The ring around the nozzle controls the width of the fan. The fan pattern in most guns is controlled by rotating the horns. The airflow is regulated either at the hose or on the gun.

THIS RING CONTROLS THE SIZE OF THE FAN ON MANY HVLP GUNS

AIRFLOW CONTROL KNOB ON HOSE (NOT SHOWN)

Drawers add an interesting problem in spraying (as do all pieces that are essentially a box, such as cabinets). The inside and outside of the piece must be finished, and usually you need to stand on your head to spray one surface. First off, leave any bottoms or backs out of the piece until after you've sprayed the drawer or cabinet. Spray the bottom edges of the drawer, then flip the drawer over, spray the top edges, then spray alternate interior and exterior surfaces. For example, with the drawer front facing away from you, spray the outside back, then the inside front. Turn the table (or move) one-quarter turn, then spray the outside side and the opposite inside side. Rotate, spray. Rotate, spray. And you're done. If you're not using a lazy Susan, set the drawer on its front (as in the photo), spray the edges, then the inside front, both inside sides and then the outside back surface. Flip the drawer over and spray the inside back, both outside sides and finally the front.

EXHAUST DIRECTION

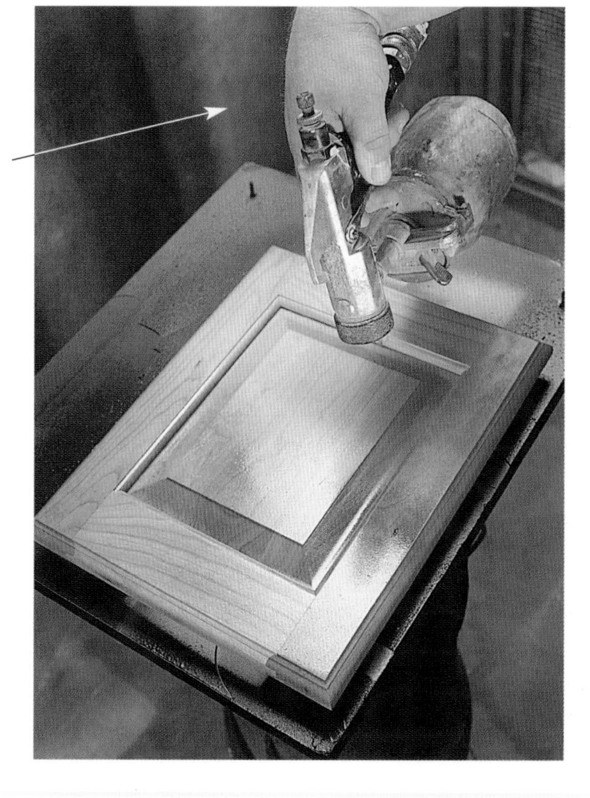

As with a shelf, a door has a good side and a less good side. Start with the good side down and spray the back, working the pattern toward your exhaust fan. Hold the gun above the piece and spray overlapping stripes across the back. Keep the gun pointing straight down and move your wrist back and forth as if it were on tracks, maintaining the distance to the piece. When that side has dried, flip the piece over and spray the edges. If you rig up a lazy Susan stand, it's easy to keep the piece oriented between you and your exhaust fan. If not, you end up dancing around the piece or misdirecting some overspray. With the edges sprayed, go ahead and spray the good face of the door. Because of the recesses formed by the frame-and-panel design, you may need to rotate your wrist slightly, moving the gun in an arc, to allow the spray to hit the inner edges.

shape of the fan (the spray shape). If those nozzles are clogged or partially blocked, the finish will not apply correctly. Another critical area to keep clean is the little hose leading from the cup to the gun itself. If it becomes clogged, air will blow through a bleeder gun but no material will be added. The best advice is to clean the gun and cup after each use.

You can probably leave the material in the cup overnight, but make sure you back the material out of the gun by lifting the gun out of the cup and pulling the trigger (with the turbine off) to allow the fluid to drain out of the gun. This isn't perfect, but will help overnight.

Even with the reduced amount of overspray from an HVLP system, it's best to work in a place that is either well ventilated or equipped with a spray booth of some type. Unlike high-pressure systems, you can use an HVLP system in your driveway without concerns of overspray (though a respirator is still a good idea). Of course, if you're spraying outside, there are trade-offs. A slight breeze will pull the slight overspray away from you and the work, but it may blow bugs and falling leaves onto your project.

What Materials Can I Spray?

You can spray all types of topcoat finishes with an HVLP system, including paint, shellac, lacquer and polyurethane. However, most home woodworkers don't have a shop that is adequately ventilated or exhausted for some of these materials. Unless you are using a tested and approved spray booth with explosion-proof accommodations, I recommend spraying only water-based finishes in an HVLP system.

HVLP systems are capable of spraying stains, as well, but spraying stains is a little more complicated than spraying a clear finish, and the cleanup usually isn't worth the mess (unless you're doing production work, like an entire kitchen). I'd recommend ragging or brushing on the stain and saving the HVLP for the topcoat.

As with most finishing products, I recommend you choose one type of finish and learn to work well with it. Lacquer is my preference, and again, unless you're properly outfitted, use a water-based lacquer.

Getting Started

After assembling the gun, use your viscosity cup to get a feel for the proper thickness of the material. It should flow about like canned pear juice — heavier than water, but not quite a syrup.

Start with the fan adjusted to its largest size, and the fluid turned almost all the way off. The air should be adjusted to fully open. Start spraying into the air, and slowly turn the fluid knob until a steamlike spray is produced and you can see the size of the fan. Now reduce the size of the fan by adjusting the nozzle until the fan is about 8" to 10" wide about 10" from the nozzle. This is a good place to start. You can refine the adjustments as you go. Now you need to learn how to move the spray pattern to get the best coverage.

Applying a Finish

With an HVLP system you need to keep the nozzle of the gun closer to the material than with a conventional system. I recommend 6" to 8" distance. On surfaces wider than 6" you'll need to make more than one pass, often many passes. You need to overlap your spray pattern to get an even coat. I recommend overlapping each pass by one-half the width.

Don't rock your wrist during spraying. Keep the gun perpendicular to the work and always strive to get an even coat on your work. The amount of finish on the piece should look wet but shouldn't hide the grain pattern. It should be a film covering. It's easier to spray three or four thin coats (which will dry quicker) than to spray two heavy coats and end up with runs or a plastic look to your finish.

Start and stop your spray passes off of the piece. Start spraying with the gun pointed off the piece, then move across the piece, continuing beyond the edge. Don't hesitate to adjust the fan orientation as you're spraying. It's a simple adjustment that lets you feel more comfortable with the movement and keeps you from having to tilt the gun, which may cause finish to build in places. You can also adjust the width of the fan for spraying edges.

When you start spraying, you need to plan the best spraying pattern to evenly cover all the surfaces of the piece you're spraying. A shelf is fairly simple, spray the back side, let it dry, then flip it over and spray the edges and front side. But doors and drawers require a little more thought.

In general you should always spray a piece starting with the edge closest to you (assuming that you have air being drawn away from you) and work away from your body. This keeps any overspray on the area you'll spray next, so it will be covered by your next pass. Another mantra to remember is to always spray the most visible piece last — the top of a table, a drawer front, the back and seat of a chair.

Finally, you have to be diligent about cleaning your gun. Read the directions and follow them religiously. If you don't occasionally strip your gun to clean it, you will be in for a rude surprise one day. Either your gun will stop spraying, or it will refuse to stop spraying, or chunks of garbage will end up on your project. So clean the gun.

That's the basics about HVLP and some tips on getting started. The rest is practice and getting to know your system and the finish you choose to apply.

To learn more about finishing and spray finishing than covered here, we recommend the following books: *Understanding Wood Finishing* by Bob Flexner, 1999, Reader's Digest; *The New Wood Finishing Book* by Michael Dresdner, 1999, Taunton Press; *Spray Finishing* by Andy Charron, 1996, Taunton Press; *Classic Finishing Techniques* by Sam Allen, 1995, Sterling Publications; *Good Wood Finishes* by Albert Jackson and David Day, 1997, Popular Woodworking Books.

CHAPTER 55

oil finishes: their history and use

BY BOB FLEXNER

Finishing is a mystery to most woodworkers, but it's not because finishes are difficult to apply. All that's involved in applying a finish is transferring a liquid to wood using one of three really easy-to-use tools: a rag, a brush or a spray gun.

Finishing is a mystery largely because of the confusion created by manufacturers in their labeling, and there's no better example of this than the mislabeling of various oil finishes.

This top group is oil and varnish blends. They are easy to apply, but they cure soft. As a result, the necessarily thin coats don't provide much protection.

This bottom group is actually wiping varnishes. They are thinned-down varnishes, and are as easy to apply as the above oil and varnish blends. However, they offer more protection and can be built up thicker.

The Background

Before the growth of the consumer market in the 1960s and 1970s there was little confusion about finishes. Fewer products were available and most were bought and used by professionals who were fairly knowledgeable about them. Manufacturers helped by listing ingredients, something few do today.

Boiled linseed oil was available, of course, and was used by many amateurs who sometimes added varnish to it to make the oil a little more durable. To make the mixture easier to apply, they thinned it with turpentine or mineral spirits so the proportions were about one-third linseed oil, one-third varnish and one-third thinner.

Linseed oil (which is from the seeds of flax plants) and blends of linseed oil and varnish are both easy to apply. Wipe, brush or spray the finish onto the wood; keep the wood wet with the finish for 5 to 10 minutes, or until it stops soaking in; then wipe off the excess and allow the finish to cure overnight at room temperature.

Next day, sand lightly to smooth the raised grain. Then apply one or two more coats, allowing each coat to cure overnight. Be sure to wipe off the excess after each coat, and leave your rags spread out to dry so they don't heat up and spontaneously combust.

Although boiled linseed oil and oil/varnish blends are easy to apply, they cure soft, so they have to be left too thin on the wood to be protective or durable. The growing consumer market created a need for something better. Shellac, varnish and lacquer were, of course, available at every paint store, but these finishes don't have the mystique of oil, and they require brushing or spraying, which makes them more difficult to apply than oil.

Oil/Varnish Blend

One replacement was prepackaged oil/varnish blend. This didn't add anything to what was already being used, but manufacturers made consumers think it did by labeling their products with enigmatic names like Danish oil (made by squeezing Danes?), antique oil (just for antiques?) and salad bowl finish.

Then they attached misleading marketing phrases to the product such as "contains resin," "protects the wood from the inside" or "makes the wood 25 percent harder" to make consumers think they were buying something more than simply a repackaged oil/varnish blend.

Tung Oil

A second replacement was a product labeled tung oil. This oil, pressed from the nuts of a tung tree, was introduced to the West about 1900. It was useful for making superior, water-resistant varnishes, especially for outdoor use.

But tung oil is too difficult for most people to use by itself as a finish. You apply tung oil just like linseed oil or oil/varnish blend, but you have to sand tung oil after every coat, not just after the first, and it takes five to seven coats, allowing two to three days' drying time between each, to achieve a smooth, attractive sheen.

Tung oil comes from China, however, so it has a certain mystique. Because few people really knew what tung oil was anyway, many manufacturers began packaging varnish thinned about half with paint thinner and labeling it "tung oil," "tung oil finish," or "tung oil varnish." Others further muddied the waters by calling their thinned varnish Val-Oil, Waterlox, Sealacell or ProFin.

Thinned varnish (more properly called wiping varnish) can be applied like boiled linseed oil or oil/varnish blend, or it can be applied with a brush like regular varnish. It makes an excellent finish because it looks good after only two or three coats, cures rapidly, and can be built up to a thicker, more protective film because it cures hard.

Wiping varnish is an improvement in protection and durability over boiled linseed oil and oil/varnish blend, but the only thing new about it is the misleading name on the can. Anyone can make their own wiping varnish by thinning any oil-based varnish or polyurethane enough so it is easy to wipe on the wood.

The Difference between Oil and Varnish

To help understand the differences in these products, you need to know the difference between oil and varnish.

Oil is a natural product. Some oils, such as linseed oil and tung oil, turn from a liquid to a solid when exposed to oxygen, so they make effective finishes. But these oils cure slowly to a soft, wrinkled film if applied thick, and this makes it necessary for you to remove all the excess after each coat. You can't build oil finishes to a thicker, more protective coating.

Varnish is a synthetic product made by cooking a drying oil, such as linseed oil, tung oil or modified soybean (soya) oil, with a resin, such as polyurethane, alkyd or phenolic. Varnish cures relatively rapidly to a hard, smooth film if it is applied thick, so you can leave the excess if you want to achieve a more protective coating.

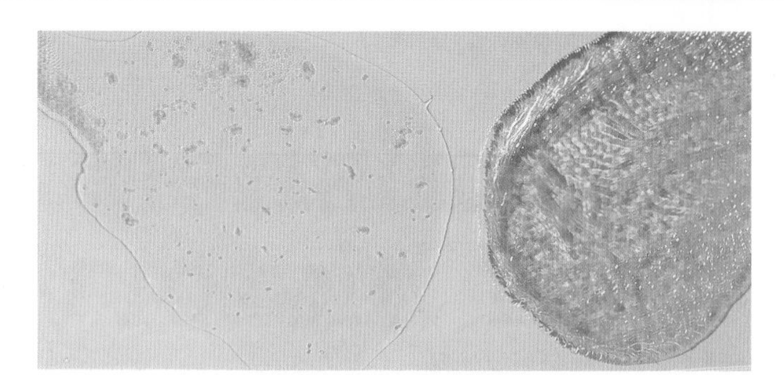

When wiping varnishes dry on a nonporous substance, such as this piece of glass, they are smooth and hard.

Oil and varnish blends, on the other hand, will cure soft and wrinkly on a nonporous surface, as shown above.

Varnish is as different from oil as bread is from yeast (an ingredient in bread). It makes no more sense to call a varnish oil than it would to call bread yeast.

How to Tell Which You Have

Because you can't trust the labeling, you have to know how to determine the difference between these products yourself.

Linseed oil is always labeled linseed oil, so far as I know, and is available in two types: raw and boiled. Raw linseed oil takes weeks to cure. Boiled linseed oil has driers added to make it cure in about a day with the excess removed. I know of no interior use for raw linseed oil.

Real tung oil has a distinct smell that clearly separates it from wiping varnish and oil/varnish blends, both of which have a varnishlike smell. Only if you are willing to go through the extra work for the increased water resistance you get in a nonbuilding finish should you use real tung oil.

Linseed oil and tung oil are always sold full strength, so if petroleum distillate or mineral spirits is listed as an ingredient, this is a clue that the finish is either wiping varnish or oil/varnish blend. To tell the difference between these two, you'll have to pour some of the finish onto a nonporous surface, such as glass or Formica, and let the finish cure for a couple of days at room temperature. If it cures fairly hard and smooth, it is wiping varnish. If it wrinkles badly and is soft, it is a blend of oil and varnish.

COMMON FINISHES

COMMON BRANDS OF FINISH:
Formby's Tung Oil Finish, Zar Tung Oil Wipe-on Finish, Val-Oil, Hope's Tung Oil Varnish, Waterlox, General Finishes Sealacell, General Finishes Arm-R-Seal, Daly's ProFin, Jasco Tung Oil

COMMON BRANDS OF FINISH THAT ARE OIL/VARNISH BLENDS:
Watco Danish Oil, Deft Deftoil Danish Oil Finish, Behlen Danish Oil, Sam Maloof Finish, Behr Scandinavian Tung Oil Finish, Minwax Tung Oil Finish, Minwax Antique Oil Finish, Velvit Oil, Behlen Salad Bowl Finish, Behlen Teak Oil, Watco Teak Oil Finish

exhausting overspray in the home shop

BY BOB FLEXNER

Spray guns, especially the high-volume, low-pressure (HVLP) type with turbine-supplied air, have become fairly popular with amateur woodworkers. Like all spray systems, turbine HVLP guns transfer the finish from the can to the wood faster than brushing and produce a more level surface (no brush marks).

Also, like all spray systems, turbine HVLP guns create overspray, though considerably less than high-pressure guns. This overspray should be exhausted to remove explosive vapors, for health reasons and to keep the dried particles of finish from settling back on the finished work and other objects in your shop. Rarely is this need for exhaust, or ways of accomplishing it, mentioned in ads for spray equipment or in articles about HVLP spray guns or spraying.

Commercial Spray Booths

Professionally equipped shops and factories use commercially made spray booths to exhaust overspray. Essentially, a spray booth is a box that's open at one end with an exhaust fan at the other and filters in between to catch overspray (see the drawing). Commercial spray booths have the following features:

- Steel construction for fire safety.
- Filters to catch and hold overspray before it is drawn into the fan.
- A chamber for collecting the air to be exhausted. This exhaust chamber makes it possible for air to be drawn uniformly through a much larger square footage of filters than just the simple, smaller diameter of the fan.
- A large enough fan to create an airflow of 100' or more per minute. This airflow is enough to pull bounce-back overspray away from the object being sprayed. The fan and motor also are explosion-proof to eliminate sparks that might cause a fire or explosion if the sparks were to come in contact with solvent vapors. (Be aware that a buildup of vapors can be ignited by a pilot light in your furnace, your water heater or from another source at home, too.)
- Side walls and a ceiling to create a work chamber or tunnel for directing the flow of air through the spray booth's filters.
- Ceiling and sometimes side lighting so the operator can see a reflection off the surface he or she is spraying. Working with a reflected light source is the only way an operator can know if the finish is being applied wet and without orange peel, runs, sags or other problems.

Commercial spray booths are an essential tool for production shops, but these booths are too large, too expensive ($3,000 to $5,000 minimum) and require too much makeup air (heated air to replace the air being exhausted) for almost all home shops. If you are using a spray gun on an infrequent basis at home and have to work inside to avoid cold, wind, bugs, falling leaves and so on, you should seriously consider building your own modified spray booth.

Making Your Own

With a note of caution that doing any type of spraying in your house, with or without a spray booth, could affect your homeowner's insurance, here's how to build a safe, inexpensive spray booth that will be adequate in the volume of air and overspray exhausted and take up very little space.

The spray booth consists of a fan with a separate motor connected by a fan belt, one or more furnace filters and plastic curtains.

Your choice of fan is determined by the amount of air, measured in cubic feet per minute (cfm), you want to move and is a trade-off between better exhaust of overspray and reducing the need to

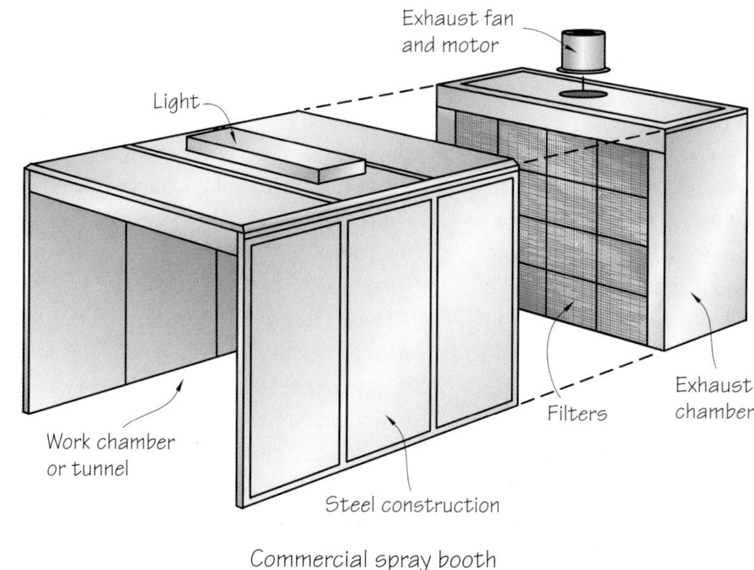

Commercial spray booth

supply heated makeup air on cold days. In other words, the more air your fan moves, the better the exhaust but the more windows you'll need to open at the opposite end of your shop and the faster the heat in your shop will be lost. Generally, the larger the fan and the more sharply angled its blades, the more air it is capable of moving.

To mount the fan, construct a box from plywood or particleboard approximately 1' deep. Both ends of the box must be open. The dimensions of the four sides should be adequate to hold the fan at one end and furnace filters, which should be efficient enough to trap all overspray particles before they reach the fan, at the other.

Cut a slot on the top of the box large enough for the fan belt to pass through and mount a motor adequate in horsepower to drive the fan on the outside of the box. A ¼- to ½-hp motor (1,725 rpm) would be typical. If you are going to spray solvent-based finishes, an explosion-proof motor is best. A standard TEFC (totally enclosed, fan-cooled) motor will do if you are going to spray only water-based finishes. Either way, the motor needs to be enclosed in a box to keep overspray from building up on it.

Place the box with the enclosed fan in a window, possibly resting on a stand just in front of the window and seal the spaces between the box and window opening. Then hang plastic curtains from the ceiling on either side of the fan, running out about 8' from the window wall. If the window is near a side wall, you could use it as one side of your booth instead of a curtain. You want the curtains to be wide enough apart so you can stand inside, or just outside, the tunnel when spraying.

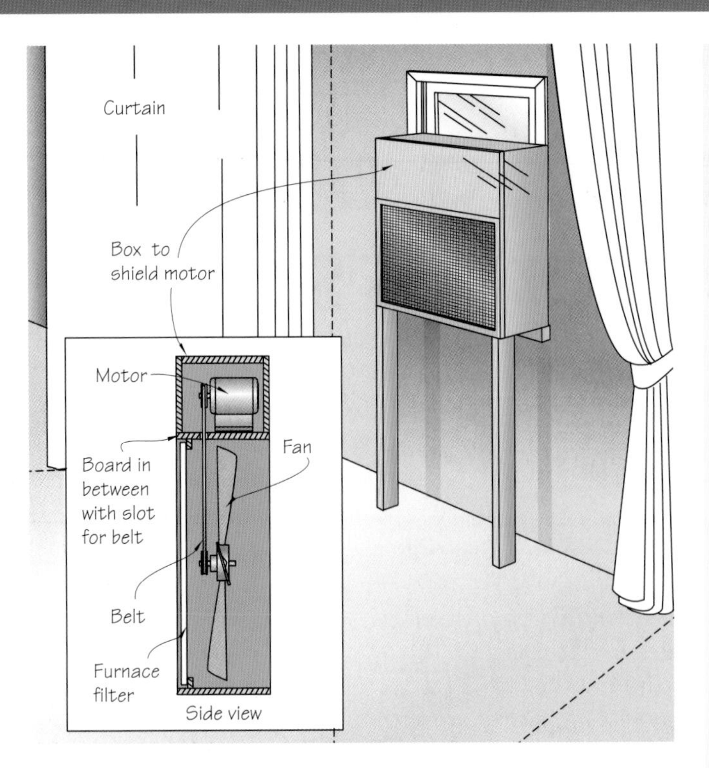

Homemade spray booth

The best curtains to use are heavy, fire-resistant industrial curtain partitions with supplied ceiling tracking that are available from auto-body supply stores, Grainger or Goff's Curtain Walls. But you can use any type of plastic sheeting, with the downside being that if the plastic is lightweight, it might be sucked in a little by the exhaust fan.

Mount the curtains to tracking on the ceiling so they can be pushed back when you aren't spraying and pulled open when you are. This way, you lose almost no space in your workshop.

Don't forget that you still need to wear a respirator while spraying with this exhaust system. I recommend a respirator with organic-vapor cartridges.

For lighting, recess a four-tube, 4' fluorescent fixture between the joists in the ceiling as close as possible to the window. Insert glass plates between the light and ceiling to shield them from overspray. For the best color balance, use full-spectrum fluorescent bulbs.

To avoid a fire hazard with your spray booth, it's essential that you keep it clean. Sweep the floor after each job and clean or replace the filter. If finish starts to cake on the curtains or fan box, clean or replace them.

SUPPLIES

Probably the biggest decision you have to make when building this system for your home is in selecting a fan. You have a few choices here.

ALL-IN-ONE UNITS: By spending a little money, you can make things simple. Grainger sells exhaust fans for areas with flammable or explosive vapors. Some examples include:

- Dayton 16" panel fan; cast aluminum blades; max cfm: 2,547; stock No. 3XK37.
- Dayton 16" exhaust fan; cast aluminum blades; max cfm: 1,979; stock No. 4C369.
- Other sizes are available.

MOTOR-SEPARATE UNITS: You also might be able to find a belt-driven fan without a motor from an industrial supply company. With these, you can mount a TEFC or explosion-proof motor outside of the path of the airflow as described in the article.

FILTERS: Use the standard blue woven furnace filters you can find at any home center store. Make sure that they are not too dense; some filters can greatly reduce your airflow. Be sure to clean the filter after each project.

paint and varnish removers

BY BOB FLEXNER

No step in refinishing is as messy and unpleasant as stripping off old paint or finish. Though stripping can't be made clean and enjoyable, it does help to know something about the stripping products available so you can choose intelligently among them.

Fortunately, in the case of strippers (unlike other finishing products), the primary ingredients are almost always listed on the container, so it's possible to make sense of the products by separating them into types.

Four types of strippers are solvents and one type is lye. You also can buy a stripper that combines two of the solvents, so actually six types of strippers are on the market today:

- Methylene chloride (MC)
- Acetone, toluene and methanol (ATM)
- N-methyl pyrrolidone (NMP)
- Di-basic esters (DBE)
- A combination of methylene chloride plus acetone, toluene and methanol (MC/ATM)
- Lye

MC, ATM and MC/ATM are available in various thicknesses, ranging from liquid to semi-paste. The thickness makes a difference in how well the stripper clings to vertical surfaces, but not in its strength or effectiveness.

Lye is available in both a powder form, which you have to mix with water, and a paste form, which is ready for use.

Methylene Chloride (MC)

The strongest and fastest-acting of the five solvent types is methylene chloride. You can identify this stripper in two easy ways: by the statement on the can that it's nonflammable and by the listing of only MC and methanol as the solvents. (A little methanol is always added to MC as an activator.)

Methylene chloride is effective at removing all types of coatings, and even though it is moderately expensive, it has been the primary solvent used in strippers for the last four decades. About 15 years ago, the Environmental Protection Agency listed MC as a probable human carcinogen, though the evidence for such a listing remains highly controversial.

Some manufacturers add acids or alkalies to their MC strippers to increase their strength, but these additives are seldom listed on the container. Almost all manufacturers add wax, which rises to the surface and retards the evaporation of the MC.

The wax residue must be washed off before finishing the wood, or the finish may not bond well. Manufacturers misleadingly call this washing step neutralizing.

Acetone, Toluene, Methanol (ATM)

The cheapest solvent stripper, ATM is essentially nothing more than lacquer thinner. It's effective at removing shellac and lacquer but is slow on all other coatings.

When manufacturers add wax to slow evaporation, they call the remover a stripper. When they don't add wax, they call it a refinisher. To use refinisher, you must work on very small sections at a time due to the fast evaporation of the solvents.

Other members of the three solvent families — ketones, petroleum distillates and alcohols — are sometimes added to or substituted for acetone, toluene and methanol to change evaporation rates, but the stripper is still in the ATM category. All the solvents used in this category are extremely flammable, and mention of this is made on the can.

MC/ATM

By combining MC and ATM in varying proportions, manufacturers produce a stripper that is in between in both effectiveness and cost. Combination strippers list a number of solvents, including methylene chloride, and also warn of flammability. These strippers are effective on all but the most stubborn coatings.

paint and varnish removers: strongest to weakest

STRIPPER TYPE	HOW TO IDENTIFY	DESCRIPTION	POTENTIAL PROBLEMS	COMMENTS
Lye	Contents list sodium hydroxide or caustic soda. Available as powder or paste. Warns of severe burns if it comes in contact with your skin.	The most effective stripper.	Damages wood. Darkens many woods and can cause finish problems.	Very dangerous to use because it causes severe burns to skin and eyes. Keep clean water close by for washing.
Methylene chloride/methanol (MC)	Contents list methylene chloride and methanol. Nonflammability is usually mentioned.	The strongest and fastest-acting solvent stripper.	Contains wax, which must be removed before applying a finish.	Fumes are a health hazard. Work outside or in a room with cross ventilation.
Methylene chloride/Acetone, Toluene, methanol (MC/ATM)	Contents list methylene chloride, methanol and a combo of acetone, methyl ethyl ketone, toluene, xylene.	The weakest and cheapest methylene-chloride stripper.	Contains wax, which must be removed before applying a finish.	Fumes are a health hazard. Fumes and liquid solvent are a fire hazard.
Acetone, toluene, methanol (ATM)	Contents list some combination of acetone, methyl ethyl ketone, toluene, xylene and methanol.	Almost as effective as MC/ATM but without methylene chloride.	Contains wax, which must be removed before applying a finish.	Fumes are a health hazard. Fumes and liquid solvent are a fire hazard.
Acetone, toluene, methanol (ATM) "refinisher"	Contents list some combination of acetone, methyl ethyl ketone, toluene, xylene and methanol.	Very inefficient as a stripper because no wax is included to slow evaporation.	Too slow on everything except shellac and lacquer.	Fumes are a health hazard. Fumes and liquid solvent are a fire hazard.
N-methyl pyrrolidone (NMP)	Contents list n-methyl pyrrolidone and possibly one or two additional ingredients.	Effective on most finishes, but two or three times slower and more expensive than methylene-chloride strippers.	Trying to rush it.	Fairly safe to use because of slow evaporation rate and nonflammability.
Di-basic esters (DBE)	Contents list "ester" or names of solvents ending in -ate, which are esters.	The slowest of the strippers.	Trying to rush it. Included water may blister veneer and warp thin wood.	Fairly safe to use because of slow evaporation rate and nonflammability.

N-Methyl Pyrrolidone (NMP)

The possibility that MC could cause cancer and the high flammability of ATM and MC/ATM strippers opened the market to two alternative solvent strippers. The more effective of the two is n-methyl pyrrolidone (NMP). It is nonflammable and is thought to be less toxic than MC and ATM.

It's not that NMP is safe to work with, but that it evaporates so slowly that the air in a room has time to replace itself several times over before toxic concentrations are reached.

Slow evaporation translates into reduced effectiveness (consider that these strippers are usually packaged in plastic containers), but an NMP stripper will remove all but the most stubborn coatings if you give it enough time — overnight in many cases.

The reasons NMP strippers haven't caught on better are their expense (about three times that of MC unless other solvents are added to reduce the cost) and the misleading claim listed on most containers that the stripper works in 30 minutes.

Claiming too much for a product may get a customer to buy it once, but rarely a second time.

Di-Basic Esters (DBE)

The first of the alternative strippers to appear on the market is based on several esters, called di-basic esters, combined with 50- to 70-percent water. These esters are very slow-evaporating, and thus weak as strippers.

DBE strippers work even slower than NMP strippers, especially on shellac and lacquer, but just as with NMP strippers, manufacturers exaggerate the speed. The problems this has caused, in addition to the damage the included water causes to veneer and wood, has led to the virtual disappearance of this stripper from stores.

Lye

Though it's rarely used, lye (sodium hydroxide) is both cheaper and more effective than the solvents discussed above. The problem with lye is that it will burn you severely if it gets on your skin, it can cause significant damage to the wood by making it soft and punky, and it may darken the wood and cause finishing problems.

You can buy lye in powder form at paint stores and sometimes at supermarkets, and mix it with water, about ¼ pound of lye to 1 gallon of warm water. Pour the lye into the water, not the other way around, or it may boil over and burn you, and use a steel container like a coffee can, not aluminum, plastic or glass. The heat that is created by the chemical reaction of the lye and water will heat the container, so don't hold it while mixing.

You can also buy lye in powder or paste form packaged with a cloth that you can apply over the lye to aid in the removal of paint or finish.

Conclusion

For difficult coatings such as paint, polyurethane and catalyzed (two-part) finishes, you should use a strong MC or lye stripper. For weaker shellac, lacquer and oil finishes, any of the strippers will work, given enough time.

the best way to reglue furniture

BY BOB FLEXNER

Of all the steps involved in restoring old furniture, regluing is by far the most important. Poorly done refinish jobs can be redone; badly made replacement parts can be remade and reinserted; sloppy touch-ups can be removed and done over — all without permanent damage to the furniture. But shoddy regluing can, and often does, lead to the complete destruction of the furniture.

Despite the importance of the regluing step, only a small percentage of professional and amateur restorers do it well. As a result, much of our old furniture is becoming unusable.

Five Methods

Five ways to reglue or tighten up furniture, in order from worst to best, are as follows.

- Use nails, screws, brackets and other metal fasteners.
- Insert white or yellow glue, cyanoacrylate (superglue), or epoxy into the joints without totally disassembling the furniture.
- Disassemble the furniture and apply fresh glue, usually white, yellow or epoxy, on top of the existing glue and clamp back together.
- Apply hot animal hide glue over the old hide glue that remains in the joints (after removing any loose or deteriorated glue) and clamp the joints back together.
- Clean all the old glue out of the joints, apply fresh glue (usually hide, white or yellow) and clamp the joints back together. In furniture with dowels, remove all the dowels that are loose and either reuse them after cleaning both them and the holes, or replace them with new dowels after cleaning the holes. Even better, replace all the dowels by drilling out those that are still tight but likely to come loose relatively soon. Then clean the holes and reglue the joints with new dowels as if everything were new.

Metal Fasteners

Inserting nails or screws and attaching metal fasteners is the worst thing that can be done to furniture. Any stress put on the joints can cause the wood to split, and sometimes cause tenons or dowels to completely break off. At best, the fasteners just hold the joints together; they don't make the joints tight.

Dowels inserted perpendicularly through a wobbly mortise-and-tenon joint are just as destructive and difficult to deal with as metal nails. Unfortunately, many people find these wooden nails somehow romantic, as if they are evidence of great craftsmanship, so they are sometimes added to old furniture.

Old furniture joints were glued with animal hide glue, which must be removed before regluing with any glue other than hot hide glue so the new glue can bond to the wood.

You can easily dissolve and wash off old hide glue with hot water or vinegar. If the glue is stubborn, scrub it with a stainless-steel kitchen scrubber and hot water.

Inserting Glue into Joints

The practice of inserting glue into joints without disassembling the furniture is widespread. Three methods are used: Drip glue at the edges of the joints and hope it runs into them; drill holes into the joints and insert the glue through a syringe; and pull the joints open just enough to expose small parts of the tenons or dowels and apply glue to them.

The glues most often used with this technique are cyanoacrylate and epoxy, though white and yellow glues are also used. Cyanoacrylate and epoxy are more expensive and difficult to use, but it's usually reasoned that they are stronger.

Though this method produces joints that usually remain

tight for a year or so, long-term soundness rarely occurs because only a part of the surface area is reglued, and it is still sealed with old glue, so the new glue doesn't get to the wood.

Disassembling and Applying Glue

A better practice is to disassemble the joints before applying the new glue — usually white, yellow, epoxy or polyurethane glue. This method exposes more surface area to these glues, so there's a better chance that the joints will remain tight for at least a few years.

But the wood is still sealed with the old glue, so just as with the previous method, whatever bond is achieved is made to the old glue, not to the wood. The bond achieved is thus no stronger than that of the remaining old glue to the wood, and that glue has already given way once. Moreover, when the joints break down again, as they surely will, proper regluing will be much more difficult because all the newly applied glue will have to be removed in addition to the original glue.

Using Hide Glue

All furniture made or repaired before the 1950s was glued with animal hide glue. This glue is made from the broth of animal skins, usually cattle, and has to be heated to about 140°F to be made liquid. Animal hide glue has the unique characteristic of dissolving quickly in hot water.

Because hot hide glue is both hot and wet, it dissolves old hide glue when applied over it, and a strong bond to the wood is usually achieved without the old glue having to be removed first.

The great advantage of continuing to use hide glue in joints glued originally with hide glue is that regluing is fast and effective. When hide glue was the only glue available, everyone used it, and this is surely a primary reason that so much very old furniture has survived so long. Most of the old-furniture joint problems you see today are the result of one of the three lesser-quality regluing methods (discussed above) having been used.

The product called liquid hide glue is the same as hot hide glue, except for added preservatives (to keep the glue from rotting for about a year) and gel depressants (to keep the glue liquid at room temperature). It can be used fairly effectively in place of hot hide glue as long as it is first heated to about 140°F.

Cleaning Joints

An even better practice than using hot hide glue over old hide glue is to clean all the old glue out of the joints before applying new glue. The strongest bonds are achieved when the wood is totally clean. This was the condition that existed when the joints were first glued.

Once the wood is clean, any glue can be applied, and the result will be strong, long-lasting bonds. The only rationale for using hide glue at this point rather than another glue is that the joints will be easier to reglue next time.

To clean old glue off of wood, you must dissolve, scrape or sand it off. Dissolving is the better method by far, because it's totally effective and doesn't change the dimensions of the parts. Because the old glue has penetrated somewhat into the wood, it's not possible to scrape or sand off all the glue without also removing some of the wood, and this creates air spaces in the joints. Tight wood-to-wood contact, which is necessary for a strong bond, is lost.

Hide glue is the easiest glue to dissolve and wash off. White and yellow glues are next. Each of these glues dissolves or breaks down in hot water or vinegar. Epoxy, urea-formaldehyde (plastic-resin), cyanoacrylate and polyurethane glues have to be scraped or sanded off because they can't be dissolved.

Not all furniture is deserving of the time it takes to reglue with one of the better methods, but all better-quality furniture is.

HOW TO REMOVE STUBBORN DOWELS

To remove an old dowel that won't budge even with a pair of pliers, first saw off the dowel just above flush.

Then drill out the center of the dowel using a brad-point drill bit 1/16" smaller in diameter than the diameter of the dowel. The brad point helps maintain center as you're drilling; the smaller bit reduces the risk of changing the location of the hole.

Use a 1/8" chisel or other sharp, narrow tool to pick away the remaining cylindrical part of the dowel. Then clean any remaining dowel or glue from the hole with the correct-size twist drill bit or a needle-nose rasp.

prevent, remove and disguise glue splotches

BY BOB FLEXNER

No finishing problem is more frustrating than glue splotches. You spend countless hours cutting, shaping, smoothing and joining pieces of wood only to have your work discolored where glue from squeeze-out or dirty hands seals the wood so your stain and finish can't penetrate. The wood under the splotch doesn't change color while all around it the wood is darkened.

Avoiding this common problem is easy with one of the following four steps.

- Keep the glue from getting on the surface of the wood in the first place.
- Wipe the glue off the surface while it's still wet.
- Identify areas of dried glue and remove it before applying a stain or finish.
- Remove or disguise the glue splotch after it has occurred.

Preventing Glue Splotches

Glue squeeze-out is a good thing when gluing boards edge to edge, because it's evidence you've applied enough glue and enough pressure with your clamps. This type of squeeze-out is seldom a problem, however, because you'll remove all traces of it when you plane, scrape or sand the surface level.

It's the squeeze-out from cross-grained joints, such as stiles and rails and legs and aprons, that causes problems, because it's hard to sand or scrape a 90° joint without leaving unsightly scratches.

The most obvious way to prevent cross-grained glue squeeze-out is to apply no more glue to the joint members (mortise and tenon, dowel and hole) than necessary to make a good glue bond. This is hard to do when working fast, however, because it's difficult to avoid getting too much glue in the joint when you're even more concerned about not getting enough to make a strong bond. The trick is to create spaces within the joint for excess glue to collect, giving you more leeway for how much glue you can apply.

To create these spaces, make your mortise or dowel hole a little deeper than necessary, chamfer the end of the tenon or dowel (most commercial dowels come this way), and chamfer the front edges of the mortise or dowel hole. When you then slide the joint together, excess glue will collect in the cavities before squeezing out.

To keep your hands clean of glue while gluing up, keep a damp cloth and a dry cloth nearby. If you do get some glue on your hands, wipe it off quickly with the damp cloth, then dry your hands with the dry cloth so you don't cause grain raising.

Glue squeeze-out is a particularly thorny problem when a joint meets at a 90° angle, such as a table leg to an apron. And because the apron is set back, it's easy to miss the squeeze-out during sanding.

Removing Wet Glue

The best time to remove excess glue is while it's still wet. Wipe with a cloth dampened with the solvent or thinner for the glue. To totally prevent glue splotching, however, you'll have to soak the wood and wipe it dry several times so you thin the glue so much that not enough is left in the wood's pores to cause a problem.

Some people remove glue squeeze-out by letting the glue dry just enough so it holds together and can be peeled off. This is a quick and easy way to remove most of the glue, but some will still remain in the pores and will have to be sanded, scraped or scrubbed out.

Identifying and Removing Dried Glue

Once the glue has dried, it's usually difficult to see on the surface of the wood. To highlight these areas, wet the entire

One way to avoid squeeze-out is to design your joints so that excess glue has a place to collect. Chamfering the ends of your tenons or using dowels with chamfered ends will help.

To find glue splotches before you stain, wet the surface with paint thinner or water. The glue will show up a lighter color.

surface with water or paint thinner, which will soak deeper into unsealed wood and leave the areas that are sealed with glue a lighter color.

Water raises the grain of wood, so if you use water, you'll have to let it dry and then sand the wood smooth again. This procedure is called sponging or dewhiskering, and it's a wise step to take anyway if you plan to use a stain or finish that contains water.

Alternatively, you can add commercial products to white and yellow glues before use that will make them show up under a black light.

When you've identified the problem areas, remove the glue by scraping, sanding or scrubbing with a solvent for the glue.

You can break down white, yellow and hide glues with vinegar or water. (Hot water works best.) You can soften white and yellow glues with acetone, toluene, xylene or lacquer thinner. You can dissolve contact cement with acetone or lacquer thinner, and you can thin epoxy and polyurethane glues with these solvents until they have cured. Then you'll either have to use a methylene-chloride-based paint stripper or resort to sanding or scraping.

Whichever liquid you use to break down the glue, it's a good idea to scrub the area with a soft, brass-wire bristle brush in the direction of the grain to help remove all the glue from the pores. Then wipe the surface dry.

After cleaning all the glue off the surface, sand it with the same grit sandpaper you used elsewhere. You need to remove all raised grain and make the sanding scratches uniform, or differences in color may show up when you apply the stain or finish.

If you scrape or sand the glue off the surface, finish up by sanding with the finest grit sandpaper you've used elsewhere to make the scratch pattern uniform.

Correcting Problems

For those cases where you don't discover the glue splotch until after you've applied the stain, sand or scrape off the glue through the stain and restain that area or leave the splotch and disguise it later, after you've applied a coat of finish.

If you sand or scrape off the glue, you may have problems blending that area with the surrounding wood. Be sure to sand the damaged area to the same grit as elsewhere before applying more stain. If the damaged area still shows, try sanding the entire part (leg, rail, tabletop) while the surface is wet with stain, then wipe off the excess.

If the part you've wet-sanded is a little lighter than other parts, wet-sand again with a coarser-grit sandpaper. Most stains lubricate sandpaper, which reduces the coarseness of the scratching.

If wet-sanding doesn't solve the problem, you'll have to strip the stain using paint stripper or the thinner for the stain. Then resand the wood and begin again with the staining step. You don't have to remove all the color from the wood if you're restaining with the same stain.

An alternative is to disguise the splotch after you've applied a coat of finish in the same way you would disguise a wood-putty repair, a burn-in repair or a rub-through. Begin by drawing in the grain using pigment suspended in a shellac or padding-lacquer binder and a very fine artist's brush. You can also use pigment in varnish (the same as thinned oil paint or glaze), but you'll have to allow a day's drying time between coats.

When you have the grain lines connected to the grain in the surrounding wood, rub lightly with #0000 steel wool to soften the lines, then apply a thin barrier coat of finish so the lines won't get smeared during the next step. Color the areas between the grain lines with either pigment or dye in a binder. When you have the splotch disguised, continue applying coats of finish.

This last step doesn't work well on oil finishes because there's no film build.

how to remove watermarks

BY BOB FLEXNER

Watermarks occur on furniture with finishes that have aged. These marks, also called water rings when they're round in shape, rarely occur in newly applied film-building finishes, even those such as shellac that have reputations for weak water resistance.

Watermarks can be either light or dark. Light marks are milky-white and are caused by moisture getting into the finish and creating voids that interfere with the finish's transparency. Dark marks are brown or black and are caused by water and metal residue penetrating through cracks in the finish and getting into the wood.

Both types are easy to remove, but the finish usually has to be stripped before removing dark watermarks. Don't confuse heat damage with light watermarks or ink stains with dark watermarks; both are usually very difficult to remove.

Light Watermarks

To remove milky-white watermarks, you need to either consolidate the finish (eliminate the voids) to the point that the transparency is reestablished or cut the film back to below the damage. Success is not predictable, but in general, a white watermark is easier to remove in the following circumstances: (1) the finish is newer, (2) the watermark has been in the finish a shorter time, and (3) the damage in the finish is shallower.

Here are the best ways to remove milky-white watermarks, arranged in order from the least damaging (and generally least effective) to the potentially most damaging.

• Apply an oily substance, such as furniture polish, petroleum jelly or mayonnaise, to the damaged area and allow the liquid or gel to remain overnight. The oil will often restore some of the transparency (by filling some of the microscopic voids) but seldom all of it.

• Heat the finish with a blow dryer or heat gun to soften the finish so it consolidates. This may restore some of the transparency if you get the temperature just right, but if you get the finish too hot, it will blister. Avoid getting the finish any hotter than is comfortable to touch.

• Dampen a cloth with denatured alcohol and wipe gently over the damaged area. The trick is to dampen the cloth just enough so it leaves the appearance of a comet's tail of evaporating alcohol trailing as you wipe. (You can practice by wiping across a more resistant surface such as polyurethane or plastic laminate.)

If you get the cloth too wet, the alcohol may soften the finish too much and dull the sheen or smear the finish. This is especially likely if the finish is shellac (used on most furniture finished before the 1930s), which dissolves with alcohol.

• Cut through the damage

To remove dark water stains, you'll usually have to first remove the finish from the piece. Oxalic acid crystals can be bought at better hardware and paint stores. Sometimes it's labeled wood bleach.

Brush the oxalic acid solution over the entire board. The dark marks will begin to fade immediately, though it might take 15 minutes or longer for them to disappear completely.

After the board has dried, remove the crystals using a wet rag or a hose. Never brush the crystals off the surface.

by rubbing with a mild abrasive such as toothpaste, or with rottenstone (a very fine abrasive powder available at most paint stores) mixed with a light oil. Fine #0000 steel wool lubricated with a light oil, such as mineral oil, is more effective because it cuts faster, but steel wool will leave noticeable scratches in the surface. Use steel wool only as a last resort.

Rub the damaged area until the water damage is gone, being careful not to rub through the finish. Then, if the sheen is different from the surrounding area, even it by rubbing the entire surface with an abrasive that produces the sheen you want.

• Spray on a lacquer retarder, such as butyl Cellosolve. Various companies package this solvent in easy-to-use aerosol cans and market them to the professional refinishing trade. The product is also available from Constantines as Blush Eraser. (Blushing in lacquer is the same microscopic-void phenomenon as a watermark.)

Lacquer retarder will soften almost any film finish enough so the water damage clears up. But use this solvent sparingly. Too wet a coat may cause the finish to blister.

• French polish over the damaged area using padding lacquer. The lacquer-thinner solvent in the padding lacquer will soften the finish (the same as if it was wiped or sprayed on separately) and often clear up the damage. Often, it will be necessary to continue polishing the entire surface to get an even sheen.

This technique works fairly well on surfaces in good condition, but it is risky on crazed or deteriorated surfaces. If the watermarks don't come out entirely with your initial application, you will seal in the remaining milky whiteness and make removing them more difficult.

If you have no experience removing milky-white watermarks, I recommend you try wiping with an alcohol-dampened cloth or rubbing with an abrasive. Both techniques are usually effective, and the risk of serious damage is minimal.

Dark Watermarks

The easiest and least damaging way to remove dark watermarks is to bleach them out of the wood with oxalic acid. This chemical is available in crystal form at pharmacies and at many paint and hardware stores. Don't confuse this bleach with household bleach, which removes dye, or with two-part bleach, which takes the natural color out of the wood.

Dissolve some oxalic-acid crystals at a ratio of 1 ounce to 1 quart of warm water or, to make it easier, just make a saturated solution by adding the crystals to warm water until no more will dissolve.

A glass jar makes a good container, but leave some air space at the top for gases to collect if you store the solution. Never use a metal container, because it will rust.

Brush a wet coat of the solution over the entire surface, not just over the stains, to keep the color even. If you are working on mahogany or cherry, which usually darken as they age, the oxalic acid may lighten the wood back to its original color.

Let the oxalic acid dry, then wash the crystals off the wood with a hose or well-soaked sponge or cloth. Don't brush the crystals into the air because they will cause you to choke if you breathe them in.

Usually, one application will remove the black marks, but you can always try a second if the first doesn't work. Often, a light brown mark will remain after the black has been removed. It can be removed easily with a light sanding.

CAUTION: Oxalic acid is toxic, capable of causing severe skin and respiratory problems. Wear gloves and goggles when using it, and don't generate airborne dust.

Oil Finishes

Dark watermarks occur easily in oil finishes because they're too thin to be effective against water penetration. Milky-white watermarks are rare, however. The lighter watermarks you sometimes see in oil finishes are almost always caused by random light reflection from raised grain telegraphing through the thin oil.

To repair light, raised-grain watermarks in oil finishes, level the raised grain with sandpaper or steel wool and apply more oil finish. Abrade the damaged area as little as possible to avoid lightening the color of the wood.

CHAPTER 61

rubbing for a perfect finish

BY BOB FLEXNER

For best results, learn to sand your finishes with wet/dry sandpaper, a block with cork backing and a lubricant (such as paint thinner).

Go to any exhibition of handmade furniture and you'll see the problem right away. The woodworking is usually impressive, but the finish on many of the pieces is horrible. It looks and feels rough because it has dust and other debris in it, and runs and sags and either brush marks or orange peel, depending on the method the maker used to apply the finish.

How is it that some woodworkers come up with finishes that look and feel great and others just can't figure it out? Is the difficulty of applying a nice finish the reason so many woodworkers opt for oil finishes, with the resulting sacrifice in protection and durability?

If you listen to advertisers and read the promotions for books and magazines ("Get a perfect finish every time"), you might think it's the product or the application tool that makes the difference, but it isn't. No product or application tool can produce a perfect finish, or even a near-perfect finish. Only one thing can — rubbing the finish, meaning rubbing with an abrasive.

You can rub a finish in one of two broad methods: the easy way and the hard way. The easy way is to rub with steel wool and maybe a lubricant. This produces noticeably better results than not rubbing at all, but not nearly as good as the hard way, which is to level the finish first with sandpaper, then rub it with abrasives and a lubricant. The hard way isn't hard to do; it just takes more time and has a greater risk of cutting or sanding through the finish and exposing raw wood.

In most cases, there's no advantage to rubbing surfaces that aren't seen in a reflected light and aren't touched. To make these surfaces (table legs, for example) the same sheen as the surfaces you're rubbing, apply a finish that produces that sheen naturally — gloss, semigloss, satin or flat.

Abrading the Finish

Abrading is easy and quick. Simply take some #000 or #0000 steel wool (I prefer #0000) and rub the finish with the grain until you achieve an even sheen over the entire surface.

Pay special attention to the edges, because the finish there is easy to cut through. To help control your strokes so you

You also can merely abrade the finish, which is not as effective as sanding. Steel wool and a lubricant such as Murphy Oil Soap dissolved in water is all you need.

stop right at each edge, take many short strokes right up to it, then connect these short strokes (on both edges) with long strokes.

On small surfaces, you can stand at the end of the piece and rub away from you and then back toward you, but on larger surfaces, you should stand at the side and rub side to side. When you do this, be conscious to not rub in an arc, which is the natural way your hand and arm want to move. Instead, think in terms of making a reverse arc, like a shallow concave, so the actual stroke is straight.

You can use a lubricant with the steel wool to soften the scratches you're putting in the finish, but you risk making rub-throughs worse, because if you do cut through (most likely on the edges), you won't see it when it first happens and stop. I suggest you not use a lubricant until you've practiced a few times.

Any liquid or paste will work well for the lubricant. The more oily or pasty (mineral oil or paste wax) the lubricant, the slower your cutting action and the higher the sheen or gloss you'll get. The more watery the lubricant (water, soap-and-water or paint thinner), the faster you'll cut and the lower the resulting sheen. (Products with names such as Wool Wax or Wool Lube, which are sold as rubbing lubricants, are simply soap in paste form — like Murphy's paste soap.)

You can use other abrasives instead of steel wool. These include Scotch-Brite pads and pumice (finely ground lava).

Gray Scotch-Brite (sold as fine) is close in grit to #000 steel wool. Pumice, which you mix into a sludge with water, paint thinner or mineral oil and apply with a felt or cloth pad, is equivalent to #0000 steel wool.

Leveling and Abrading Using Sandpaper

Rubbing the finish with steel wool, Scotch-Brite or pumice merely smooths and rounds over the imperfections. To remove them entirely, you should sand with sandpaper.

Sanding a film finish is just like sanding wood except you almost always use much finer grits (320 and up), and you have to use a lubricant to keep the sandpaper from clogging and damaging the surface. If the surface is flat, you should back the sandpaper with a flat cork, felt or rubber block. (I find cork works the best. You can make a fine rubbing block by gluing some $\frac{1}{8}$" gasket cork onto a light pine block about 1" thick and chamfered on the top side to conform to your hand.)

Choose a grit sandpaper that removes the flaws efficiently without creating greater work than necessary taking out the sanding scratches. If you don't have any idea what grit to start with, begin with 600-grit, sand a little, remove the lubricant and see what progress you've made. If you haven't completely flattened the surface with 10 or 15 strokes over the same area, drop back to a coarser grit and continue dropping back until you find a grit that flattens the surface quickly.

The most common lubricants to use are water, soap-and-water, mineral oil and paint thinner. If the sandpaper (always the wet/dry type) still clogs with water or soap-and-water, use mineral oil or paint thinner. You can mix them to control the viscosity.

Pour some of your chosen lubricant onto the surface and begin sanding. As long as you intend to move up to a finer grit, there's no reason to sand only in the direction of the wood grain. The finish doesn't have any grain, so you can sand in any direction as long as your final sanding with your finest-grit sandpaper is in the direction of the grain (to disguise the sandpaper scratches).

I usually begin by sanding in circles, except on the edges where I sand along them, not into them. By changing direction with each grit, it's easy to see when you've removed all the scratches from the previous grit and it's time to move on.

After flattening the entire surface, which you easily can check by removing the lubricant and viewing in a reflected light, remove all the lubricant and move up to the next sanding grit. To remove oil and paint-thinner lubricant, I wipe with naphtha, which evaporates very fast.

If you intend your final sheen to be that of #0000 steel wool or pumice, you don't need to sand above 600 grit, because these are equivalent. But if you want a higher gloss, you should continue sanding with 1,000, 1,200, 1,500 and even 2,000 grit until you're just below the sheen you want. Then switch to a commercial rubbing compound or rottenstone (finely ground limestone) and water or oil.

It should be obvious that perfecting your rubbing technique requires some experimentation. I recommend you make up a sample surface on a fairly decent size piece of veneered plywood by applying three or four coats of your favorite finish, and then rub it out.

If you should, by chance, complete the job the first time without rubbing through somewhere, then continue until you do rub through so you can learn how much work it takes to do this and see what it looks like.

the case for shellac

BY BOB FLEXNER

Today, shellac is the most under-appreciated of all finishes, but this hasn't always been the case. Until the 1920s, when lacquer was introduced, shellac was the primary finish used in furniture factories and small woodworking shops. It continued to be the favored finish of professionals finishing interior wood trim and floors, and of hobbyists finishing everything, including furniture, until the 1950s and 1960s.

Then polyurethane and wiping varnish (varnish thinned about half with paint thinner and often mislabeled tung oil) were introduced and widely promoted. Beginning in the 1970s, blends of linseed oil and varnish, like Watco Danish Oil, were promoted in magazines for their ease of use.

Instead of defending shellac during this period, suppliers retreated to the position that shellac was a good sealer for stains and knots. They also allowed shellac to get an exaggerated reputation for weak water resistance, and they increased its stated shelf life from one year to three years. (Shellac slowly deteriorates after it's dissolved in alcohol. After about a year it no longer hardens well enough or is water-resistant enough to be used as a complete finish on most furniture and cabinet surfaces. Always use shellac within a year of when it was dissolved.)

Now shellac is rarely used as a finish except by high-end antique refinishers (which ought to tell you something). This is terribly unfortunate, because shellac still is one of the best finish choices for most woodworking and refinishing projects.

Shellac is preferred by high-end refinishers and is a good finish for home woodworkers because it dries quickly, builds well and is easily reversed if disaster strikes.

What Is Shellac?

Shellac is a natural resin secreted by insects called lac bugs, which attach themselves to certain trees native to India and Southeast Asia. Suppliers buy the resin and sell it as flakes, or dissolve it in alcohol and package the solution in cans for you to purchase.

Natural shellac is orange (amber) in color and is your best choice when you want to add warmth to wood. Most old furniture and woodwork was finished with orange shellac. Bleached shellac (sold as white or clear) is best when you want to maintain the whiteness of a pickling stain or the natural color of light woods such as maple, birch and poplar. You can mix orange and bleached shellac to achieve an in-between color.

Natural shellac contains about 5 percent wax and will produce excellent results; but dewaxed shellac, whether pre-dissolved or in flake form, is more water-resistant. You can remove wax from regular shellac by letting it settle and then decanting the liquid.

Shellac is a very old finish, so it has an old measuring system based on the concept of pound cut. One pound of shellac flakes dissolved in one gallon of alcohol equals a one-pound cut. Two pounds in one gallon is a two-pound cut; one pound in a quart is a four-pound cut; and so on.

The shellac you buy at the paint store is almost always a three-pound cut, which is very thick for brushing or spraying. Thin this shellac by half with denatured alcohol (shellac thinner) and make adjustments from there to reach the thickness, or pound cut, you feel most comfortable working with.

To ensure maximum hardness and water resistance, make your own shellac by dissolving shellac flakes in denatured alcohol. The brown container in the middle is a light-proof collapsible container (usually used for photographic chemicals) that's great for storing shellac.

To obtain maximum freshness and thus maximum hardness and water resistance, use denatured alcohol to dissolve your own shellac from flakes, which are available from many woodworking suppliers. Start with a two-pound cut, and adjust from there.

Applying Shellac

To brush shellac, remember that alcohol evaporates rapidly, so you must work fast. Use a good quality natural- or synthetic-bristle brush, or a foam brush, and brush in long strokes in the direction of the grain if at all possible. Work fast enough on your project to keep a wet edge, and wait until the next coat to fill in any missed places if the shellac becomes tacky.

Spraying shellac is no different from spraying other finishes. Just as thinning shellac reduces brush marks during brushing, thinning reduces orange peel while spraying.

However you apply the shellac, allow the first coat to dry about two hours, then sand with gray, 320-grit stearated (self-lubricated) sandpaper just enough to remove dust nibs and raised grain. Use a light touch to reduce sandpaper clogging and to avoid sanding through the finish.

Remove the dust and apply a second coat. Add more alcohol to the shellac if you're getting severe brush marks or orange peel, or if air bubbles are drying in the film. The alcohol will slow the drying and allow the bubbles to pop out. There is no limit to the amount you can thin shellac, but you may have to apply more coats to get the build you want.

Apply as many coats as necessary to achieve the look you want. Each new coat dissolves into the existing coat, so you don't need to sand between coats except to remove dust nibs or other flaws. To see flaws like runs and sags before they dry in the film, arrange your work so you can see a reflected light in the area you're finishing. Then brush out the flaws before they dry.

If the humidity is high, or if there's too much water in the alcohol you've used to thin your shellac, it may turn milky-white. This is called blushing and is caused by moisture settling in the finish. Wait for a drier day, use a purer alcohol or both. You usually can remove existing blushing in the finish by applying alcohol on a dry day or by rubbing with an abrasive, such as a Scotch-Brite pad or steel wool.

If, at any time, you create problems you can't remove without creating greater problems, strip the finish with alcohol or paint stripper and begin again. In between coats you can store your brush by hanging it in a jar of alcohol, or you can clean it easily by washing it in a half-and-half mixture of household ammonia and water. You can reclaim brushes with hardened shellac by soaking them in either solution.

When you have applied the desired number of coats (three is minimum in most cases), you can leave the finish as is. Or you can level it using 320-grit and finer sandpaper and a flat backing block, then rub it to the sheen you want using Scotch-Brite pads, fine steel wool or abrasive compounds like pumice and rottenstone. If the rubbed finish shows finger marks easily, apply paste wax or an oily furniture polish.

SHELLAC PROS AND CONS

advantages:

- Much more water- and scratch-resistant than oil or oil/varnish blends, which cure too soft to be built up on wood.
- Better dust-free results than varnish or polyurethane, which cure very slowly.
- Less polluting, less of a health hazard and less smelly than varnish, polyurethane or lacquer.
- Easier to apply and richer-looking than water-based finishes.
- Easier to clean (with ammonia and water) than all other finishes.

disadvantages:

- Not water- or scratch-resistant enough for surfaces such as kitchen cabinets and tables that take a beating.
- Available only in gloss sheen.
- Tends to ridge at the edges of brush strokes.
- Slowly deteriorates after being dissolved in alcohol.

CHAPTER 63

understanding solvents and thinners

BY BOB FLEXNER

Finishing can't exist without solvents and thinners. Even water-based stains and finishes contain them. If you understand a little about them and how they relate to each other, you'll have more control of your work. You'll be able to speed up or slow down the drying time of your finish to compensate for the humidity or the type of project you're finishing. You'll also be able to manipulate the viscosity of your finish to make it flow better.

Though the terms *solvent* and *thinner* often are used interchangeably (and I will sometimes use the more general term *solvent* here to refer to both), they are actually quite different. A solvent is a liquid that dissolves a solid, such as a cured finish, while a thinner thins a liquid stain or finish. Sometimes a liquid just thins a finish, and other times it both dissolves and thins a finish. (See the table on the next page.)

Solvents are grouped in five families (not including the special ones used in paint-and-varnish removers): petroleum distillates, alcohols, ketones, esters and glycol ethers. Each family reacts with a finish in a different way.

Within each family, solvents differ primarily in evaporation rate, with some evaporating rapidly at room temperature and others evaporating very slowly or not at all. The most well-known family with which to illustrate this relationship is the petroleum-distillate family.

Petroleum Distillates

Petroleum distillates are composed entirely of hydrogen and carbon and are distilled from petroleum and sometimes from coal tar. They are used in finishing primarily to thin and clean up oils and varnishes.

The smallest petroleum distillate is methane, which is a gas at room temperature. Heptane and octane are fast-evaporating liquids at room temperature and are used in gasoline. Naphtha evaporates slower than gasoline, and mineral spirits (paint thinner) slower still. These are the petroleum distillates commonly found on paint store shelves and used most often in finishing.

Kerosene also is widely available, but it evaporates too slowly to be much use in finishing. Mineral oil (also called paraffin oil) and paraffin wax don't evaporate at all at room temperature. Paraffin wax, in fact, is a solid at room temperature.

You may have noticed in using these solvents that the slower the evaporation, the oilier the liquid substance. Mineral spirits is oilier than naphtha, and kerosene is oilier than mineral spirits. Mineral oil is oil. Because none of these distillations damage finishes, and because oily substances are effective at picking up dust and adding shine to dull surfaces, petroleum distillates are widely used as the main ingredient in furniture polishes.

Toluene (toluol) and xylene (xylol) make up part of naphtha and mineral spirits, and when removed leave these solvents odorless and also a little weaker in solvent strength. Toluene and xylene are used primarily as cleaners to remove oily substances from metals and wood, and to soften water-based finish, latex paint and white and yellow glue. You can remove any of these from wood by wetting and scrubbing with toluene or xylene.

Turpentine is a distillation of pine-tree sap and is equivalent to petroleum distillates in its chemical structure and uses. It is oilier and evaporates a little slower than mineral spirits, but it has a solvent strength similar to naphtha.

what dissolves and thins what

SUBSTANCE	DISSOLVES	THINS
Mineral spirits (paint thinner) Naphtha Turpentine	Wax	Wax, oil, varnish, polyurethane
Toluene Xylene	Wax, water-based finish, white and yellow glue	Wax, oil, varnish, polyurethane, conversion varnish
Alcohol	Shellac	Shellac, lacquer
Lacquer thinner	Shellac, lacquer,water-based finish	Lacquer, shellac, catalyzed lacquer
Glycol ether	Shellac, lacquer, water-based finish	Lacquer, water-based finish
Water	—	Water-based finish

Other Families

Other solvents used in finishing also are members of families, having the same relationships within those families as the individual petroleum distillates have within their family — evaporating more or less fast and being more or less oily.

Alcohols are used primarily to thin and remove shellac, and as an ingredient in lacquer thinner and many paint-and-varnish removers. Three alcohols used in finishing are common: methanol, denatured alcohol and glycol (usually propylene glycol).

Methanol evaporates the fastest and is used for thinning non-grain-raising (NGR) stains because the fast evaporation helps control the depth of stain penetration when spraying. But methanol is toxic, and respirator masks aren't effective, so it should be used only with adequate ventilation.

Denatured alcohol is ethanol (common in liquors) made poisonous so it can be sold without a tax. This is the best alcohol to use with shellac.

Glycol is an extremely slow evaporating alcohol used in water-based stains and finishes to slow their drying and help them level out. It is often sold as a flow additive. (Rubbing alcohol, sold in pharmacies, contains too much water to be useful in finishing.)

Ketones, esters and glycol ethers dissolve lacquer, so they're used as the active solvents in lacquer thinner. Acetone and methyl ethyl ketone (MEK) evaporate rapidly and are often used to remove oil from metal and wood, and for stripping paints and finishes. They are usually available in paint stores and home centers, unlike esters and glycol ethers, which aren't commonly available.

To make lacquer thinner, manufacturers choose between these solvents primarily for evaporation rate (to control the drying of the finish), with the slower-evaporating solvents being used in lacquer retarders and faster ones being used in fast lacquer thinners.

Glycol ethers are the primary solvents used in water-based stains and finishes because these solvents evaporate slower than water, which is necessary or these finishes won't cure properly.

Using This Information

Solvents and thinners help you control the finishing products you work with.

- You can control the working time of paste wood filler and glaze by choosing between mineral spirits and naphtha for the thinner.
- You can control the working properties of homemade paste wax by choosing mineral spirits or turpentine for slow drying, and naphtha, toluene or xylene for fast drying.
- You can slow the drying of lacquer so it doesn't blush in high humidity or feel sandy from overspray (especially common when spraying the insides of cabinets and drawers) by adding lacquer retarder to the lacquer.
- You can add glycol to water-based stains and finishes to increase your working time and get them to flow out better.
- You can add a little lacquer retarder to shellac to slow the drying (useful in hot weather). Lacquer thinners and retarders contain alcohol and will thin shellac.

CHAPTER 64

stripping finishes from wood

BY BOB FLEXNER

Here are the steps for using stripping products and dealing with the most common stripping problems.

1. Work outdoors in the shade or in a room where you have arranged cross ventilation provided by fans. Don't work near an open flame (such as a gas water heater or furnace) or a source of sparks if you're using a flammable stripper.

2. Remove hardware and difficult-to-reach wood parts that can be easily disassembled. Soak hardware that requires stripping in a coffee can filled with stripper.

3. Wear a long-sleeved shirt, chemical-resistant gloves (butyl or neoprene) and eye protection.

4. Spread newspapers on the ground or floor to catch the waste.

5. Shake the container of stripper, then cover it with a cloth and open the cap slowly to allow the pressure inside to escape. Pour the stripper into a large can, such as a coffee can.

6. Brush the stripper onto the wood using an old or inexpensive paintbrush. Avoid unnecessary brushing; you want to lay on a thick coat, but also minimize solvent evaporation. (Be aware that some synthetic bristles will dissolve in methylene-chloride-based strippers.)

7. Allow the stripper time to work. Test the paint or finish occasionally with a putty knife to see if you can lift it from the wood. Apply more stripper as the original dries out. All strippers will lift many layers at once if the surface is kept wet so the stripper has time to penetrate.

8. Remove the dissolved, blistered or softened paint or finish using one or more of the following methods.

• Use paper towels to soak

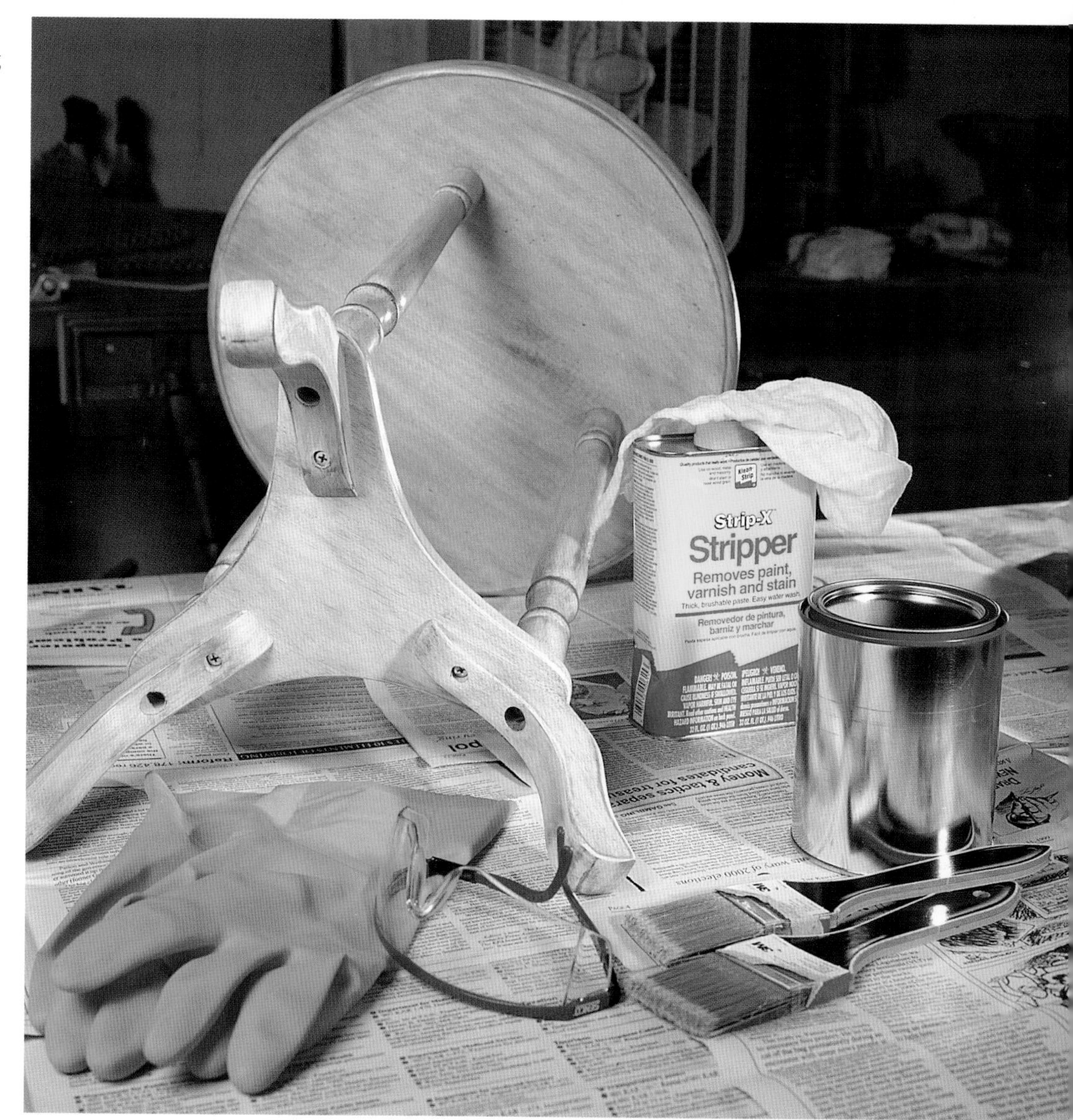

When refinishing, you should take safety precautions seriously. That means heavy-duty gloves, eye protection and even long sleeves.

up and wipe off the dissolved finish.

• Use wood shavings from a jointer or planer to soak up dissolved finish. Then brush off the shavings with a stiff-bristle brush.

• Scrape the film off flat surfaces into a bucket or cardboard box with a plastic scraper or a wide, dull putty knife. Keep the putty knife clean and smooth, and round its corners with a file so it doesn't scratch the wood.

• Break blistered or softened film loose from mouldings, turnings and carvings with #1 steel wool or a Scotch-Brite pad.

• Pull a coarse string or hemp rope around the recesses of turnings to work out blistered paint or finish.

• Pick the softened paint or finish out of cracks and recesses with sharpened sticks or dowels, which won't damage the wood as metal picks will.

9. Wash the wood with paint thinner, naphtha or lacquer thinner to remove wax residue left from strippers containing wax. You may also wash with a strong detergent and water, or simply with water if the stripper is water-washable, which means it already contains the detergent.

10. Let the solvent evaporate out of the stripping sludge, then dispose of it in the trash unless local laws forbid this. (The dried sludge is what was on the furniture before you stripped it, so it is no more polluting than tossing the entire painted or finished object into the trash.)

Common Problems

If you've ever done any stripping, you know it's seldom as easy as the step-by-step instructions suggest. Here are some of the most common stripping problems and their solutions.

• The stripper doesn't work. If the stripper you're using doesn't dissolve, blister or break the bond of the paint or finish film, either you need to allow more time for the stripper to work or you need to use a stronger stripper.

First, allow more time. Strippers work much slower in temperatures below 65°F. Keep the surface wet by applying additional coats of stripper or covering the surface with plastic wrap to prevent evaporation.

If you still have problems, try a stronger stripper. The only paint or finish that can't be removed with a solvent-based stripper is milk paint. It was used in the 18th century and in rural areas of the United States in the 19th century. You can remove it with lye.

Some modern coatings are very difficult to strip. Rough them up with coarse sandpaper to increase the surface area, then try again with a strong methylene-chloride stripper.

• You can't get paint out of the pores. Paint is softened by the stripper but doesn't come out of the pores until some mechanical force is applied to it. Stripping shops often use water under high pressure. You can use a brass bristle brush (available at paint stores), which won't damage hardwoods.

Apply more stripper to the surface, then scrub in the direction of the grain. Remove the gunk with rags or paper towels. Repeat until the wood is clean.

• You can't get the stain out. Whether a stripper removes a stain depends on how that particular stain is affected by the stripper. If the stripper doesn't remove the stain, use household bleach to remove dye stains, or scrub the wood with a brass bristle brush together with more stripper to remove pigment stains.

You don't have to remove stain, however, if you intend to restain darker than the color of the stripped wood. Simply restain right over the remaining color.

You can tell that all the finish is off when no more shiny places remain on the wood or in the pores when the wood is dry.

• The stripper streaks and darkens the wood. Lye and any stripper containing an alkali may darken wood. The darkening often shows up as ugly streaks. To bleach out the dark stains, make a saturated solution of oxalic-acid crystals, available at pharmacies and many paint stores.

Brush the solution over the entire surface, not just over the stains. Let the oxalic acid dry back into crystal form. Then wash the crystals off the wood with a hose or well-soaked sponge or cloth. The crystals will cause an uncontrollable coughing if you brush them into the air and breathe them.

Oxalic acid will also remove black water rings and rust stains. It has little effect on the natural color of the wood, except in the case of mahogany or cherry, which usually darken as they age. The oxalic acid may lighten the wood back to its original color.

• Sandpaper clogs after stripping. Clogged sandpaper indicates that some finish remains on the wood, or that the stripper hasn't completely evaporated. As long as all the finish has been removed, sanding isn't necessary if the wood is smooth. Sanding will remove the wood's patina (the appearance of age brought about by light and use).

• Wood won't stain evenly. You may not have removed all the old finish. If this is the case, you'll have to resume stripping until all the finish is removed. Uneven stain penetration can also be caused by uneven density or swirly grain in the wood itself.

• The new finish won't dry, or it peels after it has cured. Both of these problems are caused by wax left on the wood by the stripper. All strippers based on methylene chloride and acetone, toluene and methanol (ATM) contain wax. The wood must be washed thoroughly (not neutralized as most directions suggest) with a detergent or solvent for removing wax. Flood the surface, then wipe with a dry cloth, turning it frequently so you lift the wax from the wood rather than just move it around.

the keys to understanding finishes

BY BOB FLEXNER

Though you may use only one or two finishes in your work, you've surely wondered about the others and how they compare. You've probably even asked yourself if you shouldn't be using one of them instead.

To help answer this question, you may have tried to classify finishes by their resins — polyurethane, alkyd, acrylic, etc. — but then realized that this isn't very helpful. Take polyurethane, for example. It is used in oil-based varnishes, water-based finishes, some lacquers and some two-part finishes. If you've used any two of these finishes, you know that they are very different.

A much better way to make sense of finishes, so you can choose intelligently among them, is to combine them into three groups by the way they cure, then associate each of the groups with familiar objects — Tinkertoys, spaghetti and soccer balls. This may seem silly at first, but the objects make the groups easy to remember and the groups allow you to figure out the answers to most of your questions, even though you may never have used the finishes.

The Groups

The three groups are reactive, evaporative and coalescing.

Oil, varnish, and two-part finishes are reactive finishes because they cure by a chemical reaction that occurs in the finish when it comes in contact with oxygen (oil and varnish) or when a catalyst is added (two-part finishes). Since the chemical reaction causes the molecules in the finish to join up or cross-link, you can picture reactive finishes as Tinkertoys on a molecular scale that link up in a very large network.

Shellac, lacquer and wax cure entirely by the evaporation of their solvents (there is no chemical reaction and no linking up), so they are evaporative finishes. These finishes are made up of relatively large molecules that are long and stringy in shape, making the finishes resemble entangled, molecular spaghetti.

If you let all the water evaporate out of a pot of actual spaghetti, it hardens. If you then reintroduce water, the spaghetti first softens and becomes sticky, then the individual strands separate. The same happens to shellac with alcohol, lacquer with lacquer thinner, and wax with turpentine or a petroleum distillate, only on a molecular scale.

Water-based finishes cure both by chemical reaction and liquid evaporation. Like latex paint and white and yellow glue, water-based finishes are composed of tiny droplets of finish suspended (emulsified) in water and solvent. These droplets are very large compared to the molecules in the other finishes. Inside each droplet the finish molecules cure by chemical reaction, but the droplets themselves join only as a result of the water, and then the solvent, evaporating.

You can picture the droplets of cured finish as microscopic soccer balls. As the water evaporates, the soccer ball-like droplets approach each other, or coalesce, so water-based finishes are classified as coalescing finishes. The small amount of organic solvent in the water base then softens the outer surface of the droplets so they stick together when they come in contact. The solvent then evaporates and a film is formed.

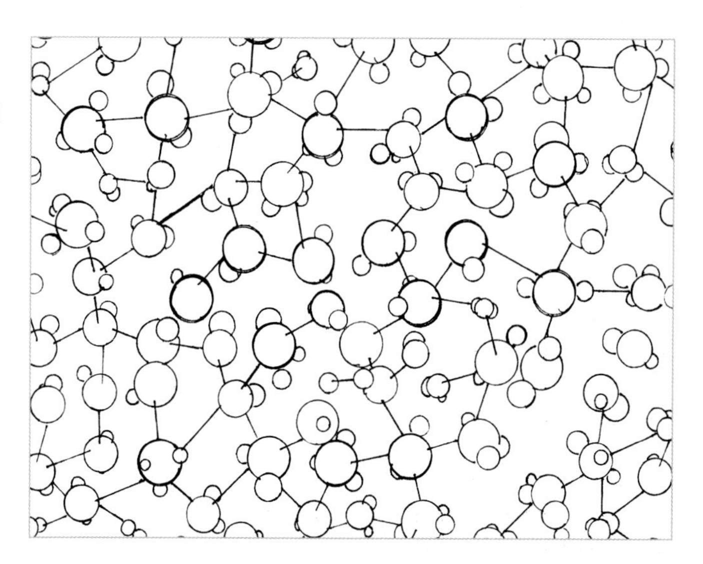

Tinkertoys: Reactive finishes (oil, varnish and two-part finishes) cure by chemical reaction after the thinner evaporates. On a molecular scale, these finishes resemble a gigantic Tinkertoy-like network when cured.

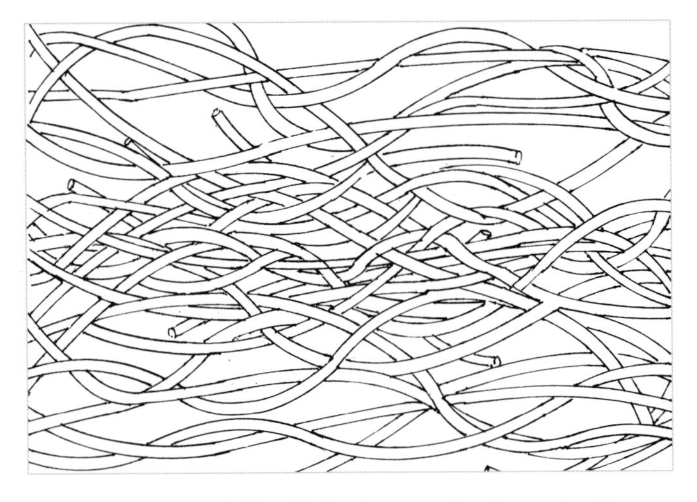

Spaghetti: Evaporative finishes (shellac, lacquer and wax) cure when the spaghetti-like molecules tangle after the solvent evaporates.

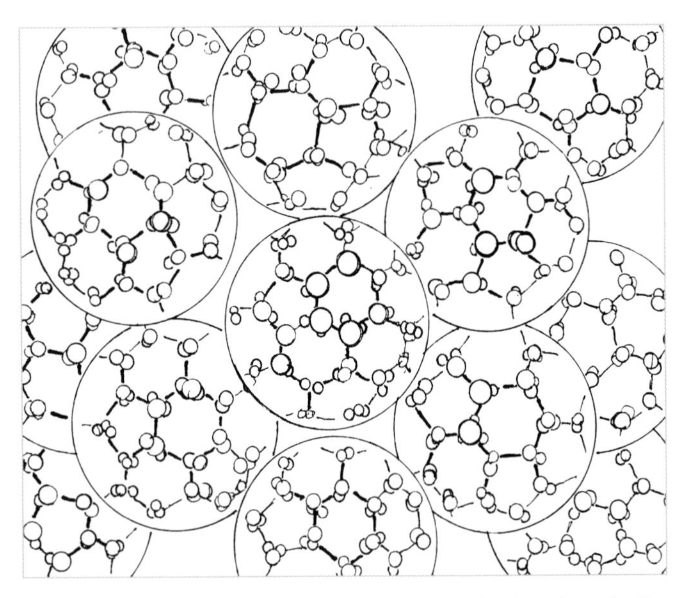

Soccer balls: Coalescing finishes (water-based) cure as droplets of reactive finish come together and stick to each other when the water and then the solvent in the finish evaporate. The droplets resemble microscopic soccer balls containing Tinkertoy-like networks of reactive finish inside each.

THE FINISHES

Even without the three groups to simplify the finishes, there are still only seven types of finishes to choose among:

• Oil, which includes raw and boiled linseed oil, pure tung oil (not the thinned varnishes often sold as tung oil) and blends of oil and varnish, commonly sold as Danish oil and antique oil. The characteristic that unites these finishes is their inability to cure hard, which makes them functional only if you wipe off the excess after each application.

• Varnish, which includes all hard-curing finishes that thin and clean up with turpentine or a petroleum distillate like paint thinner. Common polyurethane is a varnish, as are wiping varnishes (varnish thinned with paint thinner) and gel finishes.

• Two-part finishes, which, as the name indicates, are finishes that require the combining of two parts to cure. These include pre- and postcatalyzed lacquer (precatalyzed has the catalyst already added), conversion varnish, polyester, two-part polyurethane (both solvent-based and water-based) and epoxy.

• Shellac, the only finish that thins and cleans up with alcohol.

• Nitrocellulose and (water-white) CAB-acrylic (cellulose acetate butyrate) lacquers, which always thin and clean up with lacquer thinner and can be easily dissolved with lacquer thinner even after they're fully cured.

• Wax, which includes liquid, paste and solid, and always dissolves and thins with turpentine or a petroleum distillate. As with oil, you buff off all the excess to make the soft-curing wax functional.

• Water-based finishes, which include all finishes that thin and clean up with water except those that would be classified as two-part finishes.

In practice, you rarely have to choose among all seven types. You usually choose among four.

To begin with, you can eliminate wax from the seven (except for decorative objects like turnings and carvings) because of its very weak protective and durability qualities. Wax is more often used as a polish on top of another finish to add shine and scratch resistance.

Of the remaining six types, you're usually limited to oil, varnish, shellac and water-based if you aren't using a spray gun, because the other finishes dry too fast to apply with a cloth or brush.

If you are using a spray gun, you normally choose between two-part finishes, shellac, lacquer and water-based because you can achieve all the looks and durabilities you want much faster with these finishes.

Putting water back onto a cured water-based finish doesn't cause any damage, but a strong organic solvent like alcohol or lacquer thinner will make the finish sticky, and dull it or dissolve it, just like the solvent does to evaporative finishes.

Using This Information

You commonly look for five characteristics in a finish.

• Protection for the wood (resistance to water and moisture-vapor penetration);

• Durability of the finish (scratch, heat, solvent, acid and alkali resistance);

• Rubbing qualities (ease of rubbing to an even sheen);

• Reversibility (ease of repairing and stripping);

• Curing speed (ease of application without dust or sagging problems).

The Tinkertoy-like reactive finishes — varnish and two-part finishes — are protective and durable because the cross-linked molecules are difficult to penetrate or break apart. (Oil finishes offer little protection or durability because they cure too soft and are left too thin on the wood.)

In contrast, the evaporative finishes — shellac and lacquer — allow some water and moisture-vapor (humidity) penetration through the gaps where the spaghetti-like molecules bend around each other. And these finishes are easier to damage with coarse objects, heat, solvents, acids and alkalies because their molecules aren't held together by the strong ties common to reactive finishes.

(Like oil, wax is considerably weaker than shellac and lacquer because it's too soft and left too thin on the wood.)

The coalescing finish — water base — is resistant to abrasive damage because almost all the surface area is cross-linked inside the soccer-ball-like droplets. But where the droplets stick together, water and moisture vapor can penetrate; and heat, solvents, acids and alkalies can cause the droplets to separate.

This is not to say that evaporative and coalescing finishes are weak finishes, only that they aren't as protective or durable as reactive finishes. If you want the best finish for a kitchen table, kitchen cabinets or office desk, it's a reactive finish (not oil). But this degree of protection and durability is seldom necessary for an entertainment center, most woodwork or a bed.

The Trade-off

No finish can provide it all, however. You pay a price for protection and durability. Scratch resistance, for example, has the negative side of making a finish difficult to rub to an even sheen using abrasives. Solvent resistance means greater difficulty recoating, repairing and stripping. Heat resistance makes burn-in repairs less successful, and alkali resistance increases the difficulty of cleaning brushes and stripping.

At the sacrifice of better protection and durability, most refinishers and high-end furniture factories use lacquer instead of two-part finishes because of the reduced problems recoating and repairing, and because lacquer is easier to polish to a beautiful satin sheen.

Ease of Application

As a final lesson to be learned from the Tinkertoy, spaghetti and soccer ball analogy, consider that finishes are easier to apply the faster they dry and become dust- and sag-free. Fast-drying shellac, lacquer, catalyzed finish and, to a lesser degree, water-based finish, are less likely to run, sag or collect dust than varnish. If you are one of the many woodworkers who use regular alkyd or polyurethane varnish for your finishing projects, you need to recognize that you're using the finish that is most difficult to make look nice.

Ease of application is the reason factories that want the ultimate in protection and durability for objects like office furniture and kitchen cabinets use catalyzed finishes instead of polyurethane, even though these finishes are still difficult to rub to an even sheen and to repair and strip. No finish has everything.

Conclusion

Keeping all the characteristics in mind is often difficult when choosing among finishes, especially if you haven't used them all yourself. You can overcome much of your lack of hands-on experience by using the mental pictures of Tinkertoys, spaghetti and soccer balls to help keep the differences straight.

finishing walnut

BY BOB FLEXNER

Though American black walnut has lost some of the popularity it had a decade or two ago, it remains one of the easiest of all woods to finish, primarily because almost every possible stain, finish or other decorative material looks good on it — even the non-film-building finishes, wax and oil.

All wood stains, whether pigment or dye, look good on walnut, and most tend to make the wood, which has a naturally cold cast, look warmer. The pores of walnut are relatively tight for an open-grained wood, and they look good kept open with very thin finishes and also filled to a mirror-flat appearance. Two-part bleach can be used to make walnut nearly white (it can then be stained to whatever color you want), and black dye stain can be used effectively to ebonize it.

The only finishing product I can think of that doesn't always look good on walnut is water-based finish, which tends to make the wood look flat and washed out. But even this isn't always the case, because manufacturers are getting better at giving these finishes a warmer, deeper-penetrating appearance.

Choosing a Finish

The three primary qualities you look for in a finish are ease of application, durability and color. Considerations of application ease and durability are the same for walnut as they are for all finishes.

Oil and wax are the easiest finishes to apply because you wipe off all the excess. So there aren't any runs, brush marks or orange peel, and dust isn't a problem. Oil-based varnish and polyurethane are the most difficult finishes to make look nice because they dry so slowly that runs have time to develop and dust has lots of time to become embedded. All other finishes fall in between.

Oil and wax are also the least durable finishes because they never get hard. Shellac, lacquer and water-based finish are next, and oil-based varnish and polyurethane are the most durable common finishes. Catalyzed lacquer is also durable, but it is used primarily in professional shops and factories.

Color is the finish quality that has specific meaning for walnut. Some finishes darken wood more than others, and other finishes add a yellow (actually more of an orange) coloring to the wood. In my opinion, walnut looks best with this warmer orange tone.

Clear wax is the only finish that doesn't darken wood. Oil finishes tend to penetrate and darken wood more than faster-drying finishes such as lacquer. Along with orange (amber) shellac, varnish and polyurethane, oil finishes also add more yellowing than do other finishes.

Water-based finishes darken wood but they don't add yellowing. Blonde or clear shellac, nitrocellulose lacquer and catalyzed lacquer add some degree of yellowing, but not as much as varnish and polyurethane.

You can clearly see that there are real choices to be made with finishes, but all look good on walnut depending on your priorities.

Choosing a Stain

All stains look good on walnut, too. Though walnut blotches a little, it does so in a way that most people find attractive. So blotching, the ugliest effect that can occur in staining, isn't a problem with walnut.

The question is whether to stain at all, and a widespread feeling in the woodworking community is that wood, especially a high-quality wood such as walnut, should not be stained. Maybe it's all right in factories where boards are glued up randomly, but woodworkers can pick and choose boards and arrange them to achieve maximum beauty. Why would anyone want to stain walnut?

I have two answers: one general to the broader question of staining and the other specific to walnut itself.

Amateur wood finishers in the United States suffer greatly because manufacturers are so stingy (and often inaccurate) with the information they provide on their cans, and woodworking magazines and books haven't filled the void — publishing too much information that is contradictory and therefore confusing. As a result, most woodworkers don't feel comfortable with stains, finding them the cause of too many problems.

Implied here is that woodworkers would not be so adamant against staining if they had control of the process.

Specific to walnut, it has a colder natural coloring than most woods and almost always looks warmer with a stain, even if it's nothing more than an off-the-shelf walnut stain.

Dealing with Sapwood

If walnut has a problem, it is the sharp color contrast between heartwood and sapwood — and stains can be used effectively to blend these colors. The easiest method is to apply a walnut dye stain to the entire surface. But a more effective method is to apply a sap stain to the sapwood before applying a wiping stain. These methods can also be used, of course, to blend white woods such as maple and poplar to walnut.

Sap stains aren't widely available, but it's easy to make the stain yourself. Just add a little black dye stain to walnut dye stain (any type will work) so it becomes off-black. The amount you add will vary depending on the strengths of the particular dyes you're using, but think in terms of 10 to 20 percent black to begin with and adjust from there. Practice on scrap wood to get the feel.

It's best to apply the sap stain by spraying so you don't leave a sharp line at the intersection of sapwood and heartwood, but you can use a brush or cloth if you feather the stain onto the heartwood. A little sap stain getting on the heartwood isn't a problem as long as the stain is feathered out because it will be disguised by the next step.

When the sap stain is dry, apply an oil-based, walnut wiping stain, which won't cause problems with any dye stain. Finally, when this stain is dry, apply the topcoat finish of your choice.

American black walnut is considered the king of woods for its beauty and working qualities, and it should receive the same acclaim for its finishing characteristics.

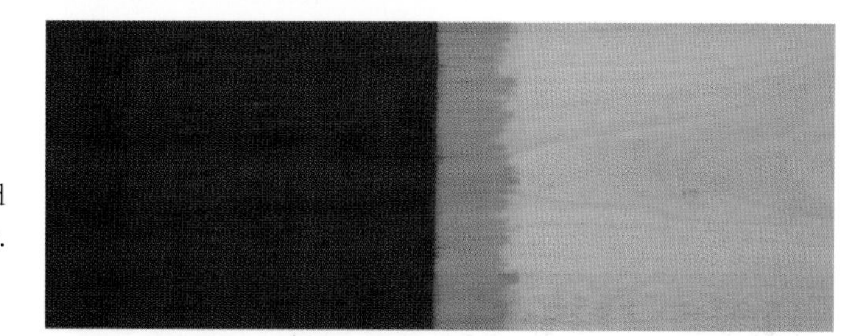

Walnut resembles ebony when dyed black (left), and it can be bleached almost white (right).

Varnish applied to the left side of this walnut board adds a warmer coloring than does the water-based finish applied to the right side.

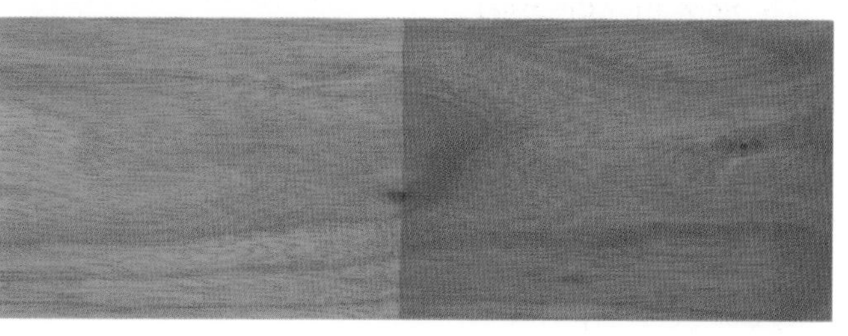

The walnut stain applied to the right side of this walnut board adds warmth to the normally cold coloring of walnut. (A lacquer finish was applied to both sides.)

The dye stain applied to the right side of this walnut board is fairly effective at blending the sharp contrast between sapwood and heartwood.

BARE WOOD | SAP STAIN | SAP STAIN PLUS WIPING STAIN | SAP STAIN PLUS WIPING STAIN PLUS FINISH

A more effective method of blending sapwood with heartwood is to apply a sap stain (first colored column from the left), then apply a walnut wiping stain and finally apply a finish.

finishing wood floors

BY BOB FLEXNER

Wooden floors used to be finished with shellac, a coating that dries rapidly, brings out a lot of depth in the wood and adds a warm amber coloring.

But shellac doesn't wear well, so it was almost always waxed to reduce scuffing and extend longevity. Keeping waxed floors in good shape was a lot of work, however, so with the introduction in the 1960s of more durable, no-wax polyurethane finishes, shellac fell out of favor.

Today, a number of durable finishes can be used successfully on wood floors, including oil-based polyurethane, water-based polyurethane, moisture-cured polyurethane and water-based finish with a catalyst (or hardener) added. Of these finishes, oil- and water-based polyurethanes are the most popular with home woodworkers because these finishes are considerably less toxic and much easier to use.

Though both of these finishes are based in large part on polyurethane resin, they differ in several significant ways. Oil-based polyurethane is more durable (meaning more wear-resistant), has a slight amber coloring and dries slower than water-based polyurethane, so application is easier.

Water-based polyurethane, on the other hand, has a much less irritating smell, is easier to clean up (with just soap and water), is nonflammable and doesn't add color at all. Because of its lack of color, water-based polyurethane generally looks better on white woods such as maple and woods that are whitewashed or pickled.

Clearly, legitimate reasons exist for choosing each of these finishes. But unless the nonyellowing characteristic of water-based polyurethane is important to you, oil-based polyurethane is your best bet for a floor because of its better durability.

Once you've chosen the finish to use, you need to prepare the surface and apply the product. Finishing floors is like finishing any wood surface — with two rather significant differences. First, the surfaces to be covered are usually very large, so different tools are commonly used to increase speed. Second, the need for perfection is reduced because flaws in the wood or in the finish aren't noticed easily.

Preparing the Surface

Just as with newly made furniture, newly laid floors are always sanded before finishing. But while already finished furniture must be stripped before refinishing, already finished floors are rarely stripped. Instead, they also are sanded and the procedure is the same as with new floors.

Special 100- to 200-lb. stand-up sanders are used, and sandpaper grits are kept fairly coarse, ranging from 36-grit to 120-grit. (Sanding no finer than 80-grit, for example, is a good idea when whitewashing floors so that more of the white pigment becomes lodged in the deeper sanding scratches.)

Rob McClanahan from Bethel, Ohio–based Tri-State Hardwood Floors, Inc., uses a stand-up sander to begin the refinishing process. This type of sander can be rented at rental stores and some flooring-materials suppliers. Look under rental in your phone book.

Varathane's ezV sander can be rented at many home centers and hardware stores. This consumer-friendly sander has on-board dust collection.

Smaller cut-in sanders are used to sand right up to baseboards, and inside corners often are scraped and sanded by hand.

All these tools, including the floor buffers mentioned below, can be rented at rental stores and some flooring-materials suppliers. These stores also stock the needed sandpaper, steel wool pads and screens, and they can provide more detailed sanding instructions if you need them.

Applying Stains and Finishes

Methods for applying stains and finishes to your floor are similar to those used on furniture or cabinets, with the major difference being the tools used for the job.

You can use a brush, of course, and this is often the best tool for cutting in near the baseboards. But for covering large expanses, a sponge mop or a similarly shaped tool with a lamb's wool pad attached is much faster. The lamb's wool will produce better results. For water-based polyurethane, a paint pad attached to a pole also is a good application tool. Each of these tools is available at hardware and paint stores.

To stain a floor, follow these steps:

1. Vacuum the floor to remove dust.

2. Pour some stain into a paint tray and apply the stain using a large brush, sponge mop, lamb's wool applicator, paint pad or simply a large cloth or sponge held in your hand.

3. Apply the stain rapidly, especially if it's a water-based stain, and wipe up the excess with a large, clean cloth, your last strokes going lengthwise with the wood. It will be helpful to have two people performing this task, one applying the stain and the other wiping up. (To avoid smearing baseboards, tape them off before applying the stain, or cut in a few inches first using a brush.)

Allow the stain to dry overnight if it is oil-based and for at least a couple of hours if it is a water-based product.

To apply finish to a floor, follow these steps:

1. Be sure the room you're working in is warm and has some ventilation — but not so much that it stirs up dust.

2. Vacuum the floor to remove dust and walk around in just your socks.

3. Pour some finish into a paint tray and apply the finish using a large brush, sponge mop, lamb's wool applicator or paint pad. There's no reason to thin the first coat, but you can if you want. The coat will dry faster, but you'll get less build.

Begin work at one side of the room and coat a 1'-wide strip up to the room's baseboard, working lengthwise with the boards. It's best if you tape off your baseboards or cut in first using a brush.

With one strip coated, begin the next, overlapping a little onto the first strip and working fast enough to keep a wet edge. That is, the first strip is still wet when you overlap with the next so you don't get a double thickness.

Work across the room in this manner, finally exiting through a door.

If you miss any small areas of the floor and the finish is beginning to set, it's best to leave them until the next coat.

Let the finish dry overnight if it's oil-based and a few hours if it's water-based. Be sure that no areas, even in corners, are tacky or soft before going to the next step.

Buff the finish using a floor buffer and a #2 steel wool pad or a 120-grit screen (a sanding product available from most rental companies) to remove raised grain and dust nibs. Don't use steel wool, however, with water-based finishes. You also can sand by hand using 120- or 150-grit sandpaper.

Vacuum the floor and apply a second coat of finish in the same way you did the first.

Buff or sand again, vacuum up the dust and apply a third coat.

Recoating Floors

You don't need to sand a floor to bare wood every time it gets a little worn. As long as you haven't let the finish wear all the way through, you can screen it using a floor buffer and apply one or two coats of finish in the same manner as described above.

You don't need to use the same brand of finish, but it's best to use the same type to avoid color differences in worn areas. Be aware, though, that you may have bonding problems using water-based polyurethane if the floor has been waxed.

You can purchase oil-based polyurethane and a lamb's wool applicator at your local home-improvement center. The lamb's wool applicator shown here requires a handle, which you also can purchase at your home-improvement center or you can disassemble an old broom.

water-based finishes

BY BOB FLEXNER

Water-based finishing products get a lot of attention in magazines and at trade shows, but these products still don't sell all that well. Most woodworkers seem reluctant to give up their familiar oil, varnish, shellac and lacquer finishes.

I think the reason for the poor sales, especially to amateur woodworkers, is the excessive hype that has raised expectations beyond what water-based products can produce. When you've been led to believe that a stain or finish doesn't raise the grain, is equivalent to lacquer or is as durable as oil-based polyurethane, and then discover otherwise when you use it, you become skeptical of the product and retreat to what you feel comfortable with.

Water-based finishing products have plenty going for them, especially for amateur woodworkers, so they should sell quite well without all the hype.

Two qualities are critical: Water-based products don't stink and don't make you feel bad, and water-based products are easy to clean from brushes (not so easy from spray guns, however). The proof of the significance of these two qualities is demonstrated by the overwhelming popularity of latex paint, which is a water-based finish with pigment added, vs. oil paint. It's likely that almost every reader uses latex paint on interior trim, kitchen and bathroom cabinets, and outdoor furniture when there is no question that oil paint would perform better. Reduced smell and easy cleanup rule with people working at home!

Other advantages you might find attractive are a reduced level of polluting solvents, reduced fire hazard and absolutely no yellowing. For the amount of finishing material you probably use, the first two are minor issues. But the nonyellowing quality can be a real benefit when you're finishing light or pickled woods. Water-based finishes are the only finishes that are totally nonyellowing.

For all their good qualities, however, water-based stains and finishes are still a relatively new technology. In contrast to other stains and finishes, improvements are still being made in the raw materials used, and some manufacturers are faster at picking up on them than others. So if you're unhappy with the results you get from one brand, try another before giving up on the entire class of products.

Water-based finishes have the distinct advantage over oil-based finishes of easy water cleanup.

Disadvantages

The rarely mentioned disadvantages are the problem, of course, because you have to know what they are or you can't overcome them. The first problem is in the naming of the products. Manufacturers often give water-based finishes the same names as totally different products that have been around for years — poly-urethane, lacquer and varnish. The intent is to make you feel comfortable with the product, but the effect is the opposite. The misleading naming sets expectations that can't be fulfilled and causes confusion because you are led to believe there are significant differences (water-based varnish vs. water-based lacquer, for example) when there aren't. The names are chosen for the market being targeted.

All water-based products should be labeled as "water-based," "waterborne," "aqua," or some other obvious water-indicating name so you don't have to read the fine print to determine what the product is.

Other significant problems common to all water-based products are grain raising, fast drying, and poor bonding over oil-based products. Let's take each in turn.

Grain Raising

Despite some manufacturers' claims to the contrary, all water-based products raise the grain of wood. How could it be otherwise? They contain a lot of water.

You can reduce the grain raising of a stain or finish in two ways. The first is to wet the wood with water, let the wood dry for several hours or overnight, then sand it with fine-grit sandpaper just enough to make it feel smooth. Don't sand any deeper than necessary or you may cut into new wood that will raise again when you apply the stain or finish. In practice you can't eliminate grain raising totally, because you can't sand evenly enough, but you can reduce it significantly.

The second is to reduce the depth the stain or finish penetrates. There are several ways to do this. Use a thicker stain or finish, one that has been slightly gelled; dry the wood quickly with heat lamps and air movement; or spray the stain or finish in a light mist coat, so it flashes dry quickly. These won't eliminate grain raising totally, and each is less effective when the humidity is high.

Without a way to totally eliminate grain raising, you have to deal with it. If you aren't staining the wood, the easiest way is to simply sand off the raised grain after the first coat of finish — the same procedure you use with other finishes. Try to apply enough finish so you don't sand through, but sanding through seldom causes a problem as long as there isn't any stain.

If you are staining the wood, you can bury the grain raising. Apply enough finish so you're sure not to sand through, then sand the surface level and apply another coat or two. To learn how much sanding it takes to sand through, practice on scrap wood by sanding through intentionally.

Fast Drying

Fast drying is an advantage when applying a finish because it reduces dust nibs, but it's a disadvantage when applying a stain. Most water-based stains are difficult to apply evenly on large surfaces because they dry too fast to get the excess wiped off.

You can use several tricks to get an even color on a large surface. Spray the stain evenly and leave it. Spray the stain and wipe it off quickly. Wipe on the stain with a large soaked rag, and quickly wipe off the excess. Stain small sections at a time. Have one person apply the stain and another wipe off right behind. Add a manufacturer's solvent, usually propylene glycol, to the stain to slow the drying. (Unfortunately, very few manufacturers supply this solvent.)

If you do get an uneven coloring due to some of the stain drying before you get it wiped off, here's what you do: Quickly wipe over the entire area with a wet cloth to redissolve and respread the stain. However, you should be aware that this might lighten the color.

Bonding to Oil Stains

To avoid both the grain-raising and fast-drying problems of water-based stains, you can use an oil-based stain, but then you have to worry about the water-based finish not bonding well. To ensure a good bond, let the oil-based stain cure totally before applying the water-based finish. Curing time depends on the stain itself, the weather and the size of the wood's pores. For example, stain on oak will take longer to cure than on maple.

Some water-based finishes bond well over some oil-based stains before the stain has cured, but there's no way of knowing for sure without trying it. The variables are the resins and solvents used in the finish and how much oil is in the stain.

To test the bonding, apply the stain and finish to scrap wood. After letting it dry for a couple of days, score the finish with a razor in a crosshatch pattern. Make the cuts about 1⁄16" apart and 1" long. Then press some masking or adhesive tape over the cuts and pull it up quickly. If the finish has bonded well, the scored lines will remain clean and little or no finish will come off on the tape.

Other Problems

Water-based finishes have other problems, as well, but they aren't serious enough to make you change to another finish except in special situations. These problems include the following: sensitivity to weather conditions (all finishes are sensitive in high heat, cold and high humidity); less durability than varnish or polyurethane (but more durability than shellac or lacquer); and greater difficulty repairing or stripping than shellac or lacquer.

The problems using water-based finishing products aren't insurmountable. But they're made more formidable by manufacturers who claim too much, mislabel their products and provide inadequate instructions for dealing with the special problems created by water.

the 16 dumbest woodworking mistakes

BY CHRISTOPHER SCHWARZ

For the record, I want it known that I had everything clamped down tight when I turned on the drill press to mix a gallon of dark brown glaze. What happened next is somewhat of a legend in our woodworking shop.

The drill press was set to run too fast, and the quill was down too low. Within seconds, the wall of the shop, all the tools within 10 feet and most of my exterior surfaces looked like we had all been dipped in chocolate at the Snickers factory.

That was five years ago. We moved the shop six miles up the highway, replaced almost all the machinery and we still find little bits of the dried glaze clinging to things just about every week.

Ask any woodworker about the dumbest mistake he or she has made and a look of pain will pass over his or her face. In our shop you'll hear stories of entertainment centers not deep enough (the wall behind it had to be punched out to make room for the stereo components) or cabinets where the knob on the last drawer was in the worst place possible.

Some of these mistakes can be fixed after the fact. All of them are avoidable. The following is a list of the 16 dumbest woodworking mistakes common to the craft. If a problem can be fixed, we show you how. But most of all, we tell you how to keep out of trouble in the first place.

1. You Measure Carefully, But Everything is a Bit Off

Problem: As you proceed though the project, small errors creep into the assemblies — errors you cannot explain. Things aren't lining up by 1/32" or so.

Next time: Stop where you are and gather all the measuring devices you've used on a project. Your tape measure, your combination square, your table saw's fence scale and your steel rules should all measure the same.

Find the problem (it's usually the tape measure or the table saw's scale) and adjust the tab on the end of the tape measure or the scale on the saw until they match your other measuring tools. If a steel ruler and a combination square don't agree, one of them has to go. Before you start a project, calibrate all your measuring tools. Plus, be aware that when ripping on your table saw, regular-kerf blades and thin-kerf blades have a different-size kerf. Pick one blade for ripping and set your fence's scale to that blade.

2. Remember the Kerf

Problem: When cutting a joint or trimming off some extra

waste, you forget to include the kerf in your measurement so your final workpiece is off by 1/8" or 3/32".

Next time: To avoid the problem, just remember what my grandfather always said: Never measure the waste piece; always measure your keeper piece. This keeps you out of trouble when the saw kerf is involved.

For additional insurance, when marking the face of a board for a cut, carry that mark onto the front edge of the board. Put the board in position on the saw and line up the mark with the blade.

3. Ending Up on the Wrong Side of the Line

Problem: You mark your mortise or crosscut, but you bore or cut on the wrong side of the line.

Next time: To avoid the problem, get in the habit of marking your waste area with crosshatches. It takes a few seconds, but it is faster than fixing this mistake.

Quick fix: There's little you can do to fix a board that's too short. To repair a round hole in face grain, never use a dowel if the area will show. You need to match the grain and color if you want to hide the repair. Purchase a set of plug cutters that cut a tapered plug. With a plug cutter you can make a bunch of plugs and compare them to the area you need to repair. Some glue and a few taps with a mallet will seat the plug firmly. Trim the excess with a flush-cut saw or sharp chisel.

4. Your Mitered Moulding is Too Short

Problem: You're trying to sneak up on a miter by nibbling at it bit by bit. You cut too far.

Next time: To avoid the problem, you can make a miter shooting board. This simple hand-tool appliance allows you to sneak up on the right fit in a more controlled manner — about 0.002" at a time.

Quick fix: Before you throw away that too-short moulding, there is a way to stretch it a tad with a sharp block plane. By planing a slight taper on the back side of the moulding (the part that attaches to the cabinet or wall), you can actually make the piece of moulding a little bit longer. If this is moulding that goes on the side of a cabinet, you want the taper to begin at the back and diminish to nothing at the miter.

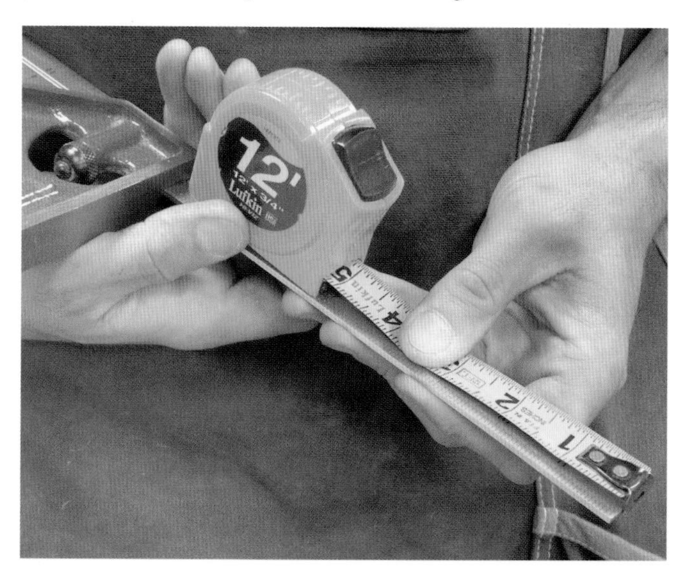

When boring a hole for a through-mortise, we ended up on the wrong side of the line. Time to get the plug cutter.

What you can squeeze out of one of these boards is limited (usually about 1/32" to 1/16" depending on the size and profile of the moulding) before things don't look right.

5. Off by an Inch — Might as Well Be a Yard

Problem: You're measuring a board with your tape measure to cut it to length. You make the mark and the cut, but your board is exactly 1" too short. The culprit usually is one of two things: You were holding the beginning of the tape at the 1" mark for a more accurate measurement. Or you were looking at the wrong number when you made your pencil mark. This second mistake is common when you have the tape measure in your left hand (reading upside down) and the pencil in your right.

Next time: There are several ways to avoid the problem in the future. First, measure everything twice (we had to say it). Second, use your combination square or (even better) a 24"-long metal hook rule to mark out small cuts instead of your tape measure.

To prevent errors from creeping into your projects, be sure to calibrate all your measuring tools against one another before you begin.

6. Gappy Joints

Problem: You glue up your case or assembly, and ugly gaps appear between the joints.

Next time: Several things can cause this, but usually it's because you didn't clamp up the project without glue first. Joints should close with minimal clamp pressure. If you have to really twist the clamps down hard, you've got some ill-fitting joints to correct first.

Always perform a dry assembly and closely inspect your joints.

Quick fix: This error is why they make wood putty.

7. Things are Not as They are Supposed to Be

Problem: You're gluing up a cabinet, a drawer or any assembly and you get one of the parts placed wrong: It could be upside down or on the wrong side, or the wrong face of the board is showing.

Next time: Use a cabinetmaker's triangle to distinguish left, right, front, back, inside and outside at a glance. Say you're building a drawer. Once you

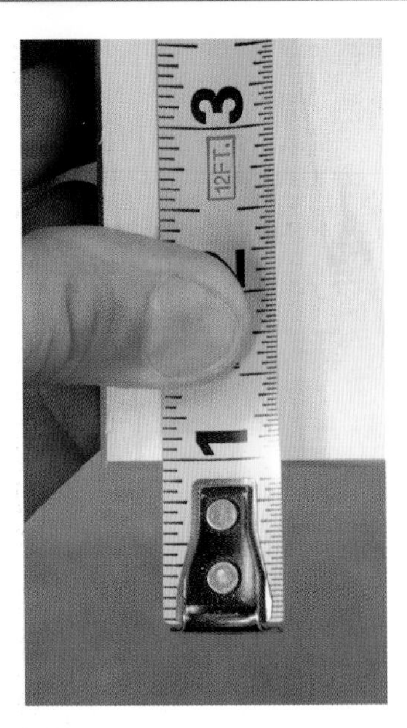

Starting your tape measure at 1" can make you more accurate. But it also can cause you to burn an inch if you're not careful. Measure things twice.

get your parts cut out, put the sides together and then place the drawer front on the end so it makes a T. Draw a triangle that spans the three parts and points to the front of the drawer. Put the back piece against the sides in a T formation and draw another triangle that spans the three pieces and points to the front of the drawer. Now you'll always know how the pieces should be oriented without labeling each joint.

The same triangle works with doors, too. Always mark the triangle on the outside face of the board and always have it point up to the top of the case.

Quick fix: If you use a slow-setting glue or hide glue (which is reversible with hot water), the obvious solution is to take the thing apart and try again. But these problems usually are discovered when it's too late.

8. Two Left Feet

Problem: You're milling the dadoes and rabbets in a case side, drawer or other box and you forget that you have left- and right-side pieces. So you make two left-hand or right-hand parts.

Next time: Again, the cabinetmaker's triangle can help avoid this problem. And you should stack your left and right pieces in different piles as you work.

9. You Drill a Large Hole That is Too Small

Problem: You bore a hole with a Forstner or hole saw that is too small, and locating the center for the next size up is difficult because there's a hole there.

Next time: You're working too fast; slow down.

Quick fix: It's easy. Cut a square plug you can pound into the round hole. Mark the center on the plug and cut your new hole.

10. Your Doors Don't Fit

Problem: Your doors are too small or crooked to fit in their opening.

Next time: To avoid this problem, rip your stiles and rails 1⁄8" wider than your cut list calls for. Then you can square and trim the door easily to size.

Quick fix: To repair your immediate problem, trim the doors so they are square — even if this results in gaps between your case and doors. Now you can fix your problem with moulding. Mill some 5⁄16"-thick by 3⁄4"-wide flat moulding and cut a profile on one edge that matches the style of your project (a bead goes well with traditional furniture; a bevel looks good with more contemporary pieces).

If you're building a face-frame cabinet, miter and nail the moulding to the inside edges of the face frame. Voilá. The hole for your doors just got smaller. If you have a frameless cabinet, miter and nail the moulding to the doors. Voilá again. Your doors are bigger.

A smaller hole is easily made bigger by pounding a temporary plug in place before drilling the new hole.

11. Pencil Line Too Fine to See or Too Dark to Remove

Problem: We all hate erasing and sanding off the pencil marks on a project, and some of us mark really fine lines to make that part of the job easier. Unfortunately, it's easy to overlook a fine pencil line and miscut. So we make the lines darker, which dents the wood and is difficult to remove.

Next time: Hold your pencil at a low angle and don't keep it too sharp when marking parts. This makes lines that are easy to read but don't dent the wood.

Quick fix: Remove all pencil lines using a rag soaked with denatured alcohol before sanding.

12. You Ruin One of the Critical Parts to Your Project

Problem: This is painful for woodworkers to discuss. After machining a part so it's almost done, something unspeakably

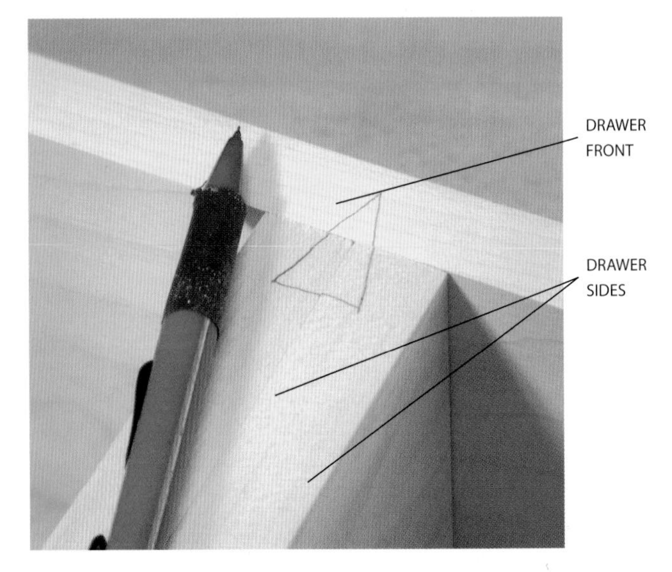

The cabinetmaker's triangle will save your bacon. The point of the triangle always faces front (or to the top). Mark all your assemblies with it before cutting your joints.

bad happens. The part is ruined.

Next time: Making replacement parts is easier if you plan for the problem in advance. First, always run out extra stock in all the thicknesses you're using (thickness is the most difficult dimension to reproduce). For the critical parts in a project, always make an extra one. For a table, make an extra leg. For a set of doors, make an extra stile and a couple of extra rails.

13. Fasteners Too Long

Problem: One of us (who shall remain nameless) once nailed a project to his father's bench with a pneumatic nailer. The nails were too long. Nails and screws that emerge where they are not supposed to emerge is sadly common. With screws this happens when you countersink too deep or the clutch is set too high on your cordless drill.

Next time: You can measure your fasteners and keep them organized to avoid this problem, but we have a better solution. Before you fire a nail or drive a screw, hold it up to the work. Fasteners should be twice as long (or a hair less) as the material they're passing through. For example, when joining $\frac{3}{4}$" material, use $1\frac{1}{4}$"- to $1\frac{1}{2}$"-long screws.

When driving screws, always measure your countersinks and start with a low clutch setting.

14. The Color of Your Finish Isn't What You Expected

Problem: Surprise, surprise, the stain color on your project looks nothing like the stain color on the can (or in your head).

Next time: Good finishing requires making a sample board beforehand. As you are sanding or planing the parts of your project, take one of your extra boards and sand or plane it the same way. This means sanding it using the same equipment, the same amount of pressure and for the same amount of time. Use this as your sample board.

Stain the board and add your topcoat finish of choice. Then take your sample board into the room where the project will be located. Daylight, fluorescent light and lamp light all make stain colors look different.

Quick fix: Get out the can of stripper or the appropriate solvent. You'll never be happy with a bad-looking finish.

Hold your pencil at this low angle and use a light touch when marking pieces (not joinery). This will keep you from denting the wood.

When we added the glaze to this cherry table it started to look like red oak. A sample board would have saved us the time spent removing the glaze.

15. When You Glue Up a Panel the Edges Don't Close

Problem: You joint the edges of the boards you are planning to glue into a panel but gaps appear between the boards' edges. You check the jointer's fence and it reads 90° to the bed.

Next time: Even if your square says the fence is at 90°, it might be a little off at other places on the fence. Or your square is off. Either way, there's an easy way to fix the problem: geometry. Use the power of complementary angles to make perfect tabletops.

For every joint in the tabletop, mark one board to edge-joint with its face against the fence, then joint its mate with the face facing away from the jointer's fence. Even if your jointer is off by some whopping degree, the two angles will cancel each other out and result in a tight fit.

Quick fix: If you glued up the panel, rip it apart along the joint lines and start over.

16. More Panel Problems: The Boards Slip at Glue-Up

Problem: You're gluing up a tabletop. As you apply clamping pressure, the boards slip up and down and refuse to line up.

Next time: To avoid the problem in the future, consider using dowels, splines or biscuits to line up the boards during critical glue-ups (though they will not add any strength to the joint).

Clamp only until the joint closes — no farther. Most woodworkers use far too much pressure when clamping. And the pipe in pipe clamps tends to bend under pressure, which also can push the boards out of alignment.

Quick fix: If you're in the middle of a glue-up, grab handscrew clamps and clamp them across the joints at each end of the panel. Then apply pressure with your bar clamps.

suppliers

ACCURIDE INTERNATIONAL, INC.
562-903-0200
Drawer slides

ADAMS & KENNEDY — THE WOOD SOURCE
613-822-6800
www.wood-source.com
Wood supply

ADJUSTABLE CLAMP COMPANY
312-666-0640
www.adjustableclamp.com
Clamps

ADS CRYOGENICS
909-338-6756
Cryogenics

ADVISOR IN METALS
603-755-9232
www.worldpath.net/~hisaim/
Cryogenics

AMAZON.COM
www.amazon.com
Woodworking books and supplies

AMERICAN SAW & MFG. COMPANY
800-628-8810
www.lenoxsaw.com
Lenox saw blades

AMEROCK CORPORATION
800-435-6959
www.amerock.com
Hinges

APPLIED CRYOGENICS
800-734-7042
Cryogenics

BALL AND BALL
www.ballandball-us.com
Hardware reproductions

B&Q
023 8025 6256
www.diy.com
Tools, paint, wood, electrical, garden

BEHR PROCESS CORPORATION
714-545-7101
www.behr.com
Wood finishing products

BLACK & DECKER
800-544-6986
www.blackanddecker.com
Power tools

BLUM, INC.
800-438-6788
www.blum.us
Drawer slides, hinges

BRIDGE CITY TOOL WORKS
800-253-3332
www.bridgecitytools.com
Woodworking tools

CMT USA, INC.
888-268-2487
www.cmtusa.com
Cove cutter, carbide-tipped tooling

COLONIAL SAW, INC.
781-585-4364
www.csaw.com
Lamello biscuit joiners

CONSTANTINES WOOD CENTER
800-443-9667
www.constantines.com
Tools, woods, veneers, hardware

CRYOGENIC SERVICES
316-545-7555
Cryogenics

CRYOTRON, LTD.
780-960-0960
Cryogenics

DALY'S PAINTS
800-735-7019
www.dalyspaint.com
Wood finishing products; ProFin

DEFT, INC.
800-544-3338
www.deftfinishes.com
wood finishing products

DELTA MACHINERY
800-223-7278 (U.S.)
800-463-3582 (Canada)
www.deltawoodworking.com
Woodworking tools

DEWALT
800-433-9258
www.dewalt.com
Power tools

DIAMOND MACHINING TECHNOLOGY, INC.
800-666-4368
www.dmtsharp.com
Diamond sharpeners

DOWN RIVER CRYOGENICS
501-397-7189
Cryogenics

EAGLE TOOLS
323-999-2909
www.eagle-tools.com
Agazzani tools

ECOGATE, INC.
888-326-4283
www.ecogate.com
Dust collection systems

FELDER USA
866-792-5288
www.felderusa.com
Machines and tools for woodworking

FORMBY'S COMPANY
800-290-1105
www.formbys.com
Wood finishing products

FORREST MANUFACTURING COMPANY, INC.
800-733-7111
forrest.woodmall.com
Carbide-tipped saw blades, dado sets, sharpening

FREUD TOOLS
800-334-4107
www.freudtools.com
Carbide-tipped saw blades, dado sets, tooling

GARRETT WADE
800-221-2942
www.garrettwade.com
General hand and power tools and supplies

GENERAL FINISHES
800-783-6050
www.generalfinishes.com
Finishing products; Arm-R-Seal; Sealacell

GOFF'S CURTAIN WALLS
800-234-0337
www.goffscurtainwalls.com
Curtain walls for finishing booths

GRAINGER
888-361-8649
www.grainger.com
Curtains and exhaust fans for finishing booths

H. BEHLEN & BRO.
866-785-7781
www.hbehlen.com
Behlen wood finishing products

HIGHLAND HARDWARE
800-241-6748
www.tools-for-woodworking.com
Woodworking tools and supplies

HILL WOOD PRODUCTS INC.
800-788-9689
www.hillwoodproducts.com
Biscuits

HOCK TOOLS
888-282-5233
www.hocktools.com
Blades for hand tools

THE HOME DEPOT
800-553-3199 (U.S.)
800-668-2266 (Canada)
www.homedepot.com
Tools, paint, wood, electrical, garden

HOPE'S PREMIUM HOME CARE
314-739-7254
www.hopecompany.com
Wood finishing products

HORTON BRASSES, INC.
800-754-9127
www.horton-brasses.com
Hardware for antique furniture

THE JAPAN WOODWORKER CATALOG
800-537-7820
www.japanwoodworker.com
Traditional Japanese hand tools; books

JASCO CHEMICAL CORPORATION
888-345-2726
www.jasco-help.com
Wood finishes and treatments

KLINGSPOR'S WOODWORKING SHOP
800-228-0000
www.woodworkingshop.com
Sanding products

KNAPE & VOGT MANUFACTURING COMPANY
616-459-3311
www.knapeandvogt.com
Drawer slides

KNIGHT TOOLWORKS
503-421-6146
www.knight-toolworks.com
Planes

KREG TOOL COMPANY
800-447-8638
www.kregtool.com
Kreg jigs

LAGUNA TOOLS
800-332-4094
www.lagunatools.com
Woodworking tools

LANGEVIN & FOREST LTE.
800-889-2060
Tools, wood and books

LEE VALLEY TOOLS LTD.
800-267-8735
www.leevalley.com
Fine woodworking tools and hardware

LIE-NIELSEN TOOLWORKS
800-327-2520
www.lie-nielsen.com
Hand tools

LOCKWOOD PRODUCTS, INC.
800-423-1625
www.loc-line.com
Loc-Line modular hose

LOWE'S HOME IMPROVEMENT WAREHOUSE
800-445-6937
www.lowes.com
Tools, paint, wood, electrical, garden

MAKITA
800-462-5482
www.makita.com
Woodworking tools

MICRO-SURFACE FINISHING PRODUCTS, INC.
800-225-3006
www.wicro-surface.com
Abrasive products

MINWAX COMPANY
800-523-9299
www.minwax.com
Wood finishing products

MLCS
800-533-9298
www.mlcswoodworking.com
Router bits and woodworking product

ONEIDA AIR SYSTEMS, INC.
800-732-4065
www.oneida-air.com
Dust collection systems

ONEWAY MANUFACTURING
800-565-7288
www.oneway.on.ca
Wolverine grinding jig system

PAXTON WOODCRAFTERS' STORE
800-332-1331
www.paxton-woodsource.com
Lumber; veneers; books and woodworking tools

PORTER-CABLE
800-487-8665
www.porter-cable.com
Woodworking tools

PRACTICAL PRODUCTS COMPANY
513-561-6560
www.practicalprods.com
Kaiser biscuits

RICHELIEU HARDWARE
800-619-5446 (U.S.)
800-361-6000 (Canada)
www.richelieu.com
Hardware supplies

ROBERT BOSCH TOOL CORPORATION
877-267-8499
www.boschtools.com
Bosch power tools

ROCKLER WOODWORKING AND HARDWARE
800-279-4441
www.rockler.com
Woodworking tools and hardware

RUSTOLEUM BRANDS
800-553-8444
www.varathane.com
Polyurethane

RYOBI TOOLS
800-525-2579
www.ryobitools.com
Power tools

SEARS
800-549-4505
www.craftsman.com
Craftsman tools

SHAPTON
877-692-3624
www.shaptonstones.com
Ceramic sharpening stones

STEVE WALL LUMBER COMPANY
800-633-4062
www.walllumber.com
Lumber

SUFFOLK MACHINERY CORPORATION
800-234-7297
www.suffolkmachinery.com
Band saw blades

TRI-STATE HARDWOOD FLOORS, INC.
513-734-4724
Hardwood flooring information

UGL: UNITED GILSONITE LABORATORIES
570-344-1202
www.ugl.com
Zar wood finishing products

ULMIA
www.ulmia.de
Workbenches

VALSPAR CORPORATION
336-887-4600
www.valspar.com
Val-Oil

VELVIT PRODUCTS
920-722-8355
www.velvitproducts.com
Velvit Oil

WOLFCRAFT NORTH AMERICA
630-773-4777
www.wolfcraft.com
Woodworking hardware and accessories

VERMONT AMERICAN
800-742-3869
www.vermontamerican.com
Power tool accessories; Ice Bits

WATERLOO INDUSTRIES, INC.
866-573-0335
www.tooldock.com
Tool Dock cabinets

WATERLOX COATINGS CORPORATION
800-321-0377
www.waterlox.com
Wood finishing products

W.D. LOCKWOOD, INC.
866-293-8913
www.wdlockwood.com
Lockwood water-soluble dyes

WOODCRAFT
800-225-1153
www.woodcraft.com
Woodworking hardware and accessories

WOOD-MIZER PRODUCTS, INC.
800-553-0182
www.woodmizer.com
Portable band-saw mills

WOODWORKER'S HARDWARE
800-383-0130
www.wwhardware.com
Woodworking tools; books and plans

WOODWORKER'S SUPPLY
800-645-9292
www.woodworker.com
Woodworking tools; books and plans

WORKSHOP SUPPLY
800-387-5716
www.workshopsupply.com
Woodworking tools; Jimmy Jigs

YORK CRYOGENICS
717-309-0639
Cryogenics

index